I0816238

ALSO BY J. D. DICKEY

The Republic of Violence: The Tormented Rise of Abolition in Andrew Jackson's America

American Demagogue: The Great Awakening and the Rise and Fall of Populism

Rising in Flames: Sherman's March and the Fight for a New Nation

Empire of Mud: The Secret History of Washington, DC

BOSTON 1776

BOSTON, 1776

A Rogue Tour of Revolution City

☆ ☆ ☆

J. D. DICKEY

DIVERSION
BOOKS

Diversion Books
A division of Diversion Publishing Corp.
www.diversionbooks.com

For more information, email info@diversionbooks.com

First Diversion Books Edition: February 2026
Hardcover ISBN: 979-8-89515-017-7
e-ISBN: 979-8-89515-019-1

Design by Neuwirth & Associates, Inc.
Cover design by Libby Kingsbury

Printed in the United States of America
1 3 5 7 9 10 8 6 4 2

To Andrew Rosenberg

☆ ☆ ☆

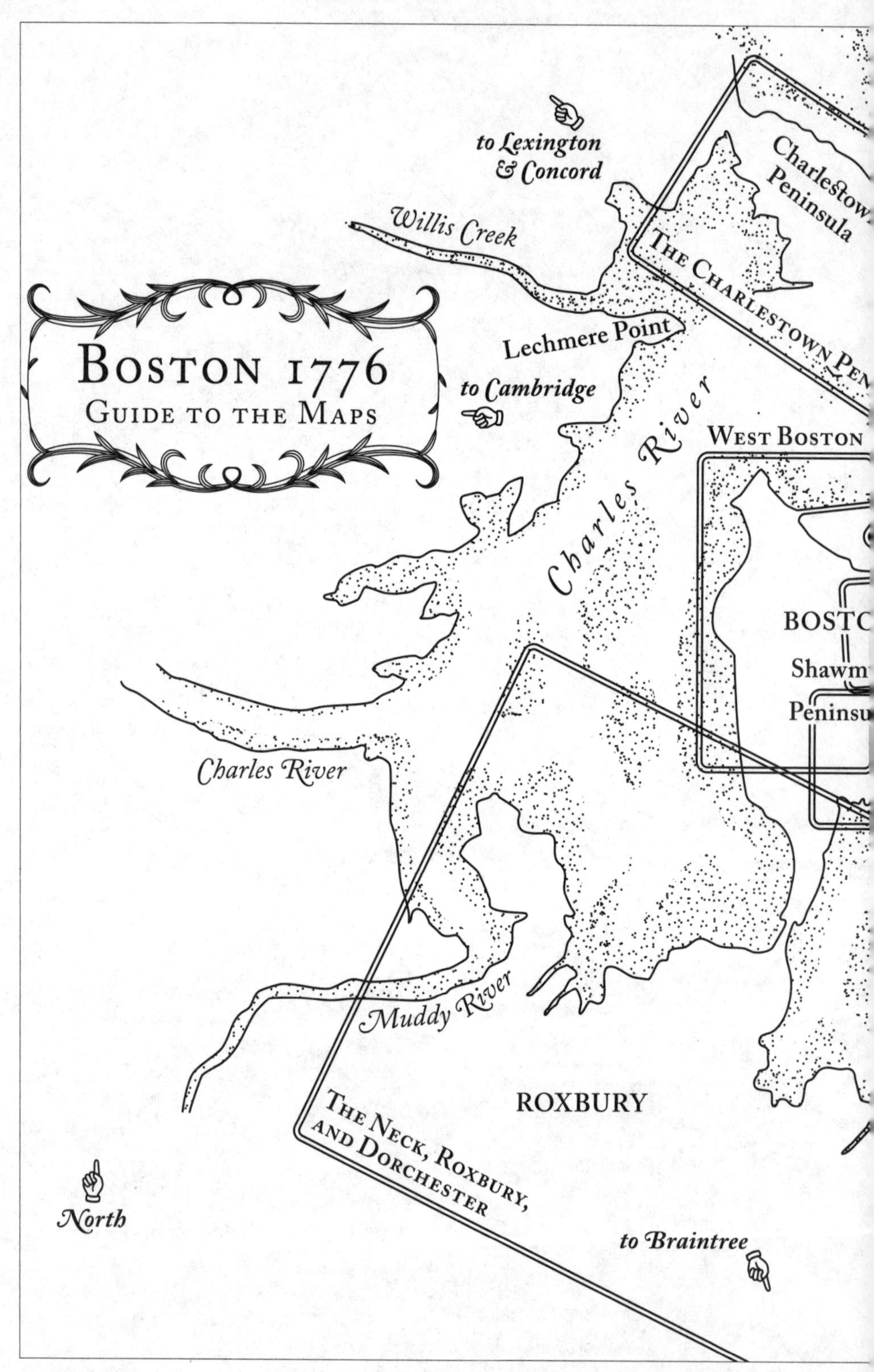

Boston 1776
Guide to the Maps
to Lexington & Concord
Willis Creek
Lechmere Point
to Cambridge
Charles River
Charlestown Peninsula
The Charlestown Pen
West Boston
Bosto
Shawm
Peninsu
Charles River
Muddy River
Roxbury
The Neck, Roxbury, and Dorchester
North
to Braintree

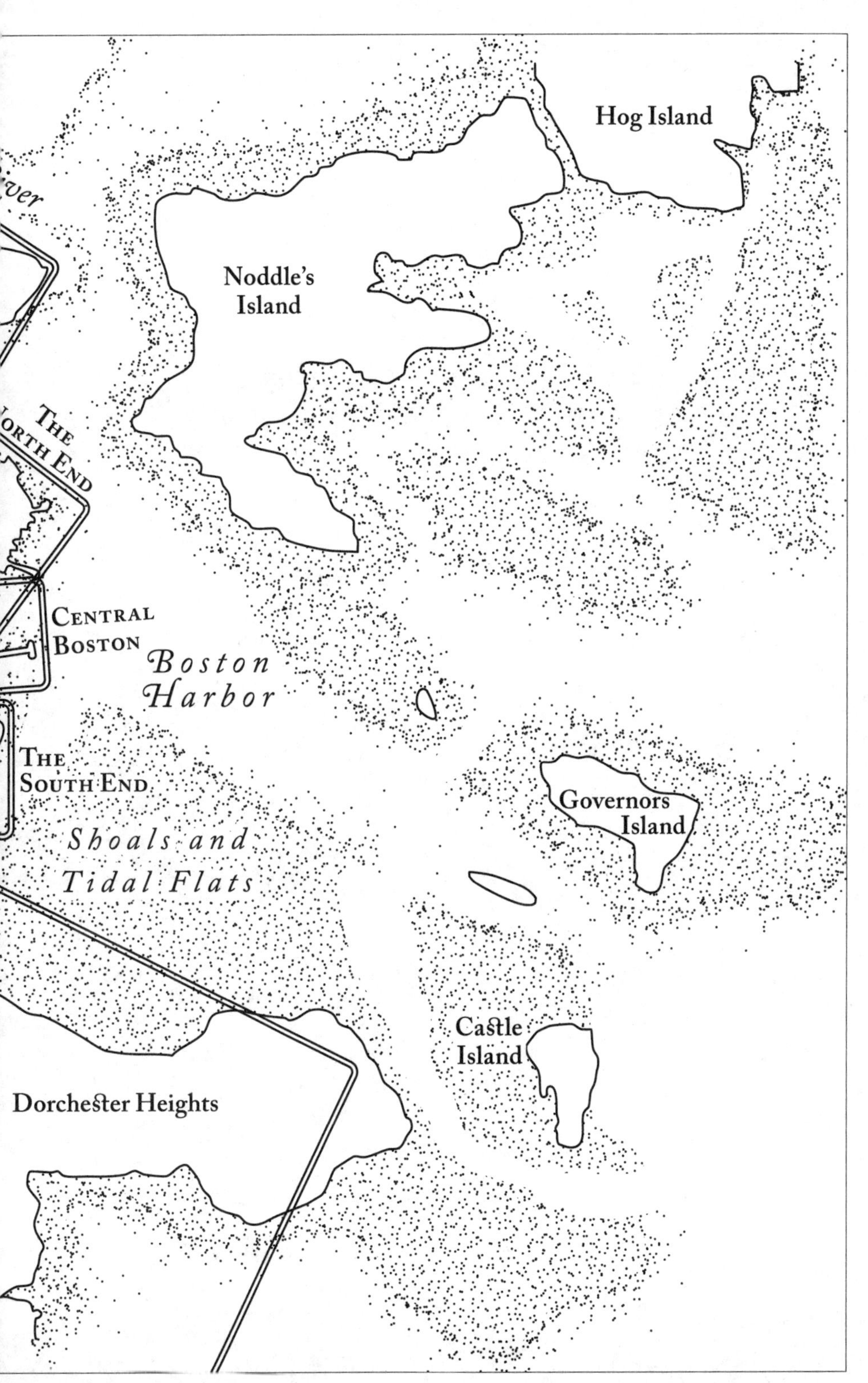
Hog Island
Noddle's Island
The North End
Central Boston
Boston Harbor
The South End
Shoals and Tidal Flats
Governors Island
Castle Island
Dorchester Heights

CONTENTS

HOW TO USE THIS GUIDE

Our journey to Boston in 1776 is designed for visitors with a flair for the dramatic, the historic, and the groundbreaking, as well as the commonplace—all in a town that has received a great deal of attention in our upstart new republic. The trip will take you to the stronghold of the American Revolution just after July 4, the day when the thirteen former British colonies renounced their loyalty to the Crown in the Declaration of Independence—a document drafted by Thomas Jefferson but brought about by the decade-long rebellion of the people of Boston.

We'll tour this Revolution City starting at the Long Wharf and proceeding through each neighborhood, stopping at the houses of the famous and the infamous, raucous taverns, contentious assembly halls, and other places key to the uprising. The last two chapters will take us just beyond Boston to nearby battle sites, and then we'll discuss the practical matters you'll need to know for your trip—lodging, transport, food, and the like.

Revolutionary Boston may not be the town you'd expect. It's much smaller than most of us envision, a little over one square mile, nearly an island. No bridges cross the Charles River, and the roads are dirt or cobbled. The town isn't a cultural hub like Philadelphia, or a citadel of commerce like New York City. Instead, it's a provincial port whose most prosperous days are behind it, but whose people's fiery spirit and unmatched civic energy have become a model for other budding American revolutionaries to follow.

The book can be read in any order because a guide to Boston need not be any more linear than a walk through its winding streets. Let impulse lead you and you'll discover a town vibrant and energetic, strange and unexpected—and with any luck, this guide can be a useful companion to your journey.

INTRODUCTION

Why is Boston in revolt in 1776?

How did this insular little town founded as a theocracy in the seventeenth century end up at the forefront of a national revolution? Did the spirit of rebellion begin with its founding in 1630 as an enclave of religious dissent? Or did it begin almost sixty years later, when the townsfolk rose up against the hated royal governor Edmund Andros and had him arrested and jailed? Or was it during the 1730s and '40s, when riots erupted over building new food markets (see p. 43) and impressing men into the Royal Navy? Or was it a combination of all those factors, or something else entirely?

Whatever the deeper reasons for Boston's contentious spirit, it was on display most visibly from the 1760s through the current 1770s—a period that began with its residents honoring a fallen monarch of the House of Hanover and now sees them destroying the arms and emblems of that dynasty. Indeed, when mourning bells rang for King George II, it was the last commemoration of a fallen British head of state in Boston, and it preceded a new era of bitter conflict that began just a few months after George III took the throne in 1760.

The time of revolution began with Bostonians suffering through "the great decay," as their once-vibrant economy fell into decline. Only a few decades before, the town was the most populous in British North America, its shipbuilding industry the envy of other American ports, and many of its tradesmen, shopkeepers, merchants, and artisans making a comfortable living. It boasted a thriving waterfront, plentiful opportunities for commerce, and a fashionable sense of style that rivaled other major towns on the Eastern Seaboard. But the good times were not to last.

By the middle of the eighteenth century, New York and Philadelphia had taken away a good portion of Boston's maritime trade and eclipsed it in population, while diseases like smallpox ravaged the health of the community. Businesses closed, unemployment rose, and fires burned down sections of the town. One-tenth of male residents died in foreign wars. Many of their widows were reduced to poverty, selling liquor by the drink on the waterfront or making ends meet as seamstresses, servants, laborers, or prostitutes. If they couldn't find a job to support their families, they might have ended up in the almshouse or the workhouse, or had to beg from door to door, town to town, as part of a growing army of the impoverished known as the "strolling poor."

The selectmen in charge dreaded the high costs of caring for the destitute—and the high taxes laid upon others to support them—and petitioned the General Court for relief, to prevent residents from moving away to avoid the increasing taxes. As the town meeting wrote to the legislature in a 1753 petition, "numbers are gone already, more are going, others are preparing to go, and unless there be some remedy, the Town must be depopulated, and the Poor perish by themselves . . . [in] this Once flourishing but now sinking Town."

In an unfortunate coincidence, His Majesty's empire was also struggling financially. Although Britain had emerged victorious in the Seven Years' War (1756–1763), its national debt had exploded to £133 million, with £10 million—about half its annual revenues—required just to pay the interest. That meant the nation and its colonies shared in the burden of servicing the debt, and a good part of that burden fell on those whose livelihoods depended on exports and imports—Bostonians.

They already paid the highest customs duties in America: nearly nine thousand pounds went out of their pockets every year into the royal treasury, almost double what New Yorkers paid. Even worse, the Navigation Acts kept British North America from trading freely with foreign countries, and certain goods like molasses, sugar, tobacco, rice, cotton, furs, hides, naval stores, and iron had to transit through a British port so shippers could pay the required tariffs. Prime Minister George Grenville cited economic and cultural reasons for keeping America dependent on Britain for its material well-being while also stifling domestic manufacturing and keeping the colonists from selling finished goods to the rest of the world. This left Britain as the central, and often the only, legal market for their exports.

Another dilemma: Boston didn't have much to offer the home country except the familiar goods of lumber, livestock, dried fish, whale products, potash, and rum—even as the British preferred rice, wheat, tobacco, and the other money crops of the more southerly colonies. So Boston faced a huge trade deficit, with exports a tough sell across the Atlantic and a flood of imports available at home at a discount. That left Boston's economy in a precarious, almost primitive, state. Or at least it would have been if not for the smugglers.

They were a curious lot, these smugglers, drawn from a variety of backgrounds and assorted political leanings, but always with this same end: to circumvent the system of customs laws and freely trade with whatever countries or territories would buy their goods. The most notable included John Rowe, a moderate merchant best known for his eponymous wharf; William Cooper, clerk of the town meeting; and William Molineux, hardware merchant turned radical patriot. The Crown also alleged the town's richest man, John Hancock, stood among them.

The smugglers knew the most lucrative markets were not in Britain but in the non-British colonies of the West Indies and Europe. There, they might unload casks of rum or whale oil in exchange for molasses, wine, textiles or tea, or a range of other commodities. Boston's version of the so-called triangle trade also proved lucrative for traders willing to traffic in human beings, sending rum to Africa, slaves to the West Indies, and molasses back to Boston. It all made for a complex and risky practice that enriched a good number of already wealthy merchants even as it infuriated customs officials who saw the trade laws openly flouted. Superior Court justice and ardent loyalist Peter Oliver put it bluntly: "The Inhabitants of the Colonies were a Race of Smugglers."

The Crown attempted to stamp out the practice with the enhanced use of vice-admiralty courts to try violators of the law, and replaced laissez-faire officials like customs collector Ben Barons with a new, more aggressive breed of enforcement officers. In 1761, one of them, agent Charles Paxton, petitioned the Superior Court of Judicature (the highest court in Massachusetts) to allow writs of assistance to inspect houses, shops, and warehouses for smuggled goods without a warrant. This policy drove former Advocate General James Otis to give a speech to the court that claimed

Parliament had no right to tax colonists without their representation and consent. A young John Adams was so impressed with the oration that he sided with the political faction known as the Whigs, who championed individual liberties against encroachment by the Crown. A number of other rising Massachusetts lawyers like Josiah Quincy II and Robert Treat Paine would follow suit.

After the writs of assistance, Boston's smugglers and customs agents became ever more hostile to each other, as Parliament passed more restrictive laws and gave customs agents new authority against those who broke them. The Revenue Act of 1764 lowered duties on foreign molasses from six pence to three pence per gallon but increased enforcement to reduce smuggling, allowing the Royal Navy to search ships up to six miles from shore and permitting the Crown, customs officials, and the royal governor to split the proceeds from any seized cargo—which many colonists saw as an open invitation to corruption. The law was more familiarly known as the Sugar Act, but Rowe and other merchants called it the Black Act.

More outrages followed. The Currency Act of 1764 extended the ban on paper money in New England to combat inflationary effects of that currency (which tended to help debtors like farmers and smallholders), and the Stamp Act of 1765 created a new tax in the form of a revenue stamp on printed materials like legal documents, licenses, diplomas, pamphlets, and even playing cards and dice. For many, that act crossed the line.

Whigs argued the law showed Parliament had no desire to protect the interests of colonists or to allow them representation in government. The royal treasury would be enriched at the expense of their liberties and cripple any hopes they might have of gaining economic self-sufficiency. To make their feelings known, colonists protested in print and on the streets. In New York, delegates met in the Stamp Act Congress to develop strategy against the act. But it was the more direct, and violent, actions of Boston's radicals that had the greater effect.

Spurred by patriot clubs like the Loyal Nine, mobs attacked the homes and property of Crown officials, directing much of their fury against the man appointed to be the new stamp commissioner, Andrew Oliver. He was the brother-in-law of Lieutenant Governor Thomas Hutchinson, so not only did the appointment smack of nepotism but it also reminded Bostonians how much power the "better sort" wielded over them. On

August 14, the mob ripped down a supposed stamp office, ransacked and vandalized Oliver's house and gardens, and later forced his resignation at the Liberty Tree—the elm on the South End that was the symbol of the growing patriot movement. Less than two weeks later, another mob led by shoemaker Ebenezer Mackintosh dismantled and almost destroyed Hutchinson's mansion, making off with much of his artwork, books, and currency, and scattering his effects along the street.

The violence had an effect. The Crown discovered the Stamp Act was unenforceable, and the next year, Parliament repealed it. Bostonians reacted with fireworks and feasting on the Common and at the Liberty Tree. The celebrants praised the radicals who'd been most vehement against the act, especially Samuel Adams. His Sons of Liberty club had assumed leadership of the patriot cause from the Loyal Nine and developed a broad network of supporters to intimidate Crown officials and act against future attempts to pass or enforce new trade and tax laws.

Nevertheless, the Crown's taxation attempts continued.

At nearly the same time it repealed the Stamp Act, Parliament passed the Declaratory Act to emphasize its sovereign right to tax any of the king's subjects. The same year, it passed the Plantation Duties Act to prohibit exports to any continental European ports roughly north of Spain. With each new law, radical patriots became more incensed. They especially condemned royal Governor Francis Bernard for enforcing the new revenue laws and the writs of assistance, with John Adams claiming that residents "are of one Mind about the Governor and absolutely hate and despise him."

The year 1767 came with yet another indignity. The Townshend Acts were a series of measures sponsored by Charles Townshend, chancellor of the exchequer, to raise additional revenue for the Crown and to enforce compliance. For Bostonians, the most repellent provisions were the new levies on tea, paper, glass, lead, and colors for painters, and the installation of an American Board of Customs Commissioners to oversee the fundraising regime—which would be based in Boston.

Residents of Massachusetts were predictably livid over the latest measures, but it was Pennsylvanian John Dickinson who crystallized opposition to them throughout the colonies. In his widely influential *Letters from a Farmer in Pennsylvania*, he claimed the measures had been enacted without local consent or representation, infringed on the rights of British subjects, enriched the salaries of royal officials, and were to be enforced by writs of assistance and other draconian methods. Dickinson's letters galvanized hostility against royal officials and those who were appointed to oversee imperial trade policy.

One of the most reviled bureaucrats was Customs Commissioner Charles Paxton, who had gone on from championing the writs to tangling repeatedly with merchants who tried to circumvent the trade laws he enforced. He and his fellow commissioners began to receive anonymous threats, with the hint of mob violence should they attempt to carry out their duties. But the most influential tactics against the Townshend Acts were devised by a group of merchants who drafted a nonimportation agreement in March 1768 to encourage domestic manufacturing and shun the import of British goods.

With the aid of the Sons of Liberty, the nonimporting merchants (who included a number of smugglers) gained public support and an advantage over their peers who didn't endorse the agreement. They also had allies like hardware merchant William Molineux—called "the first Leader of Dirty Matters"—who used gangs of teens to harass those who trafficked in British goods. His makeshift army spattered importers' houses with mud, insulted them in the streets, and laid a tar-blackened handprint on their property to mark them as suitable for—what else?—tar and feathers. Clerk of the General Court Samuel Adams did his part as well, warning in print that the Townshend duties were merely a prelude to the arrival of British troops and a new wave of Crown lackeys who would descend on Boston to enrich themselves and rob people of their liberties. In response, mobs associated with the patriot clubs paraded through the streets with cudgels and marched by the homes of officials and importers to threaten them with rough treatment.

Adams and James Otis drafted a circular letter (a widely distributed missive) to other colonies, claiming the Townshend Acts had been enacted without colonial representation and violated the right of citizens to enact their own forms of taxation. The legislative body of Massachusetts, the General Court, duly approved the letter, after which the British secretary of state, the Earl of Hillsborough, demanded they withdraw it. By a majority of 92–17, the assemblymen refused the order, and the "Glorious 92" became patriot heroes for their defiance. Silversmith and engraver Paul Revere even designed an exquisite silver bowl to honor them. But Governor Bernard dissolved the legislature, and the tension escalated.

It worsened dramatically in the spring of 1768, after shipping magnate John Hancock's employees forcibly interfered with inspectors who tried to search one of his vessels. Customs commissioners were furious over the insult to their authority and later ordered the seizure of Hancock's sloop *Liberty* for underreporting the amount of Madeira wine it carried back from Portugal. When the night came for the comptroller and port collector to take control of the vessel, sailors from the British frigate *Romney* were on hand to assist in the seizure, but a riot broke out first. The mob attacked the two officials and soon after ransacked and vandalized their homes and property. In fear for their lives, customs commissioners fled to Castle Island for protection, while press gangs from the *Romney* began forcing Boston men into service in the Royal Navy, which fueled even greater outrage. Governor Bernard felt the town was becoming ungovernable, and, with his assent at the end of the summer, the Earl of Hillsborough ordered troops to Boston to bring the town to heel.

Parliament had already directed colonial legislatures to provide housing for the British military under the terms of the Quartering Act of 1765, and three years later, commanding General Thomas Gage, at the behest of Bernard and Hillsborough, took advantage of that law. He directed troops to occupy the town by stationing the 29th Regiment on the Common, part of the 59th on Griffin's Wharf, and the 14th in Faneuil Hall and the Town House (after a debacle trying to house them at the Manufactory House). They also took positions at guardhouses, including a prominent one at the Fortification Gates on the Boston Neck, and claimed the right to question residents' movements and interrogate them to hunt down deserters and subversives.

For loyalists and Tories who had long feared radical mobs, the troop presence provided comfort, for—according to Anne Hulton, sister of a customs commissioner—"it is certain that our safety & quiet depends on the Army & Navy being here." For Whigs and patriots, the occupation was an affront to their liberties and even their pocketbooks. On their off time, soldiers took jobs at workshops, docks, and ropewalks, working for wages less than those of hometown laborers and taking jobs away from residents who desperately needed them. More alarmingly, the British troops fought with local night watchmen who dared to question their movements after dark, and they behaved boorishly on and off duty. They drank to excess, and patriot newspapers reported their transgressions in detail. One journal condemned the "drunkenness, debaucheries, and other extravagances which prevail by means of the troops being quartered in the midst of a town, where distilled spirits are so cheap and plenty."

Faced with the hostile attitudes of soldiers and royal officials, Whigs and patriots took out their frustrations on merchants who refused to commit to nonimportation. In 1769, a merchants committee demanded that the names of importers of British goods be published in newspapers, and that consumers refuse to do business with them. Mobs broke the shop windows of merchants on the list, defaced their signs, vilified them on broadsides, damaged their property, and threatened them with tarring and feathering or hanging. Even a newspaperman like John Mein, a vocal loyalist who published scathing caricatures of leading patriots and merchants in the *Boston Chronicle*, received death threats, was attacked with a shovel, and had to go into hiding in fear for his life.

By the winter of 1770, violence had become a common instrument of politics. First, a mob intimidated a local merchant, Theophilus Lillie, before attacking a customs informer named Ebenezer Richardson. When Richardson fired a weapon in his defense and killed a child named Christopher Seider, Boston patriots had a martyr to rally around and a new villain to condemn. Then another round of violence broke out at the ropewalks on the South End, as insults between rope workers and soldiers turned into fisticuffs and injuries. Many feared an even worse outbreak of mass violence would follow.

That outbreak came just a few weeks later, on an icy day in March outside the Custom House.

The episode began with insults exchanged between a sentry and a wigmaker's apprentice, but it quickly escalated as a crowd surrounded the sentry and threatened him. The fracas drew eight 29th Regiment grenadiers from their barracks to provide assistance as the crowd grew larger—up to a hundred people—and included working men from sailors and artisans to day laborers and teenage boys. The crowd hurled rocks and ice at the grenadiers, who assumed a defensive posture in a semicircle with their muskets pointed outward. After several minutes, one soldier fell, and his weapon discharged; someone may have yelled "Fire!"; and the rest of the troops fired on the crowd. When the smoke cleared, three men lay dead on the snowy cobbles, two more would soon die, and six had suffered injuries.

Patriots led by Samuel Adams channeled public outrage over the incident, calling it "the Massacre on King Street." Paul Revere made a widely distributed engraving of it. The town meeting condemned the bloodshed and demanded the reassignment of army regiments to prevent any more violence between soldiers and residents. Acting Governor Thomas Hutchinson agreed to support the request, and the military withdrew the troops to Castle Island. The grenadiers' commander, Captain Thomas Preston, faced arrest and imprisonment for his actions, as did the men under his charge.

Surprisingly, the main lawyer for the grenadiers' defense would be John Adams, ardent patriot and Samuel Adams's cousin. The younger Adams took the job to show the Whig faction was just as committed to protecting the traditional rights of British subjects (including trial by jury) as the Crown was to violating them. Through skillful legal maneuvers, Adams got a jury to acquit Preston of murder and, in a separate trial, helped five of the seven grenadiers to go free as well, though two would be convicted of manslaughter and branded on the thumbs. Samuel Adams and other radicals denounced the lenient verdicts, but the outcome did forestall another riot, at least for the moment.

Also helping lower the temperature, Bostonians learned, in April 1770, that Parliament had repealed Townshend duties on all commodities except tea. Samuel Adams claimed the effort didn't go far enough and argued the boycott of British goods should continue until all duties were removed. But the nonimportation movement across the colonies began to weaken. By the next year, it had collapsed, as imports increased by six times over what they'd been two years before, and the public eagerly bought British woolen textiles, beaver and felt hats, window glass, books, pewter, earthenware, cordage, nails, and wrought iron, as well as spices, sugar, coffee, china, and fabrics like silk, damask, and velvet. Soon, the tonnage of imports had never been higher, and Boston's trade imbalance spiked—spelling trouble for its economy. Whereas most colonies could balance the new wave of imports with exports of raw commodities back to Britain, much of New England still had to rely on smuggling from the West Indies and continental Europe to make up the difference.

By the summer of 1772, the patriot movement was ebbing. It looked as if the new hunger for consumer goods, combined with the reduced military presence, might be enough to thwart whatever rebellious tendencies the townsfolk possessed. Nonimportation was no longer a cause that appealed to the majority of citizens, mob violence lessened considerably, and loyalists and Tories began to feel confident about their political prospects. Governor Hutchinson even contrived a scheme for the Crown to pay his salary and those of appointed judges instead of having to depend on unreliable colonial legislators, who traditionally provided the funding.

The governor made a serious misstep with this plan. When word of it leaked, Samuel Adams arranged for the town meeting to draft and release a forty-three-page pamphlet-letter that claimed his proposal was a template for tyranny, and that the rights of British citizens would surely suffer at the hands of unaccountable royal officials. The letter went out to 260 other towns in Massachusetts, encouraging them to set up "Committees of Correspondence" to share news and coordinate strategy "to state the rights of the colonists and of this province in particular" against their infringement by the Crown.

While correspondence committees had first been used against imperial policy eight years earlier, only now did they achieve real momentum. Within one year, about half the towns contacted set up their own committees, and they soon appeared in most other colonies from the Carolinas to New Hampshire. Patriots praised the idea of a "government of committees" that could act as an alternative to a corrupt royal bureaucracy, while Tories called the concept "the foulest, subtlest and most venomous serpent ever issued from the eggs of sedition."

After Hutchinson's royal-funding mistake, his luck only got worse. Benjamin Franklin discovered some letters he had written to the British undersecretary of state four years earlier, when he was still the lieutenant governor. The content was explosive, with Hutchinson arguing, "There must be an Abridgment of what are called English Liberties. . . . I doubt whether it is possible to project a System of Government in which a Colony 3,000 miles distant from the parent State shall enjoy all the Liberty of the parent State." Franklin entrusted the letters to the care of Assembly Speaker Thomas Cushing, who put them in the hands of Samuel Adams, who then released them to the press. Widespread outrage followed over the governor's apparent indifference to individual rights, and he felt compelled to return to Britain to defend himself and his conduct. Before Hutchinson left, though, he would have to watch as Bostonians took the most important step on their road toward revolution.

In May 1773, Parliament passed the Tea Act to reduce the retail price of that commodity and encourage consumption of some of the seventeen million pounds of tea the East India Company had stored in its London warehouses (since the company was in a perilous state of indebtedness and needed to reduce its inventories). The plan was to ship two thousand chests of the leaf to four major American towns along the Eastern Seaboard, with "tea consignees"—approved wholesalers—signing for the cargo and selling it to other merchants. Eventually, the commodity would retail for a price comparable to the prices charged by smugglers, who mainly received their product from Dutch colonies.

The smugglers were, of course, unhappy about this turn of events. Since they provided up to three-quarters of the 1.2 million pounds of tea consumed in British North America, the economic cost to them would be huge if the Crown's latest trade gambit succeeded. In coordination with their allies in the Sons of Liberty and other patriot clubs, they raised the specter of the East India Company dumping mass quantities of tea on the American market, acquiring a monopoly over it, and distracting colonists from the even greater crime of still having to pay the duty retained from the Townshend Acts.

By the fall, opposition began to spread, and tea consignees like Richard Clarke came under pressure in print and on broadsides to resign their positions. They refused, even when threatened with injury to themselves and their businesses. So Samuel Adams resorted to the town meeting to stop the landing of the tea, first at Faneuil Hall and then at a series of mass meetings at the Old South Meetinghouse that drew up to five thousand people—a third of the town's entire population. Speakers demanded protection of colonists' political and economic rights from the Crown's latest affront, and vowed to resist "the ill effects of tea on the constitution."

Although in other major port towns efforts to avert a crisis succeeded, in Boston, they came to nothing. Governor Hutchinson simply wouldn't allow the three tea ships that had arrived (a fourth ran aground near Provincetown) to depart Boston Harbor once they had entered it.

This meant that at midnight on December 16, 1773, the product would be received whether Adams and the population approved of it or not.

A few hours before the deadline, hundreds of men in disguises marched through the South End to Griffin's Wharf, where the three ships sat at anchor. Forcing their way aboard the vessels, they intimidated the captains and crew to keep them from interfering with their plans. Over a few hours, the men took control of 342 chests of prime East India Company tea, broke them open, and scattered their contents into the water. No one was killed and few were injured, but the Destruction of the Tea, as it was known, resounded across the Atlantic in a way few riots ever had.

Parliamentarians were infuriated by what they saw as a bald-faced act of sedition. Three months later, they began passing a series of laws known as the Coercive Acts, or in America, the Intolerable Acts. Among them, the Port Act was the most punitive to the local economy, closing Boston Harbor to all but military vessels until residents repaid the financial loss of the tea. The act also moved the colonial capital to Salem and relocated the custom house to Plymouth. Even worse politically was the Massachusetts Government Act, which gave the royal governor (instead of the Assembly) the power to choose councilors by "writ of mandamus" and to appoint sheriffs and other officials, and it abolished the town meeting except by permission of the governor. Then, there was the Administration of Justice Act, which allowed for the trial of accused Crown officials to take place in England instead of the colonies, thus putting them out of reach of justice as some patriots feared. The Quartering Act, meanwhile, allowed army commanders to house troops in barns and unoccupied buildings, regardless of how their owners felt about it.

The Port Act in particular had a devastating effect. Residents refused to pay any monies to the Crown for the detested tea, so they had no choice but to see their harbor closed by force of arms. Boston spiraled into a depression, with unemployment spiking, shops closing, merchants becoming bankrupt, food supplies dwindling, and diseases like smallpox spreading. Prominent merchant John Rowe said, "Poor Unhappy Boston. God knows only thy wretched Fate. I see nothing but misery will attend thy Inhabitants." John Adams wrote to his wife, Abigail, "The Town of Boston, for ought I can see, must suffer Martyrdom: It must expire: And our principal Consolation is, that it dies in a noble Cause."

To survive, Bostonians had to relocate or rely on charity from the rest of the region. Colonies as far away as Maryland and Virginia sent barrels of pork, wheat, bread, flour, corn, and other staples by land, and residents of the countryside offered what produce they had to keep people from poverty and starvation. Still, it wasn't enough. At the harbor, the wharves stood empty, and the only water traffic came from the Royal Navy unloading new regiments to reoccupy the town. Even loyalists like Anne Hulton were shocked at the baleful effect of the law, describing Boston as "now a very gloomy place, the Streets almost empty, many families have removed from it, & the Inhabitants are divided into several parties, at variance, & quarreling with each other, some appear desponding, others full of rage."

By the middle of 1774, Thomas Hutchinson had left America and turned over his governorship to General Thomas Gage. Gage dissolved the elected Assembly, issued a proclamation threatening anyone who signed a covenant refusing to buy British goods, and revoked the charter that had governed Massachusetts since the previous century. He appointed a governor's council of loyalists and selected judges and other officials who would support and uphold his policies. But many of his handpicked favorites would not serve on the council or on a bench where they were despised by the great majority of residents, and Gage soon learned his power was limited. As one account put it: "With all the support furnished by a royal governor, royal judges, and a royal army, the courts could not sit, jurors would not serve, and the people would not obey. Sheriffs were timid, councilors resigned their places and soldiers deserted. Meanwhile the colonists were busy, maturing their plans in clubs, caucuses, and conventions."

Indeed, Gage's power over Massachusetts didn't extend much beyond Boston and Salem and whatever territory his regiments occupied. Away from his control, Whigs and patriots promoted a new boycott of British goods, especially tea, and encouraged other colonists to join them by way of the Committees of Correspondence. They also elected their own legislature, the Provincial Congress, which was held in Concord and later Cambridge, comprising 262 members drawn from two hundred towns in Massachusetts. This functional alternative government passed laws and resolutions against the interests of the Crown, despite the general's threats against its members.

Radical patriots took even stronger measures. In June 1774, Samuel Adams and Joseph Warren drafted the Solemn League and Covenant, which encouraged men and women to sign their names to a pledge to shun British goods and not do business with those who sold them. Two months later, Warren drafted the Suffolk Resolves to spur towns in Suffolk County to oppose the Coercive Acts, support nonimportation, refuse to pay taxes to Gage's government, and assist citizens to set up their own local governments and militia.

At this point, the Committees of Correspondence were sharing news and coordinating strategy among all the colonies of British North America, and patriots used them as an organizing tool to send delegates to Philadelphia for unified action against Parliament and the Crown. In August, John and Samuel Adams joined Robert Treat Paine and Thomas Cushing as the Boston delegation to what came to be known as the Continental Congress, composed of fifty-five delegates from all colonies except Georgia. The body adopted a "Continental Association" to prohibit importation from and exportation to Great Britain and its colonies. Seven thousand colonists joined inspection committees to ensure compliance with the plan, which would stay in effect until Parliament repealed all its recent duties, reduced the power of the admiralty courts for customs regulation, and quashed the Coercive Acts.

While Whig politics were taking a turn toward the revolutionary, General Gage was busy turning Boston into an armed camp. Four regiments occupied the Common, with twenty-two field pieces for three artillery companies, and he stationed additional detachments at Fort Hill, Castle Island, and other strongholds. He fortified the Neck, preventing easy access by land, and enforced martial law to allow sentries to arrest any citizens they deemed suspicious and to gain the upper hand against rebel factions Gage believed to be plotting against his rule.

Many with Whiggish or patriot sympathies attempted to leave town, either by the carefully guarded Fortification Gates or over the water, taking care to avoid British gunboats on patrol. They did so to avoid poverty or starvation, or to escape the abuse they sometimes endured at the hands of Gage's troops. More than a few soldiers drank to excess and got into regular scuffles with night watchmen and market vendors, while the loudest offenders shouted abuse from coffee house balconies—"the most vile, profane, blackguard language as ever was express'd"—or threatened to hang anyone they didn't perceive to be loyal to the king.

Gage himself was concerned enough about such behavior that he increased the severity of corporal punishment against offenders in a bid to improve relations between the military and the residents. But some of his senior officers, known as "fire and sword men," found the torments of the townsfolk perfectly acceptable, for "nothing but the Bayonet & Torch will ever Bring this Country['s] People to reason."

Patriot leaders were well aware of the threat Gage's forces presented against the colony. Accordingly, the Provincial Congress organized groups of militia drawn from men who could be ready to fight at short notice—called "Minute Men"—as well as a Committee of Safety to oversee security. Because a third of all able-bodied men in Massachusetts had already served in the Seven Years' War, and many of them had access to weapons and powder, finding potential soldiers to counter any British invasion of the interior would not be difficult. More challenging would be to find leaders who could train and command them. Nonetheless, military preparation continued until Massachusetts fielded the rudiments of an army that could hold its ground against a British incursion, or so the leaders of the Congress hoped.

However, while Americans seemed to have sufficient martial spirit, flintlock muskets, and charcoal for gunpowder, they lacked enough saltpeter and sulfur to make that powder. Two-thirds of it would have to be imported from Spanish, Dutch, and French colonies, among other sources. Parliament recognized the lack and, by the end of 1774, outlawed the transfer of munitions to the colonies to keep them from being any better armed than they already were, and to hamper colonials in a military conflict that now looked inevitable.

It was Lord Dartmouth who prompted that conflict in a January 1775 letter to Gage. As the colonial secretary of state, he ordered the general to reestablish royal authority in Massachusetts and to "arrest the principal actors and abettors in the Provincial Congress." He also promised that three more regiments and seven hundred marines were on the way to reinforce his troops. Gage received the message three months later and acted swiftly to fulfill Dartmouth's edicts. He would arrange to seize the arms depot at Concord, though he was more hesitant to arbitrarily arrest rebel leaders.

On April 15, Richard Devens, a ranking member of the Committee of Safety, learned from his Boston spy network that Gage was planning some sort of deployment, based on the disposition of the general's forces. He conveyed this news to his superior Joseph Warren, chair of the committee, who still lived in occupied Boston and did not delay in assigning men to alert the countryside that an invasion was at hand. Chief among these were the tanner William Dawes, who would take the message over the Boston Neck while it was still accessible, and the versatile artisan Paul Revere.

Revere had two of his associates ascend the steeple of Christ Church to alert patriots in Charlestown of the news, using paired lanterns to signal that British forces would be crossing the Charles River and making their way into the Massachusetts interior. To ensure his message got through, Revere rowed with two other allies across the Charles, borrowed a horse, and galloped westward to alert the countryside. He announced his message along the way, until the land resounded with drums beating and bells ringing, as part of an alarm system that Revere had helped to set up before his ride. When he arrived in Lexington, he told Samuel Adams and John Hancock, both staying at a parsonage, that they were in danger of arrest.

Around seven hundred British troops reached Lexington at dawn on the morning of April 19. They met a small force of seventy-seven rebel militiamen on the town green and ordered them to disarm. Shots rang out, and eight of the defenders lay dead before the British decided to continue on to Concord. By that point, Hancock and Adams had already escaped to safety outside the town.

At the Concord River, the redcoats secured the North Bridge and continued on to Barrett Farm in search of arms and powder, most of which had already been moved elsewhere. They burned the remnant of munitions they found before hundreds of militiamen arrived and skirmishes broke out. A few hours later, the soldiers began to retreat to Boston, but only after two thousand patriots had assembled to confront them. Taking cover behind buildings and trees, sheds and rock walls, the militiamen assailed the British troops from all sides and pursued them over eighteen miles of countryside. The soldiers eventually returned to the safety of Boston Harbor and artillery support from the Royal Navy, but by then, they had suffered a shocking three hundred casualties—versus only ninety-three for the Americans. It was an unexpected patriot victory and the first battle in what would come to be known as the War of Independence.

After the battles, fifteen thousand militiamen deployed around Boston and cut off British troops from access to the interior, leaving the only British resupply routes by sea. As doctor James Thacher wrote in his *Military Journal*, "The country militia, in great numbers, have arrived from various parts of New England; and the town of Boston is now invested on all sides, and thus is the whole royal army reduced to the humble condition of a besieged garrison."

General Gage realized the peril of this position, and he plotted strategy to gain the initiative. He suspected that countless subversives hid among the citizenry in Boston, and that patriots were only waiting for the right opportunity to advance from Roxbury by way of the Neck. He moved the troops stationed on the Charlestown Peninsula back to Boston and locked down the Fortification Gates, though he permitted Whigs and patriots to leave if they relinquished their weapons, and loyalists to return from the countryside for their own safety.

With the most prominent summits on the Charlestown Peninsula unoccupied, patriot leaders saw an opportunity to command the heights and bombard British positions. The Provincial Congress ordered the commander of the Massachusetts militia, Artemus Ward, to seize the 110-foot-tall Bunker Hill. On the evening of June 16 and the early morning of the next day, Colonel William Prescott led a force of what would become 940 troops to cross over to the peninsula and the high ground overlooking Boston.

But Prescott and his subordinates did not fortify Bunker Hill; instead, they defied the Congress's instructions and chose the much smaller Breed's Hill on which to build a redoubt—much closer to British troops occupying Boston. The militiamen worked overnight to build the earthen wall of the fortification and surrounding breastworks, and they were joined by the New Hampshire troops of Colonel John Stark, who took positions in rows behind a low wall along a beach of the Mystic River.

General Gage could not allow the rebels to hold such a position so close to his own forces, so he ordered the newly arrived General William Howe to attack the redoubt and take back control of the peninsula. Howe's men reached the area by the early afternoon of the next day, engaging in a furious series of assaults against the patriot lines and incinerating the town of Charlestown. However, they could not breach those lines: veteran troops, like the Royal Welch Fusiliers, suffered 80 percent casualties along the beach, and two successive attacks up the slope of Breed's Hill produced nothing but staggering British losses.

As the day wore on, the British received needed reinforcements while the defenders' ammunition began to run out. Howe ordered his grenadiers to make another assault up the slope. They endured even more casualties but made gradual progress until they reached the redoubt and seized it with hand-to-hand combat. The rebels made an orderly retreat toward the neck of the peninsula, with their worst loss being newly appointed General Joseph Warren, who came late to the battle to serve as a common infantryman.

For the British, the victory was Pyrrhic: a loss of more than a thousand fighting men, or two and a half times that of the rebels. In Boston, hundreds of wounded soldiers filled makeshift hospitals in private homes and taverns, and the army's feeling of invincibility gave way to the reality of having to fight a hard, relentless campaign. Within weeks, General Gage was out as royal governor, and William Howe became the commander of British forces.

Patriots soon realized their loss on the peninsula might be a kind of victory. Their troops had performed well under fire, exhibited as courageous a performance as the redcoats, and held out until they could no longer do so. But militia commanders became a target for criticism, with generals like Artemus Ward singled out as incompetent for failing to resupply Prescott's men with ammunition or to provide anything but a token amount of artillery support. Luckily, though, new leadership was on its way. And that leadership would come from a Virginian named George Washington, who would lead not a state militia but a newly organized, intercolonial Continental Army to try to drive the British out of North America for good.

In August 1775, King George III responded to the bloodshed and disloyalty of his American subjects by declaring them in "an open and avowed Rebellion, by arraying themselves in hostile Manner to withstand the Execution of the Law, and traitorously preparing, ordering, and levying War against Us." His remedy was for his officers and soldiers to suppress the insurrection and to "bring to condign Punishment the Authors, Perpetrators and Abettors of such traitorous Designs." The king's statement was dramatic but didn't change the situation on the ground, where the British were now trapped behind siege lines from which they had no easy escape.

It was a trap partly of their own making. The Neck was now nearly impregnable, artillery batteries stood at Fort Hill, Fox Hill, Copp's Hill, and the Trimountain, grenadiers occupied barracks on the Common, floating batteries prevented movement across the Charles River, and Bunker Hill's summit had been turned into a British stronghold. But for all Gage's efforts, the departing general had still left Dorchester Heights open and unoccupied.

Within Boston, the garrisons took fire from rebel batteries surrounding the town, as siege artillery sent round shot and mortar bombs into the camps and sometimes hit churches, public buildings, and private homes. The sound of gunfire echoed through the streets from skirmishes, and church bells tolled for the dead with morbid regularity, until the British military finally put a stop to the practice. Food became expensive, with low-grade meat only occasionally available, and a small cut of lamb costing a great sum. With most fruit and vegetables hard to find, scurvy and malnutrition spread among the troops and the population. As John Andrews said, dining in Boston meant eating "[p]ork and beans one day, and beans and pork another, and fish when we can catch it."

Firewood, too, was hard to find and usually appropriated for military needs, so some residents were reduced to burning twigs and branches, or even horse dung. Disease spread faster than ever, and not just the familiar plague of smallpox but "diarrhea, dysentery, food poisoning, malnutrition, pleuritical disorders, respiratory infections, arthritis, rheumatism, scurvy, and typhoid-typhus." Most Congregational ministers fled town and couldn't provide aid to the victims, but New North Minister Andrew Eliot stayed, writing, "I can do little for God & his people, but hope my tarrying here has been of use. I am continually employed in visiting the sick, who are numerous, in attending the prisoners."

Looting and crime were rampant, and some Bostonians felt it necessary to stay in town and endure the siege just to protect their property. However, they couldn't stop British officers from commandeering their homes for lodging, nor could they prevent British soldiers from tearing down their fences, trees, houses, barns, and wharves for firewood; or vandalizing the inventories of merchants; or throwing their barrels of salt, sugar, and flour into the river (perhaps in revenge for patriots doing the same thing to British tea chests).

The army resorted to arbitrary arrest and detention to punish the townsfolk, sometimes for minor "offenses" like complaining about soldiers stealing from private homes, arguing politics or questioning the war, or just walking around without a pass. The son of the headmaster at Boston Latin (closed like other schools) was arrested and charged with being a spy, and the son of the publisher Benjamin Edes was accused of storing weapons and jailed for 107 days, given only bread and water for the first sixty-three of them.

By the turn of 1776, many in the British military understood the situation was hopeless, and that their efforts to counter the rebels might be better spent elsewhere. Under the command of General Howe, they made plans to relocate to New York, but not before General Washington made a surprising move. In early March, his troops, under the command of John Thomas, used the distraction of a cannonade to occupy Dorchester Heights with hastily built fortifications and with emplaced cannon to fire upon British garrisons on the South End. The gambit worked, and Howe felt it necessary to speed up his withdrawal. Under an implicit agreement with Washington not to destroy the town if the regiments could leave without facing attack, Howe and his men prepared to depart.

In the process, they somehow vandalized Boston even worse than before. They scattered tree limbs, iron balls covered in spikes, and other impediments along the streets to prevent militiamen or subversives from chasing them on their way out. They packed up their powder stores, cannon, and ammunition, stripped workshops of their tools and valuables, and wrecked the nonmilitary boats in the harbor. Eldad Taylor, a member of a local committee of safety, reported, "The ministerial butchers have robbed the warehouses and shops of all the best goods they could carry, and destroyed what they could in their hurry. They destroyed the furniture of the houses, broke the windows, chairs, desks, tables, &c. They loaded their vessels so deep that they threw overboard much of their lumber, which floats on the water." John Rowe put it more simply: "There never was such Destruction & Outrage committed any day before this."

Once the army had moved its plundered goods into the holds of Royal Navy ships, the troops boarded those ships and took more than a thousand loyalists with them, sailing onward to New York, to Halifax, Nova Scotia, or back to Great Britain. In Braintree, Abigail Adams witnessed the massive evacuation and saw the masts of the 170 ships at sail, writing, "They look like a forest."

In the aftermath of March 1776, only a few thousand souls remained to brave what was left of Boston, but others slowly returned. They came back to find overgrown yards and gardens, missing fences, and gutted buildings. They found churches like Old North Meetinghouse disassembled for firewood and Old South Meetinghouse converted into a riding school. Abandoned wagons and carts, spiked cannon, and assorted junk littered the streets, while empty docks and pilfered stores added to the bleak atmosphere. The damage to the homes of leading patriots was arbitrary: John Hancock's mansion, occupied by General Henry Clinton, stood in fairly good shape, while Sam Adams's house had been vandalized and ruined beyond repair.

Three days after the evacuation, patriot troops at last passed through the Fortification Gates with their regimental colors flying and drums beating. Dr. James Thacher reported, "While [we were] marching through the streets, the inhabitants appeared at their doors and windows; though they manifested a lively joy on being liberated from a long imprisonment, they were not altogether free from a melancholy gloom which ten tedious months' siege has spread over their countenances."

The residents and their leaders took action to fix what was broken. In the town meeting and other civic gatherings, they laid plans to clear damage from the streets, get foodstuffs to markets, elect town officers, reopen schools, and make sure the town wouldn't burn from a lack of fire equipment. However, they also knew many homes would have to be wrecked and rebuilt, and several churches were so damaged, they wouldn't reopen for years. But the Thursday Lecture tradition was quickly revived for those seeking comfort in the promise of salvation, with Andrew Eliot the presiding minister.

And now, in the summer of 1776, the fortunes of Boston seem to be slowly reviving. More people continue to trickle back to town, a growing number of public services are available, and the townsfolk are doing what they can to aid the success of the Continental Army. About 70 percent of the men in Massachusetts will join that army, and Spain and France have authorized one million livres' worth of munitions for the patriot cause, including thirty thousand muskets, three hundred thousand pounds of gunpowder, and twenty-five thousand uniforms for the troops. Local ships and gunboats have driven the last British warships from the outer harbor, and the port of Boston is finally reopened to commercial traffic after two years of closure.

Most important, on July 18, the Declaration of Independence was read out from the balcony of the Town House to cheers along King Street and throughout town. Thirteen blasts resounded from the surrounding hills, and according to Dr. Thacher, a "detachment of artillery in King Street discharged their cannon thirteen times; which was followed by the two regiments in thirteen separate divisions; all corresponding to the number of the American United States."

BOSTON, 1776

A ROGUE TOUR OF BOSTON—REVOLUTION CITY

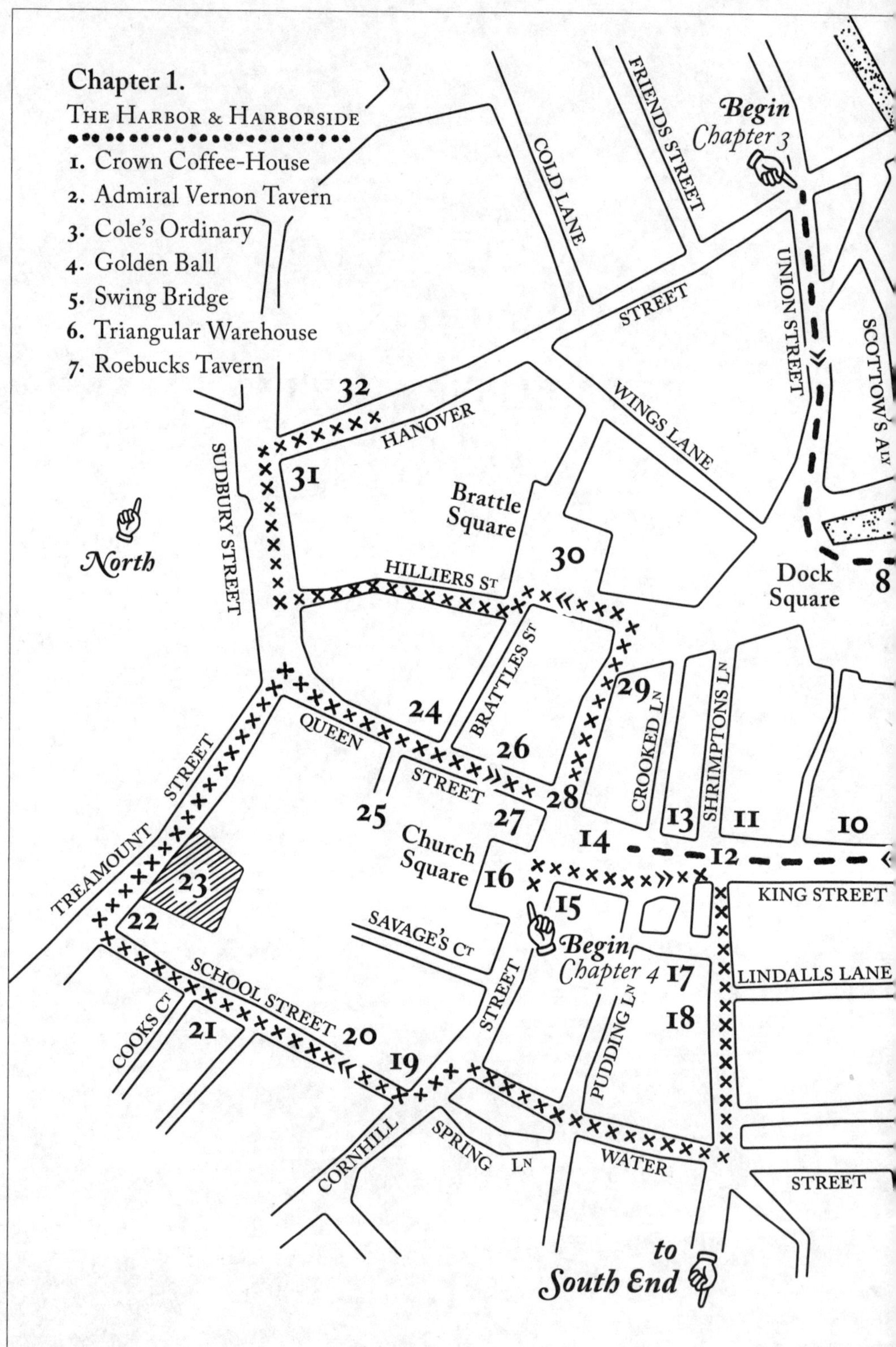
Chapter 1.
The Harbor & Harborside
1. Crown Coffee-House
2. Admiral Vernon Tavern
3. Cole's Ordinary
4. Golden Ball
5. Swing Bridge
6. Triangular Warehouse
7. Roebucks Tavern
Begin Chapter 3
Begin Chapter 4
to South End
North
Cold Lane
Friends Street
Union Street
Scottow's Aly
Street
Wings Lane
Hanover
Sudbury Street
Brattle Square
Hilliers St
Brattles St
Dock Square
Queen Street
Crooked Ln
Shrimptons Ln
Church Square
Treamount Street
King Street
Savage's Ct
Lindalls Lane
School Street
Cooks Ct
Street
Pudding Ln
Cornhill
Spring Ln
Water Street

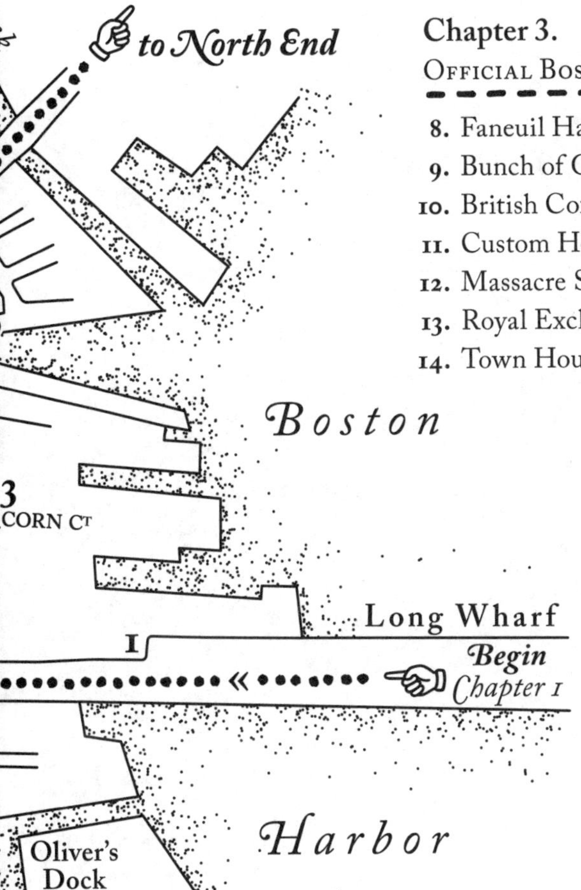

Chapter 3.
Official Boston

8. Faneuil Hall
9. Bunch of Grapes Tavern
10. British Coffee-House
11. Custom House
12. Massacre Site
13. Royal Exchange Tavern
14. Town House

Chapter 4.
The Town Center

15. London Book-Store
16. First Church *(Old Brick)*
17. Quaker Meetinghouse
18. Quaker Burying Ground
19. Apothecary *(Hutchinson Site)*
20. Cromwell's Head Tavern
21. Boston Latin School
22. King's Chapel
23. King's Chapel Burying Ground
24. Edes & Gill Print Shop
25. Queen Street Prison
26. Adams House
27. Elizabeth Murray Shop *(Former Site)*
28. Town Pump
29. Sun Tavern
30. Brattle Street Church
31. Concert Hall
32. Joseph Warren House

☆ 1 ☆

The Harbor and Harborside

It's no small challenge to visit Boston in July 1776. It's a time of war and rebellion, economic upheaval and social turmoil, and traveling will put you at hazard. To reach the town by sea, you'll sail past fortified islands and gun batteries and hostile naval fleets; to reach it by land, you'll navigate a tortuous inland route to a single point of entry on the Boston Neck (see p. 183). Either way, it's a hard journey, but well worth it. Because Boston is the seedbed of the American Revolution, and there's no place in America quite like it.

By sea, you'll arrive in Boston Harbor on a schooner, or perhaps a sloop. You might find a willing captain to give you a berth on a cargo ship, but more likely you'll have to sign on as a crew member at a dockside tavern or shipping office at one of the other American ports. (More dangerously, you can serve aboard a privateer that intercepts enemy commerce.) Be aware of the risk: Even though the last British man-of-war left the harbor in June, the Royal Navy still harasses nautical traffic in the Atlantic. If you're intercepted, you might be abducted and held prisoner, or impressed into service in the war, or face a barrage of cannon fire and go down with your ship.

Most visitors won't meet such a fate, and the odds are you won't either. You'll be in the company of ten to twenty sailors whose hard-earned experience crossing Massachusetts Bay helps them avoid its hazards. Your vessel will be carrying anything from codfish and lumber if it hails from a New England port, to tar and pitch if from North Carolina, to corn and oats if from the Middle Colonies. But it won't be carrying the goods of Great Britain. King George III has forbidden trade with his former colonies in British North America ever since he declared those colonies in "open and avowed Rebellion," and Parliament passed the Prohibitory Act to cut off their economic lifeline. As we know, the colonies have responded to these acts, and those before them, by renouncing the king and declaring their independence.

The bay stretches about forty miles from Cape Ann to Plymouth, with Boston Harbor roughly in the center. To reach the harbor, your crew will navigate a series of shallow channels and shoals. You'll pass islands with colorful names like Spectacle, Apple, Hog, and Bird, or more disturbing ones like Snake, Ragged, Hangman, and Graves. Two of the largest are Governors Island, with its expansive orchards and gardens, and, more importantly, Castle Island, a mile to the south. It's far from a pretty sight, with fortifications and outbuildings riddled with burned wood and walls scarred from fire damage. But it's well worth exploring, because this island is your entry point to the War of Independence. If you can persuade your captain to drop anchor, you'll see why.

Namely, it's a critical stronghold guarding the entrance to the harbor, essential for blockading shipping and for firing on enemy vessels. The British once emplaced two hundred guns, built towers and magazines and extensive fortifications, and named it Castle William after one of their kings. From this post, Commander William Howe oversaw the movement of eleven thousand troops, most of whom were stationed here or in the town proper during the Siege of Boston. When General Washington broke the siege and forced those troops to evacuate, Howe did his best to destroy the fort. His men incinerated the barracks and sank the ammunition in the bay, detonated what was left of the magazine, and burned everything else to render it useless for the Continental Army. As one witness described it, "in 20 minutes the whole was in flames. The repeated Shocks and Explosions of the Mines; the whole Scene most beautiful and Awful from the general Conflagration."

Surprisingly, they didn't succeed, at least not in full. Washington ordered army officer and part-time artist John Trumbull to douse the flames and take possession of the site, salvaging what he could. And as you can see, when you explore the island, most of the earthworks remain standing, 150 cannon are in various states of repair, and a team of builders and engineers is working to reconstruct the fort and its batteries. One of them might even be master silversmith Paul Revere, now holding the rank of lieutenant colonel and stationed on the island for its defense.

Away from the guns, there are the remains of barracks and quarters where soldiers and officers stayed, along with loyalists to the Crown. When he was lieutenant governor, Thomas Hutchinson found refuge here to keep a safe distance from mobs, as did other officials and their families. One of them was Ann Hulton, who relocated to the fort after the massacre outside the Custom House. As she wrote to a friend in Liverpool, "We never thought ourselves more safe from the Sons of Violence, than at present. . . . Yet our Security and the continuance of it, under a kind Providence depends on Circumstances, Chiefly the Authority & Support of Government." The government withdrew that support in March 1776, when 1,100 of Hulton's fellow loyalists were forced to flee the island along with the army, most of them never to see their home country again.

Once you've explored the ruins and reconstruction of the fort, return to the ship and secure your place on deck. Your captain will set a course for Boston proper, avoiding the Dorchester tidal flats to the south and the bars and islands to the north. Within a few miles, the town will rise into view. It's built on a two-mile-long peninsula, capped by great hills to the north and south, and adorned with a dozen church steeples. These are the tallest structures in town, up to 175 feet high, and seem to be reaching skyward to ask for God's favor.

If sufficiently inspired by the sight, you may be tempted to cry out to God yourself, as Governor John Winthrop did in a 1630 sermon, that Boston is "a City upon a Hill" where "the eyes of all people are upon us." He also warned that if the townsfolk incurred divine disfavor, "we shall shame the faces of many of God's worthy servants, and cause their prayers to be turned into curses upon us." You can decide for yourself if that prophecy has come true.

As you sail closer, northern Copp's Hill and southern Fort Hill will appear at opposite ends of a great crescent called the Town Cove. Near the center of the cove is the Long Wharf, flanked on each side by the decrepit Barricado, a failed attempt at a breakwater built in the late seventeenth century. The wood-and-stone barrier was designed to provide protection for the town, with gun emplacements to ward off the ships of European enemies and narrow entrances to allow passage for the ships of allies. It's now a ruin, collapsed along much of its length and good only for damaging the hulls of unwary vessels and providing a quarry for builders in need of heavy stones.

Sail past the Barricado and you'll reach Boston—City upon a Hill, former capital of the Massachusetts Bay Colony and Province of Massachusetts Bay, and a hotbed of rebellion. However, many of those who sparked that rebellion are not in town. The bigger names are in Philadelphia attending the Continental Congress, or fighting in Washington's Continental Army, or deployed in militia protecting the coast and countryside. But it doesn't take an encounter with a famous revolutionary to get a sense of revolution. Ask any dockman working the wharves or artisan looking for employment what they think of recent events, and they'll be glad to tell you. Most will curse the king, endorse the war, and offer their hopes for a new independent nation, even if they disagree about what exactly that might mean.

One thing is certain: Almost everyone wants the town to recover from the last decade of conflict, chaos, and financial near ruin. Not only have trade and commerce been crippled, but due to the exodus of patriots before the siege and the exodus of loyalists after it, the town has plummeted from more than 15,500 citizens to 2,700 and is only now recovering some of those residents. One of them might be you if you choose to stay and contribute your talents to its rebirth.

First, though, you'll have to debark at the Long Wharf as your crew prepares to moor. Stretching a third of a mile into the harbor, the wharf is laid out like a linear city, its north side lined with wooden shops and warehouses, the south side with docks and quays. Before the British trade embargo, the shops sold beaver hats and silks, imported fabrics and lace, among many other items. These days, the offerings are more scarce, but the wharf is still a hub of commerce where newcomers jostle with locals to secure the best deals on commodities from linen and canvas to gunpowder and snuff. Much of it comes from the ports of greater Massachusetts or other former American colonies, but every day, more merchandise becomes available from overseas, ever since the Continental Congress in April declared American ports open to the commerce of all nations—except Great Britain, of course.

One glance will tell you the Long Wharf is well named. It was built in the 1710s to be "the longest wharf on the continent" to accommodate the latest and largest vessels. Since that time, the wharf has seen its share of spectacle and drama. New royal governors made their first appearance here upon their investiture and led a procession west along King Street to the Town House. British troops disembarked here in 1768 to occupy the town and quell its rebellious spirit, marching from the wharf "with insolent Parade, Drums beating, Fifes playing, and Colours flying up King Street, each soldier having received 16 rounds of Powder and Ball." That same army left the wharf seven years later to fight the rebels at Bunker Hill and departed town for good the year after when General Washington forced them to evacuate. But despite the army's disappearance, they've left behind a deadly souvenir at the wharf and elsewhere in town: a smallpox epidemic.

The disease has been running rampant, first afflicting the king's troops and their loyalist supporters, and now affecting patriots who have returned home after the evacuation. Many Bostonians blame the army for intentionally spreading the plague and see it as part of a plot to cripple their health and spirit. No less than Washington himself has said "the enemy with a malicious assiduity have spread the infection of the smallpox through all parts of the town."

Regardless of the cause, though, all victims suffer in a similar way: first with fever, headache, and muscle pain, then with potential bleeding of the lungs and organs. A rash covers the body; wounds break and weep upon the skin; and wounds eventually become pockmarks that scar victims for life. Other effects include infertility, blindness, and death.

In response, the selectmen have taken measures to prevent it from spreading further. One of these tactics has been to prohibit visitors from arriving in, or even leaving, Boston if they are suspected of carrying the plague. Incoming vessels have to be free of disease carriers to dock, and any craft suspected of transmitting illness must be cleaned and decontaminated and its passengers sent to quarantine.

Assuming you're in good health, you can choose to get inoculated—as five thousand Bostonians have been, and as Washington has ordered his troops to be. During periods when the procedure is allowed, a physician will make a small incision in your skin with a lancet carrying the virus, and you will have to isolate yourself as you endure some milder symptoms of the disease. Once you're free of those symptoms, you will have lifelong immunity, provided there isn't a complication from the procedure. About six in one thousand people die from inoculation—a figure that might seem unsettling, but is actually far less than the fatality rate of the disease itself (one in ten).

There's one other matter to consider before you step off the boat: your captain will submit a list of passengers to the selectmen and will have to post bond for those who appear "impotent, lame or otherwise infirme." You are exempt from this law if you seem to be an "able-bodied worker of good character" and bring at least £50 in personal property. If you can't meet the standard, you may be forbidden to enter town. And even if you do enter Boston, you may not be allowed to stay, especially if confronted with the words, "I warn you to depart."

A man called a warner does this. He patrols the streets and wharves to find anyone he thinks to be a miscreant, a troublemaker, or, more commonly, a pauper, and informs them they have no more than twenty-one days to leave town. If there's any hint of you being "vicious" or having "criminal tendencies," the warner will do his best to drive you away. Other disfavored groups include immigrants from continental Europe, the frail and unhealthy, and anyone carrying "Dirt Dung Carrion or any Rubbish into the Streets or Lanes of this Town." But mainly the warners are looking for the poor, and they judge them by the condition of their faces, clothing, and goods, with an eye toward keeping them off the poor rolls and the system of charitable relief, which usually includes a stay at public expense in the Almshouse (see p. 111).

But presuming you're not carrying smallpox and don't look destitute, you can explore the town at will. As you stroll down the wharf, look around for a grand view of the harborside. At least 166 other wharves sit along the water, many of them busy with dockmen transporting cargo and merchants selling goods, others abandoned due to the bad economy. Almost all are privately owned and constructed according to a simple method: A wooden box frame is sunk into the water, built out into the harbor as far as necessary, and filled with anything from stone and gravel to wood, mud, and sand. Some of the cruder designs may even be loaded with underbrush and tree stumps. In any case, once the box is filled, it is covered with wooden planks and crossbeams and declared open for business.

Upon reaching the foot of King Street, you'll come to the Crown Coffee-House, a handsome two-story affair where you can imbibe with a mix of townsfolk and mariners. Naturally, you can have your fill of caffeine here, but as with so many coffee houses in Boston, the main appeal is alcohol. Around 130 taverns operate in Boston, and liquor is sold almost everywhere you look: in dedicated businesses like taverns, at inns where you might lodge after drinking, in dram shops catering to the poor and desperate, and by individuals on the docks and in private homes.

With so much booze on offer, John Winthrop would no doubt be shocked to see what has become of his City upon a Hill. In the early seventeenth century, he wrote of "the loathsome vice of Drunkennesse and other disorders in Alehouses," and decades later, Cotton Mather inveighed against drinking as a sign of "divine affliction, and a warning of eternal damnation." Puritan leaders called taverns "ordinaries" and sent out a "tithing-man" to inspect them for gamblers and tosspots. If caught and prosecuted, drunkards could be enchained by the ankles, clamped into stocks, repeatedly whipped, or even made to wear around their neck the letter "D" trimmed in red fabric.

These days, no one is made to wear such a scarlet letter, and most Bostonians drink with stubborn pride, whether or not they do it to excess. And even though the selectmen have identified in the taverns an increase in "idleness, drunkenness, profane cursing and swearing, and Sabbath breaking," they continue to license them liberally—so much so that the town now has more than twice the number of pubs per person than it did a century ago. Mather himself saw the change coming in his lifetime, when he remarked that every other house in Boston was an alehouse. In any case, the Crown Coffee-House is a fine place to start drinking.

Just south on Kilby Street, you can visit Oliver's Dock, once owned by and named after the rigidly loyalist Judge Peter Oliver. The dock itself is unexceptional, but it was the site where, a decade ago, Oliver constructed a brick building that, according to rumor, would serve as an office for administering the Stamp Act. It didn't last long. As one history recounts, "This small building was tumbled into the water by the patriotic mob. . . . That they instantly demolished." The crowd then turned its ire on Oliver's brother, Andrew, the Stamp Act commissioner, "and bearing each man a portion of the ruins upon his shoulder, they moved in solemn pomp to Fort-hill, where they made a bonfire in view of Mr. Oliver's house, and burnt the effigy upon it." (For more on the protests, see p. 125.)

From here, you should turn around and head north on Kilby. There are several important taverns at the intersection of King Street, which we'll return to in chapter 3, but for now, take a slight jog east along a dark and narrow path into the recesses of Merchants Row. It isn't more than twenty feet wide—no more than a glorified alley really—and you'll have to share space with horse and wagon traffic at close quarters, along with feral animals and pedestrians whose odor might best be described as fragrant. However, plenty of merchants, from grocers and furriers to apothecaries, share space along the route, along with some of the most intrepid liquor dealers in town.

The Admiral Vernon will first grab your attention, with its sprightly little figure-sign of a nautical officer holding a quadrant, but push on a few short blocks until you reach Corn Court. This was once called "a wheelbarrow-way of full five feet" and features what's reputed to be Boston's oldest tavern, "Cole's Ordinary." It's little more than an ancient-looking dive under a wooden pile, but it provides a sense of the foundations of Boston's drinking culture—though the evidence for it being the first (c. 1634), or even owned by Samuel Cole, is questionable.

More impressive is the adjacent Golden Ball, until recently owned by arch-patriot John Marston, one of several key spots where the Sons of Liberty have met to plot strategy against the British. You can spot the alehouse by the sight of its metallic orb hanging out front, and as long as you're not a loyalist, you'll find a welcoming atmosphere inside. Marston has set up drinking quarters throughout the house, with front and back chambers, an upper story, and a garret offering bottles of hard liquor, wine decanters, and shelves filled with china plates and bowls, to go along with a set of prayer books and the Bible, and an old Scottish claymore hanging from the wall.

Depending on your whim, you might be served tea or coffee in silver urns and pots, beer or cider from workaday mugs, or a meal with tableware carved from bone, ivory, or silver. Look around and you'll see handsome paintings and prints adorning the walls, the latest newspapers sitting on benches near the hearth, and the library boasting everything from Swift's essays to Defoe's *Robinson Crusoe* to Milton's *Paradise Lost*, with volumes on the history of New England, and England itself, thrown in for good measure. You might even find patriots reading the works of John Wilkes, the Whig parliamentarian who stands for personal liberty against the power of the state, or of Thomas Paine, author of *Common Sense* and the king's greatest foe of all.

Not all taverns are quite so inspired in their offerings. While Marston is a serious and committed patriot, other tavern keepers may cater to their patrons with cruder forms of amusement. These include displays of odd creatures like "cassowaries, learned pigs, learned horses," or blood sport like bear baiting and turkey shooting, or scientific curiosities like lightning rods and "elaborate clocks, moving puppets, and many mechanical contrivances." They might also invite patrons to attend a concert or gamble in a lottery. And unlike Marston's refined Golden Ball, some tavern owners advertise their wares with tawdry signs showing a dog swilling from a beer vessel (at the Dog and Pot), a dissolute god of the grape vines (at the Bacchus), or a lady without a head (at the Good Woman). However, no matter how base the appeal, few will dare hang a sign praising the monarchy. Since the war began, they've been replacing crowns and scepters with cocked hats and pictures of local heroes like John Hancock—making Boston's pubs, more than its newspapers or assembly halls, the best place to get a sense of the town's rogue spirit.

Once you've drunk your fill at Merchants Row, take a careful stagger as the street winds around to the Swing Bridge, where you come to the Town Dock. This is an enclosed cove stretching four blocks inland and ringed by wharves and markets selling meat and produce and the like. Lining the entire north side is the fish market, where small craft load and unload the harvest of New England's waters, moving anything from cod and haddock to oysters, clams, quahog, and mussels. Although some Bostonians are wary of eating too much fish, seeing it as the diet of Catholics and the poor, the market does a booming trade. You can even smell it in the air, especially during the summer months.

In fact, the odor of Town Dock will keep you from lingering. Local complaints to the selectmen say that, at low tide, the dock becomes "a very stinking puddle . . . very nauseous & offensive to all inhabitants who live near." Worse, the town's main sewer outlet opens right by the station for oyster boats, making for "a receptacle for every species of filth, and a public nuisance." More than a few citizens have pled to the selectmen to condemn the dock and fill in the cove, but with the outbreak of war and financial tumult, such a prospect seems unlikely any time soon.

You may find yourself at the Town Dock whether you want to or not. More than a few visitors have wandered away from the Long Wharf to hunt for landmarks of the Revolution, only to find themselves here instead. And if they wander any farther north, many become lost, befuddled, and enclosed by dark, narrow, and twisting alleys that seem more akin to the seventeenth century than the current one. So, considering the challenge before you, it may be a good time to take a break from your stroll and meditate on how Boston is laid out.

Of course, "laid out" implies a board of authority has planned the town and sketched out its design. This is not the case. Streets intersect at awkward angles, carry different names from one neighborhood to the next, and cannot be identified by visitors anyway because there are no signs to mark them—despite having charming names on paper like Frog Lane, Hog Alley, Elbow Alley, and Beer Lane. All of it leads to a helter-skelter visual quality in the "crowded late medieval tradition of the City of London."

Many of the avenues are similarly primitive, either unpaved or covered with pebbles, with a gutter down the center to collect rainwater and refuse. Horse manure and garbage from tailors and butchers collects along the roadside, and there are no sidewalks to avoid the mess. Still, despite the clutter, traffic crowds even the smallest lanes, and walking can be a hazard among the many carts and wagons, drays and wheelbarrows—not to mention the fast-moving carriages that can trample the slow-footed, wild dogs growling for food scraps, and uncovered wells where you might turn an ankle or break a leg. These impediments are especially hard to see at night, when the streets remain dark and unlit, aside from the dim glow of firelight from the taverns.

Yet Boston is a paradox. Despite its many hazards and eyesores, the town boasts several grand boulevards lined with dozens of elegant buildings—some among the finest in America. The mansions of the elite and better houses of artisans and merchants are the pride of their neighborhoods, and beyond them, there are scenic hills with wide vistas of the bay, fields and pastures as peaceful as anything in the countryside, and squares and plazas perfect for ceremony and celebration. You can find all of it in this town, as long as you don't mind traversing a bit of mud and chaos to get there.

Some of that mud and chaos is visible just beyond the next turn in the road. First, walk north over the Swing Bridge that crosses the inlet for the Town Dock, and you'll pass a massive triangular warehouse that looks like a French Renaissance fortress. It's rumored to store tea from the Netherlands—the kind of tea that was once smuggled into Boston before independence but can now be imported openly without a British customs officer forbidding it. Beyond the warehouse, the road descends into Roebuck's Passage, an ominous little corridor with a width of only thirteen feet in some places. In these sections, there's not enough room for two carts to pass, leaving the wagoners to decide the matter over a mug of ale at the adjacent Roebuck's Tavern. Squeeze by as best you can, because you'll not want to join them. The tavern has been called a "house of bad repute" and a "notorious resort of doubtful repute"—in both cases, a brothel.

Roebuck's is the first of many such businesses because, after the passage intersects with Ann Street, you're greeted with a slew of brothels and low-end dram shops along its entire length. One author describes it best, quoting Alexander Pope's poem "The Alley":

And on the broken pavement, here and there,
Doth many a stinking sprat and herring lie;
A brandy and tobacco shop is near,
And hens, and dogs, and hogs are feeding by;
And here a sailor's jacket hangs to dry.
At ev'ry door are sun-burnt matrons seen,
Mending old nets to catch the scaly fry;
Now singing shrill, and scolding eft between;
Scolds answer foul-mouth'd scolds; bad neighborhood I ween.

It wasn't always so. Local officials in the seventeenth century once occupied some of these wooden piles, at a time when the street featured a different cast of characters. Still, there were brothels quietly operating even then, and if their proprietors were caught, the punishments could be severe. In one case, the court fined a madam more than one hundred pounds— more than a year's salary for most workers—and sentenced her to be tied by the neck at a gallows before being stripped to the waist, strapped to a horse cart, and whipped repeatedly on her way to prison. But despite such fearsome penalties, by the early eighteenth century, prostitution had expanded its reach beyond civic authority to control it. Officials became more indulgent of it, since more than a few houses catered to a select and possibly elite clientele—to the widespread knowledge of local leaders. Cotton Mather, for one, said he was informed of "several Houses of This town, where there are young Women of a very debauched Character and extremely Impudent; unto whom there is a great resort of young men." One of them was Mather's own son "Cresy," who fathered a child out of wedlock with a prostitute.

Since then, churchmen have continued to condemn illegal sex, though the convictions have been fewer and the sentences lighter. In recent years, there have only been sixteen defendants put on trial for operating houses of prostitution, with fines of ten to twenty pounds and no whipping or other horrors, even in cases that involve patrons soliciting sex while also "quarrling fighting tipling & drinking to Excess, & otherwise misbehaving themselves." More commonly, mobs have enforced their own rules against brothels, especially if their employees solicit British soldiers. Violence erupted against several bawdy houses in 1734, 1737, and 1771, with street thugs tearing down buildings alleged to house sellers of sex, and on at least one occasion, the authorities cited several madams for "indecent exhibitions at their windows in the company of British officers." News articles reported one hundred women in the sex trade accompanying troops from Halifax to Boston and acting as camp followers for the men posted there. Officers justified these dalliances by saying Boston women were happy to entertain them—and always, they claimed, without compensation.

Now that the king's army has departed, there's less hostility against the trade, and in their more charitable moments, Bostonians will admit, "there is more Wickedness in many taverns than in any Bawdy House." For widows and younger women without any means of support, the business is a necessary evil to ward off poverty, hunger, and a trip to the Almshouse, especially at a time when the town itself is still recovering from the year-long siege and military occupation. So the illicit congress persists, in brothels and boardinghouses, in the back rooms of taverns, and in the bedrooms of private homes. Many of the patrons along Ann Street and other areas may still be drawn from the ranks of the military (albeit on the patriot side), as well as the artisan and merchant class. But by far the most common customers are mariners fresh from the sea. As one writer put it, "Wherever the haunts of sailors . . . there were sure to be houses of prostitution."

You can find many more sailors—along with the vessels of their trades, the taverns where they keep company, and their homes and churches and hideaways—as you follow Ann Street north, crossing the little bridge over Mill Creek and leading you into the neighborhood known as the North End.

The North End
Chapter 2

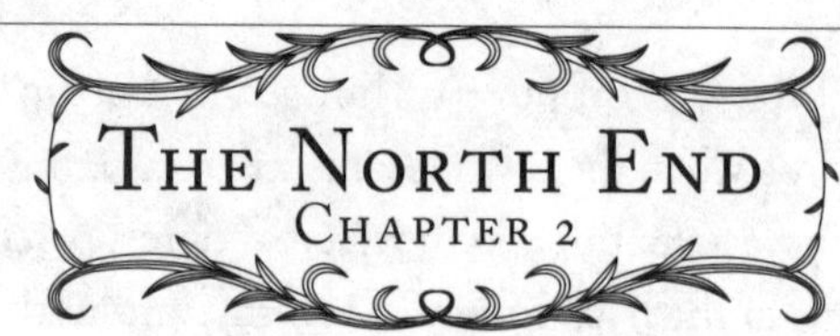

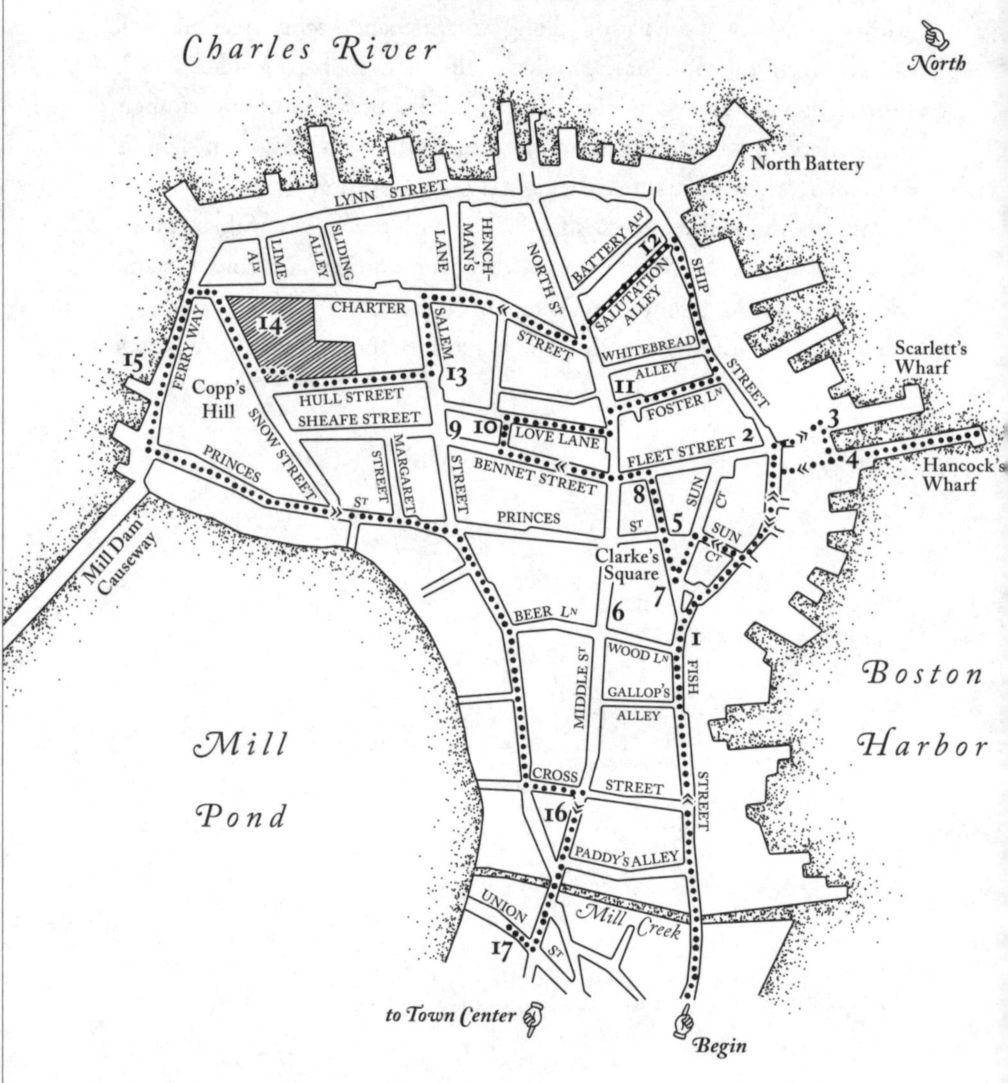

Charles River
North
North Battery
LYNN STREET
ALY
LIME
ALLEY
SLIDING
LANE
HENCH-
MAN'S
NORTH ST
BATTERY ALY
SALUTATION
ALLEY
SHIP
STREET
CHARTER
SALEM
STREET
WHITEBREAD
ALLEY
FOSTER LN
FERRY WAY
Copp's
Hill
SNOW STREET
HULL STREET
SHEAFE STREET
LOVE LANE
FLEET STREET
Scarlett's
Wharf
Hancock's
Wharf
PRINCES
ST
STREET
MARGARET
STREET
BENNET STREET
PRINCES
SUN
CT
SUN
CT
ST
Clarke's
Square
Mill Dam
Causeway
BEER LN
WOOD LN
GALLOP'S
ALLEY
MIDDLE ST
FISH
STREET
Boston
Harbor
Mill
Pond
CROSS
STREET
PADDY'S ALLEY
UNION
ST
Mill
Creek
to Town Center
Begin
1
2
3
4
5
6
7
8
9
10
11
12
13
14
15
16
17

1. Red Lion Inn
2. King's Head Tavern
3. Ship Tavern
4. Crown Tavern
5. Old North Meetinghouse *(site)*
6. New Brick Church
7. Paul Revere House
8. Thomas Hutchinson House
9. North End Grammar School
10. North Writing School
11. New North Church
12. Salutation Inn
13. Christ Church *(Old North Church)*
14. Copp's Hill Burying Ground
15. Ferry Landing
16. Lillie-Richardson Site
17. Green Dragon Tavern

☆ 2 ☆

The North End

As Ann Street emerges from the warren of darkened alleys and tenements, the road changes its name to Fish Street (an unmarked transition since there are no signs). Here, you return to the light of the waterfront and see docks and wharves stretching for a half-mile north to the edge of the peninsula. The scent of salt air mingles with the odor of tar and turpentine, and the sound of mallets and hand axes echoes across the shipyards. This is the North End—heart of the port, economic backbone of Boston, guiding spirit of the Revolution.

The North End is technically an island, cut off from the rest of Boston by Mill Creek, but connected to it by two bridges (you crossed the first of these earlier at the Swing Bridge). Within this island, up to half of the residents work directly in or support the maritime trade, but they include more just than the men who crew the ships and the teams that build them. Look around at the businesses on the street—at the shops and workshops, yards and smithies, and out on the piers—and you get a larger sense of the people who help the port run. They include the baker whose ovens turn out biscuits for the voyage, and the cooper whose barrels hold the goods for transport. The soap-maker who makes cleansers from lye and animal fat, and the blacksmith who forges the anchors and fittings. The ballast masters who load iron and stones to give the ships weight and stability, and the caulkers who seal the timbers with pitch. All these professions, and dozens more, help outfit a ship and make it seaworthy, stock it with cargo, and provision the crew. And from beyond Boston itself, hundreds of fishermen and hunters and farmers send their goods to market through the port, and thousands of other New Englanders support it with their commerce. In one way or another, they all serve the maritime trade and provide a reason why all these sloops and brigantines and schooners should fill the harbor.

Though the sea trade is the life of the region, life isn't always good. Look out at wharves like Burrell's and Haywood's, or shipyards like Lee's and Sears's, and you'll see a lot less activity than there used to be. They still build anything from brigs and sloops to ketches and shallops, but many of the slips are empty, the wharves undermanned, the cargo loads less fully packed than they could be. The ports in New York and Philadelphia have now surpassed Boston's by goods cleared, and the trade embargo has made things worse. Just four decades ago, this town had more than two dozen active shipyards with around sixty ships on the stocks at a time; now only a third of those yards are in use.

Still, some of the wharves are quite busy. Boston's chief exports are timber and dried fish, as well as potash for cleaning wool; oak planks, barrel staves, and naval stores for shipping; deerskin for gloves and clothing; hops for making beer; and, of course, rum—the most valuable commodity of all (see p. 141 for more on the industry). You might also see a healthy trade in pearl ash, fur, cotton, shoes, and ginseng. But you won't find imports of Madeira wine. The embargo has cut off the supply from Portugal, and the Continental Congress has added it to the nonimportation list, despite George Washington's well-known fondness for the drink.

As you stroll about the wharves, you might hear the sailors called "Jack Tars," or even "Jolly Tars." It's true they can have a rough look, with baggy tar-smeared breeches, short jackets and Monmouth caps, and copious tattoos, but they're as committed to the Revolution as any genteel patriot with a Harvard degree or a law office. They call themselves the Sons of Neptune (matching the more-famous Sons of Liberty) and have participated in most of the boycotts, protests, and uprisings that have animated the town over the last thirty years. None of these revolts were more violent than the riots of 1747—recalled as "the most spectacular series of impressment riots in the eighteenth century"—which countered the attempts of the Royal Navy to force sailors to serve in the fleet by kidnapping them from the streets and breaking into their homes. The old salts haven't forgotten the outrage, making just one more reason for them to serve the cause of independence from the decks or the docks.

If you don't hear sailors cursing the Crown, you might hear them speaking a unique argot, with talk of climbing ratlines (ropes as part of a ladder), using the windlass (a winch for hoisting), taking the marlinspike (for splicing rope), or complaining about the green hands (novice sailors), the lobscouse (a boiled mush for supper), or the land sharks (shoreside con men). Hundreds of men on the docks speak the language, most of them born and bred in New England, but a fair number coming from other former colonies or northern Europe. And with the war raging, new groups of seamen have arrived to seek their fortune in smuggling or privateering, hailing from southern Europe or even India and the West Indies.

Watch for the whaling vessels, too, moored at the docks. Though the business is prone to cycles of boom and bust, it holds an enduring appeal for many in the North End. Few will forget how, in the 1760s, John Hancock owned four ships that traveled the seas from Labrador to the West Indies, hunting whales for their bones and oil, before reducing their carcasses and rendering the product into blubber and oil for lighting and lubrication, among other uses. Today, as then, spermaceti, from the head case of sperm whales, is the most prized commodity, used as it is for making candles, lamp oil, and soap. But whatever the species, whaling is not for the faint of heart: killing and towing a forty-five-ton beast to the ship, cutting off its head or stripping sheets of blubber from its carcass, disassembling the flesh and bones, and boiling the blubber for days on end before cooling and rendering it into barrels. It's a filthy and dangerous business, suitable only for the most resilient mariners. Not surprisingly, whalers make for some of the fiercest and most-committed patriots in town.

Many whalers are black and find in the work a freedom they don't have on shore. Some advance up to mate or harpooner, and in a few cases, to captain. Overall, one in six sailors is black, and they make up a good portion of local residents too (one in ten). However, like most towns in America, Boston is a slave town, and the majority of the caulkers, smiths, and sailmakers you see working in the yards are not free to quit their labors or get paid for them. Some merchants are known to hold or traffic in slaves and place advertisements for buying or selling them in newspapers. Enslaved mariners often get the worst jobs in the most dangerous conditions. Free black laborers face a similar struggle but at least have the option of negotiating their wages or quitting a job if they don't like it. There are more than a few black North Enders who own cook shops or oyster stands after spending too many of their days at sea.

Black former mariners are joined by many other North Enders in selling food along the waterfront. On Fish Street, these might be anyone from fish peddlers pushing their carts while shouting out the catch of the day, to hawkers with wagons full of fruit and vegetables, to women running victualing houses to offer a taste of signature New England cuisine (see p. 209). But overall, the best place to dine on the North End, and get a sense of the neighborhood's flavor, is in the taverns.

You won't have to look far to find one. They're peppered throughout the North End and cater to every type of visitor, with a wide selection of food and liquor and stories that recall Boston's past. Take, for example, the Red Lion Inn at the corner of Fish Street and Wood Lane. It's one of the oldest alehouses in town, and its original owner, Nicholas Upsall, was a Quaker. Despite his upstanding reputation, the Puritan authorities sent him to prison, billeted soldiers at his home, and banished him from the colony under threat of execution. But he never gave up the faith. His business still stands near the wharf that also bears the tavern's name. Or head three blocks north to Scarlett's Wharf, where the Ship Tavern is a gloomy seventeenth-century pile with projecting eaves and dormers. The patrons still recall how, a century ago, royal commissioner Robert Carr assaulted a town constable within this alehouse, then refused to acknowledge the insult to local authority and ignored demands he submit to justice. Like many of the king's officials, he got away with it.

Despite the historical allure, though, the best reason to visit a North End tavern is to see how the neighborhood operates today. Across from Scarlett's Wharf, at the King's Head, you can eavesdrop on some of the conversations. Over glasses of rum or mugs of ale, you might hear a merchant trying to raise capital for a new ship by offering shares to his wealthy peers, or deciding how to outfit the vessel or insure the entire enterprise. Or you might see a captain trying to crew his ship and negotiating wages with would-be seamen—offering them generous advances or free drink—and settling debts with sailmakers, shipwrights, and rope makers. Or perhaps you'll join a group of mariners raising a glass to a successful voyage, or causing a fuss about not getting paid, or recalling how they once raised hell against royal officials.

The widow Davenport used to operate the tavern. She was one of the many women in Boston holding two-fifths of its liquor licenses, and up to half of all new licenses. This isn't unusual. Due to shipwrecks and war casualties, women outnumber men by a ratio of six to five in town, and up to a quarter of all households are headed by widows. You'll see a good number of them in the neighborhood working as seamstresses, cooks, or washwomen, operating boardinghouses and brothels, managing millinery shops, or owning other kinds of businesses.

However, the majority of widows are poor, and some of them run taverns without a license or sell individual drinks to passersby. Just walk along the waterfront and you'll see it—a woman in a ragged gown hawking beer, cider, or hard liquor for only a few pence. If you ask her why, she'll tell you the reason: to support herself or her family, and to keep off the poor rolls and out of the Almshouse.

If she doesn't sell booze on the wharves, she might operate out of her home or tenement. All she needs is a cask of rum (increasingly cheap with so many distilleries in town), and from there, it's a simple matter of "putting a shingle on her front door, and opening her home to sailors, travelers, dock workers, and whoever else happened to pass by her humble abode." However she runs her business, she has little fear of punishment if she breaks the law. Convictions are rare and incur only a two-pound fine. She might even sell to slaves, indentured servants, and Indians—all forbidden to purchase alcohol by law, but all easily able to find a dram seller who will quench their thirst. This makes liquor peddling one of the few professions that holds no social barriers and a veritable institution on the North End.

Just east of the King's Head, you can visit another institution owned by a widow, the Crown Tavern, located at the head of Hancock's Wharf. It's a lively scene these days, and there's quite a hubbub at the tables, with recruiters offering free drinks and the promise of making a fortune to any mariners willing to take a risk. Their broadsides advertise high bonuses and wages, lucrative prize shares, and "ample allotments of grog, a sailor's 'liquor of life'"—all to participate in the "legalized piracy" of privateering.

The Crown has been a rendezvous for privateers for at least thirty years, but unlike in the old days, they no longer need to operate in secret, ever since the Continental Congress in March gave them permission to prey on the commerce of the enemy. The premise is simple: For their efforts attacking and boarding an enemy ship, and stripping it of its valuable goods, privateers get to keep a substantial share of the loot, with the government also receiving a cut.

As you'd expect, this law has found great favor in the North End. So, as you leave the tavern and look around the shipyards, you'll notice many of the vessels being converted to pirate ships, their owners outfitting old brigs and brigantines with some twenty cannon and finding ammunition, in part, from the melted-down statues of British royalty. The competition for labor has been fierce because they need around a hundred sailors to board and secure an enemy vessel, and to crew it with trusted seamen who can sail the seized ship to a friendly port. Privateers have even drawn sailors from overseas to take part in the hunt for booty, and they have drawn deserters from the federal and state navies—to the consternation of Congress.

There's more to it than just money, though. Some sailors and militiamen see it as a good way to participate in the war without joining the Continental Army, while others are inspired by the example of native son Captain John Manley, who captured the 250-ton British transport *Nancy*, loaded with brass mortar and brass cannon, small arms, and ammo. However, the recruits are also aware of the risk they face, with Parliament soon to pass the Pirate Act, denying due process and prisoner exchange for those captured at sea. But it's not enough to dampen the enthusiasm. As Abigail Adams says, Boston has "a rage for privateering" in which "Vast Numbers are employed."

Vast numbers are also employed in smuggling, always one of the North End's favorite pursuits. In colonial days, this involved secretly trading in rum, wine, wool, and other goods to evade the attention of royal customs officials; since the war began, it involves importing munitions and gunpowder for the army and militia. Some of the very ships you see before you may be engaged in the practice, evading the Royal Navy blockade and hauling in crates of muskets or casks of powder and saltpeter from colonial ports in the West Indies, while European nations like Spain, France, and the Netherlands that control those ports look the other way. As with privateering, the risks are great for any smuggler caught trafficking in arms and ammunition: Parliament has decreed that any American ship found in a British port can be seized by the Crown, any foreign ship trading with the former colonies can also be commandeered, and the captain and his crew can be arrested. But despite the danger, smuggling continues to be a lucrative enterprise and offers an opportunity many North Enders are willing to take.

For a look at one of the key episodes that took place at the port, walk to the end of Hancock's Wharf. You'll pass by a few shops selling a variety of goods before you reach the end of the pilings, where you can enjoy a nice prospect of the harbor and the shipyards to the south. The wharf is John Hancock's most expensive investment in Boston and the town's second-longest after the Long Wharf. But it's not the proportions that are the most striking; it's the fact that on this site eight years ago, Bostonians first used violence against Crown officials.

They did it twice within a month. The first time, in April 1768, Hancock had moored his ship *Lydia* here only to have it boarded by a pair of customs agents. One of them, Owen Richards, quietly slipped into steerage looking for undeclared goods. After a dispute, Hancock ordered his crew to seize the agent and haul him the upper deck to prevent any further inspection, which caused some controversy when the news came out. But this was only a minor dust-up compared to the clash to come.

It began in May, after Hancock's sloop *Liberty* docked and customs officers suspected it held more than the twenty-five declared casks of Madeira wine. A month later, a tidesman, Thomas Kirk, claimed that during his inspection, he was refused access to the cargo hold and, for his troubles, was locked in a room below deck for three hours while crew members unloaded the illicit goods—perhaps four times as much wine as had been declared. Conveniently, he made the declaration while the fifty-gun man-of-war *Romney* was at the Long Wharf to deliver the first load of British troops to occupy the town. This was at a time when the Royal Navy had been impressing merchant sailors into armed service, just as it had in 1747, which raised the temperature of the townsfolk until they were ready to boil at the next provocation.

That moment came on June 10, when customs commissioners ordered the seizure of the *Liberty*, and two officials were assigned the task of taking control of the ship. Port collector Joseph Harrison and comptroller Benjamin Hallowell planned to have a group of *Romney* sailors and marines assist them in the seizure, but not before word got out to Hancock's men and a mob of hundreds of North Enders. The violence began quickly, as the mob fought the troops for control of the ship's lines to keep her moored. When that failed, and the sailors commandeered the *Liberty* and sailed it to a berth alongside the *Romney*, the mob attacked the hapless officials themselves.

They surrounded Hallowell and Harrison and the latter's son at the head of the wharf, pummeling them with fists and bricks and rocks and dirt. As Harrison recalls:

> I run the Gauntlet near 200 Yards, my poor Son following behind endeavouring to shelter his Father by receiving the strokes of many of the Stones thrown at him till at length he became equally an Object of their Resentment, was knocked down and then laid hold of by the Legs, Arms and Hair of his Head, and in that manner dragged along the Kennel in a most barbarous and cruel manner. . . . About this time I received a violent Blow on the Breast which had like to have brought me to the Ground, and I verily believe if I had fallen, I should never have got up again, the People to all appearance being determined on Blood and Murder.

Harrison and his son, along with Hallowell, escaped the frenzy with the aid of a few sympathetic locals, but the mob wasn't done with its protest. They smashed the windows of the men's homes before heading to the Liberty Tree to burn a pleasure craft belonging to the port collector. The officials, along with the customs commissioners themselves, would soon go into hiding on Castle Island; the troops of the *Romney* would continue to incur the wrath of the townsfolk; and John Hancock would be tried as a smuggler. Thanks to his lawyer John Adams, the case would eventually be dismissed.

Although the mob violence was historic, you're not apt to see much chaos on the wharf these days. Hancock no longer owns the *Liberty*, and his fleet of nine ships has been reduced to three vessels, which he keeps hidden in secluded coves away from the eyes of the Royal Navy. He still collects wharfage fees from the shippers and rents from the merchants, but otherwise, the Revolution has crushed his maritime business. Looting soldiers decimated his stores and warehouses in the vicinity, his losses have mounted since most of his loyalist debtors (like General Thomas Gage) will never repay him, and eight years of supporting the nonimportation of British goods have harmed him most of all. Yet he refuses to turn away from the movement for independence, however much it might cost him. For that reason, he may well be the most popular patriot in town. A plutocratic man of the people.

There's not much more to see farther north along the shore of the peninsula: only a few more wharves and shipyards in various states of use and the North Battery fortification that guards the approach to the Charles River. So return a block south on Fish Street and take a turn at Sun Court to see a different side of the North End.

Many artisans at the port live alongside narrow little roads just like this, not far from the merchants and shipbuilders who contract their work. A common artisan may occupy anything from a small wooden shed to a two-level house with projecting stories and a steep roof, while the wealthy enjoy mansions and gardens and outbuildings on larger lots that give them greater privacy and a buffer from other classes. Never far away are the mean shacks and boardinghouses of the "lower sort"—their usual term for the poor and less privileged.

On Sun Court, you'll pass tenements used as flops for sailors and flanked by taverns and dram shops. The street soon opens up to reveal a small triangular plaza where Moon, Sun, and Garden Courts meet, Clarke's Square (or North Square). Though it seems hidden away from the rest of the North End, the design of the streets is no accident. They all converge on the site of Old North Meetinghouse, also known as Second Church. In the seventeenth century, the meetinghouse was a simple wooden edifice with tower and steeple and private entrances for some of the pews. It was the second Congregational church in town, where parishioners came for more than sixty years to hear Increase and Cotton Mather preaching to the Puritan faithful and thundering away at sinners. Actually, they didn't have a choice. Attendance was mandatory.

Whatever fire and brimstone the Mathers may have offered, they've long since been outdone by the bombast of modern preachers. In 1770, John Lathrop offered what may have been the church's most incendiary sermon ever: "Innocent Blood Crying to God from the Streets of Boston." He preached it the Sunday after the Massacre on King Street, an "unparalleled barbarity" in which "our brethren were murdered before our eyes, and our most public streets were deeply dyed with innocent blood . . . our fellow-citizens shot to death—their garments rolled in blood, and corpses wallowing in gore." Lathrop gave voice to the fury of many of his parishioners, demanding "the justice of the divine decree, that, he who sheddeth man's blood, by man shall his blood be shed." Lathrop's words found favor not only in the pews but across the colonies, and were even printed in London, leading the British military to label his church "a nest of traitors."

The British got their revenge for his words on January 16, 1776, during the siege. As Lathrop describes it, "a number of evil-minded men, of the king's party, obtained leave of General Howe to pull down the Old North Meeting-house, under a pretence of wanting it for fuel, although there were then large quantities of coal and wood in the town." And now all that remains of it is a ruined foundation, with the beams and planks stripped away, long since burned in British ovens. There are no plans to rebuild the church, but if you'd like to call on Lathrop to learn more, you can find him where his congregation now worships, around the corner on Middle Street at New Brick Meetinghouse. It's the one with a quirky, copper-plated cockerel on the steeple.

With the old church now destroyed, Clarke's Square offers only two sights to which you should give your attention, a block north and south respectively from the plaza. The first, a few houses south on Moon Court, is the home of Paul Revere.

As imposing as you might expect, it was built in 1680 as the parsonage for Second Church and features a somber Dutch-influenced design with an overhanging second story and leaded-glass windows. Revere occupies the house but spends much of his time supporting the army and militia, also working as a goldsmith, silversmith, engraver, and part-time dentist. He once advertised his office on Hancock's Wharf (then Clarke's Wharf) as a haven for the toothless, in which those who had lost their teeth "can have them replaced with Artificial Ones that look as well as the Natural and answer the End of Speaking"—meaning the new teeth wouldn't inhibit his customers from talking or being understood.

Revere calls himself a "tradesman," but just as often a "mechanic." Even though the latter term began as an aristocratic slur against those of the artisan class, he and his peers have reclaimed the label and wear it with pride. And there is indeed much to be proud of: he's among the best metalsmiths in town, and his tea urns and silver bowls and prints struck from copper-plate engravings fetch good prices and draw a steady stream of clients. Moreover, his social world spans the classes of Boston, as he navigates the parlors of the gentry as well as the dram shops of the lower class. He's a lodge master of the Masons and a member of radical clubs like the Sons of Liberty, the North End Caucus, and the Long Room Club—a secretive group of seventeen hardened patriots, of whom he is the only mechanic.

Revere's talents have served the Revolution well, and if you travel in radical circles, you're apt to see one of his works on view, often with a political message. Famously, his Rescinders' Bowl is an exquisite silver vessel commemorating the ninety-two legislators who fought the Townshend Acts and—"undaunted by the insolent Menaces of Villains in Power"—refused to rescind their names from a letter condemning it. Even more well-known are his engravings of the landing of British troops in 1768 and the Massacre on King Street two years later, works that dramatized those events and played no small part in galvanizing local feelings against imperial authority. And this isn't to mention the sharp wit he shows in his political cartoons, which depict royal authorities as both barbarians and buffoons.

If you'd been to visit his house in 1771, the anniversary of the Massacre, you'd have seen Revere's work at its most poignant and affecting. For in the upstairs windows of his house, he illuminated three displays that North Enders still remember. The first showed the ghost of child Christopher Seider preparing to die as a martyr to the cause of liberty (see p. 38); the second showed the Massacre in all its blood and chaos; and the third depicted a figure called the "Genius of Liberty" trampling one of the king's soldiers clutching a serpent. The displays were all the more memorable for being the only illumination on the otherwise dark streets of Clarke's Square. As one account says, "the whole exhibition was so well executed, that it produced a melancholy gloom and solemn silence in several thousand spectators."

Revere would be a notable enough figure if only for his creativity, but—as we've seen—he's also been essential to the cause of independence. As a quick summary, he has (1) ridden through the colonies to inform them of major news like the passing of the Port Act and other Parliamentary outrages, (2) carried the Suffolk Resolves to the Continental Congress in Philadelphia, rallying the colonies against the import of British goods, (3) sounded the alarm in Portsmouth, New Hampshire, about British attempts to seize colonial powder stores, resulting in the colonists' capture of Fort William and Mary, (4) spied on the workings of powder mills to help the patriots create one of their own, (5) helped as a militia officer to rebuild Castle Island's fortress and munitions, (6) made his famed midnight ride to warn patriot leaders of the approach of British troops near Lexington, and (7) taken countless other actions large and small that have helped Massachusetts and the rest of America gain traction in the war. So, if you call on this master artisan and champion of the new nation, he will certainly have fascinating stories to tell you. Just don't expect him to be home. He's likely to be busy.

On the streets radiating from Clarke's Square, you're apt to find the houses of other artisans just as committed as Revere. They don't always sport the hand tools and leather aprons of cliché, and they include women as well as men, laboring either in workshops behind their homes or in other locations like the waterfront. They include the familiar masons, carpenters, bakers, butchers, grocers, woodworkers, coopers, and printers, as well as the more obscure combmakers (creating combs from animal horn), wharfingers (overseeing goods on the docks), whitesmiths (finishing iron with tin plating), and farriers (horseshoe makers).

The better-paid professions are harder to break into, but there is a hierarchy of sorts: at the top are the master artisans who own their businesses and are experts at their craft; then the journeymen who act as wage laborers and provide work for hire, and have the chance to become masters themselves; and at the bottom, the apprentices who learn their trade by living with their masters as indentured laborers on seven-year contracts, and become journeymen at the fulfillment of those contracts. Among the different occupations, there is also a hierarchy, the most well-paid being distillers, apothecaries, doctors, and lawyers, and the poorest being shoemakers and tailors. Outside the ranks of skilled trades are hawkers, peddlers, chimney sweeps, day laborers, ditch diggers, sawyers, cartmen, and draymen who do a fair share of the town's hard, physical labor.

Just like Revere, most working artisans tend toward the radical side of politics, supporting the Revolution when they can and rejecting any sympathy for the loyalists who have fled town. They especially despise the bureaucrats, customs officials, and commissioners who made life in Boston such a struggle in prewar years, and they call them no better than parasites, placemen, pimps, prostitutes, and panderers—even if those officials are homegrown Americans. Which brings us to the other side of Clarke's Square, and the former home of Thomas Hutchinson.

It's just a block north on Garden Court, a three-story Georgian mansion originally designed with Corinthian pilasters, elegant cupola, and expansive gardens that extended back to Middle Street. It's less appealing these days, with a stripped-down appearance and no hint of the gilded archway and tapestries and bronze lamps that made the house such a model for elite living. The deterioration relates to Hutchinson's role as an agent of royal power.

That power was long-vested in his family name. According to one account, "the Hutchinson family was very ancient, and highly respectable." His grandfather Colonel John Foster built the great Georgian pile in the late seventeenth century, and his father, Colonel Thomas Hutchinson, lived in it while founding some of the schools on the North End. As young Thomas rose to power, he inherited the mansion and also bought a country estate in Milton, having acquired enough assets to place him solidly among the "better class" of Bostonians. But he was never popular. What infuriated the mechanics was his open display of wealth and his privileged attitude when the town struggled economically and class divides were stark.

Crown authorities rewarded Hutchinson again and again for his loyalty—first appointing him lieutenant governor and then, inexplicably, awarding him the position of chief justice of the Massachusetts Superior Court of Judicature, despite his lacking any schooling in law. He proved himself a dutiful servant of the king, enforcing unpopular trade policies, issuing writs of assistance to allow customs officers to search merchant ships at will, and becoming "an apologist for most of their oppressive measures." He was also thought to support the Stamp Act because his brother-in-law Andrew Oliver was the stamp commissioner (though Hutchinson privately criticized it). And so on August 26, 1765, with the act due to come into force a month later, the mechanics had finally had enough.

They had already attacked Oliver's house twelve days earlier and forced his resignation. Fueled by the success, radical shoemaker Ebenezer Mackintosh led a sizable crowd on a second rampage. First, they set upon the house of William Story of the Vice-Admiralty Court, ransacked the premises, and burned the records of the Admiralty; then they invaded and looted the house of customs comptroller Benjamin Hallowell (three years before attacking him in person). But the greatest violence they reserved for Hutchinson's property.

Hutchinson would have been home at the time the crowd descended on his mansion, but for his daughter's demand to stay by his side. He couldn't allow her to face their fury, too, so they both departed the house and hoped the damage wouldn't be too great. Their hopes were in vain. As Hutchinson later reported, "The hellish crew fell upon my house with the rage of devils & in a moment with axes split down the door." Having gained access, the mob smashed through the interior walls and floors; destroyed the furniture and many of the antiques; stole portraits, clothing, books, jewelry, and £900 sterling; dismantled the cupola and tore off part of the roof; and spirited away a huge collection of historic manuscripts he had collected over his lifetime. The next morning, silver plates, gold rings, and sterling were strewn throughout the area, and Hutchinson had lost more than £3,000 in valuables.

Many patriot leaders condemned the mob action as an act of barbarism, while others remained silent. But the gauntlet had been thrown: the radicals had put royal officials on notice that, should they try to take actions like enforcing the Stamp Act, there would be violence to come. Governor Francis Bernard, always hostile to the demands of the citizenry, saw the destruction as no mere riot. Rather, it was "a War of Plunder, general levelling, and taking away the Distinction of rich and poor."

As you stroll along the perimeter of the mansion these days, you'll see that the worst of the mob's damage has been repaired, but not much remains of the house's old glory. Hutchinson sailed to Britain two years ago, the exterior ornaments are mostly gone, and the weather-beaten facade has seen better days. If you ask neighbors around the square, they aren't likely to offer much pity for the fate of the mansion or sympathy for the old royal official. The Hutchinson name is now widely reviled.

In rather better condition are the institutions Hutchinson's father helped found. Continue on to Middle Street and look down Bennet Street, where the North End Grammar School has been educating students for more than sixty years. Another block over on Love Lane, the North Writing School has stood for almost as long. The latter school is the more important: a two-story wooden structure that has served three generations of students, including budding revolutionaries like Paul Revere. Boston educates them at public expense, and the schoolmaster is the redoubtable John Tileston, also known as Johnny Crump or Master Johnny or the "patriarch of pedagogues." He's the chief instructor for two hundred students and not to be trifled with, as you can see if you'd like to witness his pedagogy in action. Though the master's hand was crippled in childhood, he uses it like an iron fist for enforcing discipline and boxing ears, and scribbling out commands for reading, writing, and arithmetic while his students sit at attention on wooden benches without desks, writing their assignments on long sheets. For his efforts, he's become as admired by adults as he is feared by youth and has been called "the father of good writing in Boston."

To be admitted, a student should have rudimentary reading ability and enough money to pay a share of the heating bill. However, boys and girls take instruction at different times, with the boys' education the more rigorous. Girls are only taught to read, unless they receive private tutelage at their parents' expense. It's an openly unequal system, and more than a few women have commented on the unfairness of it and the way it predetermines how far a youngster can go in life. Abigail Adams in her letters writes of the challenge of providing adequate education to Boston's children and sees "daughters who every day experience the want of it. . . . If we mean to have Heroes, Statesmen and Philosophers, we should have learned women."

The grammar and writing schools have reopened after the siege, but as you walk the surrounding streets, you will see many other institutions remain closed and some of the houses are damaged. The British army stripped many of planks and roofs for firewood, and dismantled others altogether. But perhaps the greatest damage, at least psychologically, was done one long block away, where Middle Street becomes North Street at Foster Lane. It didn't happen to New North Church itself—a handsome brick Congregational building—but rather to its minister.

Andrew Eliot might be the bravest preacher in town. He was one of the first to criticize the Stamp Act and has long leaned toward Whiggish politics, but he chose to remain in town during the siege and continue leading his New North congregation. It was a bold step, and he was soon serving hundreds of other Protestants whose ministers had decamped for the countryside, even providing them with food and medicine since many were lower class or poor. But the war proved too much for him. Upon witnessing the ruination of the town and the collapse of its population, he could only react in horror: "poor Boston May God sanctify our distresses which are greater than you can conceive—Such a Sabbath of melancholy and darkness I never knew." Since then, his health has suffered greatly, and if you chance to meet him, you might think the siege had never ended.

Beyond New North Church, Foster Lane leads east to more wharves and shipyards along the appropriately named Ship Street. But students of recent history may want to head a few blocks north to Salutation Alley to visit the Salutation Inn, marked by a sign of two men exchanging a deferential greeting. Despite the moderate image, the tavern has long been a hotbed of radicalism. Samuel Adams once planned strategy here with the mechanics in the North End Caucus, gathering support for candidates to elected office and taking steps to undermine royal authority; and Paul Revere led meetings from the secrecy of a private room where the caucus could arrange their plans without being overheard by British officials. The Sons of Liberty would later assume leadership of the radicals and move their meetings to the Green Dragon Tavern (see p. 38), but the Salutation remains one of Boston's prime drinking establishments for customers with a bent toward radical politics.

Instead of lingering at the tavern, head several blocks west down the alley then to Charter Street and turn south on Salem Street to reach the most famous sight in the neighborhood. It's called North Church, or Old North Church—not to be confused with Old North Meetinghouse (since destroyed) or New North Church (still standing)—even though its actual name is Christ Church. Whatever you call it, the building's claim to fame is that this is the place where, in April 1775, agents of Paul Revere hung two lanterns to warn of the movement of British troops to patriots watching across the Charles River. Revere chose his beacon well: The steeple is the highest in Boston at 175 feet, and the story bears repeating if you have somehow never heard it.

It begins with Chair of the Committee of Safety Dr. Joseph Warren receiving word from an informant that commanding British General and Massachusetts Governor Thomas Gage would be sending an expedition to the countryside to seize military stores at Concord and arrest John Hancock and Samuel Adams, both lodging near Lexington. Warren passed the message on to tanner William Dawes to carry the message overland via the Boston Neck, and to Revere to carry it by boat across the river to Charlestown.

Revere devised a backup plan—in case he and Dawes should be intercepted—whereby lanterns would be hung at the top of the Christ Church steeple to tell patriots in Charlestown of the British troop movement, beaming one light if the troops should march along the Neck, and two if they should cross by ship to Cambridge. However, access to the steeple would not be easy, since the rector, Mather Byles Jr., was a staunch loyalist and would inform Gage of any rebel activity he saw.

By a stroke of luck, Byles lost his job on the night of April 18, 1775: members of his congregation forced him to hand over his keys after already stripping him of his salary and criticizing him for his political views and management of church finances. Revere was then able to convince the Whig sexton Robert Newman and vestryman John Pulling Jr.—a member of the North Caucus Club—to open the doors, ascend the steeple, and hang two lanterns. Newman and Pulling only displayed the lights for a few moments, but those moments were enough for allies in Charlestown to get the message. What followed were the battles at Lexington and Concord, the opening salvos of the War of Independence.

Take a step back and you'll see Christ Church visually lives up to its reputation: a stately brick edifice with 2.5-foot-thick walls and a design based on Christopher Wren's architecture. Artists including Revere have featured the steeple in engravings, and if you can get inside, you'll enjoy a striking vista of the entire town and the harbor. Doing so can be a challenge, however. The church has been closed since Byles fled the town with the British evacuation. However, sexton Robert Newman still lives in the neighborhood. He may even be glad to open the doors with his legendary set of keys, show you around, and provide his account of the famous night of April 18.

Inside, the church has a distinctive look, with brass chandeliers, a grand organ, eight sonorous bells, and a crypt holding hundreds of deceased members. Note also how the church is divided: the stylish nave for the congregants who can afford their own private box pews, and a congested upper gallery where black parishioners, free and enslaved alike, worship along with indentured servants and the poor. Some have no choice, as their enslaving owners keep watch from the comforts of the boxes below. One such slaveholder was Reverend Timothy Cutler, first rector of the church, who ran it for forty years until his death in 1765. You can find him these days in a tomb under the altar, buried with honor while those he claimed to own most likely rest in obscurity at Copp's Hill Burying Ground, a block northwest.

To pay your respects to them, leave the church and head up Hull Street to reach Copp's Hill, one of the highest points on the peninsula. Like the church, the cemetery has several alternate names, including North Burying Ground and, on some maps, Corpse Hill. It's laid out in a loose hierarchy, with different social groups occupying different sections. Elite families reside in one section of the yard under elegantly carved markers; common artisans and poor folk occupy plots under more workaday stones; and free and enslaved black people lie mostly in unmarked graves.

Should you attend a funeral service, you may hear a minister offering a few words on the transience of life and the finality of God's judgment, or you may see attendees silently honoring the deceased and leaving written notes and verses at the burial site. The tradition of the wealthy handing out gloves, rings, and scarves to funeral-goers has declined since the General Court forbade the practice in 1742, though family members may privately exchange such keepsakes. The rings in particular are worth a look, since they may contain a lock of the deceased's hair and be inscribed with symbols of death and the afterlife.

Like the rings, the gravestones at the cemetery do not show the Christian cross or cherubs or other symbols you might be familiar with. Rather, because many Bostonians believe those to be signs of popish idolatry, what you'll see are skeletons and death's heads, some with wings, and other macabre images. A good number of the stones are not easy to read with broken or corroded inscriptions, and others have been dislocated or even swiped. Still, there are more than enough stones left to get a sense of the major figures in Boston history, from those the Puritans revered like

Increase and Cotton Mather, to those they persecuted like Nicholas Upsall. Intriguingly, some of the headstone carvers have cut their signatures into the base of the stones—typically below ground unless the marker has been upended. Among the most well-known artisans is the mysterious "JN," whose designs feature not just the familiar death's heads but more fanciful images like lilies growing out of urns or mermaids lounging next to them.

Outside the cemetery, across Snow Street, the northwest side of the hill terminates in a cliff about fifty feet above the waterline. British soldiers took advantage of the height by building a fortification over the Charles River, and in 1775, their batteries shelled and destroyed Charlestown during the battle of Bunker Hill. (Rumor has it they also made sport of patriot gravestones at Copp's Hill by taking potshots at them.) Upon the evacuation, they spiked and abandoned their guns, and local militia retook the high ground.

You can take a rest by the picturesque windmill before you scramble down the hill via Snow Street to reach the landing on Ferry Way. From here, you can board a single-sailed ferry, provided it's in operation, to float across the Charles to the ruins of Charlestown. Be aware that, on busy days, the ferryman will charge a double toll (two or more shillings), to the consternation of many North Enders. If you're not keen to pay the fare and leave Boston, linger at the mill house at the corner of Princes Street and get a sweeping view of the causeway that crosses to West Boston, part of the Mill Pond industrial site (explained in chapter 5).

From here, continue on Princes Street until you reach Back Street, which curves around Mill Pond until it reaches Cross Street. After a short block, you're on Middle Street again, where you'll reach the site of one of the most disturbing episodes to occur in a town well known for them. Here in February 1770, Theophilus Lillie operated a shop that offered a range of dry goods to the public—goods that likely came from Britain. Patriots claimed he broke nonimportation agreements, but he defended himself publicly and criticized his accusers in print. Still, he couldn't shake the accusation. And so on a gutter outside his store, a blackened image of a hand appeared to threaten him with tarring and feathering, and on the street, a painted and carved wooden head mocked him, along with a signboard denouncing him.

Lillie knew better than to protest the insults. One who did not was Ebenezer Richardson, an alleged customs informer who was accosted by the locals while trying to take down the signboard. Some of these tormentors followed him to his nearby house, and a growing mob began to hurl rocks and bricks through his windows. The crowd swelled to thousands of people. After his wife was hit by a projectile, Richardson asked for help from a sailor he knew, George Wilmot, and together, they loaded muskets with birdshot and blasted them at the crowd. Some of the pellets hit a pair of boys, and one of them, Christopher Seider, would die of a punctured lung (despite the intervention of Dr. Joseph Warren, who tried to save him and later did the autopsy). The mob surged into Richardson's house, seized him, and hauled him into the street. They would have lynched him, too, had it not been for the intervention of the radical William Molineux, who hustled both him and Wilmot to Faneuil Hall for arrest and detention.

Seider was only a spectator to the chaos before being shot but quickly became a martyr and Richardson an arch-villain. Samuel Adams arranged Seider's funeral at the Liberty Tree and hailed him as a hero to the patriot cause. His cortege included thirty chaises and coaches, and the funeral drew two thousand mourners. Acting Governor Hutchinson thought it the largest expression of mourning ever in America. In a trial later that year, Richardson was found guilty of murder, but his sentencing was delayed for two years, after which the Crown pardoned him, and he then fled Boston.

Although Lillie's shop has long since closed, the episode is well known for prefiguring the more famous Massacre on King Street that occurred a few weeks later. Yet it's just as important for displaying the keen political acumen and growing power of Adams himself. And the best place to be reminded of that power is just across the bridge over Mill Creek, near the junction of Hanover Street and Union Street. You'll see it marked with the sign of its namesake: the Green Dragon, a small, hammered-copper beast with a slender, slinking body and curled-out tongue. On the ground floor of this cozy brick building are wooden benches and a hearth, while upstairs is an assembly hall and an attic with sleeping quarters, where you can take your rest after a night of boozing.

The tavern has a long-running connection with the Freemasons, the secretive order combining Eastern mysticism with European Enlightenment ideals to forge bonds between men across classes. St. Andrews Lodge owns the building, and the Brethren conduct their monthly meetings here. (The Massachusetts Grand Lodge was also organized here in 1769.) Some of the members have included Paul Revere, John Hancock, William Molineux, and Grand Master Joseph Warren.

Though Freemasons are secretive by design, their processions are elaborate spectacles designed to showcase their power. If you chance to see one winding through Boston, you may spot masters and wardens marching with their officers and corps; lawyers wearing great robes; books and scrolls; swords and rods; jewels of the order on black velvet cushions; and members attired in aprons, white gloves, and stockings, and sporting mystical badges and jewels.

Beyond its Masonic ownership, the Green Dragon is best known for being intimately connected to politics, with its tavern keepers maintaining contacts among judges and lawyers and politicians, and some even becoming selectmen, town meeting moderators, tax assessors and collectors, and other employees in the public service. Naturally, the people most skilled at exploiting the politics of the tavern have been Samuel Adams and the Sons of Liberty.

Before the war, you might have found Hancock, Warren, or Adams himself sitting around these tables, working the crowd and soliciting votes for the Sons' preferred candidates for public office. And they often succeeded: By 1774, they helped elect a majority of patriots to the Assembly through their politicking, and they established ties that would prove useful for the conflict ahead. They also kept watch over British soldiers for leaked information, monitored Tory merchants who broke nonimportation agreements, and gathered intelligence on spies and saboteurs. The tactics they pioneered here became widespread, and they expanded their influence until some 20 percent of all licensed liquor dealers in Boston were members of the club.

Such tactics would also prove useful for action outside the law, from summoning crowds against the Stamp Act and other trade policies, to threatening any officials who dared get in the way. They employed tarring and feathering, hanging in effigy, targeted vandalism, and other methods to intimidate customs agents and violators of nonimportation decrees. Some even speculate that the Destruction of the Tea was plotted at the Green Dragon, weeks before the ships arrived bearing their cargo. The minutes of one Masonic Lodge meeting report a mysterious closure in November 1773, as "Consignees of Tea took up the Brethren's time."

Whatever their actions, the Sons were always happy to cast aside the old Puritan ideas about intemperance and to reject the accusations of sin the Mathers used to invoke against libertines. Instead, they celebrated the culture of drinking and encouraged artisans, laborers, and the gentry to drink out of the same vessels, like the Rescinders' Bowl of Paul Revere, to gather courage for the conflicts to come. They offered hearty toasts and praised alcohol for its salubrious effect—in contrast to tea drinking with all its elaborate rituals and ceremonies, which some saw as an effete, foreign indulgence.

This was all by design, for the Sons learned there were few better ways to attract the allegiance of the townsfolk than by offering them free liquor and festivities. The rum in their punch bowls was often complimentary, as was the wine drunk at events like the Stamp Act repeal celebrations, in which Hancock plied the celebrants with no less than ninety-two gallons of free Madeira wine. All this largesse not only appealed to the majority of working people; it drew the tavern owners, brewers, and distillers ever closer to the patriot clubs and made radical politics useful to their interests.

The Green Dragon lost a bit of its allure during the siege, when it was used as a hospital for British troops, but once it is fully restored, you might discover some of the old magic has returned. The tipplers will have found their favorite benches, and the Sons will make the rounds as they always have—this time to control the destiny of the newly independent nation. And there will surely be toasts. Before the war, the Sons praised major holidays, the anniversary of the Stamp Act riot, election days, the Liberty Tree, John Wilkes, and various Whig statesmen, and they condemned their enemies with equal vigor. Samuel Adams once offered a drink to the thought of certain figures roasting in Hell, like Judas, Nero, the pope, customs officials, and British Tories.

You may wish to offer a toast yourself if you're in such company. Just be careful to give the proper praise to the patriots before you, and avoid honoring the wrong people. For it was John Adams who saw first the power the Sons could command through their liquid camaraderie, and he also offered a hint of a warning. For with their celebrations, radical figures like his cousin Samuel "tinge the Minds of the People, they impregnate them with the sentiments of Liberty. They render the People fond of their Leaders in the Cause, and averse and bitter against all opposers."

☆ 3 ☆

Official Boston

After finishing your tour of the North End at the Green Dragon, head south on Union Street for several blocks as it curves to the west and deposits you at Dock Square. This busy plaza is close to the town center and provides a good starting point to explore the official side of Boston, home to some of the town's major civic institutions as well as its most notorious scenes of violence.

Before you begin, you'll have to make your way through the bustle of the square, where masses of carts and sleds and barrows and wagons all jockey for position to deposit their wares at the locations where they will be sold. Try to push through the turmoil to reach the adjacent stalls of food vendors offering a wide assortment of fruits and vegetables; slabs of beef and pork and lamb and poultry; and baskets of butter, cheese, and eggs, to go along with sweets and other knickknacks. Peddlers shout their offerings from their stalls, or from carts scattered over the cobbles, while a few inspectors look out for spoiled food and tainted weight scales. If you're thirsty, you won't be far from a tap: some of the houses around the square open up their ground floor rooms to marketgoers to hawk a variety of beverages—liquor being a favorite. If this is all a bit too much for you, dart to the margin of

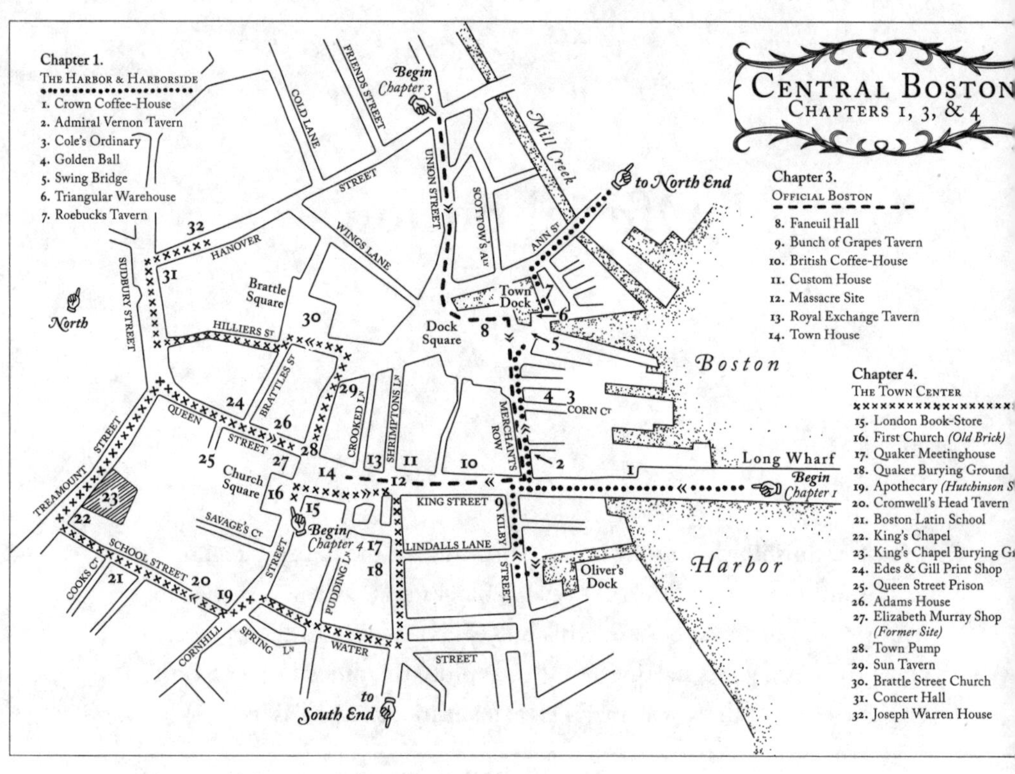

See pages 2–3 for a full-size version of this map.

the square for a quick escape, but be careful of your footing. Garbage and animal waste litter the edge, so tread carefully to avoid falling into the fetid waters of the Town Dock.

It all makes for a head-spinning spectacle of sights and smells, and an essential part of Boston that draws farmers and butchers from across the region. The selectmen aren't happy about all the disorder and would prefer to better regulate the market to make it more civil and appealing, but the vendors won't change their ways easily. For this riot of activity has its roots in an actual riot.

The conflict goes back to the seventeenth century, when food sellers had the right to travel the roads and lanes, hawking their goods from door to door. This freedom lasted until the 1730s, when the selectmen began to regulate the trade by developing markets in the north, center, and south parts of town. The peddlers saw this as a threat to their livelihood, and most of the citizens didn't support the markets, either, having no interest in trudging through wet or snowy streets to buy food that they could more easily purchase at their doorsteps. So, in the winter of 1737, some five hundred Bostonians made their feelings known.

According to a report, "the middle Market-House in this Town, together with Several butcher's Shops next the Same, were cut, pull'd down, and entirely demolished, by a Number of Persons unknown; and several Posts of the North Market House were also torn asunder the same night." To conceal their identities, some rioters painted their faces; others dressed as clergymen. Town constables made no arrests for the violence, and the markets were not rebuilt. But the selectmen were not deterred from regulating the commerce, and in 1740, they made another attempt.

Peter Faneuil offered funds for a new building. He was a shipping magnate who traded in fabric and pottery from Europe; meat, grain, and flour from the Middle Colonies; dried fish and timber from New England; and molasses, sugar, and cocoa from the West Indies. He was also a trafficker in slaves who shipped them between the Caribbean, Africa, and North America, expanding his profits in the brutal commerce until he was one of the richest men of his era. Faneuil's wealth did not endear him to the majority of citizens, who wanted nothing to do with a new market building even if they didn't have to pay for it. But in a town meeting, the merchants and politicians who supported the idea carried the day by seven votes—out of 727 cast—and two years later, Faneuil Hall took its place on the eastern edge of Dock Square.

As you can't help but notice, it's one of the largest structures in town, with a footprint of one hundred feet by forty feet, two imposing stories crowned with an octagonal cupola, brick walls decorated with Tuscan and Doric pilasters, and eight arched windows. But the most incredible aspect of the hall isn't its architectural details but the fact that it's still standing at all. Fire gutted the structure in 1761 and left only the walls standing, after which the town held a lottery to pay for its rebuilding, doubling the height of the upper story and adding galleries on Ionic columns. In a dedication speech, James Otis Jr. rechristened it as the "Cradle of Liberty" in anticipation of the inspiring things that might happen there. Still, you might be surprised upon entering. Instead of gentlemen in periwigs and breeches declaiming on liberty, the first thing you'll see is meat.

Butcher stalls line the ground floor, with vendors hawking their cuttings of beef, pork, poultry, and lamb and giving the hall the look (and smell) of a meat warehouse. They pay for a license to display their cuts here, which puts them in competition with the vendors outside at Dock Square who don't want to pay the fee. The selectmen allow the two markets to remain near each other in order to keep all sides happy and not risk another riot. John Hancock keeps a store in the Hall where his employees sell things like fabric, ribbons, shoe buckles, hardware, and coal, but seldom does he make an appearance in these gritty quarters. So, instead of lingering, head upstairs to the place where Hancock used to make regular appearances as a political leader and moderator of the town meeting.

Any committed patriot can recite for you the roll call of great revolutionary moments that took place in the assembly hall on the upper story. Like the time at the end of 1769, when a thousand townsfolk crowded inside to demand the repeal of Townshend Acts and the nonimportation of British goods. Or when Samuel Adams moved to establish the Committee of Correspondence in November 1772 to counter Crown officials through an alliance with other towns in Massachusetts, or when citizens protested the landing of the tea in 1773. Or when an array of speakers from Adams and Hancock to Otis and Joseph Warren called for the protection of individual liberty from tyranny and laid the groundwork for independence.

Because Faneuil Hall was so imbued with radical politics, it's not surprising royal officials made it one of their targets. The king's troops first entered the building in 1768 during their initial occupation and fully occupied it during the siege after Parliament had abolished the town meeting altogether. The military turned the hall into a storehouse for weapons and furniture, and later remade the auditorium into a theatre—an activity forbidden since the days of the Puritans. The soldiers created a Society for Promoting Theatrical Amusement and put on plays like Voltaire's *Zara* and various satires mocking the rebels and their leaders, including one called *The Blockade of Boston* featuring Washington in burlesque with a clownish wig and rusty sword.

But it was after a comedy called *The Busybody* when news broke of a skirmish at Charlestown in the winter of 1776. According to one report, the loyalist audience greeted the news first as if it were a farce, then broke out in a panic. "The audience at this was thrown into dire confusion, the officers jumping over the orchestra, breaking the fiddles on the way; the actors rushing about to get rid of their paint and disguises; the ladies alternately fainting and screaming." Two months later, the troops vacated the hall when Washington broke the siege. As they withdrew, they removed armament and materiel, along with portraits of George III and British officers, assuming the artwork would be headed for a bonfire if it remained on the walls.

Since then, the selectmen have made a gallant effort to clean up the hall and make it functional again as the center of local government. If you happen to look around, you'll find it a scarred but still lovely space for political debates, banquets and ceremonies, and the headquarters of the Ancient and Honorable Artillery Company, a citizen militia that's the oldest in North America. Beyond that, there are offices for town leaders and lesser officials like market clerks, overseers of the poor, sealers of weights and measures, surveyors of lumber and wheat and flax, constables, scavengers, and tax collectors and assessors.

Should you be curious about how government works in town, bear in mind Boston is not a democracy and doesn't claim to be. However, it has taken a few small steps in that direction, at least compared to other former colonial towns of a similar size. The polity is made up of freeholders: white men who are qualified to vote based on holding property worth twenty pounds (or forty pounds in provincial elections), or who can pay a fee equal to two-thirds of the annual poll tax. These freeholders choose the selectmen and lesser officers at an annual meeting in March and attend other meetings that occur throughout the year.

The selectmen are mostly drawn from the gentry while minor officers come from the artisan class. They decide all manners of things, from granting business licenses and answering pleas and petitions, to controlling nuisances like wild pigs and open wells, to outlawing noxious operations like brick and lime kilns, chocolate mills, and slaughterhouses. Poll and property taxes fund the government, though rarely sufficiently and sometimes with controversy.

Faneuil Hall seats around 1,200 comfortably, or up to 1,500 uncomfortably. Town meetings almost never get that crowded, and if it looks like they will, the meeting is held in one of the churches with a larger capacity. Regardless of size, though, the meetings offer a good opportunity to gauge the current sentiments of the citizenry. If you were here on May 30, for example, you'd have seen the selectmen read out an attack on the king: "He has licenced the Instruments of his hostile Oppressions to rob us of our Property, to burn our Houses, & to spill our Blood," and therefore "we are now constrained to consider [him] as the worst of Tyrants: Loyalty to him is *now* Treason to our Country." More commonly, though, the selectmen attend to more practical matters: the lack of food and provisions like firewood, the smallpox epidemic, the poor economy, and merchants taking advantage of depleted warehouses by price-gouging their customers. (As a recent petition signed by seventy people says, "Extortions of every kind are an abomination to God Himself.") Unfortunately, such problems aren't likely to be fixed anytime soon, so take your leave from Faneuil Hall and turn south to the dark, narrow passage of Merchants Row until you get to King Street—the axis of power in colonial times.

Walking on this grand avenue, you might be struck by the handsome brick structures lining the route, or the steeples rising above them in the distance. It may look familiar, for this view has attracted the pens and brushes of artists in America and Europe for decades. Yet the street suffers from the same challenges as any other. It's choked with traffic, from one-horse chaises to hackney coaches and drays and wagons; it's paved with beach stones that are irregularly sized and hard on feet and hooves; and it lacks any sidewalks, other than narrow footways set off with occasional posts. You're apt to get muddy, or at least mussed, if you linger too long, so keep your distance from all the traffic at the corner of King Street and Merchants Row to observe how the people go about their business. Because business is the street's main purpose.

Look into any building and you'll find clerks counting money, lawyers drawing up wills and deeds, merchants and shippers negotiating contracts, and shopkeepers trying to make sales. Royal officials appreciated the value of all this commerce and made sure to fortify the street with guardhouses and sentries, and to assess duties on the trade through customs offices. More important, they built the Town House at the end of the street and made it the center of government in Massachusetts.

While the king no longer holds sway over his namesake street, the aristocratic quality is well preserved in the fashions of the wealthy merchants you'll see passing by. The men wear tightly fitted dress coats with waistcoats underneath and ruffles at the sleeves, while their legs sport breeches and silk stockings and square-buckled shoes. They may wear a lacy jabot at the neck and a powdered periwig on their pate, or dust their tied-back hair with powder to resemble such a wig. Atop their heads, they put a smart tricorn or perhaps a broad-brimmed hat trimmed in beaver, while in their hand may be a cane gilded with an ivory or bone handle, useful for beating a passage through a crowd—or a rogue who insults their honor.

Ladies of the elite class will be less in evidence, at least on foot. If you do see them in a chaise or coach, they may be adorned with a hoop skirt or a fitted gown made with brocade or velvet or silk damask, sometimes with lace ruffles at the neck or a sash at the waist. If they're headed to a banquet or ceremony, they may be attired in a French-inspired sacque, polonaise, or some other swank costume, sporting high-heeled shoes and gloves along with a fan, parasol, or scarf. As with the men, they sport white-powdered hair, sometimes in a high and intricate coiffure, with a bonnet or broad-brimmed hat trimmed in beaver, silk, or gauze. More elaborate headgear may include plumes and feathers, garlands, pompons, and rosettes with flowers and silk ribbons.

All of it shows that while British North America may have asserted its claim to independence, the upper crust of Boston still submits to the tastes of London. As one observer said before the war, "Here we follow the fashions in England & have made great strides in Luxury & Expence . . . the young Ladies seem as smart as those we left in England." And the style craze affects all ages. Anna Winslow, a middle-class child diarist, claims to own "a droll figure of a young lady [in] a tasty head Dress," referring to a baby doll modeling the latest fashions of the imperial court.

By contrast, common artisans and laborers have neither the money nor the time to display themselves this way. Women shopkeepers and householders may wear plain gowns in muted colors, or long skirts over petticoats with linen aprons, and kerchiefs of linen or wool. Men may wear simple linen or flannel shirts, buff coats, breeches and stockings, cocked hats or woolen caps, and sometimes neckerchiefs. Sailors and laborers sport clothes with a looser fit, whether a baggy overcoat and trousers or breeches made of wool or leather. But no man of any class will have facial hair, unless he's part of the patriot army on expedition.

The rising republican mood has made the common look more stylish. Patriot icons like Samuel Adams are famed for their humble appearance, while John Adams and others decry the money wasted on the pursuit of fancy attire. He writes, "[O]ur Dress would not be So elegant—Silks and Velvets and Lace must be dispensed with. But these are Trifles in a Contest for Liberty." Editorialists in newspapers can be even harsher, hectoring men not to look foppish or affected lest they look effeminate, and chastising them for slavishly following fashion. The appearance of a dandy, according to one author, "becomes monstrous, and ridiculous" and serves to create a "Race of Coxcombs." For women, too, clothing festooned with rich and expensive ornament has been criticized by patriots who see it as a mark of excess, or even a lack of patriotism.

This is not the first time Bostonians have condemned each other for their clothing choices. Seventeenth-century Puritans passed sumptuary laws that forbade the wearing of clothes sewn with silver or golden effects, and they restricted lace and silken garments to the upper class, also advising men "they should not walk in great boots." In 1776, though, the reasoning is less moral and more economic. Imported fabric and ornamentation are not only expensive, but they also enrich the king's coffers and the British treasury.

Patriot leaders have long tried to promote homespun and woven fabric. The idea began in 1768, when the Sons of Liberty and others encouraged the practice of "spinning bees" to support nonimportation of British goods. The bees involved groups of twenty to forty women spinning wool, often in the houses of ministers, as they listened to sermons and sang hymns, with the products to be donated to charity. Some wealthy women made appearances at the wheel, too, no longer fearing social disapproval of such labors.

The spinning bees had a positive effect. An editorial in the *Boston Evening-Post* proclaimed, "[T]he industry and frugality of American ladies . . . serve to show how greatly they are contributing to bring about the whole salvation of an entire continent." Even young Anna Winslow wrote, "I choose to wear as much of our own manufactory as possible." Other children promised to learn sewing or to wear only homespun wool, and to quit drinking tea if they had acquired the habit.

Since then, voluntary spinning has fallen off, but paid work has increased. Hardware merchant William Molineux invested in four hundred spinning wheels so women could create wool for the Revolution, just as many working women have always done for their families. However, more complex garments and fashionable wear are still only available from Europe, and local industry struggles to compete with imported wool and cotton with their manufacturers' higher volume and efficiency. This economic disparity applies to other goods as well, since Massachusetts depends its survival on overseas shipments of hemp, flour, grain, meat, sugar, and other essentials, not to mention weapons and ammunition. But local patriot leaders still venerate the idea of domestic production replacing foreign imports and claim it can make the new republic a strong and viable nation, as independent economically as it is politically.

The Daughters of Liberty have been near the forefront of this movement to promote colonially made goods—and to shun those imported from overseas. Women associated with this moniker first appeared in 1770, when some three hundred "Ladies of the highest rank and Influence," according to the *Boston Evening-Post,* pledged to abstain from tea drinking and to ally "with the true Friends of Liberty in all Measures they have taken to save this Abused Country from Ruin and Slavery." Others signed their names to the Solemn League and Covenant, swearing off British imports and pledging not to patronize any merchants who didn't support the cause. One broadside against an offending merchant said, "It is desired that the Sons and Daughters of LIBERTY, would not buy any one thing of him, for in so doing they will bring Disgrace upon themselves, and their Posterity, for ever and ever, AMEN."

As revolutionary feelings spread, women have deepened their commitment in unexpected ways. New broadsides have appeared showing women in tricorns bearing muskets, captioned with "A New Touch of the Times . . . by a Daughter of Liberty." Notables such as Abigail Adams, Mercy Warren, and Hannah Winthrop have joined a women's committee that interrogates suspected loyalists about their sympathies. More militant women even take violent action against merchants who gouge them on the price of beans, cloth, molasses, salt, sugar, coffee, and other critical goods (see p. 225).

If you're sufficiently inspired by these revolutionary sentiments, duck into the Bunch of Grapes tavern, at the corner of Kilby Street, for a dose of radical politics and liquid refreshment. Elizabeth Marston runs the tavern along with her husband, John—best known for owning the arch-patriot tavern the Golden Ball—and they offer the same kind of affordable luxury to their patrons: elegant glasses and dinnerware, dramatic lighting with sconces and candlesticks, and a healthy supply of reading material for the edification of revolutionaries. It's been described as both "the chosen resort of the patriot leaders" and the "best punch house in Boston" and is decorated with a sign featuring a gilded cluster of grapes.

Like the Green Dragon, these quarters are not friendly to Tories and loyalists, and praise for the king will draw a stern backlash or get you reported to the Sons of Liberty. The radical bona fides of the Grapes are indeed beyond question. The Sons and other clubs have plotted strategy around its tables; General Washington was honored here after the occupation; and, upon the reading of the Declaration of Independence, tavern patrons made a bonfire outside the building to torch any emblems of the king they found.

By contrast, the longstanding nemesis of the Grapes patriots stands just across King Street: the British Coffee-House. Run by Hannah Cordis, the tavern offers many of the same elegant furnishings as the Grapes, but with enough space to seat seventy-two patrons and with fifteen beds upstairs for the drowsy or drunken. In that upstairs, a British army surgeon once delivered a notorious harangue from the balcony against Joseph Warren and John Hancock, while at the downstairs tables, legions of loyalists enjoyed a tipple of rum or Madeira wine. The most reliable patrons were members of the Merchants Club, which included officers of the king's army and navy, well-heeled merchants and lawyers, and gentlemen of good breeding. Naturally, this has made the tavern suspect in the eyes of Whig politicians, but not enough to keep them away from its doors. Warren and John Adams have been spotted inside meeting in secret, along with one of the most fervent patriots of all, James Otis Jr. And it was at the British Coffee-House where Otis met a most unfortunate fate.

The son of an eminent attorney, Otis once stood among the top lawyers in Boston and drew attention for his sharp wit and quick tongue, both in and out of court. However, it didn't take long for his Whiggish—or, to the Tories, seditious—sympathies to appear. When Governor Francis Bernard chose Lieutenant Governor Thomas Hutchinson over Otis's father to become chief justice of the Superior Court, young Otis resigned his position as deputy advocate general of the Admiralty Court and made public his outrage. His anger only increased the following year when Hutchinson approved writs of assistance for customs officials to enter private homes, workshops, ships, and the like without a warrant, as a means of stopping smuggling. Otis made a case against the writs, but thanks to Hutchinson's judicial maneuvers, he lost. Despite this, a growing number of local Whigs praised his words at the bench, some of which were memorable. As reported by John Adams in his "Abstract of the Argument," Otis stated:

> Every one with this writ may be a tyrant; if this commission is legal, a tyrant may in a legal manner, also control, imprison, or murder any one within the realm. In the next place, it is perpetual; there is no return. A man is accountable to no person for his doings. Every man may reign secure in his petty tyranny, and spread terror and desolation around him.

Adams was so impressed, he later wrote, "Then and there the Child Independence was born. In fifteen years [i.e., in 1776], he grew up to Manhood, & declared himself free." Otis had no way of knowing the importance of the case to the coming revolution, but he made his point so effectively that Adams and other Whigs began to see him as a champion of colonial liberties.

Otis was just as outspoken in print as he was at the bench, condemning the state of the "American peazant" forced to pay duties and taxes on imported goods that inflated their cost; arguing against the lack of colonial representation in Parliament and denying the right of that body to tax them; demanding unrestricted trade for Bostonians, including entry into foreign ports in southern Europe and the foreign West Indies; and even condemning slavery, unlike many of his peers.

Needless to say, all this talk of individual liberty and freedom versus royal authority got him into trouble. In September 1769, he castigated several customs commissioners upon the discovery of letters they'd written to England depicting Boston Whigs as insurrectionary and hinting they should be prosecuted. Otis called the commissioners "superlative blockheads," and of one of them, John Robinson, he wrote, "I have a natural right if I can get no other satisfaction to break his head." Robinson accepted the challenge. They would face off at the British Coffee-House.

Otis should have chosen another venue. At the time, the tavern was packed with soldiers and sailors friendly to the Tory side, as well as friends of Robinson himself. Nonetheless, Otis took up the fight. When the men spotted each other, they squared off and began the tussle with Robinson pulling on Otis's nose—an insult to his honor. They first used their walking sticks, then their fists, to pummel each other, and it quickly became a barroom brawl. Otis and his young friend John Gridley were greatly outnumbered, and when the violence was over, Otis had a gash to the forehead and Gridley a broken arm. Their assailants faced legal punishment and lawsuits. In the *Gazette*, Samuel Adams depicted the attack as an attempted assassination, writing, "[A]number of sticks at once were over Mr. Otis's head—a drawn sword—the cry in the room G—d d——n him, meaning Mr. Otis, knock him down—kill him—kill him." This episode heightened public animosity to colonial officials, not a difficult task in Boston, but more than anything, it greatly injured Otis's already damaged psyche.

He had never been the picture of mental stability, prone to raving during arguments and behaving erratically. The attack, though, sent him into a spiral of addiction and madness. His political arguments became confused, he quit lawyering, and drank to oblivion. On March 16, 1770, after the Massacre, he "got into a mad Freak," attacked the Town House and broke its windows and was later seen firing a weapon on the street. The next year, his association with the patriot cause ended, and he found a pleasant home in the countryside to spend his days, and lives there even today—and does not entertain visitors, if you're curious.

Loyalists like Judge Peter Oliver delighted in his downfall, calling him "a living Monument of the Justice of Heaven, by his being a miserable Vagabond, rolling in the Streets & Gutters, the laughing-Stock of Boys & the Song of the Drunkard." However, patriots have mourned his disappearance from public view. Continental Army surgeon James Thacher wrote in his journal, in 1775, "[A]ll New England is deploring the irreparable loss of the talents, eloquence, and patriotic services of this justly celebrated character."

The British Coffee-House is a quieter affair these days, with no battles between patriots and loyalists since the latter have either fled or become silent in their sympathies. So, after drinking your fill of brandy or rum, walk one block west to a sight of greater infamy, the Royal Custom House. Sitting on Royal Exchange Lane by an eponymous tavern once popular with military officials, the Custom House is a workaday pile that was once a key part of imperial bureaucracy. But it's best known as the place outside of which five people were killed on March 5, 1770, in what's come to be known as the Massacre on King Street.

Customs officials vacated the building several months ago, and it no longer holds records of shipping manifests or import duties. But that hasn't stopped people from visiting the site, so infamous is the patch of cobbles out front where British troops discharged their muskets. To take your own measure, step back a few feet onto King Street and try to imagine the scene on a late-winter day, when the ground was covered in ice and snow, but the public temper was running hot, ready to explode at the next provocation.

In previous weeks, there had been repeated episodes of mayhem at the ropewalks on the South End (see p. 153) and the killing of a child by a loyalist informer on the North End (see p. 38). British soldiers patrolled the streets and were stationed at a guardhouse a block west and in a barracks two blocks northwest. The troops were tense, anxious after facing sharp words from the townsfolk and printed attacks from the Sons of Liberty and other patriot clubs.

A sentry at the Custom House watched a wigmaker's apprentice criticize a passing captain over an unpaid bill, delivering an insult before the officer went on his way. The sentry offered his own insult to the apprentice and, after an exchange of words, struck him across the head. A crowd rushed to the scene, surrounding the sentry and calling him a scoundrel and a "lobster" and a "bloody-back." At the same time, four teenaged boys confronted a pair of soldiers at their barracks, causing a scuffle that drew up to a dozen grenadiers armed with swords and shovels to fight off the youth. Then the soldiers heard the commotion on King Street and rushed to the sentry's defense to chase away the crowd. A superior officer saw the fracas and ordered the troops back to their barracks.

As the crowd was dispersing, the peal of church bells rang out—likely due to the youth ringing them to cause mischief—which summoned a crowd of hundreds who assumed a fire had broken out. When they found no blaze to fight, some in the crowd redirected their energies to the Custom House. Merchant sailors, rowdy youth, artisans, and laborers surrounded the sentry and tormented him. His associates called for help from the 29th Regiment. Eight grenadiers then marched out of their barracks, led by Captain Thomas Preston, and took position in a tight semicircle to guard the building.

As you look up at the Custom House, try to put yourself in the position of the crowd confronting the grenadiers, those agents of a much-feared, much-hated military, aiming their loaded muskets at you with bayonets attached to the muzzles. Then turn around and take a position closer to the building. Consider the soldiers' perspective, outnumbered perhaps a hundred to eight, facing a hail of ice and snowballs and taunts, knowing you may soon be overtaken and crushed by the mob, or killed with your own weapon. Now consider what came next.

A piece of ice hit grenadier Hugh Montgomery, and he fell. He tried to recover, and his gun discharged. The crowd surged. Someone may have yelled, "Fire!" Seven or eight other muskets discharged. Crowd members hit the soldiers with heavy sticks and ice. Bayonets slashed against them. Musket balls peppered the crowd. Bodies fell and blood spilled. The shooting ended. Captain Preston withdrew his men to their barracks. And on King Street, three men lay dead, two fatally wounded, and six injured.

Among the dead was Crispus Attucks. He was a black sailor, also part Natick Indian, who had lived in the Caribbean but found work on whaling vessels and was planning to ship out soon to North Carolina. He had escaped slavery and was known to some as Michael Johnson, an alias that helped gain him freedom from bondage. He had sailed the waves for decades to maintain that freedom, and like others in the port, he despised the thought of being kidnapped again, this time by the Royal Navy. He made for a tall target at 6'2" and was hit by two musket balls in the chest. Other victims included fellow sailor James Caldwell, rope maker Samuel Gray, leather-breeches maker Patrick Carr, and Samuel Maverick, a seventeen-year-old joiner's apprentice.

When the news of the deaths came out, some called for an insurrection. Patriots had a tar barrel ready atop Beacon Hill to alert the countryside to rise up in defense of the town; the troops of the 14th and 29th Regiments stood guard against attack; and patriot leaders like Samuel Adams demanded the removal of all royal military forces. Acting Governor Hutchinson did his best to minimize any more unrest. He promised an inquest into the deaths, convinced the military to withdraw the redcoats to Castle Island, and allowed the arrest and imprisonment of Captain Preston and the grenadiers under his command.

After Hutchinson reduced tensions, Adams and his Sons of Liberty faced a dilemma in how to keep them elevated—and how to portray the event to the rest of the colonies. Royal officials had long vilified the Sons as a menace to civil order and could easily blame them for instigating the violence. So, instead of issuing threats against the military or officials, Adams appealed to the hearts of Bostonians by focusing on the victims.

The Sons arranged for the bodies to lay in state at Faneuil Hall for all the townsfolk to see, providing stirring orations about imperial oppression and violations of the rights of Englishmen. They staged a funeral procession along King Street that may have drawn more than half the town's residents to watch, as the cortege found its way to Granary Burying Ground. And one of their members, Paul Revere, created an engraving of the violent affair (based on a work by fellow artist Henry Pelham) and called it the "Bloody Massacre Perpetrated on King Street." Taking considerable liberties, Revere transformed the angry crowd of sailors and mechanics into a peaceable mass of tricorn-wearing gentlemen facing a row of soldiers firing with merciless precision. And it was this version of the event that proved to be the most influential.

The report of a town-meeting committee, signed by Samuel Adams, Hancock, Molineux, and Warren, cemented the patriot view, claiming the soldiers had "attacked the people with their bayonets; and that there was not the least provocation given to Captain Preston or his party; the backs of the people being toward them when the people were attacked." Loyalists in their pamphlets protested the claim and said the deaths were an accident caused by a violent mob attacking innocent soldiers, and the word "massacre" was "a very gross abuse of language, and highly injurious to the unhappy officer and soldiers who were concerned in this affair."

The contrasting views haven't changed much in six years. But perhaps you'll want to do your own research. If so, start by inspecting the building facades scarred here and there by gunfire, or estimating the trajectory of the musket balls and who might have been hit and where on the street. Then try to gain entry to the upper stories of the Custom House and surrounding houses, where patriot literature claims stealthy assassins aimed their weapons. As the town-committee report said, "[T]here are witnesses who swear that when the soldiers fired, several muskets were discharged from the house, where the commissioners' board is kept" and "the soldiers have been made use of by others as instruments in executing a settled plot to massacre the inhabitants." There are several other conspiratorial claims for you to pursue as well, if you're particularly obsessed with finding the truth or the version of it that suits you.

In any case, most Bostonians think they already know the truth. They commemorate the Massacre on its anniversary with tolling bells throughout the day and illuminated transparencies in street windows at night, such as those displayed at the Royal Exchange Tavern. These typically show the bloody scene in detail and depict royal officials as accomplices to murder. Orations at the Old South Meetinghouse draw up to five thousand people and have included such speakers as Hancock and Warren. And when those orations appear in print, they always find an audience eager to read them, and according to John Adams, "scarcely ever with dry eyes."

Adams would play his own role in the trial of the soldiers that followed, but to understand it (and him), you have to visit the site where the trial took place, a block west at the Town House. You won't have trouble finding it, since the building looms over the street in more ways than one. Physically, it's quite imposing—two and a half stories, 110 feet long, with classical columns, ornate arched windows, a gabled roof, and a three-story tower resembling a steeple. Historically, it's even more conspicuous. For this is the place where the colonial governor and legislature decided the affairs of Massachusetts for more than sixty years—and where some of the most important debates took place that changed the hearts of Bostonians and drove them toward revolt.

Enter at the ground floor and you'll find a covered walk where merchants and lawyers discuss partnerships and contracts and other weighty matters. Climb to the upper story and you'll be at the former heart of colonial government. Here, power was arranged by position. The east chamber was the quarters for the governor and his council, and is about as lavish as you'd expect. You won't find any of those officials today, of course, since they fled to Britain or Nova Scotia months ago, but there's still enough of an imperious air to get a sense of the sway the governor once held, and the resentment his power often inspired.

Step outside onto the balcony, which provides a wide vista of King Street, and notice the brick walls around you. They're the oldest parts of the building, having stood since 1713 and surviving a fire that consumed the rest of the structure in 1747. (It was rebuilt within soon after.) On this balcony, servants of the king would read out proclamations and announce news of great import: the death of George II, the accession of George III, the installation of new governors, and so on, often to the sound of drums beating and trumpets blaring. But notice there are no more imperial emblems stuck to the facade of the Town House. Patriots recently tore down the royal lion and unicorn that had flanked the balcony and burned them in the street.

Back inside, the central chamber is the home of the General Court, also called the Assembly. These are the quarters where, for decades, the representatives of different towns in the colony met to deliberate issues and pass legislation, and sometimes see it vetoed by the governor. Many of the major figures among Boston's patriots appeared in this chamber, none more memorably than Samuel Adams. In 1768, he helped draft the Massachusetts Circular Letter, in which the Assembly rejected Parliamentary taxation of the colonies without their consent, and said such measures as the Townshend Acts violated their inherent rights and liberties. As if that weren't enough, Adams had the letter sent to other colonies to gain their assent and form an alliance. Predictably, this drew the wrath of the Crown. Governor Francis Bernard dissolved the Assembly, riots ensued, and by the end of the year, the king's troops were occupying Boston.

After taking in the storied atmosphere, leave the hall and head to the west chamber of the Town House, where you'll find the quarters of the lesser courts as well as the Superior Court of Judicature, the highest judicial body in Massachusetts. Thomas Hutchinson famously ruled as chief justice over this body despite having no law training, and it was here where his opponent James Otis argued against the writs of assistance (see p. 51). Otis's words were even more charged in 1768 when British troops occupied the lower floor of the building and emplaced cannon at the front entry. He pushed to have the courtrooms moved to Faneuil Hall, "not only as the stench occasioned by the troops may prove infectious, but as it was derogatory to the honor of the court to administer justice at the mouths of cannon and the points of bayonets." However, the most renowned event to take place here did not involve Otis, but his protégé John Adams.

John Adams *is* Boston in many ways, which is surprising because he was neither born nor raised here. Instead, he spent his childhood in Braintree and developed into something of a prodigy by his teen years. He entered Harvard College at fifteen to become a clergyman, but after graduating, he decided to practice law and built a successful office working with deeds, contracts, and wills; trade and maritime issues; as well as criminal matters. He traveled throughout the colony taking cases, away from his wife, Abigail, and family for weeks at a time, until they all moved to Boston and settled into a home just west of the Town House.

Influenced by Otis's speeches and writings, Adams became interested in the rights and freedoms of British subjects and was incensed at their infringement by Parliament. In the *Boston Gazette* and other publications, he anonymously penned articles and essays defending liberty, condemning the rumored establishment of an Anglican bishop, and criticizing the Stamp Act and other measures. He was also a member of the Sons of Liberty, drawing up many of their public statements while working behind the scenes to advance Whiggish causes, instead of being the public face of the club as his cousin Samuel was.

John Adams avoided soliciting the favor of those in power, turning down the advocate general position in the Admiralty Court, and concentrated on his law practice. He achieved fame in patriot circles thanks to his successful defense in 1769 of sailors accused of murdering a superior officer after they'd been illegally impressed into naval service. The next year, he was elected to a seat in the Assembly. That was also the year of the Massacre.

Adams agreed to act as counsel for the soldiers accused of murder after highly regarded loyalist attorneys wouldn't take the case. Even though he had no sympathy for Tories or royalists, he accepted the role to show that Bostonians had a deep respect for traditional English rights and liberties—in contrast to colonial officials who routinely flouted them—and he would abide by his principles and provide the accused with a vigorous defense.

He worked to get the trial delayed until the public temper had calmed, later in 1770. By this time, Captain Thomas Preston had languished behind bars for more than seven months, all the time fearing the mob might storm the jail and execute him without trial. But that trial finally came in late October, after Adams had worked for many months to devise his arguments and craft a winning strategy. In jury selection, he rejected jurors with Whiggish views or who were unsympathetic to the military, and during the trial, he showed the prosecution's evidence to be either contradictory or muddled. This made the jury's decision an easy one—to acquit Preston of murder.

A month later, Preston's seven grenadiers went on trial, and due to jury selection, not a single member was from Boston. Adams let his associates make many of the arguments, but he proposed to the jury a critical idea: that it was better for a guilty man to go free than an innocent one to be executed. Moreover, he depicted King Street as a scene of chaos before the Massacre, with the mob full of sailors and foreigners "shouting and huzzaing, and threatening life, the bells all ringing, the mob whistle screaming and rending like an Indian yell." The crowd of agitators and out-of-towners was, as he described them, "A motley rabble of saucy boys, Negroes and molattoes, Irish teagues and outlandish jack tars." He appealed to the prejudice of the jury by calling victim Thomas Gray a rabble-rouser "active in the battle at the Rope walks" and Crispus Attucks "a stout Molatto fellow, whose very look, was enough to terrify any person." Then he summed up the case by saying, "Facts are stubborn things; and whatever may be our wishes, our inclinations, or the dictates of our passions, they cannot alter the state of facts and evidence."

The strategy worked, and Adams's lawyering was vindicated: five of the seven soldiers were acquitted, and the two convicted of manslaughter faced only their thumbs being branded, by pleading "benefit of clergy" (a legalistic term referring to a request for clemency or a lighter sentence). The local reaction was muted, aside from a few angry patriot broadsides and sharp words from Samuel Adams, and John called his work "one of the most gallant, generous, manly, disinterested Actions of my whole Life, and one of the best pieces of Service I ever rendered my country."

If Adams's work gave him a bit of sympathy for loyalists, it didn't last long. In 1774, the Massachusetts Government Act annulled the colony's charter, forbade town meetings without the governor's approval, gave the governor sweeping new powers in the appointment of judges and other officials, and replaced elected councilors with ones appointed by the Crown. In protest, patriot legislators departed the Town House and formed the Massachusetts Provincial Congress. Adams wrote seven public essays debating the rising rebellion with a loyalist known as "Massachusettensis" (actually a Tory councilor named Daniel Leonard). Under the name "Novanglus," Adams hailed the colonists' desire for greater freedom and attacked the despotic rule of Parliament and royal officials, comparing the struggle to episodes from the Bible, Ancient Greece, and the Roman Republic.

Since then, Adams has become a delegate to the Continental Congress and intimately involved in the war and the affairs of the nation. He nominated General Washington to be commander in chief, and now advocates for an alliance with European nations against Britain, helps to secure armament for the Continental Army, and works to build up a Continental Navy. He has also drawn up a pamphlet called *Thoughts on Government*, which has proved to be influential for the design of state governments, proposing three branches checking each other's powers to prevent tyranny. Most important, he helped developed the ideas within the Declaration of Independence and defended them with his persuasive oratory and debating skills.

Adams's ideas in the Declaration were given powerful voice on July 18, when the document was read for the first time in Boston from the balcony of the Town House. It was a scene of jubilation and euphoria, as ardent patriot and Colonel Thomas Crafts stepped out to announce:

> We hold these truths to be self-evident, that all men are created equal, that they are endowed by their Creator with certain unalienable Rights, that among these are Life, Liberty and the pursuit of Happiness. . . . These United Colonies are, and of Right ought to be Free and Independent States; that they are Absolved from all Allegiance to the British Crown, and that all political connection between them and the State of Great Britain, is and ought to be totally dissolved.

After finishing the text, Crafts shouted, "God save our American States!" and the celebration truly began. Three cheers from the crowd rent the air and cannon on the hills rang out with a volley of thirteen blasts to represent each of the states in the new union. Two regiments of soldiers and one of artillery paraded through town dressed in their regalia, as representatives, selectmen, and clergymen assembled at the Town House to honor the occasion with a banquet and their own volley of toasts. The patriot clubs allotted a generous helping of free liquor for the townsfolk as well, until there was a merry hubbub on the streets, "a great Confusion" as merchant John Rowe saw it, and, of course, a bit of violence.

The crowd destroyed every copy of the king's arms they could find, along with mortars and pestles, hearts, crowns, and symbols belonging to royalty or royalists, and lit them in a bonfire in the middle of King Street. They demanded that monarchical names of taverns and streets, including King Street itself, be changed to those of patriot heroes, and that traitors and loyalists be rooted out and exiled or imprisoned. Boston became a different place on that July day, no longer a British colonial town but the capital of a new American state.

Abigail Adams echoed the excitement of many Bostonians when she wrote to John about the happy prospect of the new nation, writing, "May the foundation of our new Constitution be Justice, Truth, Righteousness! Like the wise man's house, may it be founded upon these rocks, and then neither storms nor tempests will overthrow it!" But true to his nature, John Adams was more sanguine, even a bit wary. He had seen the compromises necessary to draft the Declaration and was anxious over the outcome of the war:

You will think me transported with Enthusiasm but I am not.—I am well aware of the Toil and Blood and Treasure, that it will cost Us to maintain this Declaration, and support and defend these States.—Yet through all the Gloom I can see the Rays of ravishing Light and Glory. I can see that the End is more than worth all the Means. And that Posterity will triumph in that Days Transaction, even although We should rue it, which I trust in God We shall not.

ear right) **ABIGAIL ADAMS.** *One of the best chroniclers of life in Boston during the siege and the early days of ependence. Her keen insight and wit are often without parallel.*

(far right) **JAMES OTIS.** *ampion of liberty, opponent tyranny, inspiration to John dams—Otis has been many ngs to Bostonians, including a tavern brawler.*

TOWN HOUSE. *Home to the legislature and the Superior Court and, at one time, the offices of the royal governor and his council, though the king's arms have now been stripped from its facade.*

(above left) **PHILLIS WHEATLEY.** *Transcendent Boston p formerly enslaved, with readers in America and Europe a champions from George Washington to Thomas Hutchins*

(above right) **OLD SOUTH CHURCH.** *Spiritual fixture of the South End whose greatest moment came in late 1773 when it hosted five thousand residents to decide the fate o British tea shipments.*

(left) **GEORGE WASHINGTON.** *Liberator of Boston and head of the Continental Army, who entrapped the British army and forced its evacuation with a daring gambit ato Dorchester Heights.*

SONS OF LIBERTY. *Famous revolutionary society that exercises power through broad social networks, public events and celebrations, propaganda, intimidation, and sometimes violence.*

CHRIST CHURCH. *Also known as Old th Church, where Paul Revere directed allies to hang lanterns in the steeple to arn against the British army's invasion of the countryside.*

(left) **PAUL REVERE.** *A metalsmith, engra master Mason, militia officer, and part-ti dentist, whose most renowned activity was taking a midnight ride to warn residents, "The regulars are coming out!"*

(above) **PAUL REVERE HOUSE.** *A good example of what most of Boston's domestic architecture looks like in 1776, with dark wooden beams and panels, an overhangin second story, and leaded glass windows.*

THOMAS HUTCHINSON. *Greatly maligned royal governor of Massachusetts who had a flair for enforcing the will of Parliament and often being indifferent to colonial liberties.*

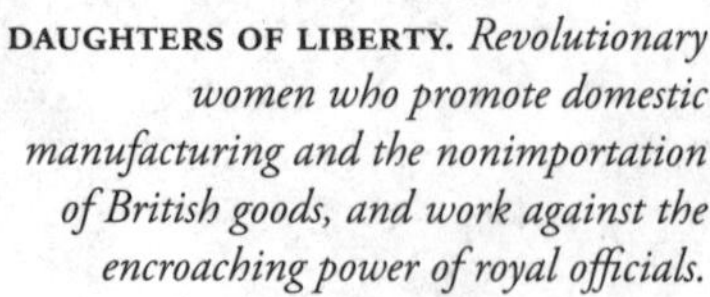

DAUGHTERS OF LIBERTY. *Revolutionary women who promote domestic manufacturing and the nonimportation of British goods, and work against the encroaching power of royal officials.*

EEN DRAGON TAVERN. *A favorite haunt of the Sons of Liberty, as well as the local order of Masons, where you can :re a mug of ale with some of Boston's most ardent patriots.*

(left) **SAMUEL ADAMS.** *Onetime maltster and tax collector who became a state and national legislator—and with the Sons of Liberty, raised public outrage to the point of armed rebellion.*

(above) **BACK ROADS AND ALLEYS.** *The anonymous back streets of Boston, where the real movement toward independence began, in the workshops and docks and ropewalks of working people.*

EBENEZER MACKINTOSH. *South End gang leader who led the annual anti-Catholic "Pope's Day" riot with effigie the pontiff and the devil, bef the Sons of Liberty found hi useful to their cause.*

JOSEPH WARREN. *Doctor turned radical politician turned major general, who treated the wounded after the Massacre on King Street and was fatally wounded himself at Bunker Hill.*

THE LIBERTY TREE. *The wooden emblem of the Revolution that's held banners and effigies, hoste speeches and celebrations, and met its fate by the blo of a British axe.*

ove left) **MERCY OTIS WARREN.** *Friend and correspondent of leading politicians and statesmen, author of poems d essays and plays, and historian planning a detailed history of the war.* (above right) **JOHN ADAMS.** *Country lawyer ned national politician who's made a name for himself as one of the most conservative of revolutionaries and an ellectual architect of the new republic.*

ove left) **FANEUIL HALL.** *Famed site of the town meeting that houses the offices of local officials, hosts assemblies d banquets, and features a market hall where you can buy fresh meat.* (above right) **JOHN HANCOCK.** *Among the hest men in the region but also a popular favorite who's galvanized support for the Revolution among both his fellow rchants and working-class patriots.*

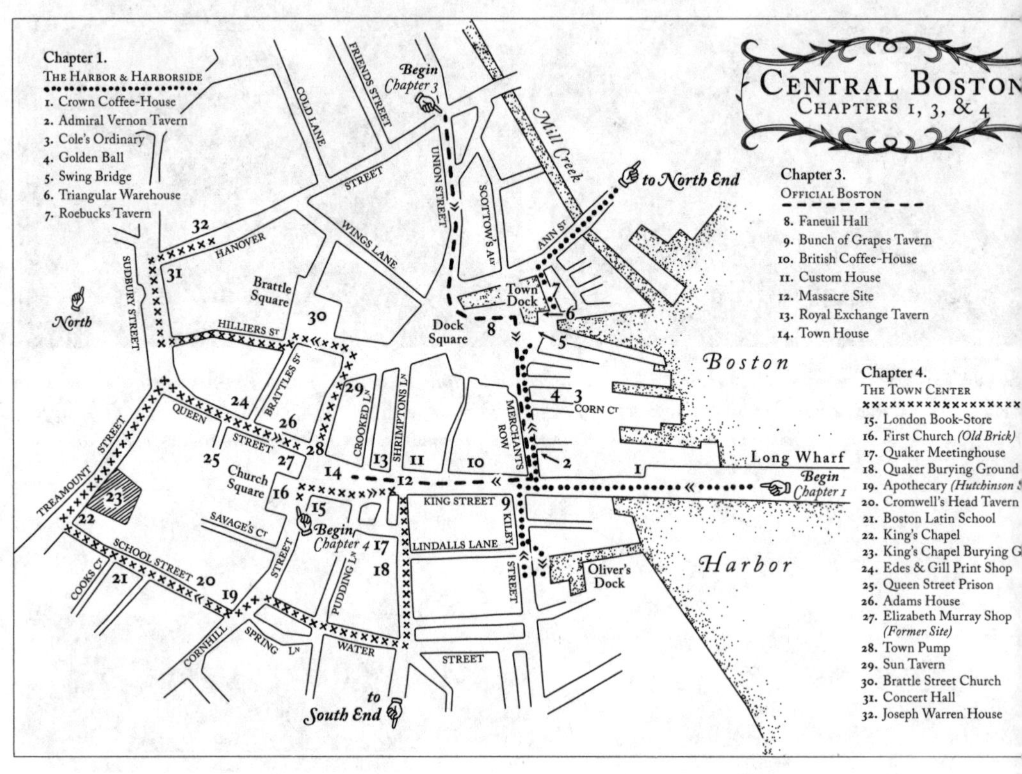

See pages 2–3 for a full-size version of this map.

☆ 4 ☆

The Town Center

The Town Center includes more than just the official side of Boston. It's the hub of its business district and the home of many of its most admired figures. It features sights that recall the darkest chapters in local history as well as the promise of an enlightened new era. And it's the place to find shops and artisans that cater to every need and whim, news offices that provide the latest updates on the war, and taverns where you can enjoy a stiff drink in a lively setting.

Begin just south of King Street on Cornhill Street, where many of the town's booksellers are located, carrying the latest political pamphlets, novels from Britain and the Continent, and an assortment of knickknacks to pique your interest. The tradesmen who run these shops have a side business in bookbinding and will take your old cheaply bound books and rebind them with gilded designs and leather covers.

The most highly regarded is Henry Knox's London Book-Store, at the southeast corner of King and Cornhill. Knox is a man of twenty-six years, large and lumbering but with a keen intellect and impressive reputation. He married into a rich loyalist family but has done much to support the rebel cause: eavesdropping on the soldiers who once frequented his shop and picking up key bits of military intelligence, conveying what he learned to his friends in the patriot clubs, and even joining the local artillery company—in which he blew off several of his fingers. Knox was on King Street on the night of the Massacre, warning Captain Preston of the trouble that would ensue if he marched his grenadiers toward the crowd: "For God's sake take care of your Men, for if they fire your life must be answerable." Preston brushed him off, and not long after, those men killed five people.

In the last year, Knox has had to step away from his business to take a larger role in the fight against Britain, recently leading a remarkable expedition to bring a caravan of mortars, howitzers, and cannon from Fort Ticonderoga to Dorchester Heights (see p. 193 for the full story). Knox's feat owed in part to his incessant reading habits, poring over his store's military and engineering titles to make himself into a martial expert. He's since become an artillery colonel in the Continental Army.

The bookstore is now shuttered, but when it's open, you'll find a wealth of titles here: classics by Locke, Pope, Homer, Virgil, Plutarch, Molière, and Voltaire; treatises on mathematics, science, anatomy, and medicine; Latin and English grammars; stories like *Tristram Shandy*, *Tom Jones*, and the *Arabian Nights*; biographies from Oliver Cromwell to Benvenuto Cellini; histories of assorted countries; tales of exotic adventure in foreign lands; primers on moral conduct; and collections of riddles and puzzles. There's also a broad range of goods for the civilized Bostonian: paper and pens, quills, inkwells, sealing wax, reading glasses, snuff boxes, desk globes, paper hangings, money scales, fishing rods, telescopes, microscopes, magic lanterns, fifes and flutes, toothbrushes, razor straps, battledores and shuttlecocks, not to mention "Hair Powder Machines," and the mercury-laden Maredent's Drops and Keyser's Female Pills.

If you're most interested in the Revolution, you'd be keen to pick up a copy of Thomas Paine's *Common Sense.* The pamphlet is only forty-seven pages long and costs but a shilling, but it has sold at least a hundred thousand copies in British North America and gone through multiple editions. Its popularity owes in part to its clear, simple language and bracing, honest perspective. You can see (or hear) it read in taverns and workshops, parlors and churches, and even military camps. General Washington has said, "I find *Common Sense* is working a powerful change in the minds of men," and indeed no writer has contributed more to the rise of rebellious American sentiments than the Englishman who wrote it.

Paine has helped sever the loyalty of the colonies from their imperial master. He's attacked the divine right of kings, calling William the Conqueror "a French bastard landing with an armed banditti" and claiming more recent monarchs are no better than rogues, with George III being "the royal brute of Great Britain." He reviles the system of government of the kingdom as much as its monarchy, calling it hierarchical and hereditary, corrupt and unaccountable, and lacking in legitimacy—yet feels confident Americans will soon overthrow that system: "The birthday of a new world is at hand."

Paine is a radical democrat, as enthusiastic about democracy as the ruling class is wary of it. He believes American government should be a simple mass assembly of the people, annually elected from nationwide districts, with no property requirements to vote or anything smacking of privilege and hierarchy. "The more simple a thing is, the less liable it is to be disordered, and the easier repaired when disordered." This idea has, however, drawn at least one formidable opponent.

John Adams published his influential *Thoughts on Government* as a counterweight to Paine, believing only checks and balances in state and federal governments, and houses split between popular and indirectly elected assemblies, can prevent tyranny. Adams appreciates the success of *Common Sense* in purging people of their affection for the Crown, but he has no use for the other parts of the program. He asserts Paine's philosophy is "so democratical, without any restraint or even an attempt at equilibrium or Counterpoise, that it must produce confusion and every Evil work." Luckily for you, both volumes are available for purchase at the London Book-Store, so you can decide for yourself which man was right.

Just as you can find books of political radicalism at Knox's shop, you can hear sermons of religious radicalism across the street at First Church, also known as "Old Brick." It's led by the redoubtable Charles Chauncy, who first made his name in the 1740s opposing the Great Awakening religious revival and now just as fervently opposes British rule in North America. The building stands three stories, with galleries supported by Tuscan columns, and two iron stoves for warmth. The organ was the first ever installed in a

Congregational church, and the clock on the bell tower was also the first of its kind.

Chauncy preaches from a pulpit located almost exactly in the middle of town, though his political stance is anything but middling. Some call his brand of religion "polemical divinity"—a militant theology invoking God as an ally in the fight—and he's honed his craft over three decades. As early as 1747, the year of the impressment riots against the Royal Navy, Chauncy warned against the monarchy and Parliament overstepping their power. His animus toward the Crown has only increased since then. When he heard a rumor after the Massacre that the king might pardon the accused captain and grenadiers before their trial, he warned of turmoil to follow—"Surely he would not suffer the town & land to lie under the defilement of blood!"—and in his 1774 *Letter to a Friend*, he went further and saw the possibility of revolution: "Force may for a while keep the people under restraint; but this very restraint may, in time, be the occasion of the outbreaking of their passions with the greater violence."

Chauncy is closely aligned with Samuel Adams and James Otis, and Benjamin Edes has published many of his tracts in the *Boston Gazette*. He's one of several radical ministers who have become so associated with the Sons of Liberty that, according to one observer, "scarcely a patriot club was without a divine who lent an odor of sanctity to what conservatives believed would otherwise have been rank treason." The firmest loyalists like Judge Peter Oliver call him part of the Black Regiment of the Revolution, ministers who encourage riot and sedition and remake their pulpits into "Gutters of Sedition" and preach "*it was no Sin to kill the Tories.*" A popular ballad adds mockery to the charge:

That fine preacher, called a teacher,
Of Old Brick Church the first,
Regards no grace, to men in place,
And is by Tories curst.
At young and old, he'll rave and scold,
And is, in things of state,
A zealous Whig, than Wilkes more big,
In Church a tyrant great.

Paradoxically, Chauncy promotes a gentle form of theology, with less emphasis on original sin and predestination and more on human agency and God's benevolence. Despite this emphasis, should you attend a service at First Church, you may find him to be pompous and aloof, and his oratory to be bombastic, prone to lengthy diatribes against the king and the evils of imperial rule. For these reasons, one might think his church would have been a primary target of the British army during the siege, but strangely enough, it remained unscathed—even as others were severely damaged, used as stables or barracks, converted to hospitals, or torn down for firewood. So, with a touch of grace, First Church endures as strongly as ever, and now Old Brick has become the nickname not just of the building but of Chauncy himself.

Return to the cobbles outside the church and you'll have the fine view of steeples and towers all around you. They represent eleven Congregational, three Anglican, one Presbyterian, and two Baptist congregations—with Roman Catholic churches being forbidden by law. Women make up the majority of these congregations, filling the pews and benches, singing in choirs, creating prayer groups, giving alms for charity. But they're disallowed behind the altar and prevented from learning theology or holding ecclesiastical title. In fact, for all their radical tendencies in politics, Boston's churches maintain a strict social divide: black parishioners are made to watch in the galleries and back pews; men and women often worship separately across the aisle from each other; and the "better sort" purchase exclusive boxes in the nave, closer to the altar and to the word of God.

One group that rejects many of these distinctions is called the "Sandemanians," founded by a Scot named Robert Sandeman. They preach a social gospel unusual to Boston: living and eating communally, handing out their wealth to the poor, washing each other's feet, and giving each other something called "the holy Kiss." They're notorious among mainline ministers (Chauncy, for one, has condemned them), but there are still enough of them to regularly meet. If you're interested in joining them for a service, you can find them at a blockmaker's workshop on Barrett's Wharf, in a dicey area just below Ann Street.

The Sandemanians are only the latest in a long line of dissenters against Boston's spiritual orthodoxy. The first were the Quakers, whose meetinghouse and burial ground are only a few blocks away. To get there, go east along King Street and turn right on Leveret's Lane, where the Society of Friends owns a plot of land just south of the site of the Massacre. They bought it earlier in the century, after a tumultuous period in the mid-1600s when Puritan judges and ministers persecuted them for heresy, sorcery, sedition, and other supposed sins, and barred them from entering the colony. Out of defiance, many Quakers challenged the law, and the consequences were often dire. Magistrates ordered them to have their ears cut off, tongues bored with hot irons, and bodies dragged behind a cart and whipped repeatedly.

Despite the oppression, Quakers refused to bend in their beliefs. They prophesied and gave voice to revelations—which the authorities called "ravings and blasphemies"—and allowed women to speak aloud in their meetinghouses (forbidden in Puritan houses of worship). They also criticized Congregational ministers in their own churches, openly accusing them of having "a covetous and deceitful rotten heart, lying lips . . . and a smooth, fawning, flattering tongue," among other things.

Four Quakers died as martyrs. The most famous was Mary Dyer, who, like the others, was executed by gallows on the Boston Neck, the same place where accused witches like Ann Hibbins met their end during the same era. However, the threat of hanging did not stop Quakers from coming into the colony. With the prospect of more executions to follow, the newly installed monarch Charles II finally put a stop to the killings and ordered the accused to be brought back to England for trial.

Happily, that period of sectarian hatred is more than a century in the past, and Quakers practice the faith in their meetinghouse on Leveret's Lane without threat of arrest or violence. It's a squat brick structure sitting behind a high wooden fence (rebuilt in recent years after being destroyed in the fire of 1760), and the Society of Friends have their meetings here monthly. You won't find more than ten families these days as members, but women still take a prominent role, channeling the inner light and divine visions, along with sitting on committees, keeping account books, serving as ambassadors to other congregations, and judging whether partners in marriage are suitable for each other. On occasion, a prominent Quaker like Rachel Wilson will offer a speech outside the meetinghouse, too—her 1769 oration in Faneuil Hall is thought to be the first time any woman spoke in front of an audience in that chamber. Behind the meetinghouse, there are around a hundred Quakers occupying the Burying Ground, which was founded a half-century after the executions and is not believed to hold any martyrs. Still, it's a peaceful sanctuary that recalls the quiet, inward aspects of the faith and gives you an opportunity to reflect on its members' strength and resilience in the face of unconscionable brutality.

To go deeper into the heart of seventeenth-century religious dissent, continue west two blocks along Water Street with a short jog south to School Street. Here at the corner of School and Cornhill sits a sturdy gambrel-roofed brick structure now occupied by an apothecary. Inside, you can get your share of tinctures and decoctions for relieving various maladies; and if the druggist feels like telling you, you can hear the story of one of the most renowned figures in early Massachusetts, Anne Hutchinson.

She sailed to the colony as a midwife in 1634, leaving the confines of England where Congregationalism was not tolerated by Anglican authorities, and with her husband built a two-story, half-timbered home on this very plot of land. Boston was then barely four years old, and she became a prominent figure in town, showing a talent for leadership and for interpreting the Bible, and hosting weekly meetings in her parlor that drew up to a hundred men and women to discuss their faith. Many of her guests were so impressed with her skills, they saw her as "a Woman that Preaches better Gospel then any of your black-coats that have been at [University], a Woman of another kind of spirit, who hath had many Revelations of things to come."

However, Governor Winthrop and other authorities didn't appreciate her talents, with the governor saying she was "a woman of ready wit and bold spirit, brought over with her dangerous errors." What troubled him and other orthodox Puritans was her assertion that salvation could come by faith alone—without good works or the guidance of ministers. This was called the Antinomian Controversy, and it excited an uproar among traditional believers. For her outspoken ways and persuasive oratory, Winthrop and his allies labeled her an "opinionist" who slandered church officials and undercut their power. They charged her with sedition and heresy and put her on trial before the General Court.

She defended herself ably, rebutting Winthrop's aggressive questions with her own and challenging the very premise of the trial and her alleged misdeeds. Nonetheless, the governor's power was too great: after she admitted to experiencing divine revelations, he persuaded the Court to convict her. The authorities imprisoned and held her in solitary confinement over the winter of 1637, before excommunicating and banishing her and her followers. She found refuge in Rhode Island, helping to establish the more tolerant atmosphere of that colony, before relocating to Long Island, New York, where, in 1643, she died during warfare between native Indians and Dutch colonizers. In the years since, she's inspired many dissenters—most famously her friend Mary Dyer, the Quaker martyr—and her descendants have been prominent leaders in the region. Ironically, the most famous of these was a champion of political orthodoxy, her great-great-grandson, Governor Thomas Hutchinson.

If all this walking through history has made you thirsty, take your leave from the apothecary and head next door to Cromwell's Head Tavern, which can serve you a mug of ale while reminding you of yet another chapter from the Puritan era. The pub is named after the Lord Protector of 1650s England, Oliver Cromwell, whose Parliamentary army of "roundheads" abolished the monarchy and assumed dictatorial power. Be careful upon entering. The sign with Cromwell's noggin hangs so low below the eave, you'll have to bow your own head to go inside—which is precisely the point. The proprietor Anthony Brackett intended all visitors to "honor" him in this way, mainly as a poke in the eye to the British military, to whom Cromwell's name still reeks with villainy for approving the execution of Charles I.

Like the witch trials and Quaker persecutions, the reign of Cromwell is a chapter most Bostonians would prefer to avoid discussing (at least with outsiders), though the Lord Protector does have his fans. His name has appeared on broadsides threatening the tea consignees; the most radical patriots occasionally invoke him as a "glorious fellow" in toasts and ceremonies; and his byline has appeared under articles in the press that promise deliverance from "tyrannical ministers" of the Crown, signed "with peculiar affection your assured friend, Oliver Cromwell."

Even if you care not a whit for distant history, Cromwell's Head might still be worth a visit. This two-story wooden house has entertained more than a few esteemed visitors, and once hosted Washington when he was still serving with the British army. You can enjoy wine, punch, porter, or rum, among many other drinks; consume a hearty meal of the local cuisine; or stay the night if the sight of the dictator's glowering face doesn't keep you up at night.

After spending your time at the tavern, continue a short distance west to Boston Latin School, which has been educating students since before the time of Cromwell. Under its pitched roof, instructors teach history, philosophy, and theology as well as classical Latin and the literature of ancient authors, with the expectation that many of their young charges will go on to get degrees at Harvard College, or find success in law, business, or politics. Figures like John Hancock, Cotton Mather, Samuel Adams, and John Trumbull have all studied here, along with Benjamin Franklin, who entered at eight years old but later dropped out. Despite the esteem accorded to the school, at the moment, it's closed because its loyalist headmaster John Lovell fled town. And like every other educational institution in the area, it's underfunded and educates only a fraction of the town's school-aged boys, while girls are disallowed entry completely.

The original building used to stand across School Street, but that two-story wooden pile had to be demolished to make way for the construction of a much grander creation: King's Chapel, a Georgian monolith to the Anglican faith with a blocky stone facade and no steeple. Inside are Corinthian columns molded from wood and box pews for those who can afford them, while the tower features a great bell cast in Britain to call the faithful to worship.

Contrary to what you might have heard, patriots are not uniformly Congregational and loyalists Anglican, but the major figures in the struggle for independence do represent those opposing sides. Fervent patriots have led churches like Old Brick and the Old North Meetinghouse, while royal officials favored this bastion of the Church of England. The king's soldiers and officers once made up a good portion of the congregation, too, occupying the pews and the galleries to hear the priest lead prayers to God and to the king—the Defender of the Faith.

Henry Caner was the most recent rector, a Doctor of Divinity who led the church for nearly thirty years, as long as the current building has been standing. In that time, he saw the reputation of Anglicanism change dramatically, from a faith with a growing appeal at mid-century, to a target of enmity by radical patriots twenty years later. This owed in part to Caner's advocacy for a bishop to be installed in North America, naively assuming this would reduce tensions between rival sects. His concerns were also practical, since ministers had to travel a six-thousand-mile round trip across the Atlantic and back to be ordained. But in pressing the episcopal cause, Caner made a grievous error. Not only has Boston long been dominated in religion by Congregationalism, in politics its citizens have failed to elect even a single Anglican representative to the General Court, and only one selectman to the town government. It didn't take long for the faith to fall under siege.

The Black Regiment was first to press the attack, with ministers like Charles Chauncy and Jonathan Mayhew warning of bishops seizing power and drawing converts from Congregationalism, leading to "the spiritual siege of our churches, with the hope that they will one day submit to an Episcopal sovereign." John Adams and James Otis also inflamed fears about the installment of a bishop, and Samuel Adams proclaimed Anglicanism was no better than "popery" and said there was "much more to be dreaded from the growth of POPERY in America, than from Stamp-Acts or any other Acts destructive of men's civil rights." Even a child like Anna Winslow became aware that "the good people of [New England] are threaten'd with & dreading the coming of an episcopal bishop."

The climate of fear worsened in the years before the Revolution, until the church became a target of widespread abuse by radical patriots and religious bigots. Caner and three other clergymen wrote to the Bishop of London in 1774 to say that their lives and property were at stake, and if measures weren't taken to ensure their safety, "we have the prospect of a fiery trial." In the countryside, violence erupted over the issue. One Anglican minister, Samuel Peters, wrote, "The Sons of Liberty have almost killed one of my Church, tarred and feathered two, abused others, and on the 6th Day destroyed my Windows and rent my Clothes, even my Gown, &c. . . . The Lord deliver us from Anarchy."

Most Anglican clergymen evacuated to Halifax or Britain after the siege. When Caner left, he managed to take the register, records, communion service, and vestments, but left behind his books and furniture. Many in his congregation joined him in shipping out, while those who remained largely joined the congregation of Christ Church. And King's Chapel shut its doors.

Ironically, the church reopened them once in recent months to host a funeral service for the patriot doctor-warrior Joseph Warren. After Paul

Revere recognized Warren's body in a common grave on Bunker Hill, it was disinterred and brought here in a grand procession in the spring of 1776. There was a military parade, elegies and prayers by Congregational clergy, and an oration from lawyer Perez Morton, who demanded "an entire disconnection with Great Britain" in calling for independence. Not long after, the gilded miters and crown that flanked the organ were taken down, and no one in the sanctuary has since offered prayers to the king, even in a place named after him.

Once you've finished looking at the stately relic of King's Chapel, continue north on Treamount Street and take a right onto Queen Street, where many of the newspapers that fueled animosity against Anglicanism have their offices. Some are still in operation, though the siege and occupation have taken a toll. Major names like *The Massachusetts Spy* have moved out of town, and some papers have ceased operation altogether (including loyalist journals like the *News-Letter*, *Weekly Advertiser*, and *Chronicle*). But there are still a few in business in the area, so you can read the latest dispatches on the war and the various activities of patriots in New England.

The two most important Whiggish journals once had their offices at the corner of Brattles Street and Queen Street. The first, *The New England Courant*, was a legendary sheet in the 1720s, best known for featuring the writing of young Benjamin Franklin, who penned interesting and provocative essays under the byline Silence Dogood. His brother James acted as publisher-gadfly, questioning government policies and the wisdom of Puritan divines like Cotton Mather. The paper failed under legal pressure, and James was jailed for printing articles that impugned the reputation of town leaders and advanced such dangerous notions as freedom of the press.

Also at this corner is the print shop for the *Boston Gazette and Country Journal*, better known as the *Gazette*. It's closed at the moment, but if you were to visit before the war, you would have found the printer or his assistants setting type, laying out paper, inking plates, and producing a range of documents from sermons and moral lectures to almanacs, advertisements, broadsides, and essays. However, the newspaper was best regarded for promoting the patriot cause.

Publishers Benjamin Edes and John Gill were long known for defending the rights of colonists and criticizing royal officials—in one case making Governor Francis Bernard so angry, he tried to have them arrested for sedition. They showcased the writing of James Otis and Joseph Warren, published sermons by dissenting clergy, and penned editorials damning the policies of the Crown and those who tried to enforce them. But their greatest impact on publishing has been in influencing the debate around major events. As one example, the official report *A Short Narrative of the Horrid Massacre* informed readers the bloodshed on King Street was a willful attempt to murder Boston's citizens, instead of a panicked reaction by British soldiers against an advancing mob. The tract found an audience well beyond New England and moved the colonists another step down the path toward revolt.

Edes is a firmly committed patriot, and his actions have gone well beyond the press. He's a member of the Loyal Nine, one of the most important patriot clubs. Among their other activities, the Nine subverted colonial tax policy by issuing broadsides against measures like the Stamp Act while privately coordinating with radicals like Ebenezer Mackintosh to carry out violent protests—tactics that would influence those of the more famous Sons of Liberty.

The Nine and the Sons have members in common, as do many of the social groups in Boston. These include the North Caucus Club, Wednesday Night Club, Massachusetts Charitable Society, Number Five Club, and Merchants Club. Although the radicals plot strategy, the majority of groups simply provide a venue for their members to chat, drink, dine, and work toward a shared purpose. The Fire Club fights blazes with ladders and leather buckets and a hand-pumped engine, and other societies devote their energies to promoting the mercantile trade, leading fishing expeditions, or training with arms and artillery.

One of the most secretive societies meets above the *Gazette* office and is named after the space where they meet—the Long Room Club. Except for Paul Revere, its members all hail from the wealthier class of doctors, merchants, lawyers, and judges, and include figures like John Hancock and Josiah Quincy. Rumor has it that the club has been behind everything from the Destruction of the Tea to the forming of the Provincial Congress, but since it doesn't share reports of its meetings, we're not likely to know much more than that.

During the siege, the British army tried to have Edes arrested, but he escaped to Watertown with his press and his typefaces and briefly published his newspaper there. With the liberation of Boston, he promises to return and restore the *Gazette* to its former eminence. Unfortunately, he will not have his partner to help him. John Gill has split from the *Gazette* to publish his own paper, the *Continental Journal.* Unlike Edes, Gill stayed in town during the occupation and was arrested for printing treason and sedition. For a month, he occupied a cell across the street—at the fearsome town prison.

Wander across Queen Street to get a closer look at that building. The brick-and-wooden pile has six cells on the first and second floors, encased by iron bars and warmed by charcoal pots, while the third story has five cells for debtors in default. You'll not want to visit the interior by choice, though the prison does provide an interesting window into the nature of crime and punishment in Boston.

It occupies the site of the old Stone Jail, a rough pen from the seventeenth century, when Queen Street was called Prison Lane. The jail held blasphemers, adulterers, sexual transgressors, servants disobeying their masters, Sabbath breakers, and truants from church services, along with violent criminals and assorted miscreants. There weren't a large number of lawbreakers at the time, as they were more often publicly shamed, but the jail stood as a warning to those who would defy God's law as it was determined by Puritan magistrates.

These days, moral and sexual crimes are less often prosecuted, and more than three-quarters of convictions are for property crimes like arson, burglary, and robbery; fraud in the form of forgery and counterfeiting; and treason and sedition. The prison is usually just a way station for the accused on their way to trial or criminals about to be punished in some other way. Farmers, merchants, and gentlemen often receive fines for their transgressions (running from one to sixty pounds), while other groups like the enslaved, the young, and the poor may face a harsher form of justice.

If the court decides a criminal deserves a strong punishment for his crime, he may be publicly humiliated by cheek branding, ear cutting, standing in the gallows, doing hard labor, or being sold into servitude. Outside the prison on Queen Street, there is also a convenient (and mobile) whipping post and pillory to shame and torture the guilty. Men and women are punished with equal severity. As Samuel Breck recalls in his *Recollections*:

> Here women were taken from a huge cage, in which they were dragged on wheels from prison, and tied to the post with bare backs, on which thirty or forty lashes were bestowed amid the screams of the culprits and the uproar of the mob. A little farther in the street was to be seen the pillory, with three or four fellows fastened by the head and hands, and standing for an hour in that helpless posture, exposed to gross and cruel insult from the multitude, who pelted them incessantly with rotten eggs and every repulsive kind of garbage that could be collected.

In the most serious capital cases like homicide, hiring a good attorney may not help the accused get acquitted or reduce the severity of his punishment—70 percent of all cases result in convictions. Despite this, administration of justice tends to be measured, or even lax in some cases, and the crime rate is fairly low. The prison is more a symbol of the old oppressive power of the Crown than the new, more enlightened regime the patriots hope to build.

A few doors east on Queen Street, two of the architects of that regime, John and Abigail Adams, own a handsome brick house. They purchased it for its location, only a short distance from the Town House and near John's office in the center of town. However, you won't find John here these days, since he spends most of his time at the Continental Congress in Philadelphia; and Abigail only visits on occasion, when she has relief from her duties at the family farm in Braintree. Should you chance to meet her, you'll find she offers a sharp perspective on the state of the town and the most prominent figures of the day. Indeed, her judgment and erudition are widely respected even at a time when the intellect and opinions of young women are often ignored or dismissed. As she writes, "[I]n this country you need not be told how much female Education is neglected, nor how fashionable it has been to ridicule Female learning."

By way of background, Abigail's mother and grandmother taught her to read and write at an early age, and she quickly showed a talent for self-education. She learned French and English, and had access to the massive library of her Congregational minister father, through which she explored classical literature and the arts as well as modern political theory. She married her match, lawyer John Adams, at the family home in

Weymouth, after which they relocated to Braintree and began raising a family.

The couple has moved back and forth between Boston and Braintree several times and occupied different homes. They vacated this one on Queen Street as tensions with the British rose in 1774, and she's only recently returned to inspect its condition, after a British army doctor squatted here during the siege. She found the house dirty and disheveled, but otherwise intact—though it does need to be cleaned to be made habitable again. It's just one more task to add to her growing list.

In Braintree, she and John have four surviving children (ages four to eleven), and she's been raising them while she manages affairs at the farm, keeping the account books and overseeing investments. To her friend Mercy Otis Warren, she has written of her considerable duties: "Frugality, Industry and Economy are the Lessons of the day—at least they must be so for me or my small Boat will suffer shipwreck." Yet despite living much of the time in the country, she understands the problems facing urban Boston. She's traveled throughout the town inspecting damage to the public buildings and houses after the occupation, and even crossed the river to Charlestown to look at the ruins: "A melancholy sight . . . which evinces the barbarity of the foe, and leaves a deep impression of the sufferings of that unhappy town."

She has taken to signing her letters to John and others as "Portia," after the faithful wife of the tyrannicidal Brutus in ancient Rome. At times, her letters offer a call to arms, a promise that women will defend the town from siege. ("We are no ways dispirited here, we possess a Spirit that will not be conquered. If our Men are all drawn of and we should be attacked, you would find a Race of Amazons in America.") At other times, she is unflinching in her view of the inequality she finds here, especially the hypocrisy of Bostonians who claim to be patriots owning slaves. ("I wish most sincerely there was not a Slave in the province. It always appeared a most iniquitous Scheme to me—fight ourselves for what we are daily robbing and plundering from those who have as good a right to freedom as we have.") She also sees the same hypocrisy at work in the relations of men and women. To John, she writes:

> I desire you would Remember the Ladies, and be more generous and favourable to them than your ancestors. Do not put such

> unlimited power into the hands of the Husbands. Remember all Men would be tyrants if they could. If particular care and attention is not paid to the Ladies we are determined to foment a Rebellion, and will not hold ourselves bound by any Laws in which we have no voice, or Representation.

Unlike many of her missives, this one did not receive a favorable response from her husband. Instead, John dismissed her concerns, and Abigail expressed her frustration to Mercy Warren: "He is very saucy to me in return for a List of Female Grievances which I transmitted to him. I think I will get you to join me in a petition to Congress."

This is no idle promise: Warren is as important a figure as she is, and just as capable of drawing attention. As the sister of James Otis and wife of legislator James Warren, Mercy Warren has corresponded with the delegates of the Continental Congress and opened her house in Plymouth to them as a forum for discussion and argument. She's also a prolific writer of drama, satire, and poems about the war and political conflicts, and she uses classical metaphor to compare the struggles of the ancient world with those of 1776. So any petition to Congress signed by Adams and Warren would be sure to gain the attention of legislators.

Most women in Boston are, of course, not as privileged as they are. You can get a sense of their struggles as you look around on Queen Street and the streets nearby, where, in some houses, women work as tutors, midwives, nurses, and wet nurses, or labor in the mansions of the wealthy as laundresses and slaves, and poor girls work as indentured servants. Even those who don't work out of their home face a long list of tasks inside of it: cooking, preserving, baking, pickling, making cakes and confections, as well as washing and ironing, sewing and knitting, and more often in the countryside, growing produce, raising stock, churning butter, and making clothes for the family.

Preparing for marriage is also a challenge. Many young women face pressure from their families to find a partner who can provide an adequate income and protect their social status. For the wealthy, the rules are even stricter, as the respective parents of the bride and groom judge their would-be in-laws' property and standing and negotiate over dowries and economic settlements. However, the rules of marriage are looser for the children of artisans and laborers, as love and affection are allowed to play a greater role than economics.

On Queen Street, you might see a young man and woman courting publicly by attending a lecture or walking to church, but it's more likely the match will be made in a private home under the watchful eyes of their elders. Sometimes, they will be given leeway to enjoy more intimate explorations. New England has a custom of "bundling" wherein a couple who hope to be married bed together for a night as a test of compatibility. Presumably they will be fully clothed (or have to deal with a sack or board put between them), but if not, there may be consequences. Despite social disapproval, it's not unusual for brides to become pregnant before the marital bond is sealed, and according to the minutes of the General Court, children are sometimes born out of wedlock and their mothers prosecuted for it.

If a woman brings wealth to a marriage, she may have her husband-to-be sign a contract or settlement to keep him from seizing all her assets and leaving her with nothing if the union fails. And should it fail, her petition for divorce will have an even chance of success before a court of law, especially if she can prove adultery or desertion. In fact, despite being hampered in their liberties, women do have certain rights within the legal code that they would not have in many other colonies and in England: they can negotiate contracts and enter into partnerships, manage financial accounts as Abigail Adams does, or be granted the title executrix and sue for damages and defend their estates.

Many Bostonian women take advantage of what liberties they have to go into business. You might see them acting as victualers or green grocers; running taverns, dram shops, or brothels; or owning or managing anything from modest inns to sizable boardinghouses. Even seamstresses, some of the lowest-paid women, may have aspirations to become milliners crafting exquisite hats or mantua makers creating large gowns with great folds and trains. Indeed, the greatest aspiration of some is to become a "she-merchant" with a large inventory and profit.

Women own 30 percent of all shops in Boston, as you can see on and around Queen Street, where the businesses carry everything from cutlery and hardware to pewter and brassware, garden seeds to dry goods, groceries, toys, and kitchenware. Head to the corner of Cornhill and Queen, and you can see the former location of one of the town's most successful female merchants. It's occupied by a different business now, but up to 1760, it housed the shop of the Scottish-born Elizabeth Murray. In these quarters, she sold petticoats, hoops, stays, earrings, necklaces, jewelry, bonnets, stockings, and dresses of fine silk and satin. She purchased her stock on credit advanced from British merchants and made a contract with her then-husband to control her own property and run her business as saw fit. She continued her work even after closing the shop, becoming a mentor to women in the local retail trade (including her nieces) and investing money in their success.

Murray has dealt with steep challenges since the war began. As a loyalist, she's met public backlash for encouraging the import of British goods, and some of her mentees like shopkeepers Anne and Betsy Cummings have faced public denunciation as "Enemies to their country" for bringing in foreign merchandise. Her current husband deserted her and got himself arrested for sedition; financially, she was nearly ruined. But instead of giving up on her adopted country, she has committed to staying here instead of departing for the Old World like so many of her peers. She may even offer you business advice, should you ask for it. You can find her at home, just across the river in Cambridge.

Not all importers of British goods were as lucky as Murray to avoid the wrath of the mob. To be reminded of what can happen to some merchants, head across the street to the Town Pump, where Bostonians draw their water from the ground for drinking or cooking, or for fighting a fire should one break out. Sometimes they also post broadsides here to alert their neighbors of people they regard as enemies—like those who have violated nonimportation decrees. The notices may warn the public to shun a particular business, such as that of the brazier William Jackson, and anyone who fails to respect the boycott "will bring disgrace upon themselves, and their Posterity, for ever and ever." These are not empty words. In Jackson's case, radical patriots raised him in effigy, tried to burn down his shop, and banished him from town.

Conveniently, you might have a word with some of the men who post these anonymous warnings (if they'll admit to it) lounging comfortably at the Sun Tavern, a block further north at the corner of Cornhill and Hilliers Streets. It's a fine three-story house that's a favorite for working patriots, and worth a visit to sample the rum and brandy, as well as more inventive concoctions made with lime juice and cinnamon water. Chandeliers light the dark space, which draws a hearty crowd of sailors and day laborers who come to drink and smoke, and perhaps to purchase one of the many clay pipes for sale. After you've drunk and smoked with them, leave the tavern and go just a few paces west to the Brattle Street Church, another pillar of the Revolution.

This impressive brick building is of recent vintage, opened in 1774 to replace an old wooden church from the previous century. The design is humble yet striking: a portico with eight Ionic columns, arched windows, and a square steeple. Inside are Corinthian columns in the nave, a mahogany pulpit, and what's said to be the largest church bell in Boston. Like many other churches, this one is under repair. The British army used it as a barracks during the occupation, removed all the pews, and left it in a "filthy and defaced condition." Notice the missing chunk of bricks on the tower where a cannonball hit during the siege; also note the name engraved on the stone corner—a dedication to John Hancock, who helped pay for the church's construction.

While there are more famous meetinghouses than the Brattle Street Church, none have been more central to the cause of independence than this one. The congregation includes Hancock, John and Samuel Adams, James and Joseph Warren, and James Bowdoin. The builder of the church was the arch-patriot Thomas Dawes. But just as committed to the cause is the minister himself, Samuel Cooper.

Cooper is no Charles Chauncy, and you won't hear him thundering away from the pulpit. Instead, he's a suave and urbane fellow with a calm and reassuring manner. If you meet him or have a chance to hear him preach, you'll find, as one contemporary did, "a voice melodious in the tones of a delicate flute, with an elegant address, in Attic diction, [as] he allured his hearers to virtue, with soothing tenderness he poured the oil and the wine into the wounded bosom." His style draws an elite class of congregants, and about a quarter of the town's upper-end merchants worship here—which is reflected in Cooper's preaching. While his treasury gives about twice as much to charity as any other church, he is also known to warn poorer congregants not to rely on that charity and to remain content in their social positions.

Patriots like Abigail Adams delight in his dulcet tones: "I rejoice in a preacher who has some warmth, some energy, some feeling. Deliver me from your cold phlegmatic Preachers, Politicians, Friends, Lovers and Husbands." Some of the leading radicals value him for other reasons too. He's a member of groups like the Sons of Liberty and the Long Room Club, Samuel Adams and James Otis have regarded him as an ally, and John Adams says, "Dr. Cooper and others were excellent hands to spread a rumor." Through an inside connection with customs commissioner John Temple, Cooper has conveyed critical news about imperial trade policy; and through his correspondence with Benjamin Franklin, he's shared sensitive information about royal officials. His brother William, the town clerk, has given him access to municipal reports, and he's learned even more from the town selectmen, most of whom attend his church. For good reason, then, Cooper's public manner at the pulpit suits his private role as one of Boston's quietest, but most effective, revolutionaries.

From the Brattle Street Church, keep heading west toward the hills of the Trimountain (covered in the next chapter). Take a right at Treamount Street and walk a block north to Hanover Street. Within sight of this corner, our tour of the town center concludes with a pair of sites that show two different sides of Boston. On the southerly corner, the brick, two-story Concert Hall is an upscale tavern that hosts balls and parties, features a dancing and fencing academy, and is decorated with stone scrolls on the facade—a symbol of the Masonic Lodge that owns it. The front hall is ornamented with Corinthian columns and mirrors on the walls, and has excellent acoustics and room for an orchestra. Should you attend a concert, you may hear an ensemble of bassoon, horn, trumpet, kettledrum, violin, viola, flute, and harpsichord, or some combination thereof. Tickets for such events are two shillings, and shows begin at six o'clock.

One local composer whose work you might enjoy is William Billings, a well-known "singing master" and friend of Paul Revere and Samuel Adams. His *New England Psalm-Singer* is an ennobling set of religious tunes with a political edge, as in his song "Chester":

Let tyrants shake their iron rod,
And Slav'ry clank her galling chains,

We fear them not, we trust in God,
New England's God forever reigns.

More controversially, Concert Hall has showcased opera in the past, with productions like *The Beggar's Opera*, *Damon and Phillida*, and selections from Handel and Italian arias. However, these shows are well in the past, and the venue hasn't presented an opera in six years. The reasons relate to the cultural preferences of the townsfolk. Unlike residents of Philadelphia, New York, or other major towns on the Eastern Seaboard, many Bostonians have long thought of musical and dramatic theatre as an evil influence, seeing it as no better than an artistic brothel. One Puritan leader even catalogued the sins of the medium:

> . . . the wanton gestures; the amorous kisses, compliments, and salutes; the meretricious songs and speeches; the lascivious whorish Actions; the beautiful faces; the ravishing Music, the flexanimous enticements, the witty obscenities, the rhetorical passages, the adulterous representations, with all the other fomentations of uncleanness in the Play-house.

These feelings are entrenched in law too. A 1759 act of the General Court forbade the practice of theatre in the colony, which "tend[s] generally to increase immorality, impiety, and a contempt of religion." The local selectmen have gone even further, forbidding everything from acrobatics and puppet shows, to mummers' plays and street theatre, to juggling and palm reading, on threat of steep fines and even imprisonment. Thanks to the influence of New England representatives, the old Puritan belief has swayed the national discourse. In 1774, the Continental Congress inveighed against "every species of extravagance and dissipation, especially all horse-racing, and all kinds of gaming, cockfighting, exhibitions of shews, plays, and other expensive diversions and entertainments." So make sure to leave your puppets and juggling balls at home when you visit.

If the lack of dramatic and operatic art at Concert Hall shows Boston at its most rigid and hidebound, the house a few doors down across Hanover Street shows how brave and fair-minded the town can be. It's a two-story,

Georgian affair with a slanted roof and pleasing symmetry that was, up until last year, rented by the patriot general and martyr Joseph Warren.

He was born in Roxbury but moved to Boston in 1764 after earning a degree from Harvard College and training as a physician. He first drew attention for working long hours as a volunteer treating smallpox on the waterfront, successfully helping around five thousand patients, only 1 percent of whom died from the disease. In later years, he would become a Grand Master of the Masonic Order, join the Sons of Liberty, and make public his feelings about Parliament's infringement on the rights of colonists. He penned poetry with stirring titles like "A Song for Liberty" and had it published in the *Gazette* and *Spy*, fueled protests over the seizure of John Hancock's ship *Liberty*, and rallied Whigs around causes like nonimportation. Predictably, Governor Francis Bernard accused him of sedition, and a Tory pamphlet asserted, "One of our most bawling demagogues and voluminous writers is a crazy doctor."

Warren became a primary participant in the major events of the Revolution. In February 1770, after a customs officer shot young Christopher Seidel, Warren tried to save the boy's life. When the child died, Warren removed the lead from his body as evidence. Just weeks later, he examined the body of Crispus Attucks after the Massacre and cowrote the town's official report that condemned the killings. He attacked imperial policies in print and worked with radical patriots to undermine them, and he gave a rousing address at the Old South Meetinghouse on the second anniversary of the Massacre, defying the rumors that said he would be arrested if he made any attempt to commemorate the victims.

Three years later, he returned to Old South to give the fifth anniversary oration, with Samuel Adams, John Hancock, and Samuel Cooper in attendance and the pulpit draped in black. This time, the stakes were higher and the threat to his safety greater: blocking the front door and filling many of the pews were rows of British soldiers, forcing him to shimmy in through the rear windows to deliver his speech, which he gave enrobed in a Roman toga. Taking the role of the people's tribune, he spoke with more fire than ever: "The hearts of Britons and Americans, which lately felt the generous glow of mutual confidence and love, now burn with jealousy and rage." And looking out into the audience, he warned against the threat of standing armies and proclaimed:

> Our streets are again filled with armed men: our harbor is crowded with ships of war; but these cannot intimidate us; our liberty must be preserved; it is far dearer than life, we hold it even dear as our allegiance; we must defend it against the attacks of friends as well as enemies; we cannot suffer even Britons to ravish it from us. . . . Our enemies are numerous and powerful—but we have many friends, determining to be free, and Heaven and earth will aid the resolution.

The patriots greeted his words with huzzahs; the soldiers with laughs and jeers. One seated near the front flashed a handful of pistol bullets to Warren as a warning, which the physician addressed by dropping his handkerchief over them. Then the soldiers began to yell, "O fie! O fie!"—an insult unfamiliar to local ears. The patriots thought they yelled, "O fire!" and panicked. The audience scrambled for the exits and leapt from the windows, and the meeting fell into bedlam—worsened by the clamor of the 43rd Regiment marching toward the church with their drums beating and trumpets blaring. This was only weeks before the outbreak of war.

Warren, by this time, had become integral to the fight. He served as chair of the Committee of Safety and president of the Provincial Congress, and he stayed in Boston at his house on Hanover Street to gather information on British saboteurs and troop movements. Upon learning of General Gage's plan to march his regiments into the countryside, Warren conveyed the news to Paul Revere and William Dawes and sent them to alert the rest of Massachusetts to the impending threat.

As we'll see in upcoming chapters, Warren fought during the last part of the battle at Bunker Hill, where instead of assuming his rank of general, he died as a common soldier and was thrown in a mass grave. With his wife, Elizabeth, already having died, he left behind four children who had to find new homes—which they did with the aid of old friends like Samuel Adams. Warren thus proved to be one of the Revolution's greatest champions as well as its most prominent casualty. As Mercy Warren (no relation) said, "[H]is memory will be revered by every lover of his country, and the name of *Warren* will be enrolled at the head of that band of patriots and heroes, who sacrificed their lives to purchase the independence of America."

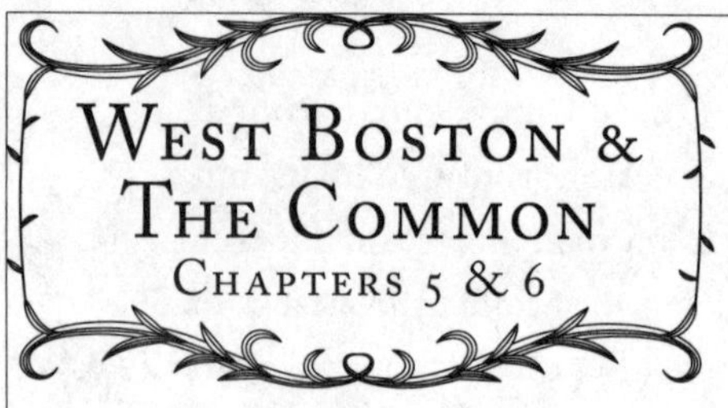

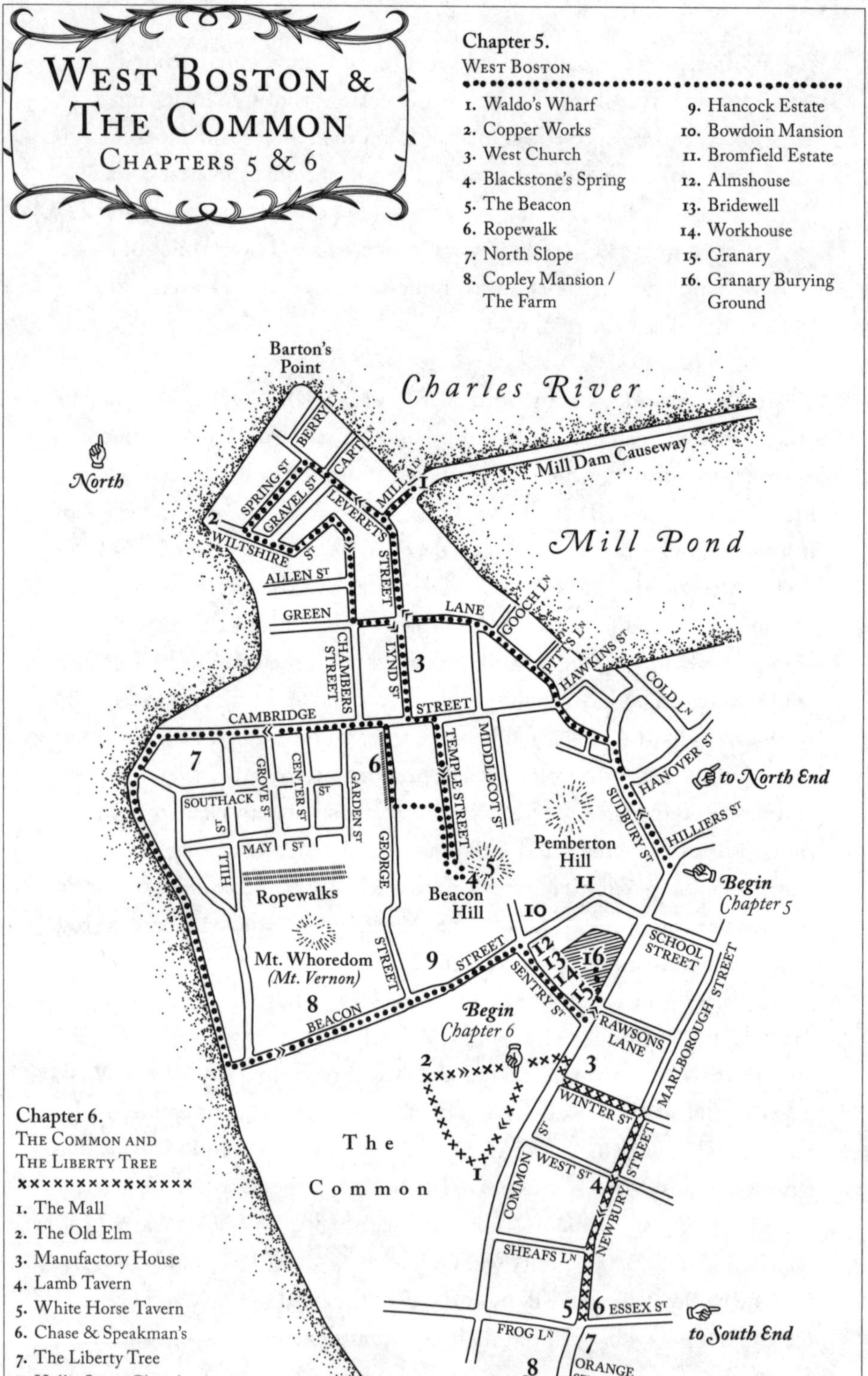
West Boston & The Common
Chapters 5 & 6
Chapter 5.
West Boston
1. Waldo's Wharf
2. Copper Works
3. West Church
4. Blackstone's Spring
5. The Beacon
6. Ropewalk
7. North Slope
8. Copley Mansion / The Farm
9. Hancock Estate
10. Bowdoin Mansion
11. Bromfield Estate
12. Almshouse
13. Bridewell
14. Workhouse
15. Granary
16. Granary Burying Ground
Barton's Point
Charles River
Mill Dam Causeway
Mill Pond
North
Berry Ln
Cart Ln
Mill Al
Spring St
Gravel St
Leverets Street
Wiltshire St
Allen St
Green
Lane
Gooch Ln
Pitts Ln
Hawkins St
Cold Ln
Chambers Street
Lynd St
Street
Cambridge
Temple Street
Middlecot St
Hanover St
Sudbury St
Hilliers St
to North End
Southack
Grove St
Center St
Garden St
St
May
Hill
Ropewalks
George Street
Beacon Hill
Pemberton Hill
Begin Chapter 5
Mt. Whoredom (Mt. Vernon)
Beacon
Street
Sentry St
School Street
Marlborough Street
Rawsons Lane
Begin Chapter 6
Winter St
Common St
West St
Street
Newbury
Sheafs Ln
Essex St
Frog Ln
Orange Street
to South End
The Common
Chapter 6.
The Common and The Liberty Tree
1. The Mall
2. The Old Elm
3. Manufactory House
4. Lamb Tavern
5. White Horse Tavern
6. Chase & Speakman's
7. The Liberty Tree
8. Hollis Street Church

☆ 5 ☆

West Boston and Beacon Hill

A for visit to West Boston, later known as the West End, isn't on the agenda for most tourists in 1776, but there's no reason to leave it off yours. While places like the North and South Ends draw most of the attention for their revolutionary politics, this neighborhood generates industrial power for the uprising. You can see it in the ropewalks that spin hemp into cordage, in the mills that grind grain and clean wool, in the foundries that smelt copper, and in all the other facilities that manufacture products so the new republic can be strong and self-sustaining in the face of the crippling British trade embargo. Rising above all this activity is Beacon Hill, the highest point on the peninsula, which not only provides a nice view of the neighborhood but gives you a broad panorama of Boston and the river and harbor surrounding it.

You'll begin your tour on Sudbury Street, which leads north away from the town center. After a few blocks, turn west onto Cambridge Street, which becomes Green Lane. The houses here are typical of the dwellings Bostonians prefer and can afford—mostly built of unpainted pine or oak, darkly weathered, with timber frames and beams. The roofs have steep gables, and the upper stories overhang the lower, with added rooms and lean-tos giving the houses a helter-skelter appearance. Boston has two thousand of these structures. Some are new but many more are old, dating from the seventeenth or early eighteenth century, built around twisting streets and alleys, pocket squares, and garden courts. More than a few are weather-beaten and dilapidated, but all are lucky to be standing, having survived the recent siege and bombing, and the periodic fires that have scorched the town since its founding (see p. 223).

For a closer look at a given house, it's worth befriending the residents, who might invite you in for a visit. If so, you may find their home to be cramped but livable, with one or two rooms built on one or two stories, a fireplace for heat, and small leaded windows for light. They may feel a certain pride at having bought it, or complain of the cost if they're just renting it. If they have a bit of wealth, they'll likely add ornamental tapestries and engraved prints to the walls, and show off their porcelain ware or silver urns and tea service. If they're artisans, around back there may be a workshop for such tasks as repairing shoes or crafting metal, or just a room set aside for needlework and finishing garments.

When you return to the street, you'll find only a few exceptions to this building style. The wealthiest homeowners (the ones who follow the architectural trends in London) have designed their mansions in the latest Georgian style, with brick facades, meticulous symmetry, tasteful decor, and grand proportions. Their lots are large, too, with fruit trees and beds for flowers and vegetables, set off from the street with posts and chains. If you're an artist or engraver, these are the kinds of houses you'll want to highlight in your work, perhaps depicting all of Boston as a great Georgian utopia or a stately brick metropolis—even if the actual townscape is mostly old dark wood.

In Puritan days, West Boston was called New Fields, and it might seem the roads haven't changed much since then. Some are cobbled, but many more are dirt and turn into quagmires in the winter from the rain and snow. It can be difficult to walk through these passageways, with drays and wagons taking up space for their deliveries, and residents throwing manure and garbage outside their homes or piling up dirt from their yard and cellar diggings. If you find yourself exhausted from jockeying around all the impediments, feel free to take a break, perhaps inside a workshop or factory to watch how the local tradesmen go about their business.

There are many options. At the distilleries on Hawkins Street and Gooch Lane, the employees ferment molasses and transform it into rum in pot stills. Around Barton's Point, the shipwrights build vessels in the yards and launch them in slipways. And elsewhere, there are shops for creating sailcloth from duck, fishhooks from iron wire, playing cards from paper boards, combs from animal horn, and redware pottery from clay. But the most eye-catching enterprise sits along the cove to the east of these businesses, at the edge of the massive catchment known as Mill Pond.

From Green Lane, take a right on Leverets Street and another right on Mill Alley for a closer look. Located behind the wharves and sheds that line the shore, the pond comprises forty-three acres of shallow water, not more than two or three feet deep, enclosed by a manmade causeway that stretches a half-mile east to the North End. If you scramble over the top of the causeway, it takes only ten minutes to reach the base of Copp's Hill. But it's not worth the effort (it's hardly a scenic walk), so have a look at the pond from here.

Millworks occupy the east, west, and south ends of the reservoir and capture the ebb and flood of the tide to pound grain and cut lumber, even to make chocolate. Near where you stand, the fulling mill by Waldo's Wharf employs a water wheel to run machines that clean the dirt and oil from wool and beat it with wooden mallets to shrink the fabric and interlock the fibers. The process is modern and efficient, but unfortunately, the wastewater and refuse go directly into the pond, as you can smell.

Mill Pond is a noxious affair, so don't be tempted to get any closer. Miscreants dump their dead animals and refuse here, and the water collects a nasty brew of sugar-refinery tailings, distillers' waste, and the outfall of sewers and privies. Every year, more silt and debris settle into the pond and make it even shallower, until it now resembles less the natural cove it once was and more a watery cesspit.

There's no reason to linger. Instead, make your way around Barton's Point before turning onto Spring Street to pay a visit to the copper works and see artisans casting handsome bells in their foundry, along with workaday bolts and fittings. Just be careful of your footing: the British army built earthworks and emplaced guns around the point during the siege that now sit abandoned, so you can twist your ankle if you don't watch your step.

If you do climb the berm to see where the soldiers once garrisoned, you'll notice how isolated you are from the rest of Boston—hemmed in by tall hills to the south, Mill Pond to the east, and the Charles River to the north and west. In part due to this isolation, the artisans and laborers have developed a fierce sense of independence, as have the merchants and shop owners, even the ministers. In fact, the man who was Boston's most radical pastor once preached in this neighborhood, as prominent in the politics of the Revolution as he was a pariah to other clergymen.

Wend your way down Wiltshire Street to Lynd Street to find his meetinghouse. It's called West Church and isn't much more than a humble, wood-framed building with a simple, squat appearance. British soldiers removed the steeple a year ago when they converted the building into a barracks, fearing rebels might use the tower to signal to their compatriots across the river. The current minister is Simeon Howard, a pleasant enough chap who has the unenviable task of preaching in the long shadow of his predecessor, Jonathan Mayhew.

Reverend Mayhew was the most formidable and controversial of all Boston clergymen. He took the pulpit in 1747, when he was only twenty-seven and West Church was only ten. Few of his peers attended his ordination, as he had already developed a reputation for dispute and unorthodoxy. At first, he gained his notoriety from chastising his fellow ministers for their dour Calvinism, presenting God as a cold-hearted brute rather than the figure of love and reason Mayhew believed Him to be. But Mayhew went much further than that when he began to criticize the Crown. His 1749 sermon *A Discourse Concerning Unlimited Submission and Non-Resistance to the Higher Powers* promoted resistance against tyranny and unjust governments, and it seemed to excuse the execution of Charles I as a necessary measure to protect English liberties—a daring claim on the hundredth anniversary of the monarch's death. The sermon was printed widely and ignited a furor on both sides of the Atlantic, but a budding group of Whigs found his words inspiring. Teenage John Adams was so influenced by the sermon, he "read it, till the Substance of it was incorporated into my Nature and indelibly engraved on my Memory."

Mayhew rejected mainline Congregationalism and said dogma like original sin was illogical and "more readily embraced by a man after his brains are knocked out, than while he continues in his senses, and of a sound mind." Instead, he praised "natural religion" that valued "beauty, order, harmony and design" because "Christianity is principally an institution of life and manners; designed to teach us how to be good men, and to show us the necessity of becoming so."

The minister's words found disfavor among his black-robed peers, who ostracized him and barred him from delivering Boston's Thursday lecture, traditionally offered to a worthy pastor on a rotating basis. He answered their actions by becoming even more unorthodox, rejecting articles of faith like predestination and the Trinity as it was conventionally preached. His boldness fueled his bravado against royal officials, too, until he was denouncing their policies and Parliamentary measures that infringed on colonial liberties—at a time when most of his rivals held their tongues.

Mayhew's politics of the pulpit reached a height of controversy on August 25, 1765, after the initial round of riots against the Stamp Act. Here at West Church, he preached that those who have no ability to affect the laws by which they are governed are the equivalent of slaves and are not obliged to submit to them. He cautioned against the use of violence but hinted that his listeners should resist unjust governments with all their strength and courage. The next day, another round of riots ensued as mobs ransacked officials' houses and nearly destroyed Thomas Hutchinson's mansion.

Bostonians stood divided on whether to blame Mayhew for the violence. While many artisans and patriots praised his sermon, more well-heeled parishioners like merchant Richard Clarke and Whig printer Benjamin Edes withdrew from his congregation. Anglican clergymen like Henry Caner erupted in fury, claiming the homily was "One of the most Seditious Sermons ever delivered, advising the people to stand up for their rights to the last drop of their Blood." Mayhew felt he had to respond, so he duly condemned the riot in a letter to Hutchinson ("from the bottom of my heart I detest these proceedings"), but he neither apologized for his words nor retracted them.

And so the rebellion found its unlikely champion, a spiritual gadfly who antagonized his peers but built a philosophical model by which they could resist tyranny. When Parliament repealed the Stamp Act, he celebrated its demise ("our soul is escaped as a bird from the snare of the fowlers") and warned colonists to be vigilant in protecting their liberties. He soon began to correspond with James Otis about resistance to royal officials and made valuable contacts among other Whigs and radicals, until he was the leading figure in the ranks of dissenting clergy.

A year later, Mayhew died of a stroke at age forty-five. The news came as a shock to his growing number of followers throughout the colonies, and his funeral became a grand spectacle, attended by hundreds and marked by a procession of fifty-seven carriages and a ceremonial military corps. Charles Chauncy delivered his eulogy at West Church and acted as one of his pallbearers, assuming the weight of his coffin as he would soon assume his leadership in the Black Regiment. In the decade after his death, Mayhew's legacy remains as powerful as ever. In the words of one historian, by his demands for the protection of individual liberty against the power of the state, and "maddening the corrupt, frightening the timid, rousing the apathetic, and bracing the patriot heart," Mayhew fired "the morning gun of the Revolution, the *punctum temporis* when that period of history began."

Mayhew is an inspiration to those with even a little patriot blood in them, but you're not apt to find too many other ministers like him in West Boston. One reason is there are no other major churches. Unlike other parts of town, the highest points in this neighborhood are not steeples but massive hills. Notice three of them to the south, collectively called the Trimountain and ranging from 80 to 138 feet tall. To the east is Pemberton Hill, in the middle Beacon Hill, and to the west Mount Whoredom—called Mount Vernon in polite company.

If you're in fair shape, you won't have trouble ascending Beacon Hill. Follow Temple Street south to a path that leads up the slope and curves around to a steep, grassy, hemispheric mound. From here, you can see pastures for cattle and horses, docks and wharves lining the western shore, and fine views out to Cambridge and Charlestown. The residents draw fresh water from natural springs along the slope, with Blackstone's Spring being the best known.

The path ends at the summit of Beacon Hill, topped by a sixty-foot-tall, four-foot-thick mast with a stone foundation. Climb the mast by the pole steps (not recommended) and you'll reach a projecting arm, off of which hangs a hook for an iron pot or barrel to be attached. During times of peril for the town, the container is filled with tar and set alight to warn the countryside it should prepare for battle and send militia to Boston's defense. Originally, Puritan leaders built the beacon to signal attack by native Indians, but more recently, patriots have regarded the British army as the primary threat. They nearly lit the barrel in 1768 when tensions were high with occupying troops, and again in 1770 immediately after the Massacre on King Street.

General Howe had no use for the beacon and had it dismantled during the siege, also building fortifications on the summit and emplacing 24-pounder cannon. After the evacuation, Bostonians rebuilt the beacon—to fire the tar should another invasion occur. Today, it stands less as an emblem of military power than a relic from an earlier age. A time when their greatest threat was the tribes on the frontier of Massachusetts instead of an imperial army across the length of North America.

As you descend the hill the way you came, you'll find that another threat is topographical. On the western slope, huge gouges have been hacked out of the earth—an ugly and aggressive excavation, which some residents fear may cause the entire hill to subside or collapse. A man named Thomas Hodson has done this to collect gravel to fill in his wharves, and the selectmen haven't been able to stop him. Indeed, other enterprising vandals have hacked away at the hills and reduced their size, transporting the dirt and rocks to enlarge the boundaries of their property and fill in the waterways around the peninsula. If the process isn't stopped, some fear the Trimountain may disappear within decades and become, to future generations, no more than a distant memory or a fanciful legend.

Once the slope evens out, turn west onto a path that crosses rough, uneven ground. The route passes through shrub and hedge, over patches of muck and gravel, but the destination is worth it if you'd like to see one of the key industrial engines that makes the town run. Near George Street, it will come into view—a thousand-foot-long shed, fuming smoke and smelling like tar, where dozens of men shout and twist and turn in elaborate motion. It can only be a ropewalk.

There are fourteen ropewalks in town, and half of them are in West Boston. Inside, workers create ropes for the nautical industry. Sailors use these ropes for rigging masts and mooring ships to shore and many other purposes, and constructing them requires building wooden sheds as long as the ropes themselves. Go inside and have a look. You'll see the rope makers with a yarn made of hemp wrapped around their waists, which they uncoil and feed into a turning wheel that twists and tightens the yarn into cordage. During the process, you'll also see them turning and "spinning" as they walk down the length of the building with willow wands to straighten the fibers. It's a strange industrial ballet that requires skill to maintain a consistent thickness and weave, after which the ropes are doused in hot tar to make them waterproof and seaworthy.

There's a good reason ropewalks occupy land at the edge of town. They can catch fire in an instant and burn down whole neighborhoods before firefighters can extinguish the flames. The same might be said for the radical politics of the workers themselves. They were among the first to enflame tensions against royal officials and spark mob violence the authorities could not control. They battled against the Stamp Act, enforced nonimportation decrees, sent customs officials running for their lives, and participated in everything from the *Liberty* riots to the Destruction of the Tea. They even carry their willow wands with them on the streets, as a handy weapon to use against loyalists and other enemies of the Revolution.

Many of them live in the houses surrounding the walks. The lots are small (often 420 square feet) and surrounded by other properties that block access to major roads, giving the neighborhood a sealed-off, claustrophobic feel. This is also true of other working-class quarters in this part of West Boston, where narrow passages and alleys (some only three feet wide) thread around the houses and huts, while hidden steps and cellar doors create hazards for walking. Outsiders can easily get lost in the maze.

From here, you can head north on George Street and west on Cambridge Street. Along this route, you might spot a few lanterns atop metal posts, offering the promise of evening light to passersby. But the lamps are dark and have been so for more than a year, with little possibility of glowing once more. The reasons for this relate to Bostonians' wariness toward new technology and the nature of life during wartime.

In the old days, iron fire baskets on poles provided illumination at major corners, but most streets stayed murky and unlit, even dangerous to travel. In 1774, the town's Committee for the Lamps devised a plan for installing proper streetlights, which were set up later that year after arriving from Britain the previous December (coincidentally, on the same ships that contained the infamous tea rebels would destroy). The burners were made of tin or iron with a reservoir for holding whale oil, an adjustable cotton or flaxen wick, and a glass casing and metal lid. The entire ensemble hung from a pole or post connected to a building, and was monitored by lamp lighters who ignited the flame in the evening with a burning reed and snuffed it out in the morning.

Some two to three hundred lamps lit up the streets afterward, and for a short time, Boston shone brighter than any town in New England. It was not to last, however. Some criticized the appearance of the lamps, weather and vandals damaged a fair number of them, and the remainder were removed or extinguished as a military precaution during the siege—and the patriots have not relit them. So, if you see evening light in West Boston or anywhere else, it likely comes from the traditional source: citizens with lanterns in hand. They may use a flint and steel to spark a box of charred linen or other tinder, and bring the fire to an encased candle made from sheep or ox tallow, or from beeswax or spermaceti oil. If you don't have your own lantern, you risk getting lost or injured.

To protect you from danger, night watchmen also carry hand lanterns. You can see them in most neighborhoods making the rounds after dark, announcing the time on the hour and shouting, "All's well!" They follow predetermined routes and are stationed out of a watch house. Among their other duties, they record encounters with suspicious or dangerous characters, as well as disorderly drunks, and will advise you to return to your lodging if the streets are unsafe. With no regular police force, Boston relies on them to maintain public order, along with constables who send miscreants to the jailhouse, summon doctors if needed, and keep spouses from abusing each other. On occasion, they will also demand that galloping carriages stop, and they will warn people not to disturb the Sabbath.

Assuming you have enough light to see, follow Cambridge Street west until you reach a village at the edge of the Charles River. This settlement provides a true glimpse of working in Boston, where artisans and laborers, both black and white, men and women, share close quarters in a setting that seems anything but favorable. The dirt roads are crooked and irregular, and the houses are a mix of wooden huts and tenements interspersed with boardinghouses, dance cellars, dram shops, brothels, and taverns.

British officials referred to the adjoining hill and this entire area as Mount Whoredom, not so much for the brothels but because they saw it as a tawdry resort for the "lower sort," who made a home here because they weren't allowed into more respectable quarters. This isn't quite accurate, since villagers on the hill's north slope often commute to the docks and warehouses of the eastern side of Boston to do their work and have created a more coherent and tightly knit community than the elite would like to admit. But life is hard here, and the locals have to contend not only with poor economic prospects but the kinds of facilities the selectmen don't want to put anywhere else—combustible ropewalks and other hazards, as well as a "pest house" for smallpox victims near the river and a powder house for explosive munitions near the hills.

Many of the villagers are black, and about 40 percent are freedmen. You can meet them in the ropewalks and shipyards, mills and workshops, and at the businesses they own. Since up to three-quarters of black Bostonians were born in Africa, their cultural traditions derive as much or more from their continent of birth as they do from New England. Sabbath markets are a popular draw for meeting friends and neighbors, buying and selling produce, and making business deals. Many people play paw paw, shaking and tossing four cowrie shells to determine good or bad fortune, and gambling on the outcome. The music in the dance halls and cellars may include flutes, drums, fiddles, tambourines, and banjos inspired by similar African instruments. And the traditional funeral processions can involve hundreds of people following a cortege that winds throughout the streets on a long circuit throughout town.

Even with the strength of their community, black residents of this and other parts of Boston face many challenges. Employers pay them less than whites, and if they own their own businesses, competitors can try to sue them to drive them out of business, knowing the law will not treat them fairly. Town and provincial statutes forbid them from carrying sticks or canes or knives, loitering on the Sabbath, and buying food in the country and selling it in town. The General Court also forbids interracial sex and marriage, and designates anyone born to such a union a "molatto bastard child." Enslaved people face greater restrictions: They can't buy or sell goods, keep hogs or swine, stay out after 9:00 p.m., defy an order from a slaveholder, or even gain their freedom without a bond posted for their release. In defiance of such laws, some bondsmen have escaped their captivity and fled to the countryside, while others have found refuge in West Boston, in neighborhoods just like this one.

Slavery has a lengthy history in Boston. The practice began in 1638 when the ship *Desire* arrived with a group of captives, gradually expanded over the next eight decades, and grew rapidly in the 1720s and '30s. Many merchants and lawyers, as well as artisans and shop owners, still choose enslaved over free laborers to work in kitchens and stables and sawmills; in upscale homes as laundresses and servants; in workshops as blacksmiths and coopers, wigmakers and bakers, tanners and soap boilers; and on the waterfront building ships or crewing ships as sailors. Most of the forced laborers are young, between eleven and thirty, and 60 percent are male. They often live on the property of those who claim to own them, sleeping in kitchens and garrets and backrooms—though familiarity provides no sense of kinship.

Most slave-trading happens on the decks of ships and inside warehouses, or in private homes and taverns, and sometimes on the wharves. The trade in human property is visible in the newspapers too. The *Boston Gazette*, for one, has, since its foundation in 1719, carried close to a thousand ads for buying and selling two thousand people of African descent, as well as native Indians. A notice might advertise "Negro Boys & Girls, duly Imported, to be Sold by Mr. George Cradock, at his Warehouse in Dr. Coock's Buildings," or "A Negro Woman to be sold at Mr. Samuel Waldo's House, or enquire at the Post-Office."

Not all white Bostonians support slavery, but many have turned a blind eye. One of the few who didn't was Samuel Sewall, best known as a judge in the Salem witch trials, who composed a pamphlet in 1700 called *The Selling of Joseph*, in which he wrote, "It is most certain that all Men, as they are the Sons of Adam . . . have equal Right unto Liberty, and all other outward Comforts of Life." Needless to say, his words did not find favor among his peers, earning him only "frowns and hard words." Even his own son went on to place ads for slaves in *The Boston News-Letter*.

Since then, a growing number of white Bostonians have followed Sewell's lead. In 1766, the town meeting instructed its representatives to the General Court to urge passage of a law forbidding slavery and slave import (royal officials rejected the idea); radicals like James Otis and ministers like Andrew Eliot have demanded the end of human bondage; and Samuel, John, and Abigail Adams have expressed disdain for it. Still, there are numerous wealthy families whose commitment to slavery is as firm as their commitment to independence. Many famous patriots, from Joseph Warren to John Hancock, have either purchased or inherited slaves.

Unlike former colonies to the south, Massachusetts permits enslaved people to own property, receive a trial by jury, and sue in court. Accordingly, they have filed suit when a slaveholder's promise of manumission is revoked, or when he subjects them to cruel and barbaric treatment. They can also petition the legislature to grant them relief. In 1773, a slave named Felix demanded that the General Court improve the welfare of the enslaved, since they were subject to oppression contrary to moral law and human dignity. The next year, another petition from a group of bondsmen said they had a right to freedom and liberty like everyone else and asked for one day a week to work for themselves, so as to gain enough money to purchase their freedom. Prompted by the petitions and by changing public opinion, the Assembly again passed a bill to ban the import of slaves into the colony—though Governor Hutchinson, himself a slaveholder, refused to sign it.

Now that the war has begun, enslaved Bostonians have offered to fight for the cause in exchange for their freedom. Some of them serve in the militia and in the Continental Army as substitutes. General Washington has changed his enlistment policy several times, but at present, Congress allows black and white men to serve together in the same ranks. Black men have fought at Lexington and Concord and Bunker Hill, and include such notable names as Peter Salem, Cato Smith, Salem Poor, Caesar Ferrit, and George Middleton—the latter a resident of West Boston and the leader of the "Bucks of America" militia, whose flag depicts a leaping stag under a tree and a field of stars.

Another notable black soldier at Bunker Hill was Prince Hall, who has done much to encourage the enlistment of men of color and to entreat the General Court to recruit them as troops. Brought up as a slave working in a tannery, he was manumitted in 1770 and learned trades from leather making to catering, later developing businesses of his own and writing anti-slavery petitions. But he's best known as a Freemason. In 1775, he was initiated along with fourteen other black men into Irish Military Lodge no. 441. They attained the degree of Master Mason so they could meet as Provisional African Lodge no.1 and conduct Masonic rites (but not grant degrees). He has plans to found an African Lodge to connect free and enslaved men, but any greater degree of organization will have to wait. Not only is creating a new kind of lodge difficult during the war, but the universal brotherhood he imagines has thus far been an illusion: local white Masons—many of them members of radical patriot clubs—have refused him entry to their lodges.

Hall may not be available for an interview since he's off fighting in the war, so wrap up your visit to the area with a drink at an inn or dram shop. Then take a turn south on Cambridge Street as it follows the shore of the west side of the peninsula, where you'll see the Charles River and its tidal flats. The landscape here is dry at low tide, which gives the impression the landscape is more expansive than it actually is. A few visionaries have even imagined filling in these flats and expanding the boundaries of the town on all sides. But with local finances at a low ebb, such a vision may have to wait until the next century to come to pass.

After Cambridge Street skirts the Trimountain, it reaches Beacon Street, home of some of Boston's wealthiest citizens. You can see their estates as you walk east along the tree-shaded path that parallels the north side of the Common. The first of these is a tasteful yellow country house with stables, gardens, and outbuildings, owned by John Singleton Copley. He's one of the town's largest landowners—unusual for an artist—with both servants and slaves in his household. On this massive tract he calls "The Farm," he's painted many of the portraits that have brought him acclaim: the elite merchant Nicholas Boylston wrapped in a green silk banyan leaning over his financial ledgers; Paul Revere dressed as an artisan while stroking his chin and holding a silver teapot; Samuel Adams in a ruddy suit and waistcoat pointing to the hallowed charter of Massachusetts; and Mercy Warren wearing a thoughtful expression and an elaborate blue dress. However, if you try to commission Copley to paint your own portrait, you'll have no luck. He departed his estate just before the war to avoid the conflict and find greater opportunities in London, where his sitters now include the sort of lords and noblemen that patriots have long despised.

A short distance east of Copley's estate is the massive estate built by merchant Thomas Hancock in 1737. Before you see the house, you'll notice the grounds: a lovely expanse of fruit trees and fences and pastures, a coach house and stables, and a summer retreat with gardens that command a wide view of the town and the harbor. The mansion itself is composed of granite block in the Georgian style, standing two and a half stories with a gambrel roof, ornamental chimneys, and decorative masonry. But the most striking thing about it isn't the architecture, but the renown of the person who now owns it—John Hancock.

Hancock is, of course, a merchant himself and one of the most important leaders in the revolutionary cause. He entertains guests in these quarters, and should you be invited in to see them, you'll find carpeted rooms with walnut and mahogany furniture, parlors adorned with paintings and engravings and European antiques, large hexagonal lanterns with iron frames and cathedral glass, a great reception hall, a dining hall that seats up to sixty, and ballrooms for card parties, dances, weddings, and all manner of celebrations.

At the moment, Hancock is in Philadelphia serving as president of the Continental Congress, but every Bostonian recognizes him when he's in town. He's thin and handsome with an aquiline nose, often sporting a white wig and the latest fashions: coats and waistcoats of velvet and silk, lacy shirts and silk stockings, silver-net knee breeches, shoes with silver buckles, coats with silver buttons, and other such adornments. His taste for luxury sets him apart from more humble patriots, and he has a taste for good Madeira wine and fine dining and entertainment. The Tories have mocked his extravagance, comparing him to an "Oriental prince" riding in a plush chariot, attended by liveried servants, and escorted by saber-wielding horsemen. No doubt jealously plays a role, since, at his height, Hancock was Boston's richest man. He owned the most land and ships, lent money throughout the region, and controlled thousands of acres in New England. More important, he used his power and influence to support the revolution, even at a cost to his fortune. His background partly explains why.

His uncle Thomas Hancock came to wealth by operating a firm specializing in mercantile trading, government contracts, and real estate, and he owned a whaling fleet that slaughtered the great mammals for their oil and "fins" (a fibrous mass used for making whips and corset supports, among other things). Young John came into his house after his minister father died when he was seven years old and Thomas adopted him. The magnate taught him the merchant trade and, in 1763, made him a partner in his firm, which John assumed control of when Thomas died a year later of a stroke. Overnight, the orphan became one of the richest men in New England.

In the years that followed, John oversaw the "House of Hancock" as it exported potash, naval stores, whale oil, and timber to Britain and imported English and Indian goods to be sold at shops on and around the waterfront. He also took an interest in politics, getting elected as the youngest of five town selectmen in 1765 and drawing closer to the Whig faction after Parliament's passage of the Stamp Act.

The act cost his firm considerable duties to the Crown and created more red tape to manage; it also made him realize the need for radical action and to abandon the moderate position he had shared with most of his mercantile peers. He allied with Samuel Adams and others in the Sons of Liberty and supported their measures to stop the importation of British goods and to take action against customs officials. When Parliament repealed the Stamp Act in 1766, Hancock set off fireworks in front of his mansion and plied the townsfolk with ninety-two gallons of free Madeira wine. His popularity surged, and he was elected to the Assembly.

The acclaim did much for his pride, and it enhanced the sense of charity he'd learned as a boy at the knee of his father. He planted lime trees along the Common, funded a fire engine for the town, paid for the construction of Brattle Street Church, provided jobs and firewood for the poor, and, when a fire burned his store and seven other buildings near Faneuil Hall, created a fund to support all the owners. He also commissioned Copley's heroic portrait of Samuel Adams and hung it alongside his own in the mansion's drawing room.

To customs officials, Hancock was no better than a showman and a smuggler. They suspected him of bringing in wine and other imports from the West Indies without paying the proper duties. In 1768, they seized his ship *Liberty*, which led to a political upheaval that ended in riots and a court case and further burnished his reputation (see p. 25 for the full story). But despite the surge in popular appeal, his business began to suffer.

Hancock obeyed the nonimportation decrees during 1768–70 (only importing the shot, hemp, and coal that were allowed), though the practice crippled his business. He faced mounting debts from English creditors, and, in combination with the loose credit he extended to Boston shopkeepers, he saw the solvency of his firm threatened. Real estate provided a backstop for maintaining his personal wealth, but the House of Hancock looked like it might totter.

Yet his commitment to the patriot cause did not waver. He became colonel of the Corps of Cadets, a local military society. He attended meetings of the Sons of Liberty in their taverns and channeled Samuel Adams in his 1774 Massacre oration, condemning those responsible for the deaths on King Street as "Ye dark designing knaves, ye murderers, parricides! How dare you tread upon the earth, which has drank in the blood of slaughtered innocents, shed by your wicked hands?"—despite the presence of British troops in the audience who likely took his words personally.

His commitment to the Revolution became irreversible in 1775, when he and Adams were staying at his childhood home, a Lexington parsonage that Thomas Hancock had built for John's minister grandfather. Under threat of arrest and with battle commencing, Adams and Hancock escaped to Philadelphia, where they took up seats as delegates in the Continental Congress. Hancock became president of that body, to go along with his presidency of the Massachusetts Provincial Congress and his more recent title of major general of militia.

Hancock's mansion survived the siege fairly well, as you can see. Some of the fences were burned for firewood and the wine cellar was pilfered by his cousin William Bowes, but the features and furnishings remained intact. This was not the case with his other local properties like rental houses and tenements, which British troops either squatted in or vandalized, leaving some with irreparable damage. Hancock has done what he can to restore them and assigned an agent to get some of his financial affairs in order—collecting rents, paying off debt, selling his ships, and letting out his waterfront stores to privateers. But it's not likely, or perhaps even possible, that he'll ever regain the full measure of his wealth. He seems resigned to it.

As popular as he is, some townsfolk with loyalist sympathies see Hancock as a businessman spouting rhetoric to protect his financial interests, or a typical wealthy merchant with his servants and small number of slaves (some of whom he has freed), or simply a tool of Samuel Adams. But he's admired by the great majority of Bostonians and New Englanders, and his national reputation is rising—and will doubtless continue to if his extravagant flourish in signing the Declaration of Independence is any indication.

After you've seen enough of Hancock's mansion, continue to walk east on Beacon Street, past the grand residence of merchant-scientist James

Bowdoin and the three-story mansion and terraced gardens of Edward Bromfield. Here, the scenery becomes more unsettling because, amid these estates and all their splendor, there is a shocking contrast. You'll see it where Beacon meets Sentry Street: a precinct for the town's poorest and most desperate inhabitants, marked by the looming silhouette of the Almshouse.

Before exploring this area, it's worth noting the relation of rich and poor in Boston. As we've seen, the fortunes of the "upper rank" have flourished through mercantile trade, smuggling and slave trading, legal maneuvering and real estate speculation. But common laborers don't have the same ways of making money. They have to work, often for long hours in workshops or on the wharves, for wages that don't pay enough to support a family. It's easy to fall into poverty, and with the war and siege adding to the challenges of the last twenty years, the ranks of the destitute keep growing.

More than 7 percent of Bostonians live in poverty, and they're the worst hit when financial calamity, fires, epidemics, or natural disasters strike. Many poor families are led by widows, some of whom sell liquor or sex in waterfront taverns and brothels (see p. 23), while others peddle fruit and vegetables on the street, and some receive alms from churches or quietly beg for charity, even though the practice is illegal. The authorities take a dim view of anyone who doesn't have a home—calling them the "strolling poor"—and they warn them out of town, sentence them to the Almshouse or Workhouse, or put them into servitude. The last punishment may be the worst of all.

You can see indentured servants throughout Boston, cooking meals and sewing garments, sweeping streets and cleaning privies, sweating in workshops and digging ditches, and doing innumerable other tasks. They're bound to a master for a contracted length of time (unlike slaves, whose labor is perpetual) and cannot say no to the work they're assigned. Their ranks may include poor boys and girls, orphans, runaway servants, the children of recent immigrants, former prisoners, and those who can't pay a fine or other court costs.

In the seventeenth century, parents could lose their children to servitude if they failed to give them the proper instruction in religion, neglected their moral improvement, or committed other sins. These days, a parent's poverty is often enough to lose control of a child, unless that parent works in an approved trade or profession (there's an official list). And they can't hide from the law either. The twelve Overseers of the Poor keep careful records of the impoverished and make a habit of inspecting private homes to determine whether the adults they find should be given charity for their destitution or punished for their idleness—and whether their children should become servants.

Which brings us back to the Almshouse. Courts have assigned more than a few children to this century-old, two-story brick building until they can be assigned as servants. If you look through the fence, you might see some of them in the yard waiting to leave or, more disturbingly, begging for change through gaps in the wooden posts. You'll likely not want to visit, but if you do, one of the Overseers can explain how the system works and offer a tour of the premises.

The Almshouse holds up to three hundred people but was only designed to lodge about half as many. The thirty-three small apartments each contain up to eight people and may be assigned to single men or women, families with children, orphans, widows, and the disabled. Wounded soldiers and prisoners of war have been housed here and, a few decades ago, Acadian refugees from Nova Scotia who were kicked out of their homes by the British military.

On-staff physicians provide treatment of broken limbs, venereal disease ("the French pox"), and mild mental health problems, while the cooks serve a regular set of meals: milk porridge for breakfast; boiled rice and molasses or beef-and-mutton soup for dinner; and salt fish and vegetables on Saturdays, alternating with beef's-head soup. Liquor is forbidden, and smuggling in spirits will get you confined to a cell.

Not surprisingly, life is difficult in the Almshouse. The selectmen do not give the Overseers sufficient funds to clean the building and relieve overcrowding, and the residents complain bitterly of what they have to face: cramped and stifling apartments, a dank and dirty atmosphere, the smell of sewage that lingers from poor drainage, and the dismal quality of the food. As one observer has said:

> [I]t is rather a dungeon than a hospital. It can neither be ventilated nor properly cleansed. And it is altogether disproportioned to the number of those, whom necessity drives to the melancholy retreat. The evils unavoidably resulting from bad air and filth, are

> notorious. These evils, neither the physician nor the overseer can prevent. As long as our poor are so ill accommodated, poverty and dependence will be the smallest of their calamities.

Next door to the Almshouse, things get worse. The Bridewell is a squat, single-story brick pile where violent and disorderly people are held until they are somehow reformed or are sent to the prison on Queen Street. They share the confines with the legally (and often criminally) insane, with a watchman to provide the "discipline of the whip" to inmates who step out of line. If you have tender ears, you may want to cross the street to avoid hearing the sounds of that discipline being enforced.

Continuing along this bleak stretch, you'll find the Workhouse—a long and narrow brick shed housing vagabonds, prostitutes, and general troublemakers, as well as mothers who a court determines have had an excessive number of children out of wedlock. Unlike the "deserving poor" in the Almshouse, the "immoral poor" here are not free to leave and have to labor in hopes of being released. The inmates cook and mend clothes and make soap, but mostly, they pick oakum—plucking oil and dirt from old ropes so they can be reused—for twelve hours a day, earning only pennies.

This block-long precinct of the poor ends at the corner of Treamount Street, where the Granary is a long wooden building that once doled out grain to the hungry at one-tenth its market value. Often drawing lines of Bostonians during times of recession or calamity, the Granary could hold twelve thousand bushels at its height and was a critical tool in preventing hunger and starvation. But it's been closed since the war began, with no signs of reopening any time soon.

Strangely, the one facility with the name of the Granary that is open for business is the cemetery behind the building. The Granary Burying Ground dates back to the 1660s and was established when King's Chapel Burying Ground across the street reached its limits and more space was needed to house the dead. This cemetery has fulfilled its function well in the century since, hosting hundreds of funeral processions and elaborate corteges, as well as common burials done at night with only a few mourners. Because the burying ground has been so successful at interring the departed, some in plots four bodies deep, the selectmen have had to open yet another cemetery in the Common to the south.

As we've already seen at Copp's Hill, many of the headstones date from the time of the Puritans and do not include crosses or other Christian symbols. Instead, you'll see winged death's heads, morbid poetry, images of the Grim Reaper, and other fatalistic emblems. Unlike the rest of West Boston, where the rich and the poor and the working classes are kept to their defined districts, in this graveyard, all of Boston can mingle in the afterlife. For here lie the town's artisans and laborers next to notables such as Judge Samuel Sewell and merchant Peter Faneuil, colonial governors, British soldiers and officers, and perhaps, someday, the leading patriots of the Revolution. Spare a moment, though, to find the graves of the victims of the Massacre on King Street: Crispus Attucks, James Caldwell, Patrick Carr, Samuel Gray, and Samuel Maverick. Because these sailors and artisans and apprentices arrived here in the grandest procession of all and were laid to rest with all the honor befitting those who brought the nation one step closer to independence and paid for it with their lives.

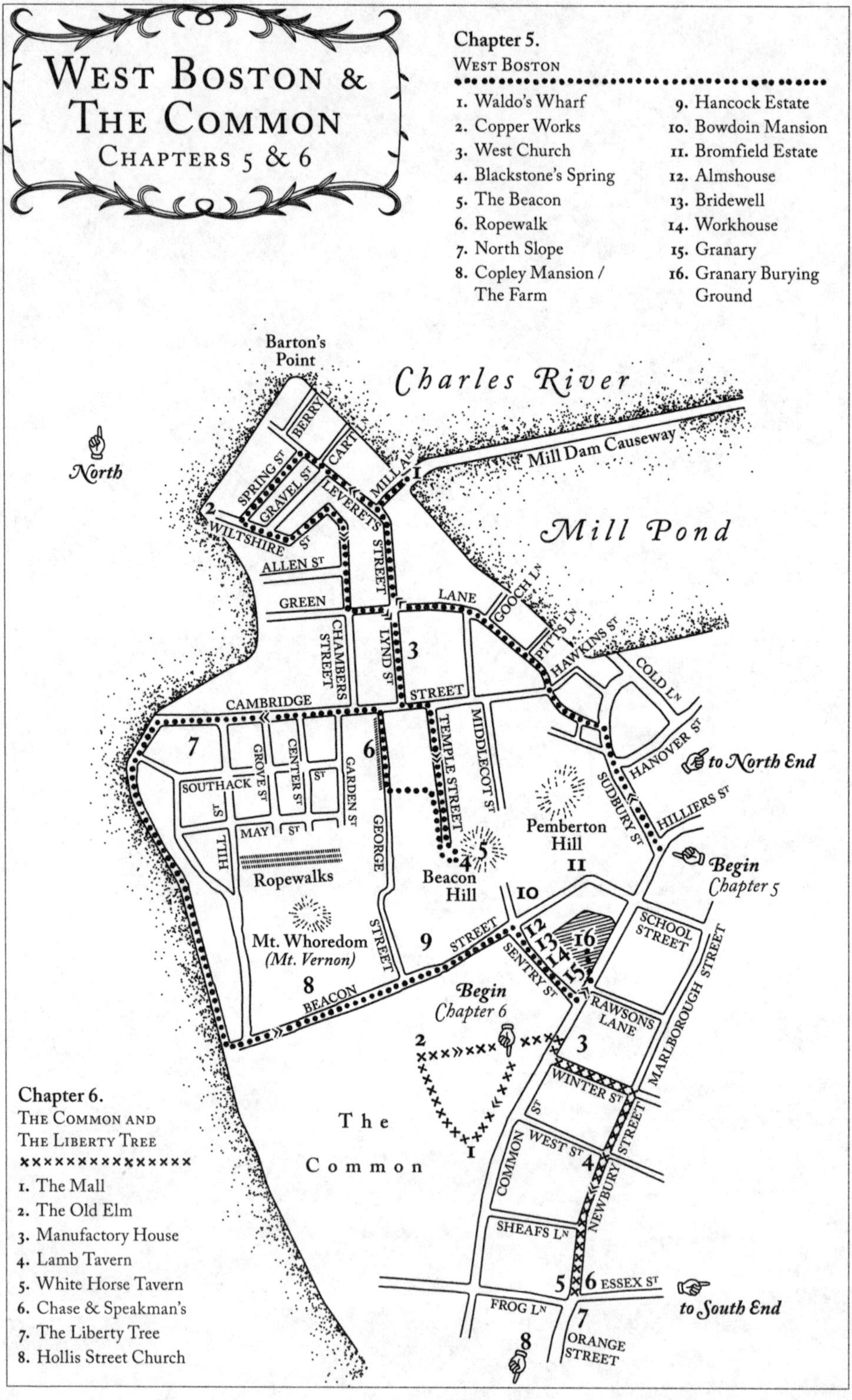

Chapter 5.
West Boston

1. Waldo's Wharf
2. Copper Works
3. West Church
4. Blackstone's Spring
5. The Beacon
6. Ropewalk
7. North Slope
8. Copley Mansion / The Farm
9. Hancock Estate
10. Bowdoin Mansion
11. Bromfield Estate
12. Almshouse
13. Bridewell
14. Workhouse
15. Granary
16. Granary Burying Ground

Barton's Point
Charles River
Mill Dam Causeway
Mill Pond
North
Berry Ln
Cart Ln
Spring St
Gravel St
Leverets Street
Mill Aly
Wiltshire St
Allen St
Green Lane
Gooch Ln
Pitts Ln
Hawkins St
Cold Ln
Chambers Street
Lynd St
Cambridge Street
Temple Street
Middlecot St
Hanover St
to North End
Sudbury St
Hilliers St
Southack St
Grove St
Center St
Garden St
George Street
Hill St
May St
Ropewalks
Beacon Hill
Pemberton Hill
Begin Chapter 5
Mt. Whoredom (Mt. Vernon)
Beacon Street
Sentry St
School Street
Marlborough Street
Rawsons Lane
Begin Chapter 6
Winter St
The Common
Common St
West St
Newbury Street
Sheafs Ln
Essex St
to South End
Frog Ln
Orange Street

Chapter 6.
The Common and The Liberty Tree

1. The Mall
2. The Old Elm
3. Manufactory House
4. Lamb Tavern
5. White Horse Tavern
6. Chase & Speakman's
7. The Liberty Tree
8. Hollis Street Church

☆ 6 ☆

The Common and the Liberty Tree

On the southeast part of the peninsula are two of Boston's quintessential sites, each so important to the story of the Revolution that they share a full chapter of this guide. You can see both on a walk of no more than a half hour. The Common and the Liberty Tree are critical not just to the town's legacy but to the course of American independence, with the former being the staging ground for the war to come and the latter being a symbol of the patriot cause, in all its knotty and tangled details.

On a walk from West Boston, the first of these two locations you'll reach is the Common: parade ground, festival zone, cattle pasture, military camp, park, graveyard, and execution site. It's been all these things and more over Boston's century and a half of existence, but more than anything, the Common has been Boston's essential green space—a historic tract that gives a window into the past while sitting close to the key sites of the current uprising.

The Common spreads across forty-five acres. The northern edge borders the homes of the wealthy on Beacon Hill; the eastern the streets of the South End; the western the tidal flats of the Charles River; and the southern a cemetery called the Common Burying Ground. Since the west side is often submerged by brackish water, you'll likely spend most of your time in the center or along the east side—a lovely area for strolling. The path designed for this purpose follows the Mall, a European-style allée with a double row of elms lining a gently curving walkway, with a few sycamores on the north end and poplars on the south. Bostonians of all classes make their appearance here in warmer weather, either showing off their finery or just looking for a place to cool off from the heat. There's not really a destination at either end of the Mall—it's flanked by the cemetery to the south and the Granary Burying Ground to the north—but the setting has its own appeal and is the best place to encounter the full spectrum of residents.

The Mall is pleasant enough but won't take more than ten minutes to walk in full. Afterward, head to a towering figure that sits close to the middle of the Common and can be seen for blocks around: the Old Elm. This massive tree is said to be older than Boston itself and offers a pleasant setting for a picnic or romantic liaison. It's been at the center of some of the most dramatic episodes in the town's history. In 1740, the evangelical firebrand George Whitefield preached here to thirty thousand people—twice the town's population—and other enthusiasts have delivered homilies to their followers and promised redemption in the world beyond. On the tree's limbs, Quakers and accused witches met their fate at the end of a rope in the mid-seventeenth century. Wampanoag prisoners and those of other tribes were similarly executed during King Philip's War. Men have fought duels to uphold their honor under its boughs, and mobs have gathered here to torment their enemies. But the history hasn't been all grim: The Old Elm has also been the site of some of Boston's grandest celebrations.

When Parliament repealed the Stamp Act in 1766, John Hancock stood outside his mansion on Beacon Street to compete in a rival fireworks display with the Sons of Liberty at a nearby stage, where "the ground was covered with beehives and serpents, and the two stages with fire-wheels of various kinds." Within the Common, a four-story pyramid reached skyward to shine with 280 lanterns, while at the pinnacle, a spectacular display of twenty-one rockets fired from a horizontal wheel, which transformed into "sixteen dozen fiery serpents." Hancock also made good use of the terrain in the early 1770s as the colonel of the Corps of Cadets, whom he outfitted with scarlet jackets, white gaiters, tricorns trimmed in beaver fur, and gilt buttons. They drilled with martial precision and provided an escort for the governor and royal officers during ceremonies—an ironic touch since half of them were members of the Sons of Liberty.

There's also been a more unwelcome military presence on the Common. The British army lodged in tents here beginning in 1768 during the town's initial occupation, which made for tense relations with residents, but nothing like the wartime situation seven years later. On April 19, 1775, General Thomas Gage deployed eight hundred men to cross the river in boats and barges to Cambridge, leading to the battles of Lexington and Concord. Soon after, he encamped three thousand soldiers in Boston, putting more than half of them in tents and improvised barracks on the Common while they built and manned earthworks and fortifications, set up guardhouses on the perimeter, and emplaced artillery at the top of hills and at the shoreline. With the outbreak of war, radical patriots fled town, and a significant number of loyalists returned, hoping the army would protect them and provide greater security than what they'd experienced during the prewar years. It didn't take long for that hope to be dashed.

Bostonians faced impoverishment during the siege, as supplies of food and firewood dwindled and patriot bombing led to confusion and panic. Floating river batteries fired at the garrison on the Common, and General Gage's regiments made no progress in finding relief from their entrapment. Tensions rose with the townsfolk, too, as restless soldiers disrupted the peace by racing horses on the lawns and playing "Yankee Doodle" loud enough to disrupt church services. They took jobs in competition with laborers at the docks and ropewalks, adopted a high-handed attitude when dealing with artisans and shopkeepers, and often drank to excess and behaved boorishly.

The reasons for their behavior related to conditions in the army and the nature of the soldiers themselves. While the redcoats acquired a fearsome reputation for their success in battle, most were poor men who lacked any better prospects. Convicted felons found their way into the ranks after being offered enlistment as an alternative to execution. Regardless of their background, soldiers found life in the garrison hard, the discipline brutal, and the pay abysmal.

Some turned to drinking to pass the time, and more than a few became addicted to it. As one major wrote to the first lord of the admiralty, "The rum is so cheap that it debauches both navy and army, and kills many of them. Depend on it, my Lord, it will destroy more of us than the Yankees will." In extreme cases, some men sold their muskets to buy alcohol, or tried to desert the regiment. If caught, they could expect to receive up to five hundred lashes to the bare back. Other punishments included hanging in chains on a gallows and being forced to ride the "wooden horse," a rigid set of planks to which an offender would be tied for a lengthy and crippling torture. The residents who witnessed such sights reacted in shock and disgust, seeing how the soldiers' agony might go on for hours until "their ribs are laid quite bare, whereby their kidneys are so affected that they become incurable." When soldiers died from such abuse, they could expect rude treatment of their bodies. Unlike their officers, who came from the upper end of British society and occupied plots in churchyards and cemeteries, enlisted men were dumped into a common grave at the foot of the burying ground.

Reminders of this grim encampment have not disappeared, even though British forces evacuated in March. Trenches and ditches still scar the Common, along with a few spiked cannon and the like. The troops tore down the fences that once graced the north and east sides of the green space and used them as firewood in the last winter, and the ground in many places is trampled with the marks of hooves and gun carriages.

Still, the occupation did not completely disfigure the site. General Howe ordered his men to keep the elms along the Mall intact, and—since returning—the patriots have been vigilant in preventing coaches and wagons from crossing the Mall and adding more damage to it. Indeed, the landscape is still enticing enough that the local militia assembles here for drills. The site also hosts one of the most vibrant festivals the region has to offer, with grand processions, marching and drilling, music and baton twirling, parades and balls and dancing. It's called Election Day, but instead of being a showcase for the wealthy, it's a celebration for the enslaved.

It occurs the last Wednesday in May, a time when the crops are all planted and bondsmen and women in the region are given a brief respite from their forced labor. Initially, slaveholders tried to manage the event, but it has since been taken over by enslaved people themselves. The purpose derives from an African tradition in which the community elects a patriarch to serve throughout the year, to represent their interests, manage disputes, and act as a liaison to the wider town. The elected governor and his officials take their vows through elaborate rituals and dress in resplendent attire with brightly colored jackets and waistcoats, silk stockings, ruffled shirts, and silver buckles on their shoes. Other celebrants may dress with flowers and feathers and ribbons, take oaths of allegiance to their leaders, feast on cakes made from fruit and wine, drink an herbal beer brewed from bark and roots, and dance to ensembles of drum, fiddle, tambourine, fife, and other instruments.

Once you finish exploring the Common, cross Common Street to reach Winter Street. Here you'll spot the Manufactory House, one of the largest structures in Boston, at two stories and 140 feet in length. The General Court intended the building to be a showcase for the town's industrial might and a means of keeping poor laborers out of the Almshouse. It didn't turn out that way, and instead became another site of conflict between the townsfolk and occupying soldiers.

The legislature funded the building's construction with a tax on carriages in 1753, with an aim to employ 150 mostly women spinners in the manufacture of linen, thus promoting domestic production and helping them earn enough money to support themselves. A year later, the building opened with great spectacle, as hundreds of spinners competed on the Common in tests of speed and dexterity. Afterward, they went to work in the Manufactory, equipped with more than twenty looms, twenty spinning wheels, and rooms for dyeing and bleaching. However, the promising start didn't augur future success. It turned out the Manufactory couldn't compete economically with cheaper foreign imports, and the General Court didn't offer enough funding to support their work. The enterprise collapsed in 1759.

For the next decade, the Manufactory housed a few weavers and spinners working of their own accord, and there were few conflicts until 1768, when freshly landed British troops had to find lodging. A dispute arose between selectmen and Crown officers over whether all the soldiers should be stationed at Castle Island. The colonel of the 14th Regiment decided to commandeer the building and boot the tenants out of their workshops. In response, the artisans barricaded themselves inside, and the colonel's forces surrounded the building and cut off food, water, and medicine. Bloodshed might have followed, if not for the governor's council seizing on a technicality to lodge the regiment elsewhere. The British army eventually did use the building as a barracks and hospital during the siege, but the evacuation put patriots back in control. The building now offers units for rent to families in need of housing, and the relief on the facade, showing a noble artisan woman with a distaff (a spinning tool that takes up the flax), has vanished.

There's not much more to detain you at the Manufactory House, so walk a block east on Winter Street until you reach Newbury Street, then another block south to West Street, where you'll come to the Lamb Tavern. It's a good spot for a mug of ale after a day of wandering and is marked with the wool-bearing creature on its sign, which fronts a charming, wooden, two-story house with plenty of windows and benches. Two blocks south on Newbury is another tavern, the White Horse, marked with another beast on its sign. More intriguing is the distillery across the street.

Chase & Speakman's doesn't look too different from the other rum-making operations in town (see p. 141 for an overview), but what makes it special is that co-owner Thomas Chase was a founder of the Loyal Nine, and inside his counting room, radical patriots held meetings to design strategy against royal officials. While John Adams heard little of this when he visited and enjoyed "Punch, Wine, Pipes and Tobacco, Biscuit and Cheese," the Nine and the Sons of Liberty have almost certainly arranged clandestine business here—they're said to have planned everything from the Stamp Act riots to the Destruction of the Tea in this little room.

Conveniently, the Nine's other base of operation sits within view of the distillery's windows, at the corner of Orange Street and Essex Street, where one of Boston's icons stood proudly until just a few months ago. The reasons for its importance, and its disappearance, are fundamental to the saga of the uprising, so take a few minutes to linger at this corner and consider the fate of the Liberty Tree.

The corner adjoins the property of the late Deacon John Eliot, who served for years at Hollis Street Church, two blocks south. Eliot's home is a large and handsome two-story building with an open gate and wood-slatted fence that surrounds a courtyard, which contained several majestic elms likely older than the town itself. The one nearest the street became the most famous, its towering limbs forming a broad canopy that lofted over the fence and attracted the eye of Bostonians. As the years passed, the elm acquired the name of Liberty Tree, and the space where you're standing below it became Liberty Hall. It was a site of protest, a place where South Enders might affix political broadsides to the bark or hang town leaders in effigy—as crude dummies dangling from the limbs. Until the 1760s, the protests were largely unorganized. That was until a journeyman cordwainer named Ebenezer Mackintosh became involved.

He's been described as a slight fellow with pale hair and a nervous demeanor. His family came from Scotland, brought here as indentured servants in the seventeenth century, and, after their release, occupied the lower rungs of Boston's social ladder. Mackintosh drifted from job to job as a young man; served some time in jail, then in the militia; and acted as a sergeant in one of the volunteer firefighting corps, Engine No. 9. He also learned the shoemaking trade, traveling from house to house making or repairing shoes, among the poorest of all artisans. Yet, somehow, he rose to fame.

He first achieved notoriety as a gang leader, channeling the town's longstanding, often vicious, feelings against Catholicism during the yearly tradition of Pope's Day on November 5. This perverse holiday commemorated the failure of Guy Fawkes's Gunpowder Plot to assassinate James I and members of Parliament in 1605. Mackintosh directed his men to gather contributions and carry out their spectacle, which often began at or near the Liberty Tree.

On the appointed day, a carriage would appear, bedecked in lanterns and transporting huge grotesque effigies of the pope and the devil—the pope sporting sleek vestments, a white wig and golden hat, and silk breeches; the devil tarred and feathered, with a long curling tail and trident. Boys dressed as imps cavorted alongside the carriage or moved the giant heads of the effigies back and forth. The bizarre parade attracted thousands of revelers, making for a colorful mix of white and black sailors, artisans, apprentices, laborers, and indentured servants, all of them beating on drums or blowing horns and conch shells, laughing, cheering, screaming, swearing, and crying out, "South End forever!" The army of mayhem then invaded the town center, reaching Union Street or Mill Creek, where they encountered their rivals, who cried out, "North End forever!" and showcased their own pope and devil on wheels.

Then the fighting began. Mackintosh and his gang members took center stage, trying to capture the North End's pope and using clubs, bricks, staves, and cutlasses to do it. Town constables would try to intervene but couldn't stop the mayhem. The men punched and gouged and flailed at each other, shouting, "[W]ith the utmost Rage and fury: Several were sorely wounded and bruised, and some left for Dead." Amid the frenzy, "pursers" appeared with little bells to collect money from passersby who looked like they had it, or from wealthier homeowners. If they refused to pay, they might receive a crack to the jaw or a club to the head, or have their house ransacked. The pursers even sang a little tune amid the violent revels:

Don't you hear my little bell
Go chink, chink, chink?
Please give me a little money,
To buy my Pope some drink.

The North Enders had always won the contest until 1764. That November night, Mackintosh's South Enders fought off the constables and seized their rivals' pope. They took all the effigies to Fort Hill, grabbing wood from stolen washtubs, tar barrels, and lumber planks along the way, and torched them in a massive bonfire. Then they retired to taverns to conclude the evening with multiple rounds of drink.

Mackintosh became a hero for his exploits that night. He earned the praise of thousands of working men in the South End and acquired the honorific "Captain General of the Liberty Tree," which gave him control over the lanterns and effigies that hung from the elm. (Thomas Hutchinson gave him a different label: "the consummate rioter.") The town meeting even elected him as a sealer of leather—an inspector who ensured that hides were properly tanned and curried—with an increase in salary and prestige. But there were also threats to his new reputation.

A child died in the 1764 fracas when a carriage rolled over his head. Property owners were incensed to see their dwellings trashed and the streets littered. And the selectmen had had enough of the violent lawlessness, which they'd outlawed repeatedly in prior decades to no avail. So they arranged the arrest of Mackintosh and other gang leaders for their role in the riot, and it looked as if the cordwainer would have to spend some time in prison. Which he might well have if some unlikely rescuers had not come to his defense—the same men who looked out on the Liberty Tree from their counting room at Chase & Speakman's Distillery.

The Loyal Nine recognized Mackintosh as a man of considerable talent and reputation, and potentially an ally in their fight against royal officials. They arranged his release from custody by standing surety for his bond and good conduct, and they began to work with him to find a greater purpose for his abilities, or at least greater than fighting over puppets of popes and devils.

The Nine's own purpose was to undermine the newly passed Stamp Act and those who tried to enforce it. From their counting room, they had been plotting ways to increase public antagonism against the act. With the aid of member Benjamin Edes, they'd printed articles and essays in the *Boston Gazette* about Parliament's transgression against colonial liberties, as well as broadsides they posted on walls and fences around town. But they needed more than that. They needed someone like Mackintosh to champion their cause.

Samuel Adams would help to secure his allegiance. In July 1765, the former tax collector turned radical patriot received a judgment against Mackintosh and his business partner Benjamin Bass for back taxes amounting to twelve pounds, ten shillings. On August 12, Adams filed a warrant for their arrest for nonpayment, and it seemed likely the cordwainer would once again be on his way to prison. But for mysterious reasons, the warrant was not executed—and two days later, Mackintosh went into action, happy to put his talents to a new purpose.

On the morning of August 14, South Enders awoke to find an effigy of stamp commissioner Andrew Oliver hanging from the Liberty Tree. Next to him hung an old boot with Satan's head popping out and his claws holding a copy of the Stamp Act. (The boot was a punning reference to Lord Bute, who supported taxation of the colonies.) Mackintosh and the Loyal Nine had helped design and arrange the display, and thousands of Bostonians who came to examine the dummies grew ever more excited as the hours passed. Realizing such displays often led to violence, the sheriff tried to have the dummies taken down, as did Deacon Eliot, but each time they tried, the crowd found ways to stop them. By nightfall, it was time for the effigies to travel.

Shouting, "Liberty, Property, and No Stamps!" Mackintosh and a mob of thousands paraded through the streets with the effigies on a rolling journey to the waterfront. Here, they destroyed a brick building they thought would be used to issue stamps before heading to the South End and burning the dummy of Oliver in front of his own house then vandalizing it and its gardens. Soon after, the stamp commissioner offered his resignation from his post. The event was a great success.

The captain general of the Liberty Tree basked in the adulation of the South Enders and many others in town. His Loyal Nine allies were pleased with his work and the outcome of the riot, which, unlike the mayhem of Pope's Day, had achieved its goal without seriously injuring or killing anyone. However, Mackintosh and his followers were not yet satisfied. On August 26, he led another huge mob into the town center, where they looted the houses of Crown officers William Story and Benjamin Hallowell before moving on to the North End mansion of Thomas Hutchinson. For many hours until the early morning, they vandalized and partly dismantled the house and stole valuable artwork, manuscripts, jewels, and money (see p. 32 for a full account). But this time, Mackintosh had overstepped his bounds in the eyes of radical patriots.

The Loyal Nine distanced themselves from the violence, and Whig newspapers' coverage was mostly hostile to the rioters and sympathetic to Hutchinson. Constables arrested the cordwainer as an instigator of the mayhem. Yet, once again, he was released and the charges dismissed, aided by public opinion and a few powerful patrons. He returned to the South End to plan his most surprising demonstration yet.

It would occur on November 1, the day the Stamp Act was to go into effect. Excitement over what might happen rose in the ranks of laborers and working folk, just as fear spread among the wealthy and royal officials. Business owners boarded their windows in the town center, people kept off the streets, and rumors spread that another outbreak of violence would surely be at hand. Soon, effigies appeared on the Liberty Tree depicting former Prime Minister George Grenville and Parliamentarian John Huske, each blamed for enacting the Stamp Act. Many in the town held their breath, fearing the spectacle to come.

Mackintosh duly made his appearance on the streets. He sported a new blue-and-red outfit, golden-lace hat, gilded military gorget, rattan cane, and a "speaking trumpet" to announce his orders. He marched at the head of two thousand protesters alongside the commander of the town militia,

William Brattle, and met his nemesis Samuel Swift—leader of the North End gang—at the Liberty Tree. But instead of exchanging insults or injuries, the two men removed the effigies and took them to the gallows on the Neck, where they condemned them before cutting them down and letting the crowd rip them apart. Many rounds of drinking and feasting followed, as the unexpected truce proved to be a success.

It was not, however, solely of their own making. The night before, John Hancock and Samuel Adams had feted the gang leaders in a "Union Feast" involving hundreds of men dining and drinking in various taverns and outfitted them in splashy uniforms. With the assistance of the Loyal Nine, they persuaded Mackintosh to maintain the truce for Pope's Day and to refrain from vandalizing the town and ransacking private property. And when the Nine pressed Andrew Oliver in December to offer a public oath that he would never distribute stamps (despite rumors to the contrary), they employed Mackintosh to escort him to the Liberty Tree to make the vow. The gang leader's status had never been higher.

In the months and years that followed, the Loyal Nine gave way to the Sons of Liberty as the leading group of radical patriots, but the Liberty Tree remained essential to the cause. After the Stamp Act's repeal in 1766, patriots decorated the elm with 108 lanterns, flags, and adornments, as cannon fired and drums pounded and bells rang from Hollis Street Church. On the August 14 anniversary of the Stamp Act riots, they hung streamers on its branches, made toasts under its boughs, sang inspiring tunes, and recited worthy poems. The Sons also ensured that, from now on, effigies on the tree would include targets beyond the pope and the devil, among them customs commissioners, royal officials, and merchants who trafficked in British goods. They attached signs that read "Love and Unity—The American Whig—Confusion to the Tories" and staged protests over events from the *Liberty* affair to the Massacre on King Street.

As the Revolution drew closer, the scene at the Liberty Tree became graver, more menacing. Detested officials were now called to resign their office at the tree or else, as broadsides threatened "parricides" with damnation for voting in the Assembly against the radical cause. Liberty Hall witnessed open intimidation, funeral processions (real and mock), and shocking episodes of violence. Perhaps the most egregious involved customs agent John Malcolm, who was widely hated among patriots for informing on violators of trade laws and for his violent temper. After he belligerently struck a child with a stick and an artisan with his cane, a crowd went to seize him from his house, then began a ritual familiar to Boston:

> [H]e was stripped Stark naked, one of the severest cold nights this Winter, his body covered all over with Tar, then with feathers, his arm dislocated in tearing off his clothes, he was dragged in a Cart with thousands attending, some beating him with clubs & Knocking him out of the Cart, then in again. They gave him several severe whippings, at different parts of the Town. This Spectacle of horror & sportive cruelty was exhibited for about five hours.

They took him here to the Liberty Tree and, after repeatedly flogging him, tried to force him to renounce his commission and promise never to hold another. But Malcolm—naked and shivering and coated with pitch—refused to promise any such thing, unlike more pliant Crown officials like Andrew Oliver in years past. So the crowd dragged him to the gallows on the Neck, put a noose around him, and vowed to slice off his ears. The last threat worked, and Malcolm complied with their demands. But the spectacle reminded less radical Bostonians just how much baleful energy a crowd could summon, and how it could use the Liberty Tree for even the most fiendish purposes.

When the news got out, merchant John Rowe wrote, "This was looked upon by me & every Sober man as an act of outrageous Violence." Most onlookers and newspaper editorialists took the same view, and even the Sons of Liberty became alarmed by how such publicity reflected badly on the radical cause, with the story drawing outrage across the Atlantic. They distanced themselves from such brutal escapades and made sure tortures like the one Malcolm endured were not repeated—at least not in the vicinity of the Liberty Tree.

By this time, the Sons had also grown impatient with men like Mackintosh. Although he'd kept the truce with the North End gang, oversaw less-violent Pope's Day events, and was repeatedly reelected as a sealer of leather, his role as a protest leader diminished. The Sons preferred their allies to be committed radicals who understood the greater purpose of the

Revolution, not troublemakers of uncertain loyalties. So they sidelined him from taking an active role in the key events of the time.

Mackintosh did not participate in the uprising on King Street that led to the Massacre, even though his wife's half-brother, Samuel Maverick, was one of those killed by the grenadiers. He lost his job as sealer of leather by the end of the 1760s and ended up in debtor's prison at the turn of the decade. While he attended the larger meetings of the Sons of Liberty and claimed credit for the Destruction of the Tea (which he said was accomplished by his "chickens"), his reputation among the radicals faded, until they regarded him as little more than a relic of primitive mob violence. In 1774, hounded by fears of being arrested by the British military, he fled to New Hampshire, where he remains today.

The next year, George Washington finally put a stop to Pope's Day by ordering his soldiers from New England to disavow the brutal custom, since it might interfere with his policy of tolerance and his overtures to potential Catholic allies in Quebec. But the tree still stood as a potent symbol of the revolutionary cause, even without violent escapades and enterprising gang leaders to draw attention to it. Inspired by Boston's example, other towns in America adopted Liberty Trees, or raised Liberty Poles to serve the same function. The original tree made appearances in Paul Revere's engravings and on his silver bowls; in songs across New England and an eponymous poem of Thomas Paine; in political cartoons in British newspapers; and on drum skins, powder horns, and flags of local militias.

All this recognition came at a cost, though. From the outset, royal officials ill-regarded the elm, seeing it as an emblem of lower-class extremism, and they condemned Liberty Hall as the place where they and their loyalist allies faced a "tree ordeal" that could threaten their jobs, their status, even their lives. Judge Peter Oliver, brother to beleaguered Andrew, said the tree was "consecrated as an Idol for the Mob to worship," and his feelings were shared by the great mass of soldiers who occupied Boston during the siege. All to the peril of the innocent elm.

Just before the evacuation, a handful of soldiers chopped it down. According to *The Essex Gazette*, "Armed with axes, they made a furious attack upon it. After a long spell of laughing and grinning, sweating, swearing, and foaming, with malice diabolical, they cut down a tree because it bore the name of Liberty." As a bit of botanical revenge, one of the men sawing away at the boughs was said to be killed when the wood fell upon him. Yet, even though the soldiers destroyed the tree, they couldn't erase its legacy. People still come to the South End to peer through the slats of Deacon Eliot's fence and gaze at the remains of the great elm. They offer their blessings and honor it for the role it's played in the struggle for independence. And as you can see, they've given it a new name, more suited to its present condition—the Liberty Stump.

STAMP ACT RIOTS. *The violent 1765 uprising that changed the course of history and alerted royal officials to the dangers of inflaming the mob.*

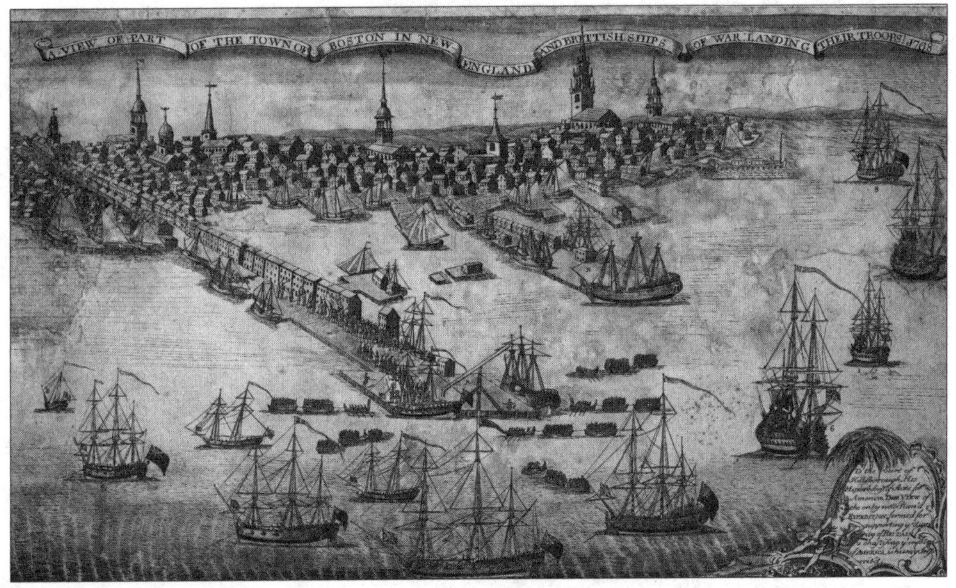

1768 TROOP LANDING. *The much-feared occupation of the town by British troops, which hardened local sentiment against imperial rule and fueled the energies of radical patriots.*

THE MASSACRE ON KING STREET. *The slaying of five Boston men on a winter's day in 1770 by British grenadiers, a seminal and still-controversial event that brought the town a step closer to revolt.*

[January, 1770]

WILLIAM JACKSON,

an *IMPORTER*; at the

BRAZEN HEAD,

North Side of the TOWN-HOUSE,

and *Oppoſite the Town-Pump, in Corn-hill*, BOSTON.

It is deſired that the Sons and Daughters of *LIBERTY*, would not buy any one thing of him, for in ſo doing they will bring Diſgrace upon *themſelves*, and their *Poſterity*, for *ever* and *ever*, AMEN.

NONIMPORTATION. *A preferred tool of radical patriots to fight the power of the Crown: refusing to purchase imported British goods and punishing those who attempt to sell them.*

TARRING AND FEATHERING. *The mob's favorite method of tormenting local officials and importing merchants—a humiliating public spectacle to force their compliance, resignation, or exile.*

THE DESTRUCTION OF THE TEA. *A few hours on the waterfront that sunk any hopes of a reconciliation between Britain and its colonies—and submerged 342 chests of tea worth almost £10,000.*

COERCIVE ACTS. *The revenge of Parliament for the tea's destruction: closing the port of Boston, stripping away popular government, and turning the town into an armed camp.*

LEXINGTON AND CONCORD. *The opening salvos fired in the War of Independence: battles between rebel militia and British regulars that forced the retreat of the king's army and the beginning of the siege.*

THE SIEGE. *A nearly yearlong period of misery, starvation, and poverty endured by residents who watched their town suffer under military control and the horrors of war.*

BATTLE OF BUNKER HILL. *Pyrrhic victory for the redcoats that turned into a moral triumph for the patriots, boosting their enthusiasm for the war and a desire for independence.*

EVACUATION DAY. *March 17, 1776, the day the Crown gave up hopes of conquering Boston and evacuated thousands of soldiers and loyalists on 170 ships—and began the next phase of the war.*

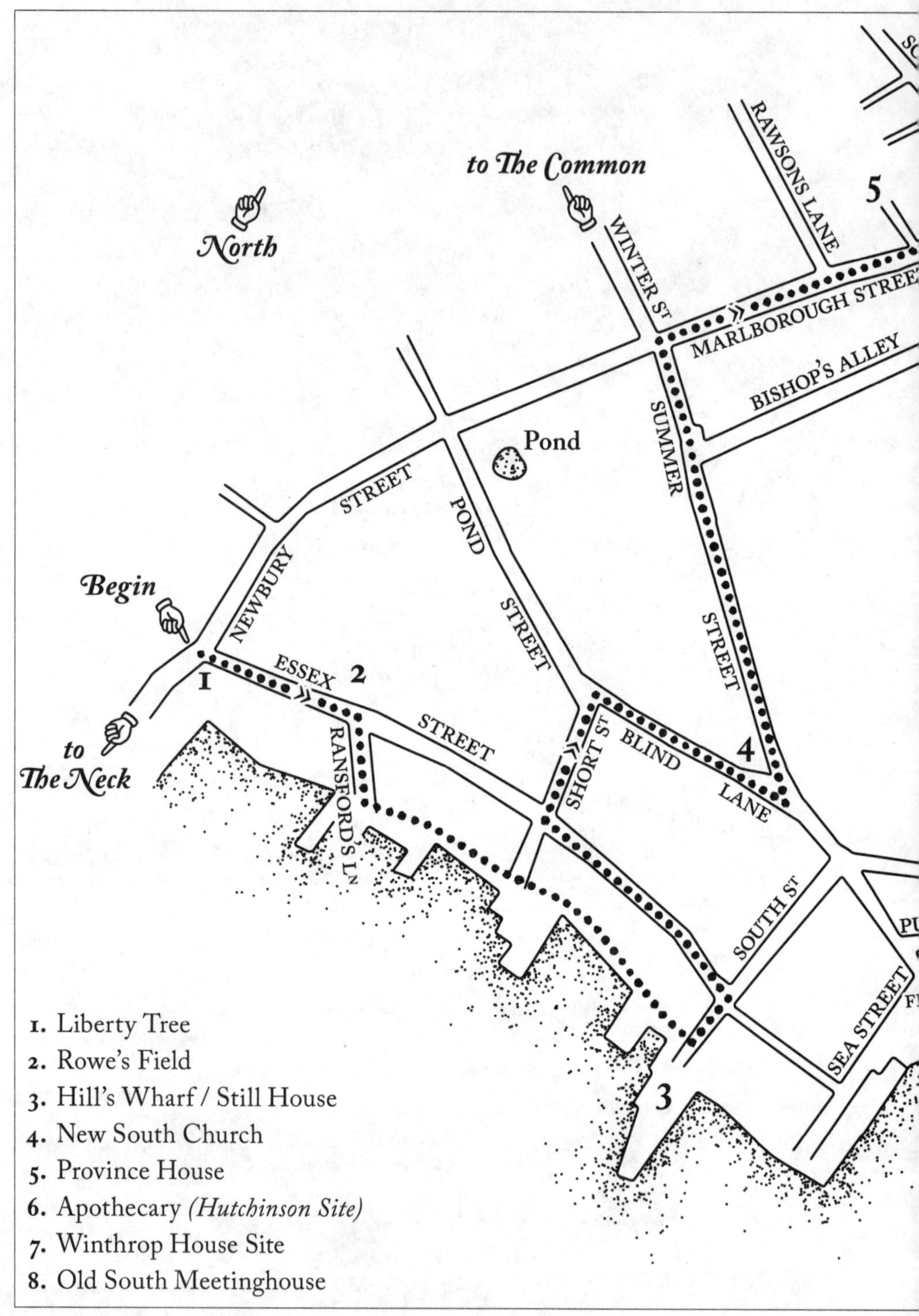
to The Common
North
Begin
to
The Neck
WINTER ST
RAWSONS LANE
5
MARLBOROUGH STREET
BISHOP'S ALLEY
SUMMER
STREET
Pond
STREET
POND
STREET
NEWBURY
ESSEX
2
1
STREET
RANSFORD'S LN
SHORT ST
BLIND
LANE
4
SOUTH ST
SEA STREET
3
1. Liberty Tree
2. Rowe's Field
3. Hill's Wharf / Still House
4. New South Church
5. Province House
6. Apothecary (Hutchinson Site)
7. Winthrop House Site
8. Old South Meetinghouse

THE SOUTH END
CHAPTER 7
to Town Center
BURY ST
STREET
ROUND LN
COW LANE
STREET
BELCHERS
LANE
Ropewalks
ATKINSON'S STREET
HUTCHINSON
STREET
OLIVER
STREET
BATTERY MARCH
BATTERY
MARCH
Fort Hill
9
10
11
12
13
14
Boston Harbor
9. Franklin House
10. Paxton House
11. MacNeil's and Gray's Ropewalks
12. South Battery
13. Military Fort
14. Griffin's Wharf
15. Samuel Adams House

☆ 7 ☆

The South End

The South End is a paradox. It's Boston's largest neighborhood by size and population, a picturesque area full of fields and pastures and estates with barns and orchards, dotted with ponds and meadows charming enough to inspire a landscape painting. But it's also where some of the most shocking episodes of revolutionary violence have occurred—brutal fights between soldiers and rope makers that led up to the Massacre, tarring and feathering of suspected spies and saboteurs, ransacking of customs officials' property, and, of course, the Destruction of the Tea on a cold December night in 1773.

Begin your journey heading east from the Liberty Tree on Essex Street, where you'll pass Rowe's Field, one of the larger green spaces, before taking a right on Ransford's Lane, which leads down to the harbor. Here you'll find some of Boston's biggest and most important distilleries, owned by major names like Henshaw, Coffin, Arbuthnot, and Walner, with Hill's Still House among the most prominent. Boston contains more than half of Massachusetts's sixty-six distilleries—out of only 140 total in British North America—producing more than 2.7 million gallons of liquor in facilities just like these. The major operations import molasses and distill it into rum, then distribute it within the region or ship it out to the rest of the world.

If you show interest, a distiller may invite you into a facility, where you can watch the employees fill large wooden tubs and vats with blackstrap molasses to ferment for up to a week. This produces a wash that they convert into rum inside a pot still before aging the distillate in casks of oak or other wood. When sampling the goods, don't be surprised to find the taste of the rum bitter or acrid, or riddled with impurities. Feel free to add sugar, fruit, or other flavorings, as locals do, to make it more palatable. But keep in mind what cousins William and Edmund Burke, in their travelogue to the New World, once said of area distillers: "[T]hey are more famous for the quantity and cheapness than for the excellency of their rum."

It's that cheapness that makes the beverage so popular. The cost is as little as two shillings a gallon, which leads many enterprising sellers to dole it out by the drink on the waterfront, or to set up a storefront in their own homes with just a single cask. In fact, the rum business is so crucial to the local economy that when paper money is scarce, waterfront traders barter for the beverage or use it as a form of currency. And any attempt to increase the cost or limit the supply of molasses may inspire a revolt.

The most famous example came in 1764, when Parliament passed the Sugar Act, which reduced the tax on molasses but dramatically increased enforcement measures to prevent smuggling from non-British colonies in the West Indies. Figures like James Otis and Samuel Adams denounced the act as an infringement on colonial liberties, with the latter writing to Boston's representatives in the General Court, "If Taxes are laid upon us in any shape without our having a legal Representation where they are laid, are we not reduced from the Character of free Subjects to the miserable State of tributary Slaves?"

Rum has made a number of merchants quite wealthy, including members of the Faneuil, Belcher, Waldo, and Cabot families. They and their associates control much of the shipping trade that exports a third of Boston's rum to foreign regions, principally Canadian colonies but also Africa. And it is in Africa where the exports of rum are tied closely to the trade in human beings.

Together with Newport, Rhode Island, Boston is New England's chief port for the triangle trade, in which mercantile ships leave town with casks of rum they sell in Africa for ivory and slaves. They take their enslaved passengers to the West Indies, where they can be traded for molasses to produce more rum back home. Any unsold or "surplus" humans sail on the same ships carrying the molasses to Boston, where they are traded on docks and in warehouses, taverns, and private homes. Most slave ports are in Senegambia, Sierra Leone, the Windward Coast, and the Gold Coast, though sometimes local shippers will trade directly for Caribbean slaves by exporting fish, livestock, wood, and whale products—but not rum, since the West Indies makes its own.

As we've seen in chapter 5, an increasing number of Bostonians have grown wary of or disgusted by the slave trade. Pressed to prohibit the practice by the town meeting, state assemblymen have tried twice to outlaw it, only to face the vetoes of royal governors. And slavery is not the only baleful effect of rum manufacture. The abundance and cheapness of the liquor have led to an increase in public drunkenness, and more than a few patriots see inebriation as inimical to the workings of a republic. The town meeting has instructed its representatives in the Assembly to discourage the drinking of liquor, because "it is destructive to the morals as well as the health and substance of the people." A contemporary observer writes of the dilemma that rum manufacturing can be both beneficial to Boston's economy and hazardous to its health, since it causes "idleness, poverty, and disgrace" and "a public benefit may, by an improper use of it, be converted to a public evil."

Beyond the still houses, the wharves continue eastward with a mix of shipyards, ropewalks, leather works, and other industrial shops. Return on Essex Street to Short Street and take a right on Blind Lane to reach the triangular plaza that hosts New South Church. The wooden Congregational meetinghouse was built in 1719 on the high ground overlooking the harbor, and offers a good spot for a respite before you continue farther into the neighborhood.

North of the church, Summer Street offers a most appealing ramble through the heart of the South End. This walk is one of Boston's gems, with stately rows of trees lining both sides of the road and connecting their branches over it to provide one seamless canopy. Beyond the trees are estates with orchards, barns and dairies, and pastures for cows and horses. At the center of each tract is typically a wooden farmhouse or a large Georgian residence surrounded by fences and terraced gardens.

At Marlborough Street, take a right, and just more than a block later, you'll come to a three-story structure built of imported Dutch brick and enclosed by sturdy fence rails and two handsome oaks. It's called the Province House, and for most of the century, it was the official residence of royal governors from Samuel Shute to Thomas Gage. (Most of them did not actually live here, but lodged their families elsewhere.) The imposing structure provides a strong sense of the Crown's authority and the many powers His Majesty's minions had to keep their subjects in line.

The last official to use the house, Major General William Howe, departed after the siege, and the mansion has been given over to the commonwealth for the offices of treasurer, secretary, and the like. The walkway toward the building follows massive freestanding stone steps, which take you across the lawn to a wood-pillared front portico topped by a balcony with an iron balustrade. From here, functionaries would stand adjacent to the carved and gilded royal arms on the facade and read official proclamations. These royal arms have since been pried off, but the initials of an early owner—merchant Peter Sergeant—still remain above the door, a reminder of the decades around the end of the seventeenth century when the house was a private residence, before it was sold to the royal government.

Before you go in, peer up at the steep roof with its dormers and decorative chimneys; it's topped by an octagonal cupola with a pedestal that supports a bronze weather vane depicting an Indian with a bow and arrow. Inside, the house is no longer as resplendent as it once was, but you can see the reception room that was once hung with tapestries and filled with dignitaries, the oak timbers supporting a grand staircase that climbs to the private rooms on the upper floors, and the wall space for portraits of men who considered themselves worthy of the highest rank. No one embodied this attitude better than the penultimate governor, Thomas Hutchinson.

Unlike his predecessor Francis Bernard, a journeyman British bureaucrat, Hutchinson was an American son of Boston, a product of the North End with a family history going back to the early days of the colony. He entered Harvard before he was a teen, was elected as a selectman in his mid-twenties, and, afterward, became an assemblyman and later Speaker of the House. As a wealthy merchant, he skillfully moved the gears of the legislature to accomplish his ends, like retiring paper money and converting the colony to hard currency, policies that often enraged the broader public.

He didn't win an election after the 1740s, but he didn't need to, since the Crown recognized his value and began bestowing favors upon him.

He was appointed lieutenant governor in 1758 and, within a few years, had collected overlapping titles like chief justice of Massachusetts Superior Court, probate judge for Suffolk County, and member of the Governor's Council. But this kind of advancement—based more on rank than merit—inspired outrage among those who called themselves Whigs, who were fiercely protective of colonial rights and suspicious of royal favoritism.

James Otis Jr. was particularly incensed when his father was passed over for the position of chief justice in favor of Hutchinson (who was unschooled in law), and many others fumed over his support for writs of assistance to permit customs officers to search merchant ships at will. Hutchinson also became part of a faction known as the Junto, made up of merchants, judges, and other men of the royalist stripe, who looked to abolish the town meeting, seeing it as a threat to public order and good government. In Hutchinson's own words, "[P]ersons of the best character and best Estate . . . decline attending Town Meeting [where] they are sure to be outvoted by men of the Lower order."

Once he became governor and settled into the Province House, Hutchinson enforced Parliament's controversial laws on smuggling and taxation, and he arranged for his salary and those of provincial judges to be paid by the Crown instead of the General Court—an attempt to reduce his dependency on assemblymen and, in the view of Whigs, a scheme to disempower them. For all these actions, radicals like the Sons of Liberty made him a target in the press and in public demonstrations, and Hutchinson did little to dispel their caricature of him as a budding tyrant.

In 1772, Benjamin Franklin gained access to letters Hutchinson had written four years before to Thomas Whately, a former undersecretary of state. They largely echoed his public statements, claiming royal officials should take greater control over the workings of local government and that a military presence might be needed in Boston. At one point, Hutchinson argued, "There must be an Abridgment of what are called English Liberties. . . . I doubt whether it is possible to project a System of Government in which a Colony 3,000 miles distant from the parent State shall enjoy all the Liberty of the parent State."

Franklin entrusted the letters to Massachusetts House Speaker Thomas Cushing, with instructions not to reveal the contents. However, Cushing soon informed Samuel Adams, who parceled out the content, knowing it would humiliate the governor. The Assembly validated the letters' authenticity and asserted that Hutchinson and his cohorts were profit-seeking opportunists aiming for "the Destruction of the Charter and Constitution of this Province" and were largely to blame for the occupation of Boston and "justly chargeable with the great Corruption of Morals, and all the Confusion, Misery and Bloodshed which have been the natural effects of this Introduction of Troops."

When the *Boston Gazette* published the letters in mid-1773, Hutchinson's humiliation was complete. The Assembly drew up a petition that demanded his removal, and the governor requested leave to go to London to defend himself and his conduct. The request would take months for the Crown to approve, and by the time Hutchinson stepped away from his position in the summer of 1774, the Destruction of the Tea had occurred, Parliament had passed the Coercive Acts, and British North America was on its way to war.

Even before he left, Hutchinson's name had fallen into such disrepute that those who tried to honor him for his service faced censure. In a signed statement, 123 residents wrote about the "entire satisfaction we feel at your wise, zealous, and faithful administration" and praised him for "having discharged your trust with fidelity and honor." Radicals were quick to mock the signers as minor businessmen who toadied to the Crown to advance their interests, while a letter from a correspondence committee of merchants claimed they were "worthless wretches" no better than prostitutes. The "addressers" were widely condemned and ostracized, with some being forced to apologize or to issue pained excuses for their signatures.

Though Hutchinson now resides in Britain, memory of his governorship still inspires rancor among many Bostonians. Should you dare to offer a toast to him, you may hear hissing or booing. According to merchant John Andrews, "Such is the detestation in which that tool of tyrants is held among us." Mercy Warren has castigated him as "dark, intriguing, insinuating, haughty and ambitious, while the extreme of avarice marked each feature of his character."

However, the critique is too harsh, as Hutchinson did exhibit sound judgment at times (such as in the aftermath of the Massacre) as well as a fair amount of tolerance for those who vilified him. His greatest sin was that he governed as if he belonged to a different era, when royal prerogatives held sway, elite merchants and Crown officials held all the power, and "men of the Lower order" could be held in open contempt by their betters. But as any good patriot knows, that time, like Hutchinson himself, has long since vanished.

(As a geographical coincidence, the memory of another Hutchinson haunts the corner of School and Cornhill Streets, a block north. The apothecary is described in chapter 4, occupying the land where the governor's great-great-grandmother Anne Hutchinson once lived a century and a half before. In a strange parallel, she too faced censure for her actions, saw her name and reputation blackened, and was ultimately driven out of the colony.)

After you've looked around the Province House, cross Marlborough Street to the site where the second governor of the Bay Colony once lived. Actually, you won't see more than an empty lot, but this is where John Winthrop's home stood on what was called Governor's Green. It was a two-story cedar pile that served him well in the later years of his life but was left to decay during the current century and was dismantled by British troops for firewood during the siege. Though the home may be gone, the grand church that stands on the site of Winthrop's former garden remains—Old South.

This majestic brick structure was built in 1729 as a replacement for the original church (then called Third Church). In the old building, young Benjamin Franklin was baptized, and Judge Samuel Sewall made a public plea for forgiveness for his role in the Salem witch trials. The new version is a bit more eye-catching, with its square clock tower, arched windows, and symmetrical design, and has hosted the sermons of many renowned preachers who called the faithful to worship during times of distress. But more than that, Old South is best known as a site of political protest.

If you were to come inside during such an event, you'd find the box pews and galleries filled with an incredible mass of people—five or six thousand, according to some reports—all hearing the speakers give voice to the issues of the day, as the audience gave their own opinions in return and voted on petitions and legislation. These massive assemblies of "the Body of the People" dropped property requirements for voting and allowed a much broader range of citizens to participate, including the poorest artisans and laborers. Selectmen called such meetings when the subjects for debate were especially critical or controversial, and when Faneuil Hall (the usual site of the town meeting) couldn't accommodate the greater number of attendees.

Royal officials cast a wary eye upon these assemblies, with Thomas Hutchinson seeing one such meeting as "consist[ing] principally of the lower ranks of people and even journeymen tradesmen were brought to increase the number and the rabble were not excluded." The Crown's representatives distrusted the meetings' democratic qualities and how effective they were in driving allegiance to the patriot cause, making for some of the most legendary moments in recent history:

June 1768. James Otis condemns the seizure of John Hancock's ship *Liberty* and the Royal Navy's campaign to kidnap local sailors into service. He moves for the adoption of a petition to Governor Francis Bernard and raises the passions of the crowd, saying, "[W]e are called on to defend our liberty and privileges, I hope and believe we shall, one and all, resist unto blood," though he prayed God would intervene so bloodshed wouldn't be needed.

March 1770. Samuel Adams puts pressure on royal officials to withdraw two army regiments after eight soldiers kill five citizens. With threats of insurrection in the air, Lieutenant Governor Hutchinson allows for the withdrawal, which Adams announces to wild huzzahs from the crowd. Subsequent anniversary orations at the church commemorate the event with blazing rhetoric, with Hancock's and Joseph Warren's among the most memorable (see p. 110 and p. 92).

November 30, 1773. In the second of a series of tea-related meetings, Adams moves that the tea within the newly arrived ship *Dartmouth* be refused by its consignees (approved wholesalers), that no import duty should be paid, and that the cargo be returned from whence it came. The sheriff tries to break up the meeting without success, and the painter John Singleton Copley—whose relatives include three of the consignees—tries to meditate but fails to negotiate a compromise with the parties. Adams mocks now Governor Hutchinson as a "Shadow of a Man, scarce able to support his withered Carcass or his hoary Head!" and merchant John Rowe asks, "Whether a little Salt Water would not do it good, or whether Salt Water would not make as good Tea as fresh." In summary, Hancock says, "My

Fellow Countrymen, we have now put our Hands to the Plough and Woe be to him that shrinks or looks back."

December 16, 1773. At the last tea assembly, all three ships have arrived, and time is running out before the military intervenes and sells the cargo at auction. Adams demands ship owners, consignees, and revenue officers take no steps to allow the tea to be landed. Others say the tea should be burned or the chests broken open with axes and chisels, "then we shall have Tea enough without paying any Duty!" One ship owner, Francis Rotch, asks for clearance for his ship to leave the harbor but Hutchinson refuses. In response, Adams declares, "This meeting can do nothing more to save the country." Passions erupt, and the galleries empty out. With war whoops resounding in the sanctuary, the meeting ends, and the Destruction of the Tea begins.

Upon learning about such stirring episodes, you might be tempted to go inside the church, sit on a pew, and imagine the scenes that took place here. But you will be in for a shock once you proceed through the doors—for the church is a complete wreck. The altar stands disfigured, the pews ripped out, the floor covered with dirt and gravel, the walls damaged and vandalized. The destruction is owed to General John Burgoyne, who, like other British officers, understood the role the church had played in the coming of the Revolution. During the siege, he allowed his light dragoons to do their worst to the sanctuary, and he set up an indoor riding school where horsemen could leap over obstacles and impress their friends. Officers set up a tavern in the gallery, torched the church ledgers, and stole or burned the priceless books in the tower library. Since the evacuation, there has been no time to repair the damage, so the building remains closed, with no hope of hosting preachers or selectmen or the Body of the People any time soon.

The parishioners have been forced to scatter, with many finding new homes at other Congregational churches. Among the displaced is one of Boston's key authors, Phillis Wheatley, who has achieved a greater measure of fame than most of the town's other writers. Her first volume of poems was published only three years ago, a remarkable feat since she was enslaved when she wrote it.

Wheatley's story is both inspiring and depressing. She was seized at a young age in Senegambia and taken aboard a slave ship, most likely transiting through the West Indies. As "surplus" cargo, the child ended up in Boston around 1760 and was given a first name that matched the ship that kidnapped her, along with the last name of the family that purchased her. Her owner John Wheatley worked as a tailor and was, like his wife, Susannah, and daughter, Mary, an evangelical Christian who justified human bondage as part of God's plan to Christianize the African continent.

Young Phillis arrived small and sickly and wrapped in a carpet swath, and the family raised her to be a domestic like other enslaved young women in town. What was unusual in her upbringing, though, was Susannah and Mary's interest in teaching her to read and giving her access to literature. She took to the pursuit and, within a few years, began writing her own poetry that drew from classical and biblical sources, as well as more contemporary writers like Milton and Pope.

Through the Wheatleys' connections, Phillis met many of the region's leading ministers and proselytizers, among them evangelical celebrity George Whitefield, revivalist Sarah Osborn, and antislavery champion Samuel Hopkins. She also visited the homes of the wealthy to read her poetry to the likes of Thomas Hutchinson, Andrew Oliver, Harrison Gray, and James Bowdoin. However, the family did not allow her to associate with other slaves and domestics, and she soon found herself isolated: in bondage like her peers but largely keeping company with the affluent, who welcomed her talent while maintaining a distance from her socially.

She felt divided by the Revolution. Many who championed her work were loyalists, yet her political sympathies lay with the rebels. She struggled with the contradiction but, in the end, became one of the few writers in Boston to conjoin the struggle against racial slavery with that of political slavery, as in her poem "America":

Tis thus with thee O Britain keeping down
New English force, thou fear'st his Tyranny and thou didst frown
He weeps afresh to feel this Iron chain
Turn, O Britannia claim thy child again

She likely witnessed many revolutionary events as they occurred, describing them in poems about the occupation like "On the Ships of War and Landing of the Troops" and the martyrdom of the child Christopher

Seider, killed by a customs agent, in "On the Death of Mr. Snider Murder'd by Richardson":

> *In heavens eternal court it was decreed*
> *How the first martyr for the cause should bleed*
> *To clear the country of the hated brood*
> *He whet his courage for the common good*

Still, in the years before the war, she couldn't afford to alienate her Tory readers, so she took care to honor King George III and Great Britain with her verse. She traveled with the Wheatleys to London in 1773, meeting figures like abolitionist Granville Sharp and William Legge, Earl of Dartmouth, while he was secretary of state for the American colonies. In her ode to him, she wrote of her life in bondage:

> *I, young in life, by seeming cruel fate*
> *Was snatch'd from Afric's fancy'd happy seat:*
> *What pangs excruciating must molest,*
> *What sorrows labour in my parent's breast?*
> *Steel'd was that soul and by no misery mov'd*
> *That from a father seiz'd his babe belov'd:*
> *Such, such my case. And can I then but pray*
> *Others may never feel tyrannic sway?*

The transatlantic visit was a success and secured the loyalty of important figures like Selina Hastings, Countess of Huntingdon, who helped arrange the publication of Wheatley's first book, *Poems on Various Subjects, Religious and Moral.* An even greater triumph came when Phillis gained her freedom after returning home from London, as the Wheatleys relinquished their control over her. In response, she wrote, "I am now upon my own footing and whatever I get by this is entirely mine, & it is the Chief I have to depend upon."

The initial crate of her books arrived in Boston in November 1773, in the hold of the ship *Dartmouth*—the same ship that contained the tea that patriots would later toss in the harbor. Luckily, her poems had already been unloaded by that point, but the episode did not bode well for her future success. With the outbreak of war, many of her loyalist advocates fled to Britain and Canada, and any patronage she might have expected left with them.

She's since bolstered her support for the Revolution and written poems about Continental Army generals, including "Generalissimo" George Washington, to whom she wrote a letter of praise and a corresponding ode. In response, he sent a letter inviting her to his Cambridge headquarters, writing, "[Your] style and manner exhibit a striking proof of your great poetical Talents. . . . I shall be happy to see a person to favored by the Muses, and to whom nature has been so liberal and beneficent in her dispensations." Even with such fulsome praise, she's struggled to achieve greater renown in the climate of war and faces many of the same struggles as other black Bostonians. If you'd like to ask her about plans for a next volume of verse, you'll have to inquire among local ministers who know her best, since her spiritual home at Old South lies in ruin.

Once you've seen enough of what remains of the church, cross Milk Street to find the boyhood home of one of the people Wheatley befriended in London, Benjamin Franklin. (He wrote of her, "I went to see the black Poetess and offer'd her any Services I could do her.") As you know, he's done great service to the nation as a diplomat, scientist, inventor, printer, author, and signer of the Declaration of Independence, and he will soon be the ambassador to France. You might say his rise started here at this simple, two-story wooden house where he was born in 1706. He took classes at Boston Latin (later dropping out), wicked candles at his father's chandlery, and apprenticed to his brother James as a "printer's devil" for *The New-England Courant*, to which he also submitted articles under the pseudonym Silence Dogood. But at seventeen, young Ben escaped his brother's control and left for Philadelphia, a town he has since made all the more famous by his presence.

From Franklin's childhood home, head east for several blocks past a few fields and pastures and estates until you reach a row of tumbledown wooden houses. Take a right on Hutchinson Street (not named after the governor) to visit several sites important to the Revolution. The first is a pleasant, three-story brick affair, the only house in the vicinity, which had the misfortune to be rented for a time by one of the most hated men in town, Customs Commissioner Charles Paxton.

In the view of countless patriots, Paxton "bought office with money, and was as rapacious as the fabled harpy," while John Adams saw him as so effective at collecting revenue that he acted as "Governor, Lieutenant-Governor, Secretary, and Chief Justice" all at once. As a customs agent, Paxton won the infamous 1761 writs of assistance case, allowing the inspection and confiscation of private property without a warrant. Seven years later, Paxton helped engineer the seizure of John Hancock's ship *Liberty* and encouraged the military occupation of Boston. He denounced colonists for evading the various acts of Parliament and urged a hardline policy against them.

Paxton's efforts did not go unnoticed. The *Gazette* mocked and lambasted him, and South Enders hung his effigy in protest and made him a target of the Stamp Act riots. Though he fled the house you see before you, the mob didn't find his absence satisfactory and threatened to burn and loot the place. They were only dissuaded by the negotiating skill of the house owner, who offered to buy them off with free punch at a nearby tavern. They accepted, and the structure remained untouched. Paxton has since escaped Boston so as not to meet the same fate as his dummy, dangling helplessly from the Liberty Tree.

Look across the street to find several more sites critical to the uprising. You'll be familiar with their appearance from your tour of West Boston: ropewalks, the long wooden sheds where smoke rises and men spin in circles to produce cordage from hemp yarn. Two of them stand next to each other, MacNeil's and Gray's, but the latter is the more important. For it was here in the early days of March 1770 that a conflict broke out over a lone British soldier seeking part-time work to supplement his meager income. In the patriot view of the episode, a simple argument led to soldiers attacking and "threaten[ing] vengeance on the defenceless workmen." In reality, the episode was a bit more complicated.

The ropewalk owner John Gray and his workers were famed for their militant anti-British attitudes. So, when the soldier asked for a job, a worker on-site responded, "Well then, go clean my shit house!" The soldier protested, and another worker tripped him and swiped his cutlass, after which he left the scene but returned with eight or nine comrades. They were outnumbered by more than a dozen spinners and retreated but returned with thirty more soldiers bearing weapons. A crew of workers fought them off, and the next day, the violence flared anew, this time at MacNeil's facility.

Seeing how the escalating battles would surely result in death or injury, John Gray and Lieutenant Colonel William Dalrymple arranged a truce, but it wasn't enough to calm tensions. Soon after, the Massacre on King Street took place, leaving five men dead outside the Custom House.

In the vicinity of the ropewalks, there are other factories and workshops surrounded by the simple wooden houses of those who labor in them. Some of the structures are missing walls or even roofs, or have been disassembled and the wood burned in piles. Once again, this destruction owes to the policies of the British army during the siege, when, on several occasions in 1775, the troops "began taking down houses at the South End, to build a new line of Works" to protect themselves from patriot attack. Such actions inspired rancor among Bostonians, which fueled the cycle of animosity between them and the king's soldiers, until outbreaks of violence came to seem inevitable.

General Howe had a difficult time controlling the behavior of his troops. As recorded in his orderly book, he had to contend with men carousing and being "seen drunk in the Streets & about the different Wharfs," as well as widespread looting and intimidation of residents. As the book reveals, "Houses have been forced open and Robbed. [Howe] is therefore under the necessity of declaring to the Troops that the first Soldier who is caught Plundering will be hanged on the Spot." He also had to issue orders preventing the killing of the local pigeons, "Cutting & defacing the King's & Queen's Pictures, & destroying the Records & other public Papers," and committing acts of arson. As one chilling note says, "Any Person detected setting Fire to the Town without Authority will suffer immediate Death."

The general was in a difficult position to have to take such measures. He sympathized with the widespread hostility of his troops to the townsfolk who tormented them with insults, barred them from employment, and even physically attacked them, but he had to prevent his redcoats from stealing and vandalizing private property in return. He saw that such behavior "tends to destroy discipline among the Troops, and to lose them the Affections of the People." Moreover, he didn't want to antagonize any loyalists or keep them from seeing the soldiers as liberators instead of oppressors. But however he tried, Howe often failed to control the rogues under his command. Ultimately, he became so frustrated that he ordered an executioner to travel with the provost marshal throughout town—to summarily hang anyone caught stealing combustible or explosive materials from private homes.

For another chapter in military history, return to Milk Street as it becomes Battery March and leads up and around Fort Hill. This is a large knoll ringed by houses with terraces, with a mall offering attractive views and a military post standing above it all. The hill's slope is gradual, but it terminates in a precipice overlooking the harbor and the guns of the South Battery.

The creation of the fort was a product of the Puritan era, when it was meant as a stronghold to protect Boston from invasion by sea. Ironically, the site became best known for protecting the much-hated Governor Edmund Andros from colonists who overthrew his rule in 1689. He was arrested and held captive at Castle Island before he was allowed to return to England. In more recent times, the South End gang led by rogue shoemaker Ebenezer Mackintosh built a massive bonfire with wood they salvaged from a dismantled building on Kilby Street (see p. 12) and beheaded and burned the effigy of Andrew Oliver on the hill. They did worse to his house lower down the slope, ransacking it and the gardens.

During the siege, General Howe fortified the hill by strengthening its works and deploying four hundred soldiers on site while readying the thirty-five guns of the battery to prevent a harborside attack. Yet none of this did any good to prevent his troops' surrender after General Washington emplaced guns atop Dorchester Heights to force their evacuation. Since then, American troops have occupied the works and kept the cannon pointed seaward, this time to prevent a British return.

Continue on Battery March as it curves around the hill and make your return to the southern edge of the South End. Here, the road becomes Belcher's Lane (named after an early settler, not a digestive habit), where you'll find the site of the most important event leading to the Revolution. It's a series of old pilings in the harbor covered by a weathered deck, "in a decayed situation and constantly washing away." But it was here at Griffin's Wharf where colonists set an irreversible course of revolt against the British empire, in the episode known as the Destruction of the Tea.

Return to the account mentioned earlier in the chapter for the lead-up to the event (p. 149), when, on the night of December 16, 1773, the town meeting at Old South Church ended with people scrambling for the exits.

Many made their way southeast through the neighborhood toward this wharf, where three ships lay at anchor: the *Dartmouth*, which had arrived in late November; the *Eleanor*, which showed up a few days later; and the *Beaver*, which had been quarantined for smallpox and only allowed to dock the day before. Each contained a mixed cargo that included around 114 chests of tea (or 342 in total), none of which had been registered by customs officials or had a duty paid by their merchants.

The timing was critical. It was early in the evening, but when midnight came, it would be twenty days since the *Dartmouth* had dropped anchor, the maximum time allowed by customs law for duty to be paid on its cargo. Should that not occur, the cargo would be subject to seizure and auction—meaning the tea would be landed and rebels' resistance overcome. Those in the crowd were well aware of the pressing deadline, and as the minutes passed, they grew in strength until two thousand people stood watching around the docks and quays.

As they arrived, some people shouted, "A tea-pot tonight!" and "Hurrah for Griffin's Wharf!" while elsewhere there was a "hideous Yelling in the Street . . . some imitating the Powaws of Indians and others the Whistle of a Boatswain." Soon, a parade of men marched down Fort Hill holding lanterns and torches. They dressed in what they believed to be the look of Mohawk Indians, with faces covered in paint and bearing clubs and cutlasses or other weapons. As observer John Andrews saw, they were "cloth'd in Blankets with the heads muffled, and copper color'd countenances, being each arm'd with a hatchet or axe, and pair pistols." Other men came, too, their faces hastily blackened with coal dust, or wearing old frocks and caps or gowns, or without any costume at all. Among them were merchants and a few radical politicians, but most were journeymen and apprentices, determined to take action outside the law to prevent the landing of the tea.

Out in the harbor floated ships full of British sailors and marines, ready to intervene and put a stop to any mischief that might arise. Hutchinson could have applied pressure to their officers to deploy them to shore, but he resisted such a measure, knowing that bloodshed might result. And so, without any intervention from the authorities, 150 or so would-be Indians went to work.

They divided into three boarding parties, one per ship, led by a commander who gave the orders and a boatswain who summoned men with a whistle and secured the keys to the holds. Many in the parties had previously worked on docks or had experience as joiners, carpenters, blockmakers, and other maritime jobs, and understood all the steps they had to take to make the plan a success. They warned away the customs officers observing at shore and promised safety to the ships' captains and crew members as long as they didn't interfere with the operation and gave up their ropes and hoisting tackle. They also promised not to touch any cargo that wasn't tea.

And what tea it was. Three-hundred-and-forty-two chests full of prime Bohea, Congou Singlo, Souchong, and Hyson, courtesy of the East India Company, with each chest weighing up to four hundred pounds, for a total of forty-five tons of loose leaves—all ready to be brewed at the bottom of the harbor. As Peter Edes, son of the publisher Benjamin, saw it, "Some were in the hold immediately after the hatches were broken open, fixing the ropes to the tea-chests; others were hauling up the chests; and others stood ready with their hatchets to cut off the bindings of the chest and cast them overboard." Still, dumping all the contents proved to be hard work, and the operation took hours to execute.

One other complication: the tide was low and the water so shallow that the loose tea formed piles above the surface. The men had to break up the piles with poles or wade into the flats to scatter the leaves or stomp them into the mud. In the confusion, a few miscreants decided to swipe some of the tea for themselves—a violation of the plan of action. One apprehended thief was stripped, dragged through the mud, and beaten, while others were merely threatened. However, for the most part, the men kept their pockets clean and completed their work by 9:00 p.m., on schedule and without any damage to the ships. They even replaced a padlock they'd broken.

The Destruction of the Tea amounted to a loss of £9,659, far beyond any common worker's salary and six times what Governor Hutchinson made annually. The men left the wharf in files and dissolved into the neighborhood, while the ruined tea settled underwater or bobbed in open chests under the moonlight. When word got out of the destruction, royal officials knew the repercussions would be great and lasting. Hutchinson wrote a few months later, "If we have not passed the Rubicon this winter, we never shall." But Whigs and patriots of all stripes were pleased. The day after the event, John Adams wrote:

> This is the most magnificent Movement of all. There is a Dignity, a Majesty, a Sublimity, in this last Effort of the Patriots, that I greatly admire. The People should never rise, without doing something to be remembered—something notable and striking. This Destruction of the Tea is so bold, so daring, so firm, intrepid and inflexible, and it must have so important Consequences, and so lasting, that I can't but consider it as an Epoch in History.

Tight secrecy ensured that the names of the participants would never be known, even long after the event. We can only speculate that men like Paul Revere, Thomas Chase, and William Molineux might have been in the holds, hoisting the tea chests and then dumping their contents overboard. But there's little doubt the radical clubs of which they were members, among them the North End Caucus and the Sons of Liberty, took a firm hand in guiding the event and may have planned it to the minute.

Yet one of the most radical Sons was not there. He was back at Old South Church wrapping up the town meeting when the destruction began and didn't need to shout orders or direct traffic at the waterfront because he already knew what the destroyers would do and when they would do it. Most likely he just walked home, which coincidentally was just a few blocks west of the wharf. And if you continue along Belcher's Lane as it gives way to Purchase Street, you'll find it—the family estate of Samuel Adams.

It's a sizable property, two stories high and 258 feet long, running down to a wharf and including a garden and orchard, with a rooftop observatory giving an expansive view of the harbor. It stands as one of the largest estates in the area, though it does look a bit ragged these days (as we'll see) and not as impressive as it was when Samuel Adams's father, also named Samuel Adams, bought it as a symbol of his wealth and stature in the community.

The elder Adams was a much-admired Congregational deacon, also serving as a selectman, justice of the peace, and assemblyman at the General Court. He was a maltster, too, soaking and drying barley in a malthouse on his property, and an active member of business and social clubs, communing with everyone from common laborers to wealthy merchants and royal officials. He championed Whig values, supported colonial rights against their encroachment by the Crown and Parliament, and combined political action with the moral spirit of Puritanism.

His son Samuel was born in 1722, and the elder taught the younger ideas and strategies to prosper in business and politics. Most of young Samuel's siblings died in childhood, but he survived and did well as a student, graduating from Boston Latin School and matriculating at Harvard at age fourteen, like many of his classmates. Seven years later, he would return for his graduate degree, which required him to answer a philosophical question with a formal response. The question was, "Is it lawful to resist the Supreme Magistrate, if the Commonwealth cannot otherwise be preserved?" He argued it was.

As he matured, Adams worked as an apprentice in a counting house and a shopkeeper but ended up living at home subsisting on income from the malthouse. At the time, his father was waging an all-consuming battle with royal officials over his plan for a land bank, in which farmers and smallholders would be given bank notes against the value of their land. This paper currency would allow them to make capital improvements without going into debt to lenders charging high interest rates. The idea was popular in rural Massachusetts and unpopular among merchants who preferred the established method: advancing credit backed by hard currency like gold and silver. The merchants had the support of royal governors and Parliament, which outlawed the land bank in 1741 and held its directors personally liable for the debts of the organization. Unfortunately, Deacon Adams was one of those directors.

The family faced ruin, with the deacon forced to sell off many of his holdings as he struggled to maintain ownership of the property. The malthouse later failed as well, and the Adams name fell from the ranks of the genteel, with lawsuits and creditors a constant presence and the threat of bankruptcy looming. When the deacon died in 1748, his debts did not die with him, and the younger Adams was forced to wage two more decades of court battles before he could free himself from his creditors. He never forgot the unfairness of Parliament's action and the way it punished small debtors and families like his to benefit the wealthy.

Adams could not, however, rebuild his wealth with a career in business, since he had no faculty with financial ledgers and account books, so he turned to politics. He began as a clerk of the town market before being elected town scavenger to keep the streets clean, then tax collector. In this role, he was able to collect 3 to 12 percent of delinquent taxes from those who owed them, though the job engaged him in numerous legal battles at a time when he was still managing those of the land bank. Nonetheless, politics suited him, and from his home on Purchase Street, he made the daily rounds collecting taxes while conversing with residents of different classes. In taverns and social clubs, he met artisans and apprentices with whom he enjoyed spirited discussions, exchanging ideas about the betterment of the colony and how it was governed. He attended Old South Church with his neighbors and dressed in common clothing, unlike the "better sort" who strolled about in stylish coats and wigs and shoes with silver buckles.

In 1764, when Parliament passed the Sugar Act and the following year the Stamp Act, the voice of Samuel Adams became louder. He attacked the new laws in newspaper columns and in speeches, and he quietly coordinated with his friends in clubs like the Loyal Nine to vilify royal authority on broadsides and in street demonstrations. His efforts peaked with the Stamp Act riots, in which a mob destroyed a building on the waterfront, forced the resignation of would-be Stamp Commissioner Andrew Oliver, and ransacked the homes of Crown officials. For his efforts, Adams rose to greater fame among Whigs and new infamy among the ruling elite.

In 1766, he was elected clerk to the Assembly with the job of record-keeping as well as communicating with other assemblies and the Massachusetts agent in London. The job enabled him to use his talent with the written word to advance the Whig cause and to beat back attempts to curb the rights of British citizens. He arranged for a gallery to be installed in the Assembly to allow the public to hear the orations of the delegates, which became ever-more-fiery as Parliament passed new acts to tax the trade of colonists and curtail their liberties.

From his seat at the General Court, Adams inveighed against the Townshend Acts, the seizure of John Hancock's ship *Liberty*, the military occupation, the importation of British goods, and the Massacre on King Street. He wrote columns in the *Gazette* and acted as moderator of the town meeting, ensuring Bostonians would know his opinions and his preferred course of action. At the same time, he continued to grow the power of the Sons of Liberty, which established bonds with artisans and laborers through events rich with drinking and feasting, while also coordinating street demonstrations, distributing propaganda, and punishing enemies like Crown officials and importers of British goods. Under the pseudonym Vindex in the *Gazette*, Adams said the purpose of a leader was to "keep the attention of his fellow citizens awake to their grievances; and not suffer them to be at rest, till the causes of their just complaints are removed."

Not surprisingly, men invested with power like Thomas Hutchinson saw him as a menace, wondering "whether there is a greater incendiary in the king's dominion or a man of greater malignity of heart." In return, Adams despised such men with equal passion, seeing them as traitors to the charter of Massachusetts and the rights granted to its citizens. His feelings only deepened when the Crown moved to pay judges from customs duties rather than from the Assembly, which Adams saw as an attempt to circumvent local government and wield the "iron Hand of Tyranny." He worked with the town meeting on a pamphlet-letter to send to other towns in Massachusetts to communicate news and build strategy against such measures. In so doing, Adams took the first step to creating the Committees of Correspondence that would help form a union among the colonies and a sense of shared national purpose.

Crown officials viewed his actions as near sedition, the work of a firebrand who had become a threat to public order. Judge Peter Oliver saw him as a Machiavellian who "understood human Nature, in low life, so well, that he could turn the Minds of the great Vulgar as well as the small into any Course that he might choose." A loyalist painter was reported to say that if he wanted "to draw a Picture of the Devil, that he would get *Sam Adams* to sit for him." And John Andrews wrote, "The ultimate wish and desire of the High Government party is to get Samuel Adams out of the way."

Among local patriots, he couldn't have been more popular. They valued him "for his *good* sense, *great* abilities, *amazing* fortitude, *noble* resolution, and *undaunted* courage," and Thomas Jefferson would later call him "truly the *Man of the Revolution*." He maintained his appeal even as he passed the age of fifty and his Puritanical notions of morality began to seem a bit stodgy to many of his peers, such as his disdain for fashion, theatre, and popular amusements and his declaration that "We may look up to Armies for our Defence, but Virtue is our best Security."

When he was chosen as a delegate to the Continental Congress in 1774 to establish ties with some of the most esteemed leaders on the continent, some of his friends worried his rumpled, disheveled appearance might do him discredit. One evening at this house, he was dining with friends when a series of artisans knocked on his door to take his measurements. Days later, a trunk arrived containing several outfits for him to wear in Philadelphia: stylish suits and shoes with silver buckles, gold knee buckles and buttons, a cocked hat and gilded cane, and a red cloak. He would now have a fine wardrobe to match the quality of his rhetoric.

Adams proved a skillful politician in Pennsylvania, forging new alliances and avoiding pitfalls set for him by opponents. But by 1775, his reputation as a radical threatened his freedom, as rumors spread that he would be arrested and jailed for subversion or sedition. In April, he had to flee Boston and go to Lexington just before war broke out; when Governor Thomas Gage offered a pardon in 1775 to any rebels against the Crown, he made a notable exception for Hancock and Adams, "whose offenses are of too flagitious a nature to admit of any other consideration than that of condign punishment."

Despite the threat, Adams escaped that punishment. He attended the sessions of both the Continental Congress and the Provincial Congress of Massachusetts and influenced the legislation of both bodies, signing the Declaration of Independence in July. Earlier in the year, he returned to Boston for the first time since he'd been forced to flee two years before. He went to the family estate you see before you to check on its condition. British officers had occupied it during the siege and made their feelings about him known—doing to the house what they couldn't do to him:

> [They] wantonly mutilated the interior, destroyed the out-houses, and, with spiteful hatred of the proprietor, had cut into the window-panes obscene and blasphemous writings, some of them ridiculing his religious habits. Caricatures were displayed upon the walls, and the garden was completely ruined. . . . Many windows were broken out, doors unhinged and burned for fuel, and every species of wanton destruction was visible.

Adams tried to repair the damage, to no avail. As you can see from its damaged facade, splintered walls, and mutilated rooms, the house lies in ruin with little hope of restoration. So he relocated to the countryside of

Dedham, where he now bides his time with his family before he returns to Philadelphia, waiting for the day when he can once again come back to Boston—to build a new home in the town where he kept his fellow citizens awake to their grievances, and in so doing helped fuel a Revolution and forge a new nation.

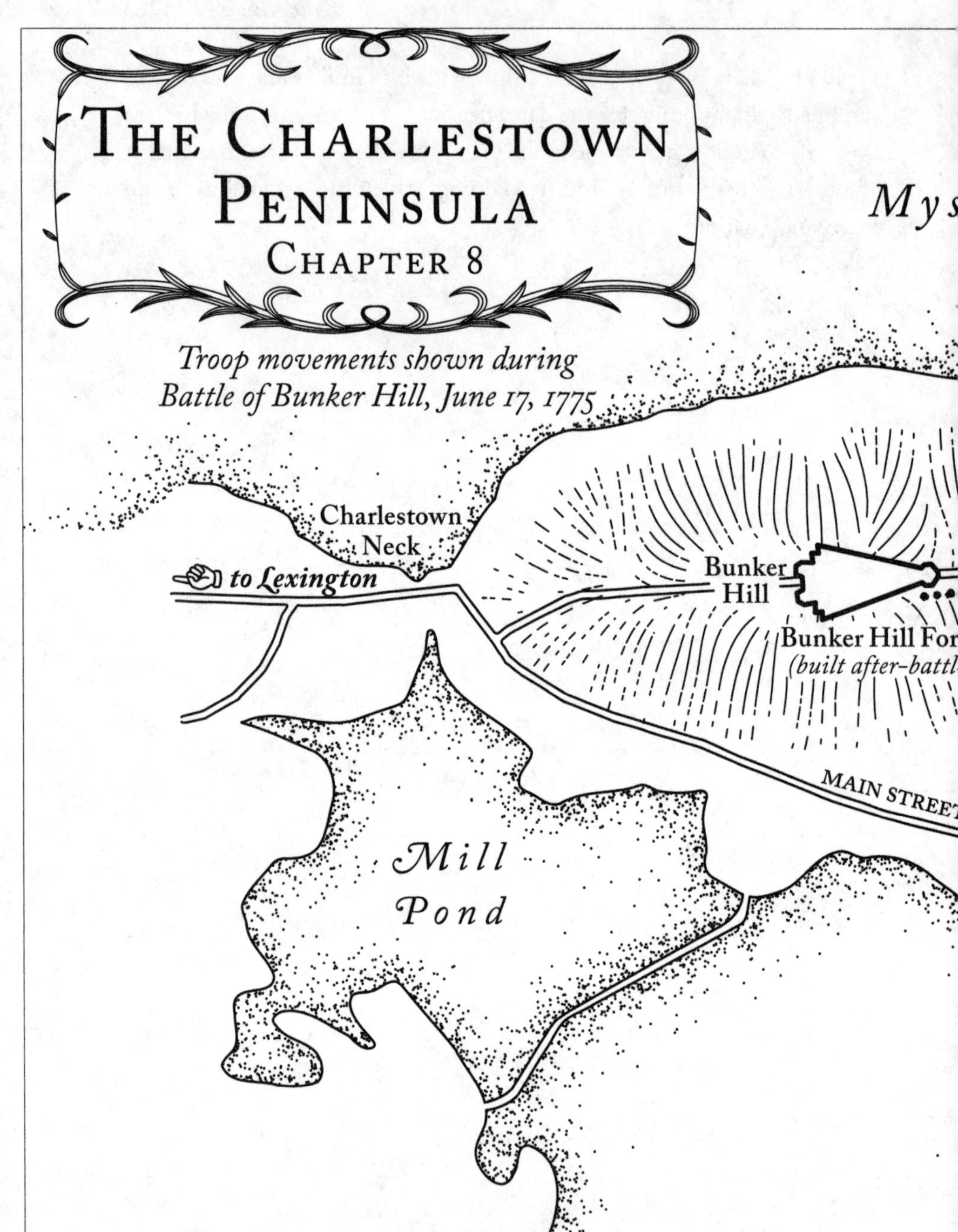
The Charlestown Peninsula
Chapter 8
Troop movements shown during
Battle of Bunker Hill, June 17, 1775
Charlestown
Neck
to Lexington
Bunker
Hill
Bunker Hill For
(built after-battl
MAIN STREET
Mill
Pond
North
Mys

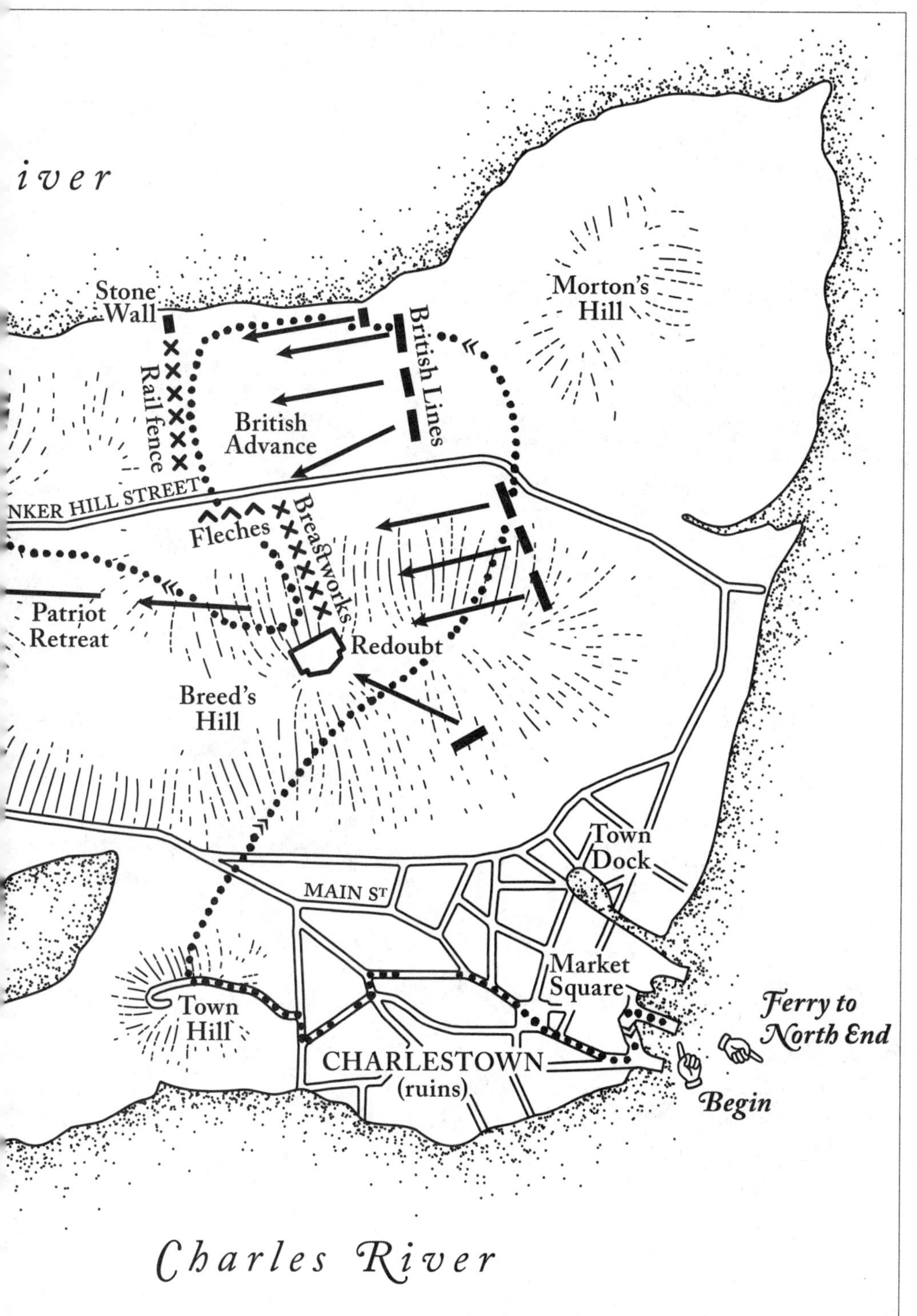

iver
Stone Wall
Rail fence
British Lines
British Advance
Morton's Hill
NKER HILL STREET
Fleches
Breastworks
Patriot Retreat
Redoubt
Breed's Hill
Town Dock
MAIN ST
Market Square
Town Hill
CHARLESTOWN (ruins)
Ferry to North End
Begin
Charles River

☆ 8 ☆

The Charlestown Peninsula

North of Boston proper, the Charlestown Peninsula sits at the confluence of the Charles and Mystic Rivers, with land access over an isthmus called the Charlestown Neck and a ferry to the North End. The peninsula once hosted a busy port with its own thriving community and industries, but since the war, it now lies in ruins. Despite the obliteration, you'll be well rewarded with a lengthy walk around, since no other place around Boston shows the high stakes of the war and its devastating cost in human life and material loss.

Begin your journey at the North End, where the ferry landing at Princes Street offers intermittent service. If the ferry boats are not in operation, you can inquire about renting a rowboat at one of the slips or ask the nearest wharfinger about your options for crossing the Charles River. If all else fails, you can take the twelve-mile-long overland route south of town over the Boston Neck, although this option does come with its own hazards (see p. 183). Provided you do find a boat, you'll be in the best position to appreciate the most historic crossing in recent memory—the April 18, 1775, journey of Paul Revere to Charlestown, where he began his famed ride to Lexington.

In chapter 2, we saw how Revere devised a way for his allies to convey news of British troop movements to patriots in Charlestown using lanterns in the steeple of Christ Church, but this was only part of a larger plan. After they received the message, his allies would then have to send a messenger to the countryside with the news, hoping he wouldn't be intercepted along the way by soldiers. As a backup, Revere himself would cross the river to ensure the countryside would know how and where British troops would be deployed. It turned out to be a prescient move because, as patriots feared, the first messenger never arrived at his destination.

Revere made his way in the evening hours to a wharf where he met up with two other men who uncovered a rowboat below the piers. Sometime after 10:00 p.m., they embarked and rowed into the Charles despite the presence of British warships in the channel. The most menacing of them, HMS *Somerset*, stood guard against ferries, canoes, and other watercraft since an official edict prohibited civilian traffic on the river after 9:00 p.m.—reflecting authorities' well-justified fears of patriot subversion against the occupation.

A bright moon rose over the river. Usually the illumination would be enough to lead to their interception and arrest, but the moon was oddly low hanging, lingering behind some of the taller structures in Boston that would provide valuable cover for the men to row across. They passed into the moon shadow of the *Somerset* as well, seeing the silhouette of the 64-gun warship up close and trying to row both quickly and silently past the behemoth. Eventually they arrived at the Charlestown ferry landing, and Revere met up with his allies to prepare for the next stage of his journey. A Congregational deacon named John Larkin loaned Revere his saddle horse, Brown Beauty, for the ride. Revere headed through the Charlestown Neck and turned west on the road to Lexington, where John Hancock and Samuel Adams lodged at a parsonage. Once he arrived, Revere shouted, "The Regulars are coming out!" to tell them the British army was on its way.

As you make your way one-third of a mile across the river, you won't have to dodge British warships, but passage can be difficult during storms and foul weather, so be careful as you go and preferably find someone to row with you. Once you come closer to the shoreline, you'll have to search for the ferry landing. It's near the center of town, among other wharfs and docks in a state of decay or ruin but might provide just enough moorage for you to tie up your vessel and go exploring.

After disembarking, you'll find no signposts to guide you. The old houses, workshops, warehouses, and other buildings of Charlestown are all either blackened shells or piles of rubble, with empty lots here and there. You may see a few property owners picking through the remnants to search for valuables or heirlooms, but for the most part, you'll have the streets to yourself in this haunted village. Just two blocks from the ferry landing, you'll come across the longest and widest road—appropriately called Main Street—along which the town began and where it may someday rebuild.

Main Street begins at the ghost of a plaza, once a market square that acted as a center of commerce. It was here in 1629 that Puritans founded Charlestown—named after Stuart monarch Charles I—in an attempt to build a colony in the New World. Unimpressed by its prospects, the majority of settlers soon departed to build a proper theocracy on the Shawmut Peninsula to the south, but for the stragglers who remained, Charlestown became their hardscrabble home. They mostly lived in tents and thatch-roofed cottages but did manage to erect a building they called the Great House as a civic and religious center. They would later construct a meetinghouse with a tall, thin steeple; a courthouse and government offices; shops for shipwrights and ship chandleries; and warehouses and wharves, with a ferry linking the town to the rapidly growing rival settlement of Boston just across the river.

In 1635, the Great House became a tavern known as the Three Cranes. It would later become Charlestown's equivalent of Boston's Green Dragon, a place for patriots to plot strategy and where British officials could expect to receive a rude welcome. The site was well-equipped with a kitchen, brewhouse, and wine cellar; an inn with stables for travelers on horseback; taps where drinkers could fill their mugs; and spaces for playing shuffleboard and lawn bowling and even dancing. But more than anything the tavern enjoyed popularity among local Whigs and radicals, who might arrive for a glass of posset (milk, rum, and spices) or a tankard of ale, take a breakfast of cornmeal mush or a dinner of meat stew, smoke a pipe, and discuss colonial affairs with their brethren by the hearth or in the quieter nooks.

Unless you'd like to poke around in the rubble for an artifact (not recommended), you're well advised to take a wider look at the old town center among the battered walls, chimneys, and foundations. Try to imagine the town at its height a few years ago, when two thousand residents occupied five hundred buildings in a successful community. Along the Charles, the wharves saw a busy trade in fur, lumber, staves, and whale products, and there was both a Town Dock several blocks from the shoreline that moored a range of vessels and a dry dock where those vessels could be repaired out of the water—the first dry dock built in America, in 1679. Nearby workshops and industrial operations included brickyards, distilleries, leather-working shops, and potteries. The latter produced some of the area's finest redware, finished with a fine lead glaze. It's still found on the shelves of local homes and taverns.

Of course, if your imagination fails you, all you'll see will be burned-out shells and broken pavements. In that case, follow Main Street northwest of the town center, then wend your way west to the gentle rise known as Town Hill. The better homes once occupied the perimeter, and a colonial fort and windmill stood at the summit, but as with the rest of Charlestown, there's not much left. However, the hill does provide an excellent vantage point to help you understand the events of June 17, 1775—the day of the Battle of Bunker Hill.

It won't take you long after climbing the hill to notice the battle was misnamed. For the peninsula's three most prominent peaks run from the northwest to the northeast in descending order of height—Bunker, Breed's, and Morton's—but most of the fighting took place on and around Breed's Hill. This is evident from the scars of bomb damage along its slopes, which rise above the townscape less than a half-mile north of the town center.

The origins of the battle owe to a curious decision General Thomas Gage made after the fighting at Lexington and Concord. He and the rest of British army leaders faced conflicting options for how to position their forces, some of which were garrisoned on Bunker Hill. Admiral Samuel Graves, whose ships had recently carried soldiers across the Charles River for the attack on Concord, encouraged Gage to destroy Roxbury and Charlestown and fortify the heights of Bunker Hill and Dorchester. But Gage refused, worried about an uprising within Boston itself and a patriot attack by way of the Boston Neck. He ordered the garrison on the Charlestown Peninsula to relocate to the Shawmut Peninsula and left the hills of the former largely undefended.

Gage's strategy had its limitations, letting the hillsides be exposed to rebel incursions and even allowing patriot General Israel Putnam to parade two thousand troops through Charlestown to mock the British sailors watching on the HMS *Somerset* and other vessels. By the time a trio of fresh British generals—John Burgoyne, Henry Clinton, and William Howe—arrived in May to serve under Gage, the strategy required dramatic, and much more aggressive, revision.

The war council's new approach was to fortify Dorchester Heights and the hills around Charlestown, and from there invade the Massachusetts countryside in a great pincer movement. The target would be Cambridge, center of rebel activity and home to military stores and thousands of troops. With the colonial militias sufficiently weakened or pulverized by the attack, the rebels would be forced to sue for peace from the British government, which could then impose a settlement to its liking. The action was due to begin on the morning of June 18.

Patriot spies reported the plans five days before they were to be executed. Sufficiently alarmed, the Provincial Congress ordered the commander of the Massachusetts militia, Artemus Ward, to protect the heartland from any such assault. To that end, Congress directed that Bunker Hill "be securely kept and defended . . . [and] be maintained by sufficient force being posted there."

The hill stood 110 feet high and was an easy choice for defense. Any attacking troops would have to march uphill against what would doubtless be lines of entrenchments and breastworks to reach a redoubt of high earthen walls and thousands of rebels defending it. Even worse, the fortification would stand above the range of British artillery, leaving any assault force susceptible to mass casualties in the face of a what could be an impregnable patriot position.

That was the idea anyway. But after Colonel William Prescott marched 940 troops through the Charlestown Neck into the interior of the peninsula on the evening of June 16, a very different plan emerged—a plan that would lead to the first major engagement with the British army after Concord and ignore the carefully laid plans of the Provincial Congress.

Around midnight, Prescott held a conference with Colonel Richard Gridley, a skilled engineer who'd already begun building a defensive wall atop Bunker Hill, and General Putnam, a volunteer who led his Connecticut forces under a separate command that was not answerable to Prescott or even General Ward himself. No one can be sure what words were exchanged at the conference, but at the end of it, Prescott decided to disregard his official orders and build his redoubt on Breed's Hill.

As you look up at Breed's Hill from the summit of Town Hill, you can see what an odd choice this was. Unlike its counterpart, Breed's was much squatter—only seventy-five feet tall—and well within the range of artillery from Royal Navy warships on the Charles River. It was closer to the British garrisons in Boston, and thus more easily surveilled and bombarded by them, and right by the center of Charlestown, exposing the town to much greater risk of destruction. But a fort atop Breed's Hill did have one advantage over one on Bunker Hill. It would put British warships within cannon range and expose the garrisons in the northern part of Boston to bombardment as well. So, in the dark early morning hours of June 17, Prescott ordered his men to dig.

Colonel Gridley oversaw the construction of a fortification with six-foot-high earthen walls, a rough square with each side running 136 feet. The troops worked through the night and into the morning to construct it and accomplished the task with surprising speed. The parapet encompassed a thick wall for protection from British cannonades, steps that helped soldiers fire over it, a sally port at the back to allow a quick escape if needed, and a line of breastworks running north to repel attacks from the east. It stood a half mile above the center of Charlestown with only a cart path to reach it. Colonel Prescott ultimately had 1,140 men to defend the position, including Captain Thomas Knowlton's two hundred volunteers from Connecticut.

Once the British high command spotted the rebel activity, there was some debate over how to proceed. General Clinton wanted either to cut off the neck of the Charlestown Peninsula and force the rebels to defend a siege, or to outflank them with attacks from both the Charles and Mystic Rivers, to the south and north of the peninsula. But General Howe, who would lead the assault, did not want to divide his forces or attack the rebels piecemeal. He wanted a direct engagement to prove the king's army could overwhelm any ragtag colonial army and to make up for their inability to do so at Concord.

Howe led a force of 2,400 British soldiers positioned in a broad arc on the eastern side of the peninsula, with the left flank of that force to climb the low slopes above Charlestown. To see what they encountered in the early afternoon of June 17, you'll have to leave Town Hill and make your way northeast across the high grass and tortured terrain of the battlefield itself.

Along the way, you may see damage to the landscape. A Royal Navy cannonade pummeled the terrain with bar shot and chain shot to maim and kill the infantry, and round shot from 24- and 18-pounder guns to shatter the fortifications. However, the guns could not breach the earthen walls, and the redoubt withstood most of the blows inflicted on it.

It was 95 degrees on a sweltering early summer day when Howe's men climbed the slope, encumbered by heavy knapsacks and other gear while wearing thick woolen coats and bearskin hats. As you'll see, it's very difficult terrain to cross, especially when making a frontal assault. Uncut hay prevented easy marching while bogs, potholes and divots, rail fences, and abandoned brick kilns forced the troops to scramble around them. By the time the British did get within musket range of their enemy, they faced a brutal onslaught.

Defensive fire from the redoubt cut down scores of them. Dead and injured, they fell into the hay and became new obstacles for troops in the rear to navigate around. Men broke up their ranks and crashed into each other, becoming prey for rebel sharpshooters, and officers in their colorful uniforms made for even riper targets. The troops also took fire from below, as patriot snipers occupied empty buildings in the town and shot any unwary soldiers who came within range.

British musket fire mostly went high and sheared off the limbs of treetops above the redoubt, while the defenders aimed low and usually found their mark. Surprisingly, rebel troops succeeded with almost no artillery support (due to a lack of functional cannon), even after defenders fled or were redeployed elsewhere, bringing their numbers down to six hundred—a quarter of Howe's forces.

Bostonians watched the spectacle across the Charles River from trees, rooftops, and hillsides, and may have even spotted Colonel Prescott defying death by jumping atop the parapet to shout encouragement to his men while cannonballs flew by him. As Colonel Josiah Willard, Prescott's loyalist brother-in-law, said to General Gage during the attack, "Prescott will fight you to the gates of hell." As Prescott himself said, "I will never be taken alive. The Tories shall never have the satisfaction of seeing me hanged."

Now stop and turn your attention back to the ruins of Charlestown. This was the point in the battle in which General Howe finally reached the limits of his patience with the snipers there. General Gage, in the weeks before the fighting, had already threatened the inhabitants with destruction should the rebel army occupy the town or allow works to be thrown up around it. The threat was enough to make most of them flee to the countryside. Now, encouraged by Admiral Graves, Howe made good on Gage's promise. He ordered his artillerymen to destroy it.

The Royal Navy unleashed superheated cannonballs to ignite anything they could hit, while the batteries atop Copp's Hill fired at the mostly wooden buildings with "carcass balls"—a combustible mix of gunpowder, saltpeter, pitch, and tallow. Before long, most of the shops, distilleries, shipyards, warehouses, and private homes were on fire, with the meetinghouse steeple a pillar of flame above them all. General Burgoyne saw "great pyramids of fire" spreading throughout the town, while the Royal Marines torched buildings the artillery hadn't yet destroyed. Soldiers watched in astonishment as an immense cloud of black smoke rose above the battlefield and a rain of cinders fell for miles around. As patriot army surgeon James Thacher saw it:

> Fire was communicated to a number of houses, which, being wafted by the wind, soon reached the sacred temple, when the flames issued from its lofty spire; while from the conflagration and the embattled field, smoke mingled with smoke in majestic columns, and ascended to the clouds. This, with the roaring of cannon, sheets of fire from the musketry, and the awful slaughter, formed a spectacle, which for sublimity and grandeur has never perhaps been exceeded.

Only fifteen houses near the Charlestown Neck survived the inferno, along with grave markers at the cemetery, cattle fences and stone walls, and a few farm buildings. But Howe failed to achieve his objective with the incineration. The patriot snipers simply relocated to an abandoned barn and kept shooting at the attackers.

By mid-afternoon, the temperature was roasting—from the burning town, the hot weather, and the general heat of combat. The British army had failed in its initial assault, and things had been even worse at the center and right flank of Howe's army. To see what they experienced, keep walking through the hay and obstacles of the slopes below Breed's Hill until you pivot northward to the brick kilns at the foot of Morton's Hill.

It was here where Howe and his staff first saw that the defenses of the rebel army amounted to more than they expected. They came to the realization just before the initial attack on the redoubt, while trying to outflank the enemy position by deploying along the Mystic River. Instead of seeing an open field and shoreline, they saw a new defense line the patriots had erected in only a few hours.

Keep walking west along the Mystic and you can see the remains of it. At first, it may be hard to tell that there's much of a defense line at all, just an old rail fence to keep cattle hemmed in and a low-lying wall of rocks on the shore. It's nothing like the formidable earthwork atop Breed's Hill, and it might not be much of a barrier at all for any army that had done the proper reconnaissance and preparation. But this was not the British army on the afternoon of June 17.

Howe actually had to pause his battle plans to assess how to handle the unexpected obstacles. (It didn't help that many of his field guns at Morton's Point had been supplied with overly large cannonballs, thus rendering them useless for this phase of the attack.) The rail fence was perhaps the more familiar impediment: wooden farm posts and rails that rebels had stuffed with dirt, rocks, and hay to make for a more robust defensive position, with a ditch stretching in front of it, from the beach up to the northern slopes of Breed's Hill. But the low stone wall on the shoreline was something else entirely: a few courses of cobbles only about knee high that any soldier with two functioning legs could step over with ease.

Colonel John Stark had ordered his New Hampshire volunteers to create the wall after they'd arrived as reinforcements. He expected an assault by way of the Mystic River and used whatever materials he could to protect against it, lining up his men in triple ranks behind the stones to surprise the attackers when they arrived.

The tactic worked. The Royal Welch Fusiliers, the light infantry assigned the task of assaulting the position, approached to within fifty yards of the wall before Stark's troops hit them with a hail of lead balls. The three lines of men fired in sequence, rapidly and almost continuously, to fell many of the fusiliers at waist or leg level until their bodies littered the beach in their royal blue uniforms. A second assault proved just as deadly, until four out of every five in the unit were either dead or injured.

Closer to the rail fence, the rebels used similar tactics and fired up to ten rounds per minute—an unheard-of rate of speed. To plug a gap in the breastworks, they constructed "fleches," V-shaped structures built of rails, dirt, and sticks that not only provided defensive cover but allowed patriot troops to shoot from multiple angles. General Putnam even came down from Bunker Hill, where his own troops were positioned, to direct the use of a single cannon to blast away at Howe's men with shocking effectiveness.

Howe himself was one of the few around him left standing, his uniform splattered with blood and gore from the wounds of his staff members. He saw hundreds of well-trained grenadiers strafed by musket fire and fail to get close to the rebel works. To protect themselves, some British soldiers even resorted to piling up the bodies of their fallen comrades and hiding behind the ghoulish mound as "a horrid breastwork to fire from."

Monitoring the scene behind patriot lines, Colonel Prescott was encouraged by his troops' success but remained unsettled. He knew the men lacked not only numbers to counter the attackers but also ammunition, so he shifted his firepower from one flank to the other, taking advantage of the British not assaulting the works in coordination. The desperate strategy worked and, in combination with the other tactics, caused the enemy to lose between eight and nine hundred men and remove more than two-thirds of the British force from action. If the battle had ended at this point, it would have been a decisive patriot victory. But Howe had more reinforcements on the way, and instead of withdrawing to the safety of Boston, he decided to summon the troops that remained and order another assault on Breed's Hill.

As you stand on the beach of the Mystic River, or on the slopes below the redoubt, try to imagine the carnage the British troops witnessed. The bodies have been taken away, but enough remains of the scarred landscape to tell the story. Along the hillside, you may find spent ammunition or a cannonball or two, and the degraded rail fence still speaks to the strength and tenacity of the rebels. Now ascend Breed's Hill closer to the redoubt to take in the final act of the battle and how the British turned what might have been shameful defeat into a costly victory.

It was by this time late in the afternoon when Joseph Warren arrived at the fortification. He'd been roused from his sickbed in Cambridge, where he'd been suffering from a headache and exhaustion, to go to the battle site, grab a musket, and serve in the infantry. Though he'd been promoted to major general and was also president of the Provincial Congress, Warren said it would be an honor to serve under Colonel Prescott as a common soldier. He promised that thousands more reinforcements were on their way to support the defensive action.

Those troops never arrived. Instead, Prescott would have to rely on his now battle-hardened militiamen to keep the British grenadiers at bay. The defenders were down to 150 men, and their ammunition was running very low. The colonel told them to conserve it until the British were only fifteen yards from them, and to prepare bayonets in case the attackers made it over the parapet and into the redoubt.

General Howe, watching from below, knew that a failure in the next assault would likely result in a catastrophic loss and another black mark against the British military. He ordered his men to remove their knapsacks and other encumbrances. Some grenadiers took the initiative to toss aside their heavy red coats as well. He had only a thousand troops left in fighting condition, to face an unknown number of defenders with an unclear amount of ammunition. Some expected that going up the hill one more time might result in the worst slaughter yet, but most of the soldiers accepted their duty.

In looking up at the hill that rises before you, try to imagine how grim conditions had become. The air was hot and the skies black with smoke, and most of the attackers were exhausted or at least discouraged. Not only had they lost a significant amount of comrades, but once again, they would face rebel muskets loaded with lead balls as well as buckshot known as "Yankee peas," to add to the bloody effect.

Howe rearranged his troops into a formation of lengthy columns only eight men wide and ordered them to march. They reached their closest distance yet before they heard the crack of musket fire. The first row of the column went down and as more followed them, men in the second and third and rows also fell. But the column of grenadiers kept coming until it reached the parapet wall. One man thought he heard patriots inside calling for more powder, that they were running out, and this inspired a last desperate charge.

Yelling, "Fight, conquer or die!" the British breached the parapet and descended on the defenders full of brutal energy. The rebels and grenadiers engaged in close combat inside the redoubt, stabbing each other with bayonets, cutting with swords, flailing with knives and hatchets, fighting with anything they had, from musket butts and rocks to fists.

It was a contest of 1,000 versus 150. As more and more defenders fell, and as the Royal Navy broke up the breastworks with artillery fire, Prescott knew his troops couldn't hold out much longer and ordered a fighting retreat. The rebels left through the sally port and made their way off Breed's Hill in a steady withdrawal. Colonel Stark repositioned his volunteers from the rail fence and used cannon and musket fire to cover the retreat. Even more attackers went down in the pursuit of the patriots and added to the casualty count.

Many of the defenders died, but only thirty were captured. Colonel Prescott and other officers made their way to safety with various injuries, but the exception was Major General Warren. Less than sixty yards outside the redoubt, he took a blast to the head and died in the field. The British would mutilate his body and dump it in a shallow grave, where it would lie for almost a year, until their evacuation in March 1776. It was then that Paul Revere helped dig up the patriot hero, identifying him by an ivory tooth he'd installed in Warren's mouth just a few months before the battle, as his dentist.

There's not much left of the redoubt these days. You may see some mounded earth and a later fortification built by the British, but by and large, the summit is bleak and windswept, a faded emblem of war that's nothing like a tourist destination. And Bunker Hill itself is even less so. Continue northwest along the peninsula and you'll come to its slopes a half mile away. The height may be imposing, but the main contribution the hill made to the battle named for it was as a place for militiamen to provide cover fire for the rebel retreat. In an ironic touch, only after the British seized control of Bunker Hill did a proper fortification finally get built on top of it—a defensive colossus with magazines, barracks, guardhouses, entrenchments, and bastions. But the Americans never dared to storm it, and the king's troops departed from it in March 1776.

In the aftermath of the battle near Bunker Hill, Colonel Prescott asked the Provincial Congress for another 1,500 men to return to the Charlestown Peninsula and reconquer the lost territory. Henry Clinton pushed for an attack on Cambridge to seal the victory and send the rebels into disarray. But neither Artemus Ward nor Thomas Gage had the stomach for another bloody engagement, so the sides dug in, and the siege of Boston began.

In the end, the American defenders of Breed's Hill took 440 casualties, nearly one-third of the troops engaged, and the British attackers suffered 1,054 losses—almost half of the troops in the field, with one soldier killed or wounded for every acre of ground captured. In Boston, the streets filled with wounded and dying men of the British army, and many taverns, private homes, and public buildings became infirmaries and makeshift hospitals. One observer called it "the most melancholy scene ever beheld in this part of the world. The Saturday night and Sabbath were taken up in carrying over the dead and wounded, and all the wood-carts in town, it is said, were employed—chaises and coaches for the officers. They have taken the workhouse, almshouse, and manufactory-house, for the wounded."

In Charlestown, any buildings that had escaped firebombing were systematically torched to prevent rebels from occupying them, or were dismantled for firewood for the coming winter. At least two thousand residents were left homeless and £117,000 assessed as damages to property, though, in most cases, no compensation was given. Almost none of the thirty Americans taken as prisoners survived by the end of summer, due to their cruel treatment in custody.

In a note of triumph, King George III said, after the battle, "The die is now cast, the Colonies must either submit or triumph." But Thomas Gage's view was more pessimistic: "The loss we have sustained here is greater than we can bear." Patriots throughout the colonies had a mixed view, seeing their own troops as heroic for fending off the king's army through pluck, guile, and bravery, yet doubting the ability of leaders like Artemus Ward to command them with any degree of competence. But with George Washington on the way to take command of a new and reorganized Continental Army, many hoped for a more favorable outcome in the months ahead.

That outcome, as it turned out, would be helped greatly by General Gage himself. Because, only days after the slaughter at Bunker Hill, he canceled the planned assault on Dorchester Heights, reasoning that his naval guns had enough firepower to control the heights if needed and that the greater threat lay in a patriot invasion via the Boston Neck. It turned out to be a false assumption, and one that would have a dramatic impact on the next round of fighting in Roxbury and Dorchester, and the ultimate evacuation of British troops from Boston.

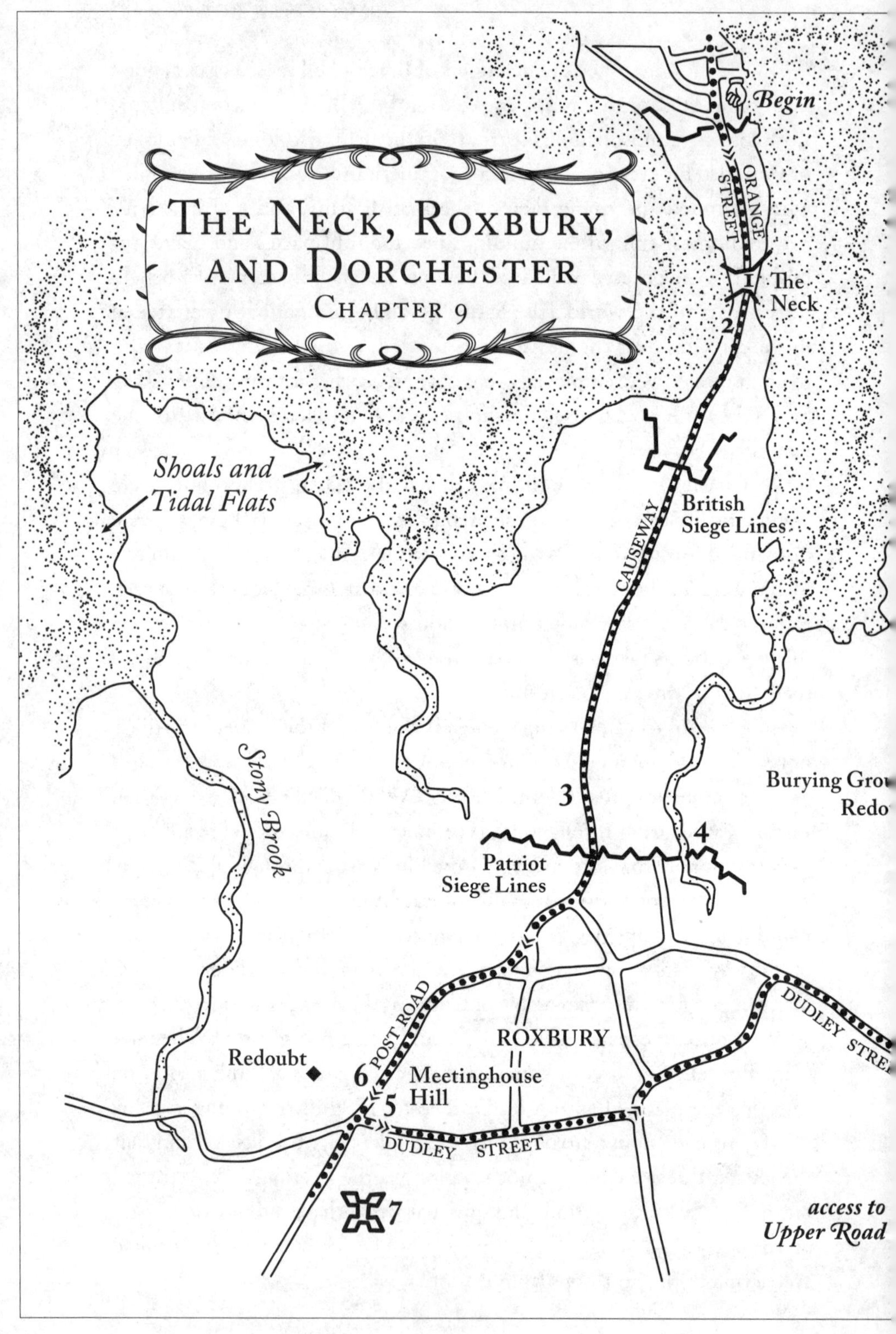
The Neck, Roxbury, and Dorchester
Chapter 9
Begin
Orange Street
1
The Neck
2
Causeway
British Siege Lines
Shoals and Tidal Flats
Stony Brook
3
4
Burying Grou
Redo
Patriot Siege Lines
Post Road
Roxbury
Dudley Street
Redoubt
6
5
Meetinghouse Hill
Dudley Street
7
access to Upper Road

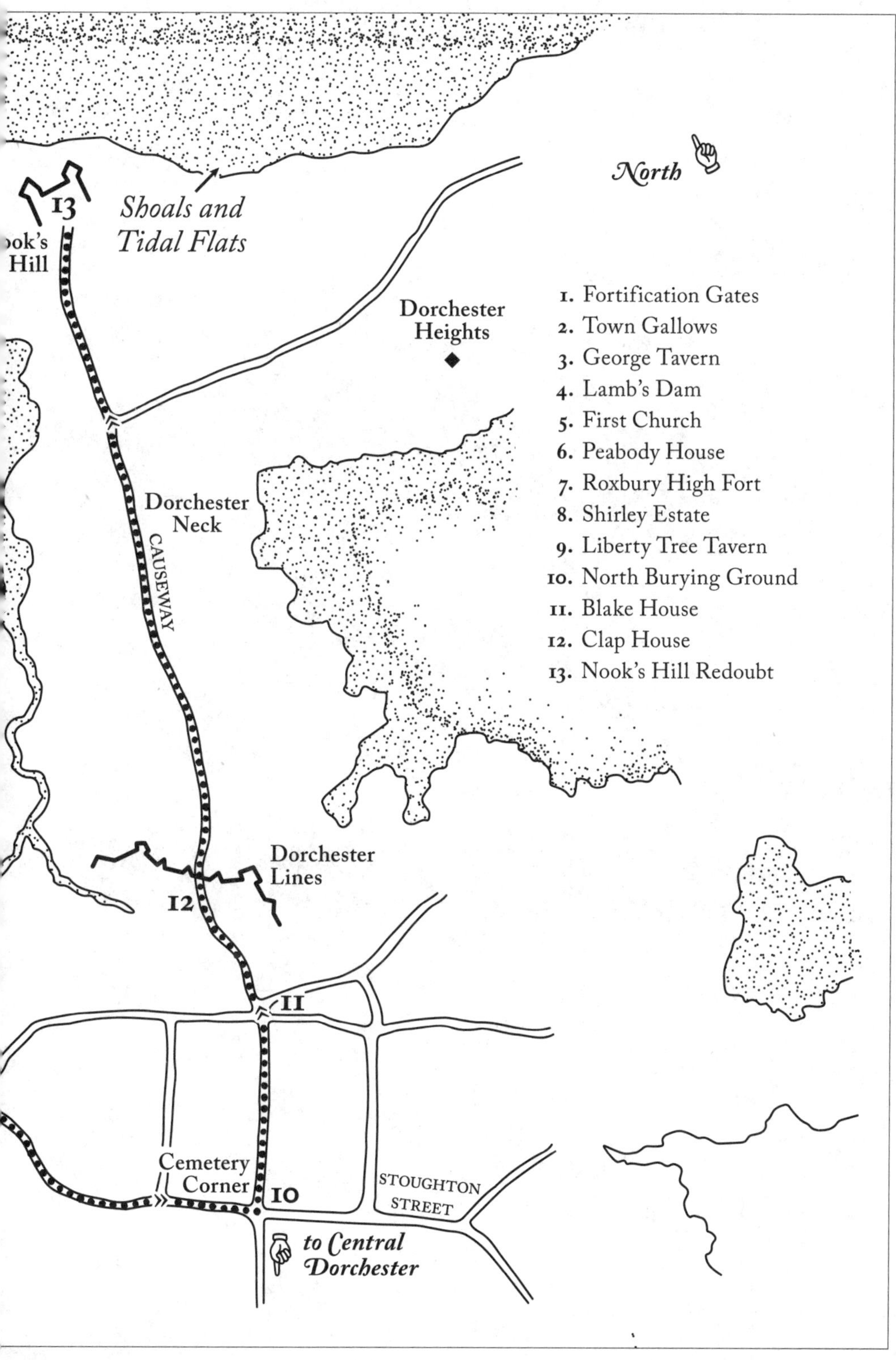

North
Shoals and Tidal Flats
13
ook's Hill
Dorchester Heights
1. Fortification Gates
2. Town Gallows
3. George Tavern
4. Lamb's Dam
5. First Church
6. Peabody House
7. Roxbury High Fort
8. Shirley Estate
9. Liberty Tree Tavern
10. North Burying Ground
11. Blake House
12. Clap House
13. Nook's Hill Redoubt
Dorchester Neck
CAUSEWAY
Dorchester Lines
12
11
Cemetery Corner
10
STOUGHTON STREET
to Central Dorchester

☆ 9 ☆

The Boston Neck, Roxbury, and Dorchester

If you were to design an ideal city, you probably would not strand it on a peninsula connected to the mainland by only a narrow, windswept, often underwater land bridge. Yet, when God and nature conspired to create the landscape that would become Boston, that is exactly what they did, surrounding the site with water and linking it to the mainland with only a thin isthmus that would come to be known as the Boston Neck. The isthmus is both a no-man's-land and a vital military corridor, where, during the siege, the Continental Army severed overland supply lines and reduced the British-occupied town to a state of penury and starvation. You can see the wider impact as you venture south of the Neck into the town of Roxbury, now itself severed with siege lines and disfigured by war, and into Dorchester, where the siege ended with one of the most daring military exploits of recent history.

To explore the Boston Neck, head south on Orange Street from the Liberty Tree. Here, the number of shipyards, taverns, and wharfs begins to thin out, and the shoreline creeps toward you from both sides. Soon you'll find yourself on the isthmus, only fifty yards wide, with the tidal flats of the Charles River to the west and a harbor channel to the east. Don't arrive during a storm, when wind-spray will blow in your eyes and numb your skin, or during high tide, when the water will top your bootlaces or even crest at your knees. Foul weather especially punishes the cobbled roadway, leaving it submerged or washed away in places.

Once you've traveled a few more blocks, you'll reach the Fortification Gates, the remnants of a formidable barrier that Puritan Boston erected to protect itself from Indian attack in the seventeenth century. The original design, still visible under recent modifications, includes brick and stone walls with dual gates for pedestrians and wheeled vehicles. The parapet is twelve feet thick, with platforms for cannon pointing southward. During the occupation, British sentries would man the gates, question travelers, and inspect their loads. Sometimes, army deserters would attempt to sneak through as well, and could face execution if they were caught in the attempt.

The most famous event to occur at the Fortification Gates was the passage of William Dawes on the evening of April 18, 1775. He was a tanner who made regular appearances here bringing goods by cart and wagon, and he was a Whig trusted by Joseph Warren, one of the few patriot leaders left in town. Warren had learned of General Gage's plans to burn the military stores at Concord, and he needed several men to convey the news to the countryside. Paul Revere would be one, arranging lantern signals at Christ Church before rowing to Charlestown to begin his midnight ride (see p. 168), while Dawes would be the other, carrying the message by way of the Neck.

Dawes arrived on a slow horse hauling saddlebags, dressed like a farmer in a floppy hat. Luckily, he knew the guard stationed at the gates that night and managed to talk his way through as if he were on a journey for his business. He passed over the Neck and made his way to Roxbury, Brookline, and Cambridge before eventually reaching Lexington a half hour after Revere did, taking three hours to travel seventeen miles in the dark countryside among British spies and sentries.

The Neck soon took on a vital military importance. After the battles of Lexington and Concord, General Gage moved many of his regiments into town and strengthened the Fortification Gates. He negotiated with the Committee of Safety so civilians could leave the Shawmut Peninsula, provided they turned in their weapons and swore not to join the Continental Army, and he arranged for loyalists to return from exile. On their way out, the townsfolk relinquished 1,800 muskets, 600 pistols, and 1,000 bayonets, while incoming allies of the Crown occupied their old homes or took ownership of vacant ones. Soon, though, Gage tightened the rules, requiring those who departed to leave behind property or a family member as a sort of collateral. By June, they could only flee if they had smallpox or were destitute. This policy left seven thousand Bostonians trapped.

Parliament did allow the shipment of food and medicine by water, but Gage forbade it, so all traffic had to go through the Neck. This clogged up the isthmus with wagons and carts, and it greatly reduced the supply of food and other essentials. Those given clearance to pass through the gates were the picture of misery, hauling the few possessions they were allowed to bring and suffering from disease and hunger. Merchant John Andrews saw "the streets and Neck lined with wagons carrying off the effects of the inhabitants, who are either afraid, mad, crazy, or infatuated, imagining to themselves that they shall be liable to every evil that can be enumerated if they tarry in town." Most became refugees, staying with friends or family in the region or living off charity.

As the number of Bostonians allowed to leave became ever fewer, Gage strengthened the army's position on the Neck until it became almost impregnable. You can see this fortified complex alongside the old gates: multiple lines of entrenchments, ramparts, and bastions, with platforms for 24-pounder and other cannon, six howitzers, and a mortar battery. A trench has been cut to allow seawater to flow through, slicing off the Neck and making Boston technically an island. In the tidal flats, abatis and pits with upturned stakes prevented amphibious assault, and 6-pounder naval guns sat atop nearby flatboats in the Charles River for additional firepower.

As impressive as these fortifications seem to be, they no longer serve a function since the redcoats evacuated in March. Still, enough remains of the site that you can see just how much money and effort the British invested in hardening the Neck, and how concerned Gage was about an overland attack after the Battle of Bunker Hill—not appreciating the greatest threat to his army stood in the heights of Dorchester to the southeast, as we'll see later in the chapter.

South of the fortifications, don't expect to find scenery any more appealing; instead, you'll see the town gallows. While people have been hanged in various places in Boston's history, this scaffold is something of an institution, a place for the authorities to put criminals to death and for radicals to stage protests, symbolically hanging both their enemies and their ideas. In the 1760s, gang leaders from the North and South Ends came here after a night of violent revels to burn effigies of popes and devils; and during the year of the Stamp Act riots, they joined in truce to destroy dummies of enemies like a Parliamentarian and a prime minister. Radical patriots also intimidated customs agents and spies by hauling them to the gallows and tying a rope around their necks, sometimes adding a whipping or a tarring-and-feathering to make their point.

Mostly, though, the gallows has been the place where the judicial system has meted out capital punishment to convicted criminals. On execution day, the authorities will bind the condemned in a cart on a journey along the major streets, stopping at the scene of the crime along the way. Once at the gallows, residents will gather to hear the sheriff read out the death warrant and a minister deliver an execution sermon. The condemned himself may then give a speech admitting his guilt and offering repentance or, in some cases, defying the judgment against him and vowing he has never committed any such crime. If he's lucky, he'll receive a pardon from a higher official, yet clemency is rarely granted, and pardons sometimes arrive after the condemned drops from the scaffold.

The crowd will greet the execution with a mix of fascination and trepidation, though for children whose parents have brought them here to impart a moral lesson, horror is the most common reaction. Once the deed is done, the executioner will strike down the body from the noose, and family members will take away their loved one to be buried. If the condemned is not well loved, gravediggers will find a place for the corpse in a field near the gallows. The soggy turf around this part of the Neck also holds the bodies of those who have killed themselves and were denied a Christian burial, since suicide is a grievous sin in Congregational teaching.

If the spectacle is dramatic enough, or the criminal's act especially notorious, you may see broadsides appearing throughout town with eyewitness accounts, or even songs and poems, about the event; and ministers will publish their execution sermons to ensure they receive a wide readership. Less than three years ago, one such execution became the most popular in the town's history, with half of all residents turning out to witness the death of Levi Ames. According to a broadside, "the terrors of a frowning God" and "Hell's Eternal pain" awaited Ames for the crime for which he'd been condemned—burglary.

Other than actual criminals, the gallows have served as the execution site for heretics and dissenters who incurred the disfavor of colonial officials. In the 1650s, Quakers like Mary Dyer became martyrs for their refusal to be expelled from the community or to keep quiet about their beliefs (see p. 76), while accused witches like Ann Hibbins faced execution on the thinnest of evidence. Due to her supposed "turbulent and quarrelsome" nature, the wealthy widow's neighbors charged her with witchcraft: "The jury brought her in guilty, but the magistrates refused to accept the verdict; so the cause came to the General Court, where the popular clamor prevailed against her, and the miserable woman was condemned and executed."

Unless you have a morbid flair, it's best not to loiter at the gallows, so continue south along the Neck past cattle pastures and a few industrial sites like a brickyard, salt works, and clay pond. The road here is unpaved, unlike the section north of the fortifications, and walking can be a slog over the mud, especially when the tide comes up. The scenery is also quite grim, littered with the remains of houses and barns destroyed during the siege. Only five structures survived the crossfire, a faint reminder of the few dozen families once bold enough to live along the Neck. One of those families was the Perrys, who operated a sort of boardinghouse for outcasts the authorities had "warned out" of town at the risk of prosecution. Many were strolling poor with just enough money to stay the night or travelers looking for a stopover before continuing on their way. It was a helpful service, but the Perrys and their boardinghouse have long since vanished, so you'll have no luck finding a place to rest—not that you should want one.

The Neck has the well-earned reputation of being the site of assaults and robberies, with unwary travelers subject to a club to the head or a knife in the ribs. Some of these tales are invented, but enough crimes have occurred that you should be quick in your step through this mile-long passage and always consider the risk before you make the attempt. According to one observer, the place is "desolate and forbidding in the extreme, especially to a nocturnal traveller."

Once you reach the southern end of the Neck, you'll find the remnants of one of Boston's largest drinking emporiums. The George Tavern was a massive complex set on eighteen acres with orchards and gardens and fine views of the harbor, plus workshops and rooms for lodging. In 1721, it even housed the General Court while the rest of Boston faced a smallpox epidemic. In later years, it offered grand feasts and entertainment that included men standing on horses' backs while they galloped at full speed and an outdoor enclosure for the blood sport of bull baiting, in which the great beast would be tethered to a rope while a team of vicious dogs tried to bite it to death and spectators wagered on the outcome. The bulls found relief from their suffering on July 30, 1775, when the British army burned the complex on their retreat northward up the Neck.

Adjacent to the tavern site is the advanced line of the American siege works. It's part of an impressive system of defense running twelve miles from Brookline to Dorchester, a collection of entrenchments and redoubts protected by abatis—tree branches sharpened into outward-facing spikes. At their closest point, the British and American lines stood only eight hundred yards apart, too far for accurate musket fire but well within the range of cannon and mortar. The works in some areas are seventeen feet thick, so if you don't find a breach, you may have to convince a guard to let you through. From that point you'll enter into the town of Roxbury to see how this charming old hamlet has survived the war.

It's not a pretty sight these days. The siege lines cut right through the middle of town, severing the central streets with fortifications stretching from Lamb's Dam on the eastern edge to Meetinghouse Hill in the center and Stony Brook to the west. Even the cemetery has been fortified as the Burying-Ground Redoubt. Troops in the Continental Army once lodged by the thousands in tents and barracks in town, but most have since moved on to follow General Washington to fend off the anticipated British attack on New York City.

It's difficult to approach the town with the mind of a tourist, but there are some historic details worth knowing. Roxbury was named for its rocky soil, largely puddingstone, and settled by a group of Puritans in search of a haven for their budding theocracy. Two prominent hills flank each side of town, while "dismal swamps" and tidal flats mark the upper boundary. The streams in the vicinity run rich with smelt, and the springs are known for their tastiness. As one early visitor reported, "I never drank wine in my life that more refreshed me, nor was more pleasant to me as I then absolutely thought."

Despite its name, Roxbury became famed for its productive soil, which allowed its residents to grow ample crops and cultivate fruit trees in great orchards. They built houses of heavy oaken timbers and planking, with two stories and one to two rooms on each, and windows of small leaded-glass panes or oiled paper sheets. (A few of the better dwellings sport gambrel roofs and twin chimneys.) These days, most houses near the front have structural damage from cannon fire or broken windows from explosions, much of the greenery has been stripped or trampled, and a hundred of the once-prized apple trees have been felled to become rows of sharpened spikes.

Roxbury has suffered £24,412 worth of damage. When Abigail Adams came to visit, she was shocked by the conditions you see before you, writing to John, "Roxbury looks more injured than Boston, that is, the houses look more torn to pieces. I was astonished at the extent of our lines and their strength." Another writer put it in more detail:

> Nothing struck me with more horror than the present condition of Roxbury. That once busy, crowded street is now occupied only by a picket-guard. The houses are deserted, the windows taken out, and many shot-holes visible. Some have been burnt, and others pulled down to make room for the fortifications. A wall of earth is carried across the street to [an] old house, where there is a formidable fort mounted with cannon.

There's less damage farther to the west. Follow the post road, which leads to Dedham, to see the Congregational meetinghouse, First Church, standing on Meetinghouse Hill. Here, a green space called Roxbury Common hosted civic meetings while the stately home of Governor Thomas Dudley stood nearby. The governor's estate, unfortunately, was a bit too close to the siege lines, so the Continental Army dismantled it and used its brick basement walls to build up their earthworks. Yet the meetinghouse on the hill remains.

This is the fourth version of a church on site, with a large, flat, circular stone in front of the facade, a wooden frame supporting a tower and belfry, and the familiar box pews inside. The first incarnation of the church dated from 1632, when residents were required to live within a half mile of it to make the community easier to defend from Indian attacks, and all men had to attend worship services armed with a musket or other weapon. Worship has now been suspended due to the war, and the structure acts as an army signal station, its role evident from the scars of bomb damage on the walls.

Across the street is another example of how Roxbury's religious buildings have been reconfigured for war. This fine house, with its gambrel roof, abundant windows, and three dormers, was built as a parsonage for Reverend Oliver Peabody, and was put to more recent use by General John Thomas, who commanded the right wing of Washington's army. Thomas, with more combat experience than nearly any other American officer, lodged here and took advantage of the excellent views from its top floor to survey Boston Harbor and Dorchester Heights. His troops constructed the works atop those heights during a single night in March 1776 (see p. 194), before he unexpectedly died three months later of smallpox.

From here, military enthusiasts may wish to venture a half-mile south along the post road to the Roxbury High Fort, a European-style bastion built by Henry Knox as one of the most formidable structures in the region. It's a rough square with bastions at each corner, sitting atop the highest hill in town, with sweeping views of the region. Washington thought it the best of all the works in the defense line. You won't be able to get too close, but, even from a distance, it's worth a look to survey the quality of military architecture in New England in 1776.

If you have no interest in the fort, head east on Dudley Street from Meetinghouse Hill to leave Roxbury. Outside of town, intersecting paths and lanes lead north to salt pans and tidal flats, as well as the kind of businesses that have often been banned in Boston: tanneries, slaughterhouses, chocolate mills, and other operations seen as noxious, malodorous, or incendiary. After a mile, however, the scenery changes and you'll reach the estate of former Governor William Shirley.

Standing on a parcel of thirty-three acres, the house was built in 1747 with oaken beams and bricks of multiple sizes shipped from Britain at great expense. It features a lovely symmetry in the style of sixteenth-century Italian architect Andrea Palladio, wooden pilasters with Corinthian capitals, and a hipped roof topped with an observatory. If you were to visit the two-story mansion at the height of its prestige, you'd have walked over stone steps flanked by iron railings and entered the premises to find a grand staircase, hallways tiled with marble, fireplaces adorned with Dutch tiles, and a commanding vantage of the town and harbor, while enjoying musicians performing for guests on a balcony. Outside, you'd see twin piazzas, a majestic lawn with surrounding ponds and brooks, and gardens abundant with fruit trees and flower beds.

Governor Shirley was best known for engineering the capture of the French fort at Louisbourg during King George's War, but otherwise, patriots recall his tenure in office unfavorably. He oversaw the demise of the Land Bank, which Parliament dissolved in 1741, leaving farmers and smallholders without a source of paper currency and families like Samuel Adams's in economic distress (see p. 159). And he was in power during Boston's impressment crisis of 1747, when the Royal Navy's habit of abducting mariners from Boston's streets and docks resulted in rioting (prefiguring similar crises in 1768 and after). His turn as commander of British forces in North America ended in failure in the Fort Niagara expedition, and he fell from power, later becoming governor of the Bahamas before returning home and dying in 1771. After Shirley's death, the house came into the hands of a loyalist, but it was later confiscated from him, and, during the siege, General Thomas's troops used it as a barracks before they marched to Dorchester Heights. If you gain access, you'll find most of the furnishings damaged, the rooms rearranged or ransacked, and the lawn and gardens in no better shape than the rest of Roxbury.

From here, you have two options: the first is to head south to reach the public highway known as the Upper Road, which runs toward the Milton River (aka the Neponset River), where there are mills for paper, grist, and chocolate and other industrial works. After three miles, you'll reach Fuller Street and come across the Liberty Tree Tavern (aka Robinson's Tavern), a two-story farmhouse surrounded by fields and pastures. At this friendly pub, the Sons of Liberty used to throw massive parties on the August 14 anniversary of the Stamp Act riots. The most notable such festivity came in 1769, when more than three hundred Sons rode here in a mile-long procession of 137 carriages, coming to feast on three barbecued pigs as cannons fired and flags flew. They sang merry songs and offered forty-five toasts to the likes of radical Parliamentarian John Wilkes, historian Catharine

Macaulay, and the Glorious 92 assemblymen who refused to rescind their names from a letter against the Townshend Acts. The Sons made sure to add condemnation toasts to their enemies like importers of British goods and "State pirates, thieves, robbers and traitors," and promised "strong halters, firm blocks, and sharp axes to all such as deserve either." John Adams attended and said of the event, "This is cultivating the Sensations of Freedom."

The second option from the Shirley mansion is to continue on Dudley Street as it curves around fields and pastures until it becomes Stoughton Street and reaches the onetime focus of settlement at Cemetery Corner (later Upham's Corner). This inauspicious name refers to the adjacent North Burying Ground that holds the bodies of early Puritan settlers. They came here in June 1630—a few months before the establishment of Boston—largely from Dorset, England, to build a home in the wilderness. Actually, the Massachusett people had settled here long before them, but the Puritans introduced smallpox to the native tribe and killed many of them before securing the land title with treaties and claiming the area as Dorchester Plantation.

In the vicinity, there are about 200 houses that are home to 1,300 people, though many of these residents have left to avoid the war; only a smaller group of die-hards remains. The most interesting relic is the James Blake House, five blocks north, a two-story, gabled-roof structure with heavy timber frames built in 1661. The owner was a deacon, constable, and selectman whose farm and tannery sat on ten acres, with attractive orchards and a garden. It's since been subdivided by his heirs and its trees cut down for abatis for the Continental Army.

First Parish Church, an old log-cabin meetinghouse, was once nearby, but the congregation has relocated and built a new church a mile south. Rather than going in that direction, make your way north from the Blake House along the causeway that leads to Dorchester Heights. You'll first see the charming house of Lemuel Clap, an elegant two-story affair with a gambrel roof, whose tanner owner now serves as a captain in the local militia. The house has the misfortune of only being a block away from a sizable earthwork the locals have built to ward off the British, and the building itself is often filled with soldiers, so don't come expecting an open door. Instead, try to talk your way past the militiamen stationed at the works and follow the causeway up the Dorchester Neck, where you'll be rewarded with a magnificent vista and a keen insight into how the Continental Army forced British troops out of Boston.

The journey, needless to say, can be a challenge. The Dorchester Neck isn't as narrow as the Boston Neck, but it's just as sodden. The causeway crosses a cow pasture and marshes and leads past the shattered remains of orchards until you get to a rocky shelf ascending to a pair of drumlins. These hills are composed of glacial sediment about 140 feet high, close to the level of Beacon Hill but more striking since they stand alone southeast of Boston, at an elevation that proved critical to the military success of the rebels.

The story of Dorchester Heights begins in May 1775 in New York, where the combined forces of Ethan Allen and Benedict Arnold captured Fort Ticonderoga and Crown Point and, with them, sixty cannon, howitzers, and mortars. The rebel army had a better use for them around Boston, where the British army was encamped, and patriots were short on firepower to evict them. So twenty-five-year-old Henry Knox volunteered to transport the weapons from the forts to the front lines. He was a former bookseller turned artillery officer who learned most of what he knew from the pages of military and engineering volumes he carried in his shop (see p. 71). Despite having less than six months of wartime experience, Knox gained the trust of George Washington, who allowed him to make the attempt.

Knox arrived in New York in early December 1775. He and his men removed the guns from their stone embrasures with chisels and sledgehammers while packing up thousands of musket balls and hundreds of cannon balls as well. They secured the heavy artillery onto boats to ferry them over Lake George, finding it a challenge to keep the vessels afloat with water overlapping the decks. After reaching shore, they lashed the weapons to forty-two ox- and horse-drawn sleds to transport them amid high winds and miserable conditions. They encountered blizzards and had to push through three-foot-deep snowdrifts. They ventured across iced-over rivers only to have some of the sleds break the ice and sink into the chilly waters, from which they had to be rescued. Worst of all, they had to pass over mountains, using ropes and chains tied around tree trunks to ascend the slopes, and block and tackle to descend them. The teams crossed the Hudson River to cheers from locals and traveled into Massachusetts via post roads and

Indian trails, occasionally offering demonstrations of the cannons' firepower to onlookers who toasted the spectacle. After they deposited the guns at Framingham, Knox went on to Washington's headquarters in Cambridge and informed the general of what his men had accomplished—hauling sixty tons of weaponry over three hundred miles in forty days. Knox then learned he'd been promoted to artillery colonel.

With the feat accomplished, Washington had the guns he needed for an assault on the occupying British forces. He proposed an attack from Cambridge across the frozen Charles River, deploying four thousand Continentals against British garrisons on the Common and Barton's Point. However, the general's war council argued strongly against it, imagining the high odds of disaster when attempting an amphibious assault against nearly nine thousand hardened redcoats. So Washington reluctantly acceded to their preference to fortify the heights of Dorchester, which General Gage had left unoccupied since making his critical decision to fortify Boston instead, after the brutal fighting on the Charlestown Peninsula during the previous June.

But first, Washington needed a distraction. On March 4, he ordered the patriot artillery to begin a cannonade of 18- and 24-pounder guns that fired shot and shell into British camps from positions at Lechmere Point east of Cambridge and Lamb's Dam at Roxbury. The bombardment damaged buildings throughout Boston and could be heard and felt throughout the region. Abigail Adams at the family home in Braintree saw the walls shake and listened to the roar of explosions, but she also knew a decisive moment in the war was coming, writing to John, "I hope to give you joy of Boston, even if it is in ruins."

For Selectman Henry Newell, the cannonade felt "as if heaven and earth were engaged" as multiple rounds of fire sent the British forces running for cover and provided a useful screen for Washington's primary aim—to drag Knox's guns up the drumlins of Dorchester and secure a decisive advantage over the enemy. To that end, he planned to fortify Nook's Hill, which looked out at Boston and the Shawmut Peninsula; and Strawberry Hill and Middle Hill, which sat in range of Castle Island.

As you climb the rocky slope of Nook's Hill, you begin to get a sense of the audacity of Washington's gambit. This isn't easy ground to cross on foot, let alone with teams of oxen and horses hauling tons of supplies and weaponry. But despite the challenge, on the night of March 4 and the morning of March 5, the Continental Army made the attempt.

In the first wave, General John Thomas oversaw the deployment of 800 troops who occupied the hills to make ready for the larger operation to come. In the second wave, 1,200 men brought up a series of "chandeliers": timber frames filled with bundled sticks called fascines and packets of stone and gravel. These had been prepared in Milton to provide the building blocks for fortifications—not strong enough to counter a cannonade but sufficient to deter small arms fire and make an impression on the enemy.

Four hundred ox-drawn wagons and carts hauled the chandeliers under cover of darkness, while support troops laid hay bales alongside the vehicles to create a blind to ensure British military scouts wouldn't see what the patriot army was trying to accomplish. The ground was frozen to a depth of several feet, and walking on it was surprisingly noisy. So, to cover the racket of the train of draft animals, troops laid straw across the causeway to dampen the sound and wound wisps of plant fiber around the wheels. The ongoing blasts of the cannonade also proved helpful, to deafen anyone who might hear the rustle of troops trying to build the forts.

Dray horses brought up the prized possessions—Knox's New York cannons—while artillerymen secured them onto wooden platforms and aimed them at the harbor and peninsula. All the while, teams of oxen kept heading up and down the slopes to transport cartloads of hay, timber, abatis, entrenchment tools, provisions, and other materials. Included in the loads were defensive weapons like casks filled with stone and sand to roll down the hills at any potential attackers, "to break the ranks and legs of the assailants as they advance." As you rise up the slope, you'll see furrows still scarring the terrain from all the wagon trains, a record of the event carved in a thousand ruts.

By 4:00 a.m. on March 5, three thousand soldiers arrived in relief and took their posts inside the newly constructed forts. The whole time, General Washington was there to observe his troops, cajoling and encouraging them to work hard because there was more at stake than the battle alone. Six years to the day had elapsed since the Massacre on King Street, and a triumph on Dorchester Heights would do much to "avenge the death of your brethren."

As the day dawned, the smoke and fog created a veil through which onlookers could clearly see the forts atop the hills. Stunned, some British officers thought Washington had built them with up to twenty thousand men; others thought they looked like they'd been conjured by a genie. General Howe said, "The rebels have done more in one night than my whole army would have done in a month."

Howe's troops did not use their awe as an excuse for inactivity. Instead, they tried to level the forts with a cannonade of their own, sending seven hundred cannon shot toward Dorchester Heights and even sinking the back of their gun carriages into the earth to provide a better trajectory to reach them. The heights were too high for the bombardment to achieve its goal, so Howe decided to attack the fort nearest Castle Island with a bayonet charge. An untimely storm thwarted his plans and scuttled any attempt to seize the high ground. With his redcoats running low on supplies and provisions, that left only one other option: withdrawal.

Howe had an assistant send a notice to the rebels informing them his imperial army would be departing from Boston, and "he has no intention of destroying the Town, unless the Troops under his command are molested, during their embarkation, or at their departure by the armed force without." Washington did not acknowledge the notice since it was not properly authenticated, but the improvised truce held, and the evacuation commenced. Within nine days, the British high command oversaw the removal of 8,900 troops and their armament, 1,200 dependents, and more than 1,000 loyalists, embarking on 78 ships from the Long Wharf, Castle Island, and other sites in the region.

As you'll see once you reach the summit of Nook's Hill, the fortifications are still there, improved with timber and stone and standing more proudly than ever, along with the soldiers who man the garrison and the batteries that look out on the harbor. So the renown of Dorchester Heights is well deserved. The front may have moved on to more difficult terrain in New York, but it's here on these windswept hills where the patriots showed they could achieve what some thought impossible and stand a fair chance of winning the greater war.

CURRENCY. *After being prohibited by Parliament for decades, federal and state governments now print their own currency—Massachusetts's is designed by Paul Revere himself.*

LANTERNS. *Elegant lights such as this once adorned the Liberty Tree, along with streamers, banners, and the effigies of hated royal officials.*

to said Eftate, in Order for Settlement.

WANTED,

One or two good Hands to work at a Grift Mill: Thofe who are acquainted with grinding Wheat, will be preferred: Enquire of the Printers.

TO BE LETT.

A convenient Dwelling-Houfe, fituate at the Weft Part of the Town, having two Rooms and a Kitchen on the lower Floor, with a good Yard, Garden, &c. Inquire of Edes & Gill.

To be Sold, a likely Negro Boy, about 9 Years old, who has been in the Country about two Years, and talks good Englifh. Inquire of Edes and Gill.

To be Sold for want of Employ,

A ftrong healthy Negro Fellow, of a good Character, that underftands Houfe and other Bufinefs; inquire of Edes & Gill.

All Perfons that have any Demands on the Eftate of *Peace Cazneau*, late of *Bofton*, deceas'd, inteftate, are defired to bring in their Accounts. And thofe that are indebted to faid Eftate,

NEWSPAPER ADS. *In papers like the* Gazette, *readers can find houses to rent, jobs to be filled, and sales of tools and medicine and furniture—as well as enslaved people.*

An ADDRESS *to the* INHABITANTS *of* BOSTON,
(*Particulary to the thoughtless YOUTH:*)
Occasioned by the Execution of
LEVI AMES,
Who so early in Life, as not 22 Years of Age, must quit the Stage of action in this awful Manner.
He was tried for BURGLARY on the 7th of September, and after a fair and impartial examination of Facts, the JURY went out but soon return'd, who upon their Oaths pronounc'd him GUILTY.
Learn to be wise by others Harms, and you shall do full well.

EXECUTIONS. *State-sanctioned killings draw hundreds or even thousands of spectators to the gallows, followed by widely printed sermons about—and speeches by—the condemned.*

ROYAL ARMS. *The lion and the unicorn, the arms of King George III, used to be found throughout town but are now no more than a relic of imperial power.*

A In *Adam's* Fall
We Sinned all.

B Thy Life to Mend
This *Book* Attend.

C The *Cat* doth play
And after slay.

D A *Dog* will bite
A Thief at night.

E An *Eagles* flight
Is out of sight.

F The Idle *Fool*
Is whipt at School.

ALPHABETS. *Primers for reading sometimes overlap with guides for moral conduct, so children can discover the terrible fate of sinners while also learning their ABCs.*

JOSHUA BRACKETT
CROMWELL'S HEAD, SCHOOL-STREET
BOSTON

	£	s	d
Board	1	18	
Lodging		7	6
Eating			
Wine			
Punch			
Porter			
Liquor		17	
Horse-keeping	1	17	6
Oats		15	
Lemmons	1	4	
Entered	£6	1[illegible]	0

TAVERN BILLS. *You may find basic room and board at a tavern like Cromwell's Head unappealing, but until you get established in town, it may be one of your few options.*

RAVESTONES. *You won't find too many ngels and crosses on the gravestones of a raditional Boston cemetery. Instead, be prepared for winged death's heads and skulls and crossbones.*

Earthquakes,

Tokens of GOD's Power and Wrath. The Di[illegible]
of the prefent World ; and the approaching Co[illegible]
tion, when all Things fhall be burnt up : With[illegible]
Defcription of the drowning the oldWorld, and Chrift's
coming to Judgment. Being a Warning to Sinners and
Comfort to the Children of GOD

FAST DAYS. *Should a calamity like a fire or earthquake strike, Bostonians will fast and pray for God's forgiveness, assuming their sins brought about His unexpected wrath.*

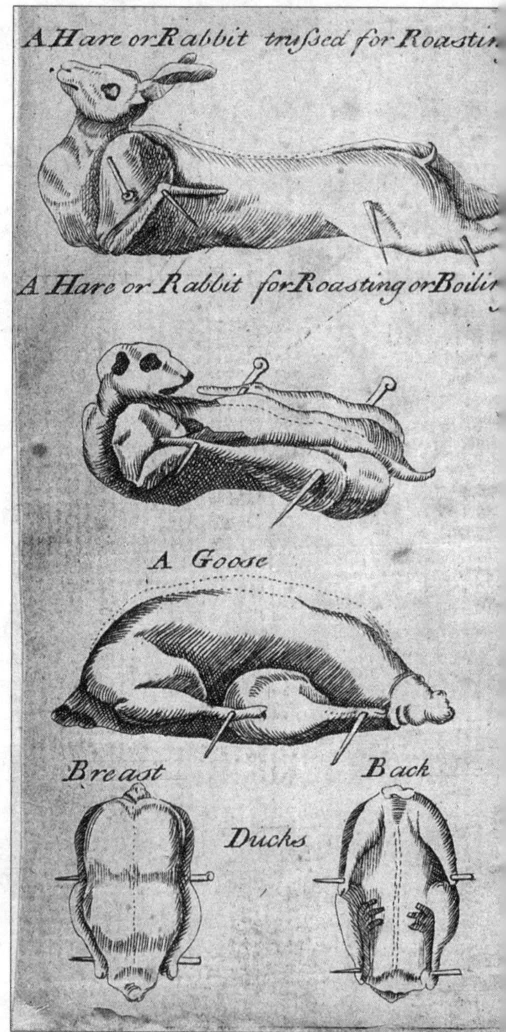

COOKING. *Guides to British cuisine appear on the shelves of bookstores, but true gourmands know the best place to sample New England fare is at an upscale inn, banquet, or private home.*

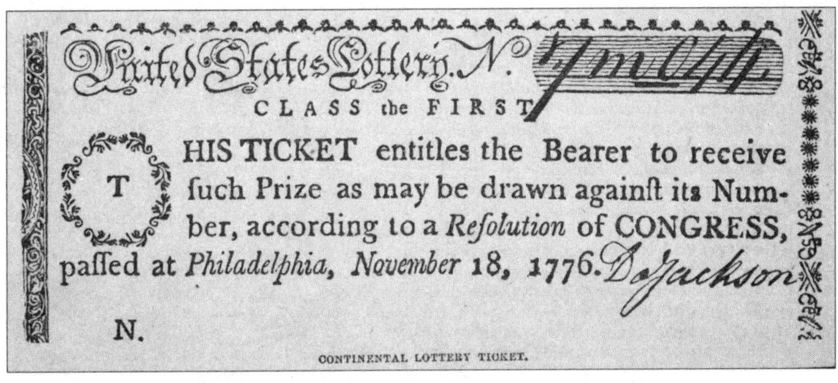

United States Lottery. No.

CLASS the FIRST

THIS TICKET entitles the Bearer to receive ſuch Prize as may be drawn againſt its Number, according to a *Reſolution* of CONGRESS, paſſed at *Philadelphia, November* 18, 1776. D. Jackson

N.

CONTINENTAL LOTTERY TICKET.

LOTTERY TICKETS. *The Continental Congress needs $1.5 million to finance the war, so it has resorted to planning a national lottery. Tickets are affordable, the prizes tempting.*

CARTOONS. *Few political critiques have nettled royal officials more than cartoons mocking and vilifying them. Paul Revere wields a particularly sharp stylus as his weapon.*

PRACTICAL MATTERS

Congratulations! Journeying to Boston in 1776 makes you an intrepid traveler, willing to experience one of the most dynamic and interesting towns in North America. It will be something of a challenge to make the effort, however, since opening hours may be erratic, numerous businesses have closed, and a fair fraction of the town has been damaged from the war. So attend to practical matters closely and plan to change your itinerary should complications arise.

TRANSPORT

You have three possibilities for getting to Boston. The most unlikely is by ferry across the Charles River from Charlestown. As we saw in chapter 8, the Royal Navy incinerated that town with combustible artillery shells during the Battle of Bunker Hill, and it has not yet been rebuilt. Any ferry service will therefore be intermittent if it is available at all.

The second means of transport is by ship. A journey by sea is described in chapter 1 and will likely involve getting a berth on a sloop or schooner, perhaps one carrying grain from New York or transporting lumber from another seaport in New England. Don't attempt a journey from a port too distant from the Eastern Seaboard, much less across the Atlantic, since you risk being intercepted or sunk by a British warship. Privateers are also a significant danger, taking your cargo while putting your life at hazard, should you resist.

You will arrive at the Long Wharf or Hancock's Wharf, both accommodating ships with deep drafts, unlike most other wharves in town. Since Boston is in the midst of a smallpox epidemic, only vessels free of the plague will be allowed to moor and their passengers to debark. Not only should you be free from disease, but your appearance should be sensible and clothes tidy. If you appear to be a pauper or in need of charity, a public official called a "warner" will bid you leave and give you twenty-one days or less to do so. But provided you meet the standard, you'll find sufficient options along the wharves for dining, drinking, and accommodation.

The third means of transport is by horse. Stagecoaches and stage wagons operate once or twice weekly, traveling on regular routes and often bearing mail. They connect to such towns as Salem and Marblehead, as well as Providence, Rhode Island. Depending on the distance, the fee may be ten to fifteen shillings one way. Horses will be changed out at stage stations, while taverns and inns offer meals and beds for the night. One of the speediest routes covers forty-four miles from Providence in a mere five hours, arriving at Crown Coffee-House on the Long Wharf. However, the longest route, covering sixty miles from Portsmouth, New Hampshire, is not currently in operation—its terminus was the Three Cranes Tavern in Charlestown, which now lies in ruins.

Coaches and wagons are not particularly comfortable vehicles. They carry four to twelve people with teams of four to six horses, but the seats are simple benches, all facing forward, with no doors for easy access. Passengers will have to climb in above the front wheels and clamber over each other with their luggage to find a place to sit. Since the coach does not have springs, the ride can be bumpy and unpleasant, especially over rough country roads, and the leather curtains provide only limited protection from wind and rain. Ladies tend to take a seat near the rear of the vehicle, where there is a rest for back support, and gentlemen toward the front, sometimes riding on the same bench with the driver.

Once you arrive in town, you'll see many more horse-drawn vehicles of various shapes and sizes—too many, in fact. The selectmen routinely condemn the amount of traffic and the difficulty of walking the streets because of drivers moving too fast and haphazardly. Public officials known as Surveyors of the Highways attempt to clamp down on scofflaws, but they face a steep challenge trying to contain Bostonians' desire for speed.

A wide range of vehicles occupy the roads, among them coaches and chaises, each led by a team of two to four horses, country wagons hitched to two to four oxen, and simple carts with a single draft horse. Other conveyances are curricles and calashes of various sizes and styles; a "chair" without a roof, attached to one or two horses; and a phaeton with four wheels and no roof, often the fastest and most dangerous vehicle on the road. Elite Bostonians may also choose chariots for their riding pleasure, featuring intricately carved and painted woodwork, glass windows, and embroidered seats with a silken fringe. However, as a tourist, you'll probably have to settle for a hackney carriage. For a few shillings, these light vehicles will haul you around town at a brisk speed, though pickup spots can be irregular. (One of the most longstanding is near the Orange Tree Tavern at Hanover Street and Treamount Street.)

The most practical means of seeing Boston is on foot, and this guide has been designed accordingly. However, if you have luggage or other encumbrances, you might want to unload them at your preferred lodging before you go strolling. The roads are mostly dirt or cobbled, and quite narrow, and some spots are choked with garbage and refuse from animals and tailings from workshops. The footway, when there is one, may be separated from vehicle traffic by posts and chains, though you might also have to share the space with feral dogs and pigs and young boys roughhousing and darting in and out of traffic. If you have a friend in town, you might try to borrow a horse. Otherwise, you can rent from a livery at one of the public stables, but this isn't recommended: Boston takes less than an hour to walk from end to end, making horse rental an unnecessary expense.

LODGING

However you plan on getting to Boston, you'll doubtless need somewhere to stay if you're coming for more than a day. It helps to have a friend in town who can lend you a room, but if you have no such contact, you'll choose from the assortment of paid lodging on offer. Inns and taverns are the most common places to find that lodging, and the cheapest places to bunk down. Across the river, Charlestown used to offer a range of clean, affordable rooms, but since it was destroyed during the Battle of Bunker Hill, you'll have to settle for what you find in Boston proper.

Accommodation costs one to three shillings per night in an inn or tavern, but if you're looking to have your own room with a bath, you'll be disappointed. Almost all rooms—and even beds—are shared. Men and women may sleep in segregated quarters, or there may be a single bed to hold up to four people. Sometimes, you'll share the space with the landlord or landlady and their family members, or more often an assortment of travelers in various states of sobriety. Rooms can be noisy from all the high-spirited drinking you can hear through the walls, and bedmates can wander in at any time of night—and you'll be expected to wake and make room for them. Also concerning to those in need of their slumber, the common lack of shades or curtains means east-facing rooms will have the morning sun blasting through the windows, making it hard to fall back asleep.

Sanitation is not ideal, and the linens and pillow covers may go months between washings and collect the stains and grime of previous visitors. Aside from dirt, at the lowliest dives you may even find insects or other vermin in the sheets. Some of these haunts acquire a notorious reputation, so it's best to ask around for advice on avoiding them and finding the better options. But if the town is particularly busy with overnight guests, there may be few other choices, and you'll have to settle for what you can get.

Once you've rested among strangers for a night or two, you'll doubtless want to find a cleaner and more hospitable space to stay. If you've come to visit for several weeks, you might consider renting a room. Because of the lean economic times, many residents have no choice but to let out rooms in their homes as another source of income. Indeed, people from shopkeepers to teachers, government officials to common laborers and artisans, may host an extra person or two or up to a dozen lodgers. Even John Hancock owns a rental house a few blocks east of his Beacon Hill mansion. Rooms on offer can range widely, anything from the outbuildings of grand estates to private bedrooms and servants' quarters to the meanest garrets and tenements.

Whatever room you rent, it's likely to be small and cold, and you may have to share a bed, since Boston has one of the highest occupancy rates of any town in the former colonies. Typically, the house owner's family will occupy one part of the floor and designate bedrooms for other guests. These may include sailors and roustabouts, European travelers, country folk visiting relatives, widows and mariners' wives, unattached men and artisans' apprentices, or the family's enslaved and indentured servants. Whatever the case, tenancy tends to be dynamic, with people moving in and out of a house with regularity, but always keeping it close to full. If the place is particularly raucous, authorities may cite the owner for housing "lewd and idle and dissolute persons," which can mean anything from criminals to rowdy drunks to women selling sex.

In the North End, there's a sizable brick tenement on Fish Street that has plentiful housing for sailors and other itinerants, as well as other large boardinghouses near the waterfront. However, six out of every ten rental properties are located on the South End, and since they have a somewhat better reputation for cleanliness and hospitality, that neighborhood should be your first destination for any extended visit. You can find either furnished or unfurnished houses or rooms for rent by consulting the newspapers or by word of mouth. Some units are meant to be shared only by single men or women, though more than a few can be shared by both. A common destination is the government-owned Manufactory House, which has rooms for rent as well as a historic legacy in the years before the Revolution (see p. 121).

Finally, if you find Boston quite to your liking and have enough cash to purchase your own home, you might want to seek residency in order to vote or hold public office, among other privileges. You'll need the approval of selectmen or a vote of the town meeting, and recommendations from others who can speak to your virtue and character. If they attest that you're an industrious and upright citizen, that's a good start to being approved; even better is your own promise to invest money to build a new business or provide other capital to help bring the town back to its feet.

CURRENCY

The prices in this guide are in pounds, since that's the most familiar currency to Bostonians. However, the pound itself is difficult to find in circulation, and specie is forbidden by law to leave Great Britain. The economy doesn't function by coin exchange, and Boston lacks a modern commercial banking system. So it's thought of more as a basis for transactions than something you'd have in your pocket, with units of twelve pence to one shilling, and twenty shillings to one pound.

Goods are often paid for in kind or through barter. It's a crude but complicated system, and one of the less widely known causes of colonial dissatisfaction with the Crown. It may require, for example, exchanging a measure of cloth for a sack of grain, or a length of chain for a cask of rum, or any other transaction in which the buyer and seller are known to each other and can agree on the roughly equal value of their commodities.

Establishing credit is critical under the system, so your debits can be recorded in a ledger, and you can be held to account for them. This applies to businesses as well as individuals. Shopkeepers like Elizabeth Murray and countless others in Boston once received generous credit from merchants in London, by which they could bring overseas goods to market at wholesale cost, mark them up at retail, and make enough profit to pay down their debts and build wealth. This system has since broken down, and with advance credit from Britain no longer possible, the former colonies have developed a new means of commerce.

Massachusetts now issues its own paper currency, after years of being denied the privilege by Parliament, and is intent on having people recognize its shilling and pound notes as valid, with penalties built into the law if you refuse to accept them. But also circulating is Continental Currency, established by the Continental Congress, paper bills denominated in dollars with engravings by Paul Revere. If this isn't confusing enough, many people remain wedded to the old system and question the worth of any of these notes and may not accept their face value. So you might attempt to pay for, say, a bundle of market goods with a 36-shilling note, but the vendor may claim it's only worth half that. You might want to haggle or even go to the authorities in such cases, but for the most part, it's not worth it, since the dispute is so common. Instead, assume the paper currency you possess has less actual value than the amount printed on it and accept it as simply the way of doing business.

Another danger is the ever-present threat of inflation. The war has made importing goods more difficult and raised the costs of most commodities, and it's alleged that loyalists have sought to undermine the value of paper currency through hoarding goods in warehouses and marking up the prices of those they do sell. Sometimes, riots have occurred in protest (as noted under "Safety"), with common Bostonians breaking into warehouses and seizing goods merchants have withheld in order to charge high prices for them later. The Continental Congress has tried to outlaw such practices with a system of price-fixing and a prohibition on withholding goods from market, but it hasn't achieved success. State and federal notes are worth less by the month, many Bostonians don't accept their face value, and money has become one of the most vexing problems the new republic has yet to face.

Criminals have tried to take advantage of the situation by creating their own fake money, despite counterfeiting being a crime punishable with a fine and a whipping session and, for repeat offenders, execution. Other states have similar laws, making the illegal printing of currency a dangerous pursuit. Still, some scoundrels do make the attempt, so look closely at any paper note that circulates and judge the integrity of the person giving it to you as much as the look of the bill itself.

If the idea of judging money and arguing over its value doesn't appeal to you, you might try a more immediate means of getting rich: the new Continental Lottery, which has been devised by Congress to raise $1.5 million to help fund the war. Tickets are ten to forty dollars, and cash prizes run anywhere from twenty dollars to fifty thousand dollars, depending on the ticket class you select. Colonies have run their own lotteries before, but there's never been one with this wide a scope or with so much at stake. If you'd like to try your luck, the drawing is to be held on November 18, 1776.

FOOD

Inns, taverns, boardinghouses, and similar lodgments will provide at least a meal or two with your stay, which will likely be your first encounter with local cooking. But it should not be your only one. For a better taste of Boston, try to sample the wide range of foodstuffs available from individual merchants and vendors, commercial kitchens, and even private homes.

Groceries feature fresh and preserved products brought from the New England countryside or shipped in from ports in Europe and the West Indies. These are not the places to buy meat, and you can find better options for produce at markets and green grocers, but the dry goods are well stocked, and the selection can be overwhelming. Jolley Allen of Marlborough Street, for example, offers muscovado sugar, salt, tea, pepper, coffee, indigo, raisins and currants, ginger, mustard and flour, along with pipes, playing cards, and clothing like Brunswick jackets and summer waistcoats. Other such retailers may traffic in beeswax, tobacco, seeds for cooking, vinegar, soap, dried figs and prunes, alum, brimstone, as well as hardware and cleaning supplies.

The widest selection of fresh food is available at town markets, and the greatest marketplace is Faneuil Hall. It hosts vendors inside the building on the ground floor and sits by a helter-skelter of stalls near Dock Square. The produce varies by season and may encompass apples and plums, peaches and cherries, pears and berries, plus vegetables like beans, corn, squash, turnips, onions, carrots, and cabbage. Herbs are also on offer, such as rosemary and garlic, nutmeg, ginger, cinnamon, celery root, horseradish, parsley, chives, mint, thyme, and even sassafras, pennyroyal, and liverwort.

Other market vendors sell live animals and cuts of meat from slaughtered ones. You'll see an assortment of birds—anything that flies or floats or bobs around the waters of Massachusetts Bay or the inland streams and ponds. Bostonians especially have a taste for passenger pigeon, as well as pheasants, chickens, partridges, ducks, and woodcocks. Cuts of meat from large and small mammals are for sale, too, typically mutton and rabbit and venison, and, on occasion, you may find frogs and marsh turtles. Milk and butter are pricier than the locals would prefer, along with cheese, with imported varieties like Cheshire the most expensive.

The most sought-after meats are pork and beef, which are salted or otherwise preserved through smoking, pickling, or curing. Surprisingly, however, you won't find many butchers in Boston. To escape high taxes and regulations on their messy business, most have relocated to the Brighton market and slaughter grounds five miles west of town, but they still bring their products here to market. Pigs and cows are traditionally killed in late fall and winter with the onset of cold weather, to help preserve the meat.

Prices for animal products have been rising due to the war, but they start at eight to twelve pence per weighed pound of meat, with butter twice as much. Birds fetch around six to eight pence per unit, though fattened ducks may cost a full shilling. Costs for produce vary, but you can acquire enough vegetables and greens for a meal for under ten pence. As for fraud at the market—with marketeers intentionally overweighting or selling inferior product—public officials in charge of weights and measures make regular inspections to protect customers from being fleeced.

Faneuil Hall and Dock Square aren't the only places to buy food in the area. Farmers sell directly to the public on the street from their carts and wagons, and merchants may do the same from their warehouses and wharves. Hucksters are still a common sight, selling "small meat" like chickens and pigeons from carts, baskets, and saddle bags, and shouting their wares to passersby.

If you'd like to dine right away, victualing houses are the places to stuff yourself on a bench with other hungry gourmands. There are about a dozen in town, which you can find in the town center and on the North End near the waterfront. Unlike a tavern or boardinghouse, they don't provide accommodation, but they can be quite handy for getting food on the go. They even provision ships for voyages with potted meat that can travel a long distance without spoiling.

Bostonians prepare their meat just about every way you can imagine. Some of the dishes include mincemeat pie, roast beef, dried or boiled tongue, hare pie, roast mutton, bacon and sausage, pork foot ragout, stuffed calf's head, venison hash, and pasties with various fillings. If you'd like to try making a dish yourself, the following is a good example, borrowed from *The Frugal Housewife, or Complete Woman Cook* by Susannah Carter:

BEEF RAGOUT

Take a buttock of beef, interlarded with great lard, rolled up with chopped spice, sage, parsley, thyme, and green onions; put it into a great saucepan, and bind it close with coarse tape. When it is half done, turn it; let it stand over the fire on a stove twelve hours. It is fit to be eat cold or hot. When it is cold, slice it out thin, and toss it up in a fine ragout of sweet-breads, oysters, mushrooms, and palates.

In contrast with beef and pork, fish is seen in some American quarters as the diet of Catholics and the poor (except for sturgeon, which the wealthy enjoy). But for most people in Boston, fish is important both to their livelihoods—with dried fish as a key export—and to their dinner tables. Live and freshly caught varieties include cod, quahogs, panfish, oysters, clams, mussels, haddock, and lobsters. You can find fishermen and mongers selling their product at the markets, on the wharves, and at Oliver's Dock and the Town Dock.

Most fish isn't expensive, just a few pence per weighed pound, but it can cost more than a shilling for a prime cut of sturgeon. Fish recipes are wide-ranging and creative, everything from simple roasted, fried, or smoked dishes to savory cakes and chowders, pickled smelt and eel stew, and curiosities like fish bladders boiled in milk and served in a cream sauce.

OYSTER PIE

Parboil a quart of large oysters in their own liquor, mince them small, and pound them in a mortar, with pistachio nuts, marrow, and sweet herbs, and onion and savory seeds, and a little grated bread, or season as aforesaid whole. Lay on butter and close it.

Another staple of the Boston diet is beans, which can be stewed or pickled, or made into a fricassee or a porridge. If you truly love legumes, try to take part in the Saturday ritual that occurs in taverns and inns, in which community members mix their own ingredients in pots and cook them all day long in ovens while gabbing and drinking with their friends. Each family has its own recipe, but one of the more common includes beans, molasses, beef or pork fat, and salt.

As for grains, wheat can be costly depending on the season and is imported from the mid-Atlantic states, so the price ranges from one-third more to twice as much as that of corn and rye. Consequently, Boston cuisine relies heavily on the latter two. Among the favorites are johnnycakes (corn cakes made with scalded milk) and a rich brown rye bread. Note that free or low-cost grain is no longer available from the town granary near the burying-ground; it's been shut down and is not likely to reopen any time soon.

Since baking is the preferred technique in Boston kitchens, there are countless savory pies and custards and cakes that residents enjoy cooking, among them baked puddings with a starch like bread flour or rice added and other combinations.

A POOR MAN'S PUDDING

Take some stale bread; pour over it some hot water, till it is well soaked; then press out the water, and wash the bread; add some powdered sugar, nutmeg grated, and a little salt; some rose water or sack, some Lisbon sugar, and some currants; mix them well together, and lay it in a pan well buttered on the sides; and when it is well flattened with a spoon, lay some pieces of butter on the top; bake it in a gentle oven, and serve it hot. You may turn it out of the pan when it is cold, and it will eat like a fine cheesecake.

After a hearty meal, Bostonians will indulge their sweet tooth, choosing from an array of sugary confections. Sugar itself is expensive and largely comes from the West Indies; locally, it is sold in hard forms like cones and loaves (not cubes). Less expensive sweeteners include molasses, such as the dark and tangy blackstrap variety; honey and maple syrup from area beekeepers and sugar-makers; and—cheapest of all—treacle, a by-product of sugar refining.

Some of the treats you may see on local countertops include molasses gingerbread, plum cake, raspberry cream, almond custard, orange fool, trifles, and pies and puddings made with apples, pears, berries, and carrots—as well as potatoes, rice, and suet. Syllabubs are a curious concoction like a mousse but made with white wine, and flummeries are a starchy pudding that may include oatmeal or some kind of meat. On the shelves of grocers, you'll come across horehound and peppermint drops, molasses sweets, candied flowers, glazed and sugared almonds, and macaroons.

A WHIPT SYLLABUB

Take two porringers of cream, and one of white wine, grate in the skin of a lemon, take the whites of three eggs, sweeten them to your taste, then whip it with a whisk, take off the froth as it rises, and put it into your syllabub-glasses or pots, and they are fit for use.

For guidance on making a recipe, pick up one of the cookbooks available from booksellers or on the shelves of residents' homes. In a volume like Carter's *Frugal Housewife*, you can discover how to make beef and pork entrées, as well as dishes featuring geese, snipes, larks, ortolans, and other creatures. The book also has instructions for assembling gravies, sauces, and soups, and fricassees and hashes made from everything from ox palate and pig's ears to sweetbreads, tripe, calf's head, and brain cakes. Sweet delights like cakes, tarts, jellies, and custards round out the book, along with tips on preserving and pickling produce and fermenting your own wine from raisins, birch, oranges, currants, or cowslip flowers.

DRINK

Boston has a wealth of things to drink, be they alcoholic or stimulating, herbal or tonic, pleasurable or medicinal. There are public drinking societies devoted to raising fraternal spirits, as well as the private society of conversing among friends over beverages in a parlor or tearoom. So you're never at a loss to find something to imbibe and to enjoy the company of others doing the same thing, especially on cold winter nights when a comforting elixir fills your belly as you sit around a hearth warming your toes.

Alcohol is the most prominent beverage consumed, and there are taverns for every sort of drinker. Some like the British Coffee-House once catered to Crown officials and loyalists; others like the Bunch of Grapes have long had a radical bent. Still others like those on the North End waterfront may draw Indian and black patrons excluded from other taverns, while unlicensed dram shops may appeal to those without much money.

As for what you will drink, the options are many. Beer is always a popular option. To make it, a brewmaster will take a grain such as barley and crack it by hand, soak the grains in warm water to create a mash, separate out the liquid in a wooden barrel, and boil that liquid in a copper kettle, adding wild hops and yeast before placing the mixture into casks. There, the liquid will ferment for several weeks until it becomes beer. You'll see different versions known as ale or porter or other names, but, generally, beer can be brewed strong or weak. The brew will feature different degrees of malting, to add color, flavor, and aroma, and that process, like the rest of beer-making, is its own science. Samuel Adams's father, for example, was a successful maltster who thrived in the first half of the century. The younger Samuel took over the operation only to see it fail within a few years, which was one of the reasons he was prompted to leave business life and take up a career as a politician.

TO MAKE ELDER-ALE

Take ten Bushels of Malt to a Hogshead, then put two Bushels of Elder-berries picked from the Stalks into a Pot or earthen Pan, and fit it in a Pot of boiling Water till the Berries swell, then strain it out and put the Juice into the Guile-fat [wort], and beat it often in, and so order it as the common way of brewing.

A fermented beverage need not be made from grain, and countless alternatives have quenched the palates of Bostonians. Some may be drawn from the wood of trees like pine, birch, spruce, hemlock, and fir, or be brewed with herbs and spices like sassafras and ginger, or produce like pumpkins, artichokes, and persimmons. But the cheapest and most popular beverage is cider, which makes use of New England's abundant apple crop. One loyalist in the countryside before the war reports having "made 90 Barrels of Cider in one Year, & at same time consumed 100 Bushels of Apples in the Family."

The drink can be made crudely with a mortar and pestle at home, or in a large-scale cider mill. In the industrial process, the fruit is crushed into mash, then pressed to remove the juice, which is then fermented and aged, and later sold for consumption. Cider routinely fills two-quart tankards for communal drinking in taverns, but it can also be enjoyed in smaller vessels and quaffed at any time, including before breakfast. You'll find the drink at weddings and funerals, ordinations and church raisings, formal gatherings and street celebrations. For good reason, John Adams will say, "If the Ancients drank Wine as our People drink rum and Cider it is no wonder We read of so many possessed with Devils." The most possessed lovers of the fruit can also imbibe the more potent applejack—a brandy distilled from the mash—as well as seasonal variations based on peaches (called "peachy"), pears ("perry"), honey and spices (mead or "metheglin"), elderberry and juniper mixed with grains ("ebulum"), and other such libations.

When grapes are fermented, the beverage is known generally as wine (though the term can refer to any number of different fermentations). It's nearly as popular as cider: Bostonians of means keep a wide selection of their favorite vintages at home, but even working- and middle-class families savor the beverage, bottling it by hand from the cask and stamping the bottle with their own seal. In recent years, some of the finest vintages have been harder to obtain due to the various trade embargoes. Madeira wine is one of them, but other popular wines you may or may not see on shelves are those from the Canary and Azores Islands, Spanish sherry and Málaga, Portuguese port, and French clairet, Burgundy, Champagne, and Bordeaux.

Wine and cider have an enduring popularity that appeals to all generations, including the youngest. With their parents' permission, children can be served the drinks, usually at home, with perhaps a less generous proportion of alcohol. The young diarist Anna Winslow is not unusual when she reports that at one family gathering, "our treat was nuts, raisins, Cakes, Wine, punch, hot & cold, all in great plenty. We had a very agreeable evening from 5 to 10 o'clock."

TO MAKE BIRCH WINE

> In March bore a hole in a Tree, and put in a Faucet, and it will run two or three days together without hurting the Tree; then put in a Pin to stop it, and the next Year you may draw as much from the same hole; put to every Gallon of the Liquor a quart of good Honey and stir it well together, boil it an hour, scum it well, and put it in a few Cloves and a piece of Lemon-peel; when 'tis almost cold, put to it so much Ale-yeast as will make it work like new Ale, and when the Yeast begins to settle, put it in a Runlet that will just hold it; so let it stand six Weeks or longer, if you please; then bottle it, and in a Month you may drink it. . . .

For those a bit older, or with a stronger constitution, only distilled spirits will do—and the most common of them is rum. In the early days, it was called rumbullion or kill-devil, and acquired a reputation as a hellacious by-product of Caribbean sugar refining. Since then, rum production has become a valuable part of Boston's economy and one of its prime exports. Yet, for all its economic importance, local rum is not very tasty. The product distilled in the West Indies is widely judged superior, and the New England variety is regarded more for its cheap price than for its uneven, sometimes bitter flavor. So you may want to cut the rum with another liquid and add spice to make it easier on the palate and the stomach.

Rum mixes well into other drinks, the most popular of which is punch. This concoction isn't only colorful and eye-catching but has also played a large role in patriot celebrations. It contributes a lively communal air to taverns, with the bowl often passed around and enjoyed by a table full of drinkers. It can be made from rum and arrack or cider or brandy and sweetened with lime, orange, lemon, and other citrus fruits, and sometimes enlivened with wine or other spirits. It's served with a ladle and strainer and glasses, or drunk straight from the bowl. Other variations of rum drinks include grog, sling, and toddy—comprising rum and water, and/or sugar and nutmeg—each with its own champions and detractors.

The most interesting mixed drink is flip. This is made by filling a mug or tumbler two-thirds with beer then adding molasses, sugar, eggs and perhaps cream, and a measure of rum, then plunging a red-hot iron poker (or loggerhead) into the solution to stir it around and give it a pleasing burnt taste. There are other, even more unusual mixtures you can find outside of Boston, but beware of some of the things you find in country taverns. One of them is called "blackstrap," which comprises rum mixed with the sticky black tailings of sugar refining and may prove too much for urban dwellers not used to its aggressively acrid flavor.

Other spirits aren't as popular as rum, though most taverns do sell brandy for drinking neat or, more commonly, for mixing in drinks like those already mentioned. The quality of brandy tends to vary, especially during wartime, but if sufficiently doctored, the spirit is usually palatable enough to enjoy. Domestic whiskey is much less in evidence, though with the Royal Navy now intercepting shipments of molasses, grain distillation may be on the upswing. Imports from Britain like Scotch and gin are uncommon on tavern shelves, though you may find a few wealthy merchants who keep them on hand as curiosities.

The cost of fermented and distilled products in Boston is not high. You can find rum for five to seven pence a gill in a tavern down to half that on the docks from a seller of single drinks. Cider and beer are similarly inexpensive, but brandy and more complex drinks will cost a bit more. For nine or ten pence, you can sample flip, while one pound gets your table a full bowl of punch, and two pounds or more will afford you a fine bottle of Madeira or other top-shelf wine.

TO MAKE CHERRY BRANDY

To every four quarts of Brandy, put four pounds of red Cherries, two pounds of black, and one quart of Raspberries, a few Cloves, a stick of Cinnamon, and a bit of Orange-peel, let these stand a Month close stopped, then bottle it off, put a lump of Sugar into every bottle.

If you've had your fill of strong drink and would rather enjoy a concoction to stimulate your spirit, you might sample a caffeinated beverage. The most popular is, of course, tea, which continues to gain enthusiasts even as it attracts controversy. Many writers have praised its healthful properties, that it encourages healthy living without inebriation, while others have warned that it agitates digestion and contributes to idle and dissolute behavior. Whatever the case, it has retained its appeal even after being protested, destroyed, and otherwise condemned by patriot clubs and the press, and will likely continue to remain one the town's most desired drinks, even in times of hardship.

Bostonians have an affection for Dutch Bohea black tea, one of the most smuggled teas before the Revolution, which takes pride of place during a tea service, sometimes with other choice varieties. During such a ceremony, you're apt to see elegant ceramic cups and saucers imported from London, silver tongs, sugar bowls, creamers, canisters, and other artful objects well suited to conversation in a parlor. The host will typically be a woman of the middle or upper class excluded from a tavern who serves the beverage to enjoy the company of her friends and intimates. For good reason, then, tea has been called "the Ladies favorite Liquor," and you may want to sample it, too, if you're invited to the event. But in workaday taverns, especially of the radical patriot stripe, you're better off asking for coffee if you don't want to start an argument.

If you do want coffee, be aware that many taverns are labeled as coffee houses but mainly serve alcohol. Still, there's at least a coffee mill for grinding the beans and a copper pot for brewing them, along with coffee cups and dishes suited for the beverage. The varieties of coffee on offer can be hard to predict—depending on what shippers can acquire—and the taste can vary depending on territory of origin, season, and other factors. But the stimulant is popular, and it's hard to imagine some revolutionaries making their efforts to overturn British rule without it.

Another choice drink is chocolate, prepared in a variety of ways. Martha Washington enjoys steeping the cacao shells in hot water to provide a mildly stimulating beverage, but most Bostonians prefer to buy it in blocks or cakes of ground nibs. Should you purchase one, simply grate the cake with sugar into hot milk or water, and add spices like cinnamon, clove, and nutmeg to your taste. Or you can simply steep the grounds with hot water for a bitter and refreshing jolt, or rely on a coffee house to do the work. Regardless of how you go about consuming it, chocolate will activate your senses and keep you awake during the long summer days and cold winter nights.

Finally, if you'd prefer not to get intoxicated or stimulated, there are any number of milder brews that offer a subtler effect on the mind and that may act as a refreshing alternative. You can find clove water or mint water at a few taverns, but more appealing are sassafras tea (said to be a cure for syphilis!) or the leaves of goldenrod, strawberry, blackberry, or other plants brewed into tasty herbal elixirs. Among the more unusual is vinegar, molasses, and ginger stirred together to make "switchel," which is occasionally topped with rum for an added kick.

If you feel ill, you might also sample medicinal infusions brewed from peppermint, spearmint, pennyroyal, rose, cinnamon, or Jamaica peppers, or herbal wines featuring ingredients like gentian root, pepper, and lemon peel, or more questionable components like antimony, tar, and quicklime. These are detailed in various cookbooks, including Eliza Smith's *Compleat Housewife*, from which this and previous recipes have been borrowed.

AN OPENING DRINK

Take Pennyroyal, red Sage, Liverwort, Horehound, Maidenhair, Hyssop, of each two handfuls, Figs one pound, Raisins stoned one pound, blue Currants half a pound, Licorice, Aniseeds, Coriander-seeds, of each two ounces; put all these in two gallons of Spring-water, and let it boil away two or three quarts; then strain it, and when 'tis cold put it in Bottles. Drink half a pint in a Morning, and as much in the Afternoon; keep warm and eat little.

HEALTH

The greatest danger to your health during a sojourn in Boston comes from smallpox. The town has been plagued with the malady for most of its existence but especially during the current century, when each wave of the disease in 1702, 1721, 1730, 1752, and 1764 killed hundreds of people—usually about 1 to 6 percent of the population. The current 1776 outbreak has afflicted more than five thousand, with the selectmen taking desperate measures to clean and smoke vacant and abandoned houses, and Abigail Adams writing to John, "I am fearful of the small pox, or I should have been in [to Boston] before this time."

Smallpox is a brutal disease that spreads through respiratory action, with symptoms appearing around two weeks after transmission: fever, headache, and muscle pain for most, then possibly vomiting and convulsions, and potentially organ hemorrhages and rashes across the skin that become weeping pustules. Long-term dangers are permanent disfiguration, blindness, and death.

To try to relieve the suffering, in 1721, doctors developed a practice called inoculation, in which they would draw a length of string through a victim's suppurating wound, incise the skin of a healthy patient, apply the contaminated string to the patient's cut, and cover it with a plaster. It wasn't foolproof: many patients would still get sick and about one in fifty would die from being exposed to the live virus (as opposed to one in ten who died the old-fashioned way). Those who survived gained lifelong immunity, after a stay in quarantine to prevent further transmission to others.

Even as it boosted odds of survival, inoculation proved to be controversial: selectmen periodically outlawed it, and some residents condemned the doctors who practiced it. However, over the course of a half-century, it gained traction with every new outbreak, until the majority of residents now accept it. It also helped that the death rate from inoculation dropped by three-quarters, to around one in two hundred people. George Washington ordered his Continental Army troops to undergo it and encouraged the townsfolk to do the same.

The latest technique involves doctors dipping a lancet in a viral solution and making a tiny cut in the patient's epidermis. This provokes an immune reaction without the same number of side effects or the higher risk of death as in earlier approaches. The latest numbers show only about six in one thousand patients succumb to inoculation. If you'd like to undergo the treatment yourself, keep in mind that hospitals that offer the procedure are still banned in many areas, depending on the decision of county courts. If you do find one, you'll be laid up for a month in quarantine, and when you leave, you'll have to disrobe and be washed in rum or vinegar, then fumigated.

Other maladies can prove to be just as deadly as smallpox. Dysentery, typhus, and other fevers and infections ran rampant during the occupation, often originating in or near soldiers' barracks, and poor sanitation also afflicts patriot camps and the areas around them. An aide to General Washington writes of one of them, "[T]he Offal near many of the Commissaries Stalls, still lay unburied, that much Filth and nastiness, is spread among the Huts, which will soon be reduced to a state of putrefaction and cause a Sickly Camp." Within town, the selectmen have repeatedly tried to clean up the streets and lanes and prohibit dumping of "Dirt Dung Garbage Carcass Carrion Shavings Rubbish or Soil."

Aside from poor sanitation, Bostonians blame the season and climate for the spread of disease, as well as filthy air and putrefying animal and vegetable matter. Contemporaries warn against "malignant Vapours proceeding from dead Bodies, or from the Sinks of common Shores of great Cities, or standing Waters"—with the fens of the Charles River said to be a particularly noxious spot.

If you should contract an illness during your stay, doctors will treat you with assorted pills, ointments, and plasters. Among the most highly regarded, Dr. James Lloyd is the rare loyalist who still lives in Boston, with a sterling reputation, a convenient office on Treamount Street, and a high fee for his services—often a pound sterling or more. Other, less-talented physicians are content to charge just a few shillings.

Should modern medicine lack appeal, you might instead try a folk remedy for your ailment, which could be anything from taking herbs infused with vinegar, to not eating or drinking to excess, to avoiding breathing the night air outside and getting your feet wet. Alternately, there are the cures of patent medicine such as "Pectoral Balsam of Honey" for consumption; "Negro Caesar's Cure for Poison" for recovery from toxins and rattlesnake bites; and "Bishop Berkeley's Tar Water," said to fix anything from smallpox and pleurisy to asthma, loose teeth, and eye inflammation. Other options, available at your local apothecary, are Dr. Bateman's Pectoral Drops; an opium product; Maredent's Drops and Keyser's Female Pills, both containing mercury; and Godfrey's Cordial, featuring a kick of laudanum.

SAFETY

Fire

Apart from threats to your health, Boston also presents a range of dangers to your safety. Perhaps the most notorious in this century has been fire, with the town suffering from fifteen major blazes that have wiped out entire blocks or neighborhoods in a few hours. Conflagrations are a continual hazard in a place largely built of wood, and longtime residents still remember the worst of them all, the "Great Fire" of 1760, which incinerated 175 businesses and about as many homes—one in ten of the town's total structures. The damage cost Bostonians £100,000, which they could hardly raise on their own, so they had to rely on assistance from other Massachusetts towns and from Britain to rebuild. Another lethal fire the next year gutted Faneuil Hall and surrounding businesses, and most recently, in May 1775, an ammunition explosion at a barracks for British troops consumed thirty warehouses.

Fires arise from a range of causes, but the selectmen typically blame outbuildings full of dry hay, unattended woodpiles, and other combustible sites; workshops like smithies that use high heat in their operation; and businesses like chocolate mills, lime and brick kilns, and ropewalks. To contain the danger, the town is divided into sixteen fire wards, each with a publicly chosen captain, and eight engines to direct water to the blazes. Members of fire clubs also pledge to do their part, individually equipped with two leather bags and buckets, which can be filled at public wells like the town pump. Another source of fire comes from dirty chimneys, which are prone to emit sparks, and which only a licensed sweep is allowed to clean. The sweep does a dirty job, bracing and climbing inside the brick walls while scraping soot and collecting it in a bag.

However, the greatest danger you'll have to face in Boston comes not from the heat but the cold. This is why some chimneys can be so large, featuring a great hearth, a chimney corner with seats to warm yourself and others, and a brick oven for cooking. Without these furnaces, area houses might be close to uninhabitable during the winter, and even with them, the warmth largely escapes through the flue and scarcely reaches the other side of the room, much less the entire building. And so the bedrooms of houses tend to be small and chilly while public rooms like parlors are left unheated and closed off. In such cases, food and water, and even beer and wine, will freeze on tables overnight and have to be thawed in the morning.

Crime

Another significant hazard is crime. Although Boston is relatively safe to explore during the day, some areas should be avoided after dark. The Neck has a reputation as being a site of assaults and robberies, and you should keep away from it if possible, along with the nearby gallows. You might also be robbed in one of the seedier dives near the waterfront, where dram shops and brothels offer cheap amusement to sailors and rowdies. Certain industrial stretches of the South End and West Boston can also put you at hazard, especially near the docks and ropewalks, which have, in recent years, been sites of crowd violence.

Conversely, you might find yourself accused of breaking the law. Prosecution tends to focus on those who commit property crimes like arson, burglary, and robbery, along with treason, forgery, counterfeiting, and violent crimes. The old morality laws against adultery and sodomy are only occasionally enforced, and the same is true for laws against fornication and bastardy—with the accused more often punished if they belong to different races.

Assuming you are arrested and arraigned, if you plead not guilty, you'll stand an even chance of being released. But if convicted and punished, you can expect to serve a sentence at the prison on Queen Street or, more likely, a public whipping. Less common punishments include indentured servitude, branding, having an ear sliced off, and standing at the gallows with a rope around your neck. The burden of corporal punishment tends to fall hardest on the poor, with wealthier defendants often let off with a fine. Note that the court system only functions irregularly, when it functions at all, due to the ongoing Revolution and the recovery from the siege.

Riot

Mass violence is more tolerated in Boston than it is in other towns to the south. The combination of bleak economic conditions, the ready availability of cheap alcohol, the presence of violent gangs, and general hatred against royal officials and an occupying military has made for a combustible mix—and the incendiary atmosphere has continued even after the British evacuation.

Forbidden under English common law, riot is defined as three or more persons engaged in an act of public violence. Rout and unlawful assembly are other variations, and in the colonial era, treason was defined as "levying war against the King." Despite these prohibitions, Boston has long led other towns in British North America in its number of riots. (Even before the revolutionary era, in 1764, it had already experienced twenty-eight of them.) Some of the reasons for mass violence have been the establishment of central markets, men forced into service in the Royal Navy, class resentments, fears over prostitution, and anti-Catholic bigotry—and, of course, Parliament's imposition of customs duties and taxes.

Should a riot occur during your stay, you'll likely see artisans and laborers in the streets, with perhaps a few middle-class shopkeepers and tradesmen among them. In the past, wealthier merchants and gentlemen also took part, such as during the first Stamp Act riot, and prominent Whigs and patriots are known to have planned and participated in the Destruction of the Tea. There's a significant overlap between the members of mobs and militias too. On one occasion, in an attempt to control an unruly crowd, Sheriff Stephen Greenleaf tried to raise the state militia, only to be told they'd already been raised.

With the majority of men inducted in the Continental Army and militia, women make up a third of all contemporary rioters, taking to the streets to protest high prices for commodities and merchants' hoarding of them in warehouses or monopolizing their sale. Along with grain and produce, some of the price-gouged goods include "Rum, Sugar, Molasses, Cotton-Wool, coffee, Cocoa, &c. & most Kinds of Clothing." At a time when such commodities are costly and in short supply—but no less essential—this behavior invites outrage. One example occurred when a mob of a hundred women descended on the property of merchant Thomas Boylston and accused him of hoarding coffee so as to charge a steep price for it. As Abigail Adams wrote in a letter to John:

> There has been much rout and Noise in the town for several weeks. . . . A number of females some say a hundred, some say more assembled with a cart and trucks, marched down to the warehouse and demanded the keys, which he refused to deliver, upon which one of them seized him by his neck and tossed him into the cart. Upon his finding no quarter he delivered the keys, when they tipped up the cart and discharged him, then opened the warehouse, hoisted out the coffee themselves, put it into the trucks and drove off. It was reported that he had a spanking among them, but this I believe was not true. A large concourse of men stood amazed silent spectators of the whole transaction.

Tarring and Feathering

By far, the most extreme weapon in the rioter's arsenal is tarring and feathering. Imported from Europe, the practice found its most popular expression in New England during the Revolution, with two dozen documented attacks taking place in and around Boston in the last decade. Mobs have tarred and feathered customs informers and loyalist merchants, shopkeepers, artisans, and the like. However, royal officials like Thomas Hutchinson and customs commissioners were more often targeted with property destruction or hanging in effigy at the Liberty Tree.

Merchant John Rowe describes a typical tarring and feathering in 1769: "In the evening, a large mob assembled and got hold of one George Greyer, an informer, who they stripped naked and painted him all over with tar, and then covered him with feathers and put him in a cart and carried him through all the main streets of the town, huzzahing, etc., and at nine dismissed him—this matter occasioned much terror, etc., in some fearful people among the inhabitants." Which, of course, was exactly the point.

Crowds engaged in the practice may grow quite large and enjoy the quiet support of wealthier patriots, such as in 1770 when a mob attacked customs inspector Owen Richards. Some two thousand people turned out for the spectacle, and John Hancock paid the legal bills of one of the men accused. However, after the shocking, horrific tarring and feathering of customs agent John Malcolm in 1774 (see p. 127), many patriot leaders condemned the action, and the press castigated it as a relic of ancient barbarity unsuitable for the current age.

Needless to say, you do not want to be tarred and feathered. Pine tar is a substance used to waterproof ships, among other uses, and when it's smeared on the skin, it can blister it and adhere rigorously when it cools. To get it off, you'll need a scrub brush, possibly turpentine or another solvent, and can expect to be marked with nasty scars, depending on whether the crowd elects to tear off your clothes. The worst victims have suffered frostbite from being hauled around town in a cart in the chilly air, or seen their skin come off in strips along with the tar. Even in the best case, you might be covered in grease with a smattering of feathers and be made to bide your time overnight at the bottom of a dry well, until pulled up from the hole in the morning.

FESTIVALS

Crowd action need not be violent in Boston, and the locals enjoy peaceable community festivals and holidays as much as people anywhere else in North America, though what they celebrate might be a bit different than what you're used to. You'll see the expected grand dinners and drinking parties, fireworks and parades, and other such revels for the major events, but the holidays can also be quiet and contemplative, shared by family members and intimates and kept out of public view. Still, keep watch on the calendar, because if you're here on an important day, you might want to celebrate with the locals and get a truer sense of who they are and how they act.

In the summer of 1776, they will most assuredly not be celebrating royal festivals, such as the birthday of Queen Anne and other monarchs, much less the widely hated George III and his ministers. This wasn't always the case. Up until the revolutionary era, they at least paid homage to British heads of state, mentioning them in their toasts and sometimes keeping their images and emblems on the walls of taverns and private homes. Since the reading of the Declaration of Independence from the Town House balcony, though, nearly all such icons have been stripped away, and few will dare honor the memory of past monarchs and the accession of their successors.

You're more likely to see triumphs of military victories over the king's troops and celebrations of his misfortunes. To that end, the festivities center on the anniversaries of major events like the Stamp Act riots or the Destruction of the Tea, or commemorate tragic episodes like the Massacre on King Street, with orations and processions at the major churches.

Outside the town proper, you'll find a number of local celebrations, most notably Forefathers' Day in Plymouth, established in 1769 to commemorate the 1620 landing of Pilgrim dissenters. The townsfolk honor the memory with a great feast that may include a "large baked Indian whortleberry pudding, a dish of sauquetach [succotash], a dish of clams, a dish of oysters, and a dish of cod fish, a haunch of venison, a dish of sea fowl, a dish of frost fish and eels, an apple pie, a course of cranberry tarts and cheese."

This is not to be confused with the days of thanksgiving that are periodically observed in Boston. This solemn religious event occurs after a period of hardship or at harvest time, during which ministers give praise to God for the bounty He delivers, and parishioners reflect on His providence with a communal meal. Food on offer may include venison, turkey, hen, or some other meat; onions, potatoes, bread, and beans; and various savory and sweet puddings and pies. By contrast, fast days in New England are another way to honor God, this time through humility after a calamity or terrible event such as a drought or an earthquake (such as the one striking Cape Ann in 1755). To repent for the human sin that apparently invited God's vengeance, people will go without food for a certain amount of time and offer prayers of repentance.

As for other religious holidays, Bostonians of the Congregationalist stripe reject all days that honor saints and either ignore or minimize most liturgical events on the Roman Catholic calendar, including Easter, Ascension Day, Epiphany, and so on. A local minister may, in a sermon, allude to such a holiday, or even reflect on its meaning and purpose, but they are not major public events, and more than a few residents are wary of such holidays and do not expect to celebrate them in their meetinghouses.

The most fraught is Christmas. Congregationalists disparage it as a time of revelry, if not excess, and in some ways, the recent occupation has only hardened their views. John Andrews reports on one episode that especially offended the townsfolk, after soldiers' Christmastime revels had been rowdy and boisterous. On January 6, 1775, a group of colorfully dressed sailors paraded with an effigy "completely tarred and feathered, representing a he Devil, together with a She Devil, and an attendant, each furnished with a bag to collect money, stopping every person of genteel appearance to request a remembrance of Old England, wishing 'em a merry Christmas."

Massachusetts's tense, even hostile, relationship with Christmas predated the occupation. Both in England, where the holiday was banned under Oliver Cromwell's autocratic rule in 1647, and in the Bay Colony, which followed a dozen years later, Puritans and their descendants have seen it as a pagan holdover—an excuse for hedonism and debauchery with no spiritual purpose whatsoever. They couldn't find the date December 25 in the Bible but knew ancient church leaders had established the holiday to supplant the depraved Roman Saturnalia, and thought the replacement wasn't much of an improvement. As English bishop and martyr Hugh Latimer said, "Men dishonor Christ more in the twelve days of Christmas than in all the twelve months besides," and later Congregational leaders agreed, establishing a five-shilling fine as the "Penalty for Keeping Christmas."

However, Charles II ultimately forced them to recognize the holiday, and it was made legal in Boston in 1681. But in the century since, it has not found any more acceptance among the majority of townsfolk, at least those with Puritan roots. They think of it as a Catholic festival of idolatry, a time for gluttony, drunkenness, and sexual license, which they claim people use as an excuse to indulge in the worst sort of behavior. They even fear it, since one unfortunate tradition involves groups of "Anticks" (or mummers) barging into middle- and upper-class homes and singing loudly or putting on an impromptu play, only promising to leave once they are paid off or given sweets and strong drink. For good reason, then, the holiday has something of a checkered reputation. It's true that Anglicans, some working-class families, and others do celebrate it as well as Easter and other holidays shared with those of the Catholic faith. But you'll find few, if any, public displays or commemorations that do the same. The schools and stores stay open, and the churches remain closed.

Boston prefers its homegrown traditions to those brought over from the Old World (though the perverse and violent "Pope's Day," adapted from Guy Fawkes Night, is an exception; see p. 123). Residents most vigorously take part in secular holidays like Training Day, in which militiamen parade for spectators and drill and fire their weapons with martial precision; Election Day, honoring the installation of representatives to the General Court; and Commencement, reveling in the graduation of students at Harvard College in Cambridge. All of these events will include the requisite feasting and drinking, and sometimes fireworks on the Common and marches through the streets. Enslaved Bostonians also have their own holiday to elect leaders of their community, which takes place every year on the Common (see p. 120). And in years to come, Bostonians will doubtless celebrate July 4, which marks the signing of the Declaration of Independence; Evacuation Day, on the March 17 anniversary of the end of military occupation; and Bunker Hill Day, on June 17, honoring the militiamen who fought in that battle.

If you'd like to review the litany of holidays and "remarkable days" that Boston honors or remembers throughout the year, pick up a copy of *Bickerstaff's Boston Almanack*, which provides a rundown of the most important. It includes helpful astrological charts and the timing of eclipses, and can help you decide which days might be the worthiest (or luckiest) to visit town. There's a wide range of religious holidays, along with anniversaries of revolutionary episodes like the repeal of the Stamp Act, reminders of election days and legislative sessions, predictions of weather, charts for high and low tides and the phases of the moon, and the beginning and the end of Dog Days. And with any luck, those days of heat and oppression that Bostonians have long endured will be ending when you come to town, and a new, better time will emerge soon after.

VISITING BOSTON IN 2026 VS. 1776

On the 250th anniversary edition of this book, it's worth noting how Boston has grown up since 1776. The capital of Massachusetts has exploded in size and population to become more than just a town, and its people incorporated it as a city in 1822. Developers have created new neighborhoods where there were once only streams and tidal flats, hills like the Trimountain have been leveled or lopped off, and the urban boundaries have expanded considerably. Looking at a modern map, it can be difficult to discern the original outline of the town since so much within it has been redesigned, rebuilt, and reimagined; the streets and neighborhoods have been given new names; and almost all of the old wooden townscape has been destroyed or remodeled beyond recognition. The waterways, too, scarcely bear resemblance to their colonial forebears: countless streams and creeks and town docks and mill ponds have vanished, and once disparate islands are now connected as part of a sprawling metropolis that extends well into the harbor. And the same is true inland, as the city has annexed dozens of towns and neighborhoods and extended its land mass from just over one square mile during the Revolution to more than forty-eight today. Indeed, Boston is no longer a near island on a vulnerable peninsula, struggling to maintain its population of fifteen thousand, but the center of a vast complex of five million people, one of the largest such conglomerations in the nation.

So what can you see in 2026 that's authentic to 1776? Remarkably, about two dozen sites and structures survive more-or-less intact from the colonial era. About half of these are viewable on the Freedom Trail, which leads visitors over two and half miles past historic churches, houses, parks, and cemeteries to get a sense of the town in its early years—though gaining this perspective can be difficult when sites are shoehorned in between modern office complexes, chain pharmacies, and glass-and-steel high-rises. Still, costumed interpreters and docents do their best to immerse you in "ye olde Boston" with a range of themed tours and events throughout the year.

As for individual attractions, following their order in the guide, you can first visit Castle Island. The name has become a misnomer, since the old military post is now connected to South Boston by peninsula. But the site does provide a sense of the remoteness and defensive capability of the fort, even if the architecture is mid-nineteenth century rather than colonial. Closer to downtown Boston, the Long Wharf is a pleasant enough place for a stroll, though harborside fill has reduced its length by half, and the shops and restaurants are much more sedate than the taverns and merchant traders of old. By contrast, Faneuil Hall is among the most engaging sites for visitors, with adjacent Quincy Market adding to the options for commerce and entertainment. The building features vendors on the ground level, the historic assembly hall on the second story, and, on the fourth, a museum and meeting space for the Ancient and Honorable Artillery Company, founded in 1638. Note, however, that offices for city officials are now a block west at the unloved concrete behemoth of City Hall.

Two blocks south, another colonial stalwart—the Town House—has stood for more than 315 years in various incarnations. Now known as the Old State House, it's the oldest public building in the city and a lovely relic from an antique era—once the seat of colonial government, then the state capitol, then the city hall, and now a museum and access point for the MBTA subway. Outside the east face of the building, there's a granite circle commemorating the victims of the Boston Massacre, though the actual killing occurred closer to the Custom House, which has long since disappeared.

Several blocks south, at the corner of School Street and what's now Washington Street, is the former apothecary that's almost as old as the Old State House. It sits on a plot of land once belonging to Anne Hutchinson, but it is now called the Old Corner Bookstore for all the publishers and booksellers that operated there in the nineteenth century. On the western end of the block is another holdover, King's Chapel, its sturdy stone facade ornamented with classical columns, and its denomination Unitarian instead of Anglican. The chapel's adjacent burying ground is also venerable, and worth a look. However, Boston Latin School, which once stood near the chapel, relocated in the nineteenth century, and it now occupies space three miles away on the Boston campus of Harvard, its longtime academic associate. It claims to be the oldest school of any kind still operating within the United States.

Elsewhere in the area, there's a trio of eighteenth-century relics that do not appear in the guide but may be worth a visit for historical completists. John Hancock built the sturdy brick Ebenezer Hancock House, at 10 Marshall Street, in 1767 for his brother to occupy. During the war, Ebenezer served as an army deputy paymaster and disbursed funds from the building, though the Georgian edifice later came into the possession of a series of shoemakers. It now houses business offices and puts on occasional events. Across the street, the Boston Stone is an eighteenth-century millstone embedded in a brick wall and considered to have historic value by many tourists. However, it was largely unknown during the Revolution and only came to public attention in the 1830s as an apocryphal survey point. Finally, just around the corner at Hanover and Union Streets, the Bell in Hand Tavern is said to be the oldest bar in central Boston; it was founded in 1795 but has only occupied this building since the mid-nineteenth century. (Another nearby bar with an old-timey appeal, the Green Dragon, is a modern replica of the famous haunt of the Sons of Liberty.)

In the North End are several survivors from the era of revolution, none better than the Paul Revere House. Not only is this vernacular wooden house from 1680 an excellent museum and tribute to the life of its namesake, but it's a telling reflection of the type of domestic architecture once so prevalent across colonial Boston. Also rewarding a visit is the adjacent Pierce-Hichborn House, among the earliest brick structures to appear in town, from 1711; when it's intermittently open, the house is tourable on the same admission ticket as its more famous neighbor.

The church most associated with Revere, Christ Church, is better known as Old North Church and still stands in an excellent state of preservation. It's long been a Boston landmark for its famed steeple, but other aspects can be seen up close in a range of tours from the crypt to the bell chamber. Within the same complex is the Edes & Gill Print Shop, which is a replica of the shop that published the *Boston Gazette* from a long-vanished office near the Town House. Another casualty of time is the original quarters of the North Writing School, though the school lives on today as the

Eliot K-8 Innovation School, spread over three different facilities in the North End. Also living on, a bit more ironically, is Copp's Hill Burying Ground, which still features its macabre Puritan-era gravestones in various states of disrepair, as well as more recent crosses and obelisks.

A mile south, another cemetery, Granary Burying Ground, has grave markers with a similar look, though the names of the departed will be more familiar to visitors—among them John Hancock, Samuel Adams, Paul Revere, James Otis Jr., James Bowdoin, and the five victims of the Massacre on King Street. The adjoining Common also has its own cemetery, Central Burying Ground, though the main appeal of this splendid urban park is its shaded walks, sports fields, seasonal ice-skating rink, plaza and bandstand, assorted statues and monuments, and the lovely Public Garden addition to the west. The legendary Old Elm that once stood in the center fell during a storm in 1876.

The Common stands in the shadow of the great Massachusetts State House, finished in 1798 after the Revolution and part of a wholesale reconstruction of Beacon Hill. In the nineteenth century, most of the Trimountain was leveled, and the ropewalks and heavy industry removed, to make way for elegant brick townhouses and mansions of the wealthy. Most of the African American community on the North Slope relocated, but the key sites of the neighborhood are still preserved on the Black Heritage Trail. The stops of the route date from after the Revolution, though the George Middleton House, from 1787, is relevant to the era. Its owner fought at Bunker Hill and was the commander of the Bucks of America militia of black soldiers.

As with the West End, the South End of Boston has been dramatically transformed, its fields and pastures giving way to mass development, with only a few remnants of the eighteenth century remaining. Foremost among these is the Old South Meetinghouse, whose role in the Revolution is commemorated with museum exhibits and well-preserved architecture that provides a sense of the fiery debates that took place in the days and weeks before the Destruction of the Tea. That event, known popularly as the Boston Tea Party, occurred on Griffin's Wharf several blocks to the southeast, along a shoreline that's since been filled in. But not too far away, an attraction known as the Boston Tea Party Ships & Museum depicts the episode with reenactments and interpretive exhibits on two replica vessels that float in a harbor channel.

North of the old Shawmut Peninsula, there's nothing left of revolutionary Charlestown since that town was destroyed during the war. However, this current neighborhood of Boston does feature the city's oldest bar, the Warren Tavern, dating from 1780, as well as a stirring monument and a fine museum devoted to the Battle of Bunker Hill. Most tourists come to Charlestown to see the USS *Constitution*, or Old Ironsides, a three-masted frigate dating from 1797.

In the southern part of modern Boston, towns like Roxbury and Dorchester were swallowed up by the metropolis in the post–Civil War era but still offer a handful of surviving buildings from the colonial and revolutionary eras. The First Church of Roxbury is the fifth incarnation of a meetinghouse on the site, with a congregation established nearly four hundred years ago and an 1803 design in a tasteful Federal style. Across the street, Oliver Peabody's 1750 parsonage for the church has been preserved as the Dillaway-Thomas House, partly named after General John Thomas, who commanded the right wing of Washington's army during the pivotal Dorchester Heights campaign. It's been restored several times and now acts as a museum offering period furnishings and exhibits. Similarly, the Shirley-Eustis House is a Roxbury museum that features restored architecture and compelling exhibits, showing the splendor in which mid-eighteenth-century royal governor William Shirley lived, as well as the grim conditions endured by his slaves.

In Dorchester, the historic North Burying Ground displays the increasingly worn-away headstones of town founders and more than a thousand others—though the nearby intersection no longer carries the Cemetery Corner moniker but is now known as Upham's Corner. Just north, the James Blake House is the oldest in Boston, dating from 1661, with a medieval-style timber frame and simple rustic design. A bit more fetching, the wood-shingled Lemuel Clap House stands along what was once the causeway to Dorchester Heights, which has become a residential stretch known as Boston Street. Along with the Blake House, the Clap House is under the protection of the Dorchester Historical Society and no longer sits in the shadow of a massive defensive earthwork, as it did during the war. In fact, most of Boston's fortifications and strongholds from that time have been lost to history. What was once an armed camp under constant siege has emerged as a stronghold of art and culture, education and commerce, medicine and technology—a vibrant urban setting with a cosmopolitan appeal, yet still an essential part of the formerly new, now quarter-millennium-old, republic.

ACKNOWLEDGMENTS

I'd most like to thank my wife, Teresa, for her thoughts and support in the development of this book, and to my parents and other family members for their kind words and encouragement. My friends, too, have provided valuable thoughts and feedback and deserve many thanks.

My manager Adam Chromy was essential in helping me get this project off the ground, with his own keen insights and strategy. At Diversion, I'm also grateful to Editor-in-Chief Keith Wallman for giving a book like this a chance to find a market, for guiding the project and contributing creative and thoughtful ideas, and for helping focus it on Boston instead of a wider, more diffuse view of the Revolution. I'd like to thank Leigh Grossman for his excellent work copyediting and fact-checking the manuscript, and for his valuable suggestions; Nina Smetana for assisting in the publication of the project; Daniel Huffman for creating the maps; and Amy Martin for managing the project.

Further, institutions and organizations like the Massachusetts Historical Society; the Museum of Fine Arts, Boston; the American Antiquarian Society; Historic New England; Revolutionary Spaces; the Boston Public Library; the Dorchester Historical Society; the West End Museum; and the Library of Congress provided useful suggestions, or helped me find sources when I needed them. The staff at sites like the Old State House and the Paul Revere House, and churches like Old North and Old South, allowed me to take a close look at their premises, glean what information I could from them, and peel back historical layers to uncover the differences between 1776 and today. Bostonians, too, helped me in some cases to discover quiet historic gems or unexpected angles on the city that I might not have otherwise considered.

To give a deeper thanks, I appreciate all that Andrew Rosenberg did some years ago to help me realize my potential as an author, not only in crafting travel guides at the outset of my career but to shape my writing and make it smarter, sharper, and more concise—and to offer his support with wit, kindness, and forbearance. I am forever grateful.

ILLUSTRATION CREDITS

PEOPLE AND PLACES

Abigail Adams. *Portrait by Benjamin Blyth, courtesy of Library of Congress*

James Otis. *Courtesy of Library of Congress*

Town House. *Courtesy of Boston Public Library*

Phillis Wheatley. *Courtesy of Library Company of Philadelphia*

Old South Church. *From the book* Rambles in Old Boston *by Edward G. Porter*

George Washington. *Courtesy of Library of Congress*

Sons of Liberty. *Courtesy of the Metropolitan Museum of Art*

Christ Church. *From the book* The Memorial History of Boston, v.2

Paul Revere. *Portrait by John Singleton Copley, courtesy of Museum of Fine Arts, Boston*

Paul Revere House. *From the book* Rambles in Old Boston *by Edward G. Porter*

Thomas Hutchinson. *Courtesy of New York Public Library*

Daughters of Liberty. *Woodcut from the poem "A New Touch on the Times" by Molly Gutridge; Courtesy of New-York Historical Society*

Green Dragon Tavern. *Courtesy of Boston Public Library*

Samuel Adams. *Portrait by John Singleton Copley, courtesy of Museum of Fine Arts, Boston*

Back Roads and Alleys. *From the book* Rambles in Old Boston *by Edward G. Porter*

Pope's Day. *Courtesy of Library of Congress*

Joseph Warren. *Courtesy of Library of Congress*

The Liberty Tree. *From the book* A History of Boston, the Metropolis of Massachusetts *by Caleb Snow*

Mercy Otis Warren. *Portrait by John Singleton Copley, courtesy of Museum of Fine Arts, Boston*

Faneuil Hall. *Courtesy of Library of Congress*

John Adams. *Portrait by Benjamin Blyth, courtesy of Massachusetts Historical Society*

John Hancock. *From the book* An Impartial History of the War in America *by James Murray*

REVOLUTIONARY EVENTS

Stamp Act Riots. *From the book* Cassell's History of the United States, vol. 2

1768 Troop Landing. *Courtesy of American Antiquarian Society*

The Massacre on King Street. *Courtesy of American Antiquarian Society*

Nonimportation. *Courtesy of Library of Congress*

Tarring and Feathering. *Courtesy of Library of Congress*

The Destruction of the Tea. *Courtesy of Library of Congress*

Coercive Acts. *Courtesy of Library of Congress*

Lexington and Concord. *Courtesy of Library Company of Philadelphia*

The Siege. *Courtesy of Boston Public Library*

Battle of Bunker Hill. *Courtesy of Library of Congress*

Evacuation Day. *Courtesy of Library of Congress*

ASPECTS OF BOSTON

Currency. *Courtesy of American Antiquarian Society*

Lanterns. *Courtesy of New York Public Library*

Newspaper Ads. *Boston Gazette*, April 20, 1767; *Courtesy of Massachusetts Historical Society*

Executions. *Courtesy of Library of Congress*

Royal Arms. *Courtesy of Massachusetts Historical Society*

Alphabets. *From the book* The New-England Primer Enlarged; *Courtesy of New York Public Library*

Tavern Bills. *Courtesy of American Antiquarian Society*

Cooking. *Courtesy of American Antiquarian Society*

Fast Days. *Courtesy of New York Public Library*

Gravestones. *Photo by Rhododendrites, Creative Commons*

Lottery Tickets. *Courtesy of Historic New England*

Cartoons. *"Wicked Statesman" by Paul Revere, courtesy of American Antiquarian Society*

BIBLIOGRAPHY

PRIMARY SOURCES

Adams Family

Adams, Abigail, and John Adams. *The Adams Papers, Adams Family Correspondence*, vol. 1, December 1761–May 1776, Lyman H. Butterfield, ed. Cambridge, Mass.: Harvard Univ. Press, 1963.

Adams, Abigail, and John Adams. *The Adams Papers, Adams Family Correspondence*, vol. 2, June 1776–March 1778. L.H. Butterfield, ed. Cambridge, Mass.: Harvard Univ. Press, 1963.

Adams, Abigail, and John Adams. *The Adams Papers, Adams Family Correspondence*, vol. 3, April 1778–September 1780, L. H. Butterfield and Marc Friedlaender, eds. Cambridge, Mass.: Harvard Univ. Press, 1973.

Adams, Abigail, and John Adams. *Familiar Letters of John Adams and His Wife Abigail Adams, During the Revolution, with a Memoir of Mrs. Adams.* Charles Francis Adams, ed. New York: Hurd and Houghton, 1876.

Adams, Abigail, and John Adams. *My Dearest Friend: Letters of Abigail and John Adams*. Margaret A. Hogan and C. James Taylor, eds. Cambridge, Mass.: Belknap Press, 2007.

Adams, John. *The Adams Papers, Legal Papers of John Adams,* 3 vols. L. Kinvin Wroth and Hiller B. Zobel, eds. Cambridge, Mass.: Harvard University Press, 1965.

Adams, John. *The Adams Papers, Papers of John Adams,* 20 vols. Robert J. Taylor, ed. Cambridge, Mass.: Harvard University Press, 1979.

Adams, John. *Diary and Autobiography of John Adams*. 4 vols. E. H. Butterfield, ed. Cambridge, Mass.: Harvard University Press, 1961.

Adams, John. *Thoughts on Government: Applicable to the Present State of the American Colonies*. Philadelphia: John Dunlap, 1776.

Adams, John. *The Works of John Adams, Second President of the United States,* 10 vols. Charles Francis Adams, ed. Boston: Charles C. Little and James Brown, 1851.

Letters, Memoirs and Diaries

Andrews, John. Letter to William Barrell, December 18, 1773. Andrews–Eliot Correspondence. Massachusetts Historical Society, Collections Online. Accessed on January 22, 2025. https://www.masshist.org/database/viewer.php?item_id=6605.

Andrews, John. "Letters of John Andrews, Esq., of Boston: 1772–1776." Winthrop Sargent, ed. *Massachusetts Historical Society Proceedings* 8 (July 1865): 316–412.

Boudinot, Elias. *Journal or Historical Recollections of American Events During the Revolutionary War*. Philadelphia: Frederick Bourquin, 1894.

Breck, Samuel. *Recollections of Samuel Breck, with Passages from His Notebooks*. Philadelphia: Sherman & Co., 1877.

Chipman, Ward. "Ward Chipman Diary," Joseph B. Berry, ed. *The Essex Institute Historical Collections* 87 (July 1951): 211–242.

Cooper, Samuel. "Diary of Samuel Cooper, 1775–1776." *The American Historical Review* 6, no. 2 (Jan. 1901): 301–341.

Cooper, Samuel. "Letters of Samuel Cooper to Thomas Pownall, 1769-1777." *The American Historical Review* 8, no. 2 (Jan. 1903): 301–330.

Curwen, Samuel. *Journal and Letters of the Late Samuel Curwen, Judge of the Admiralty, etc….* 3rd ed., George Atkinson Ward, ed. New York: Leavitt, Trow & Co., 1845.

de Chastellux, François Jean. *Travels in North America, in the Years 1780–81–82. . . .* New York: White, Gallaher, & White, 1827.

Eliot, Andrew. Letter to His Son, April 23, 1775. Massachusetts Historical Society, Miscellaneous Manuscripts. MHS Collections Online. http://www.masshist.org.

Franklin, Benjamin. *Papers of Benjamin Franklin,* vols. 18–21, William B. Willcox, ed. New Haven, Conn.: Yale University Press, 1974–1978.

Graydon, Alexander. *Memoirs of His Own Time, with Reminiscences of the Men and Events of the Revolution*. John Stockton Littell, ed. Philadelphia: Lindsay & Blakiston, 1846.

Hamilton, Phillip. *The Revolutionary War Lives and Letters of Lucy and Henry Knox*. Baltimore: Johns Hopkins University Press, 2017.

Hewes, George R. T. *Traits of the Tea Party; Being a Memoir of George R. T. Hewes, One of the Last Survivors*. New York: Harper & Brothers, 1835.

Hulton, Anne. *Letters of a Loyalist Lady*. Cambridge, Mass.: Harvard University Press, 1927.

Hutchinson, Thomas. "The Correspondence of Thomas Hutchinson, Volume 1: 1740–1766." John W. Tyler and Elizabeth Dubrulle, eds. *Colonial Society of Massachusetts* 84 (2014): 90–494.

Hutchinson, Thomas. "The Correspondence of Thomas Hutchinson, Volume 2: 1767–1769." John W. Tyler and Elizabeth Dubrulle, eds. *Colonial Society of Massachusetts* 92 (2020): 28–457.

Hutchinson, Thomas. "The Correspondence of Thomas Hutchinson, Volume 3: 1770 (January–October)." John W. Tyler, Margaret A. Hogan and Jane E. Ward, eds. *Colonial Society of Massachusetts* 94 (2021): 20–443.

Hutchinson, Thomas. "The Correspondence of Thomas Hutchinson, Volume 4: November 1770–June 1772." John W. Tyler, Margaret A. Hogan and Jane E. Ward, eds. *Colonial Society of Massachusetts* 95 (2022): 14–399.

Hutchinson, Thomas. "The Correspondence of Thomas Hutchinson, Volume 5: July 1772–May 1774." John W. Tyler, Margaret A. Hogan and Jane E. Ward, eds. *Colonial Society of Massachusetts* 99 (2023): 27–514.

Hutchinson, Thomas. *The Diary and Letters of His Excellency Thomas Hutchinson, Esq.* Peter Orlando Hutchinson, ed. London: Sampson Low, Marston, Searle & Rivington, 1883.

Jefferson, Thomas. *The Papers of Thomas Jefferson, Retirement Series*, J. Jefferson Looney, ed. Princeton, N.J.: Princeton University Press (2016).

Mather, Cotton. *Diary of Cotton Mather*, Volume II, 1709–1724. New York: Frederick Ungar, 1957.

Nantucket Historical Association. "Francis Rotch's Account of the Boston Tea Party." *Historic Nantucket* 23, no. 3 (January 1976): 21–23.

Newell, Timothy. "A Journal Kept During the Time That Boston Was Shut Up in 1775–6." *Collections of the Massachusetts Historical Society* 4, no. 1 (1852): 261–276.

Nichols, Charles L. "Samuel Salisbury—A Boston Merchant in the Revolution." *Proceedings of the American Antiquarian Society* (April 1925): 46–63.

Paine, Samuel. "Letter of Samuel Paine Upon Affairs at Boston in October, 1775." *New England Historical and Genealogical Register* 30 (July 1876): 369–373.

Rowe, John. *Letters and Diary of John Rowe, Boston Merchant: 1759–1762, 1764–1179*. Anne Rowe Cunningham, ed. Boston: W. B. Clarke, 1903.

Sewall, Samuel. *Diary of Samuel Sewall*. Collections of the Massachusetts Historical Society, vol. 7. Boston: Massachusetts Historical Society, 1887.

Wheatley, Phillis. Letter to David Wooster, October 18, 1773. Massachusetts Historical Society, Collections Online. Accessed on July 12, 2024. https://www.masshist.org/database/771.

Winslow, Anna Green. *Diary of Anna Green Winslow, a Boston School Girl of 1771*, Alice Morse Earle, ed. Boston: Houghton Mifflin, 1894.

Winslow, Edward, et al. *A Relation or Journal of the Beginning and Proceedings of the English Plantation Settled at Plymouth in New England* [Mourt's Relation]. London: John Bellamie, 1622.

Government Records

Adams, Samuel. Instruction to Representatives Upon the Following Draft . . . May 15, 1764. Boston Public Library, American Revolutionary War Manuscripts Collection.

"The Articles of Association." In *Journal of the Proceedings of the Congress, Held at Philadelphia*. Philadelphia: William and Thomas Bradford, 1774.

Board of Street Commissioners, *A Record of the Streets, Alleys, Places., Etc., in the City of Boston*. Boston: City Printing Dept., 1910.

Boston Committee of Correspondence. Letter to New York Committee of Correspondence, May 30, 1774. New York Public Library, Bancroft Papers.

Felt, Joseph B. *Annals of Salem*, vol. 2. Salem, Mass.: W & S. B. Ives, 1849.

The Journals of the Provincial Congress of Massachusetts in 1774 and 1775, and of the Committee of Safety. William Lincoln, ed. Boston: Dutton and Wentworth, 1838.

Massachusetts House of Representatives, "Resolves Respecting Certain Letters, Signed Tho. Hutchinson &c." Massachusetts Historical Society, Robert Treat Paine Papers, vol. 2.

"Record of the Boston Committee of Correspondence, Inspection and Safety, May to November, 1776." *New England Historical and Genealogical Register* 30 (July 1876): 441–444.

Records of the Governor and Company of the Massachusetts Bay in New England, vol. 4, 1650-1660. Nathaniel B. Shurtleff, ed. Boston: Massachusetts Govt. Printing Office, 1853.

A Report of the Record Commissioners of the City of Boston, Containing the Boston Records, 1660 to 1701. Boston: Rockwell and Churchill, 1881.

A Report of the Record Commissioners of the City of Boston, Containing the Boston Town Records, 1742 to 1757. Boston: Rockwell and Churchill, 1885.

A Report of the Record Commissioners of the City of Boston, Containing the Boston Town Records, 1758 to 1769. Boston: Rockwell and Churchill, 1886.

A Report of the Record Commissioners of the City of Boston, Containing the Boston Town Records, 1770 Through 1777. Boston: Rockwell and Churchill, 1887.

A Report of the Record Commissioners of the City of Boston, Containing the Selectmen's Minutes from 1764 Through 1768. Boston: Rockwell and Churchill, 1889.

A Report of the Record Commissioners of the City of Boston, Containing the Selectmen's Minutes from 1769 Through April 1775. Boston: Rockwell and Churchill, 1893.

A Report of the Record Commissioners of the City of Boston, Containing the Selectmen's Minutes from 1776 Through 1786. Boston: Rockwell and Churchill, 1894.

Military Affairs

Bowdoin, James, Joseph Warren and Samuel Pemberton [Town Meeting Committee]. *A Short Narrative of the Horrid Massacre in Boston. . . .* Boston: Edes & Gill, 1770.

Dearborn, Henry. *Revolutionary War Journals of Henry Dearborn, 1775–1783*. Lloyd A. Brown and Howard H. Peckham, eds. Chicago: Canton Club, 1939.

Edes, Peter. *Peter Edes, Pioneer Printer in Maine: A Biography. His Diary While a Prisoner by the British at Boston in 1775. . . .* Samuel Lane Boardman, ed. Bangor: private press, 1901.

A Fair Account of the Late Unhappy Disturbance at Boston in New England. London: B. White, 1770.

Fresh News from Boston. Copy of a Letter from a Person of Distinction at Cambridge, to a Gentleman in This City, dated Cambridge, March 21, 1776. New York, 1776. [broadside]

Gage, Thomas. Proclamation of Amnesty in Boston, June 12, 1775. Library of Congress. Accessed on Dec. 17, 2024. https://www.loc.gov/item/2016660912/.

Greenman, Jeremiah. *Diary of a Common Soldier in the American Revolution, 1775–1783*. Robert Bray and Paul Bushnell, eds. DeKalb, Ill.: Northern Illinois University Press, 1978.

Howe, William. *General Sir William Howe's Orderly Book at Charlestown, Boston and Halifax, June 17, 1775, to May 26, 1776*. London: Benjamin Franklin Stevens, 1890.

Kemble, Stephen. "Journals of Lieut.–Col. Stephen Kemble, 1773–1789." In *Collections of the New-York Historical Society for the Year 1883*. New York: New-York Historical Society, 1883.

Kimball, James. "Orderly Book of the Regiment of Artillery Raised for the Defence of the Town of Boston in 1776." *The Essex Institute Historical Collections* 14 (1877): 60–76, 110–128.

Percy, Hugh. *Letters of Hugh Earl Percy from Boston and New York, 1774–1776.* Charles Knowles Bolton, ed. Boston: Charles E. Goodspeed, 1902.

The Revolution Remembered: Eyewitness Accounts of the War of Independence. Dann, John C., ed. Chicago: University of Chicago, 1980.

The Spirit of 'Seventy-Six: The Story of the American Revolution as Told by Participants. Henry Steele Commager and Richard B. Morris, eds. Reprint. New York: Bonanza, 1983.

Stirke, Henry. "A British Officer's Revolutionary War Journal, 1776–1778." S. Sydney Bradford, ed. *Maryland Historical Magazine* 56, no. 2 (June 1961): 150–175.

Taylor, Eldad. "Evacuation of Boston, 1776, By an Eye Witness." *New England Historical and Genealogical Review* 8 (July 1854): 231–232.

Thacher, James. *A Military Journal During the American Revolutionary War, from 1775–1783.* Boston: Cottons & Barnard: 1827.

The Trial of William Wemms, James Hartegan, William McCauley. . . . Transcript of Superior Court of Judicature, November 27, 1770. Boston: J. Fleeming, 1770.

Upham, William P. "Extracts from Letters Written at the Time of the Occupation of Boston by the British, 1775–6." *The Essex Institute Historical Collections* 13 (July 1876): 153–236.

Washington, George. *The Papers of George Washington*, Revolutionary War Series, vols. 1–4, Philander D. Chase, ed. Charlottesville, Va.: University Press of Virginia, 1988.

Political Speeches and Writings

Adams, Samuel. *The Writings of Samuel Adams,* 4 vols. Harry Alonzo Cushing, ed. New York: G. P. Putnam's Sons, 1904–1908.

The American Revolution: Writings from the Pamphlet Debate, 2 vols., 1764–1776. Gordon S. Wood, ed. New York: Library of America, 2015.

British Pamphlets on the American Revolution, 1763–1785, 4 vols. Harry T. Dickinson, ed. New York: Routledge, 2007.

Declaration of Independence, July 4, 1776. National Archives, America's Founding Documents. Accessed on March 26, 1969. https://www.archives.gov/founding-docs/declaration-transcript.

George III, "A Proclamation, for Suppressing Rebellion and Sedition." August 23, 1775.

Gutridge, Molly. *A New Touch on the Times: Well Adapted to the Distressing Situation of Every Sea-port Town*. Danvers, Mass.: Ezekiel Russell, 1779 [broadside].

Hancock, John. "Oration Delivered at Boston," March 5, 1774. In *Principles and Acts of the Revolution in America*. H. Niles, ed. Boston: William Ogden Niles, 1822.

On Tuesday Night Arrived in This City, a Gentleman, Who Came Express from Boston, with the Following Interesting Intelligence viz. Boston, December 16. New York, 1773 [broadside].

Otis, James, Jr. *The Collected Political Writings of James Otis*, Richard A. Samuelson, ed. Indianapolis: Liberty Fund, 2015.

Otis, James, Jr. *The Rights of the British Colonies Asserted and Proved*. Boston: Edes & Gill, 1764.

Paine, Thomas. *Common Sense; Addressed to the Inhabitants of America, on the Following Interesting Subjects. . . .* Philadelphia: T. Bradford, 1776.

Pamphlets of the American Revolution, vol. 1, 1750-1765. Bernard Bailyn and Jane N. Garrett, eds. Cambridge, Mass.: Harvard University Press, 1965.

Revere, Paul. Sons of Liberty Bowl [Rescinders' Bowl] Inscription, 1768. Museum of Fine Arts Boston. Accessed September 1, 2024. https://collections.mfa.org/objects/39072.

Sewall, Samuel. *The Selling of Joseph, A Memorial*. Boston: Bartholomew Green, 1700.

"Sons and Daughters of Liberty Unite to Boycott William Jackson." Boston, 1769. [broadside] Upton, L.F.S. "Proceedings of Ye Body Respecting the Tea." *The William and Mary Quarterly* 22, no. 2 (April 1965): 287–300.

Warren, Joseph. "Oration Delivered at Boston, March 5, 1772." In *Principles and Acts of the Revolution in America*. H. Niles, ed. Baltimore: William Ogden Niles, 1822.

Warren, Joseph. "Oration Delivered at Boston," March 6, 1775. In *Principles and Acts of the Revolution in America*. H. Niles, ed. Boston: William Ogden Niles, 1822.

Religion

Chauncy, Charles. *Civil Magistrates Must Be Just, Ruling in the Fear of God*. Boston: Massachusetts Bay House of Representatives, 1747.

Chauncy, Charles. *Seasonable Thoughts on the State of Religion in New-England.* Boston: Rogers and Fowle, 1743.

Chauncy, Charles. *Trust in God, The Duty of a People in a Day of Trouble.* Boston: D. Kneeland, 1770.

Cutler, Timothy. Sermon to the Society for the Propagation of the Gospel, 1754. Massachusetts Historical Society, Old North Church Records, Box 24, Folder 27.

Eliot, Andrew. *An Evil and Adulterous Generation. A Sermon Preached on the Publick Fast, April 19, 1753.* Boston: S. Kneeland, 1753.

Lathrop, John. *A Sermon Occasioned by the Horrid Murder . . . on the Fifth of March, 1770.* London: E. and C. Dilly, 1770.

Mather, Cotton. *Grace Defended. A Censure on the Ungodliness, by Which the Glorious Grace of God, Is Too Commonly Abused.* Boston: B. Green, 1712.

Mather, Cotton. *Sober Considerations, on a Growing Flood of Iniquity.* Boston: John Allen, 1708.

Mayhew, Jonathan. *A Discourse Considering Unlimited Submission and Non-Resistance to the Higher Powers.* Boston: D. Fowle, 1750.

Mayhew, Jonathan. *Observations on the Charter and Conduct of the Society for the Propagation of the Gospel in Foreign Parts.* Boston: private press, 1763.

Mayhew, Jonathan. *A Sermon Preached in the Audience of His Excellency William Shirley, Esq.* Boston: S. Kneeland, 1754.

Mayhew, Jonathan. *Seven Sermons Upon the Following Subjects. . . .* Boston: Rogers and Fowle, 1749.

Mayhew, Jonathan. *The Snare Broken. A Thanksgiving-Discourse, Preached at the Desire of the West Church.* Boston: R. & S. Draper, 1766.

Norton, Humphrey. *New-England's Ensigne: It Being the Account of Cruelty, the Professors Pride, and the Articles of Their Faith, Signified in Characters Written in Blood. . . .* London: G. Calvert, 1659.

Pike, Samuel. *A Plain and Full Account of the Christian Practices Observed by the Church in St. Martin's-le-Grand, London, and Other Churches. . . .* Boston: Z. Fowle, 1766.

T. W. [Charles Chauncy] *Letter to a Friend, Containing a Concise, but Just, Representation of the Hardships and Sufferings. . . .* Boston: Greenleaf's Printing Office, 1774.

Winthrop, John. "For Preventing Drunkenness." Massachusetts Historical Society. Papers of the Winthrop Family, vol. 1 (1627). 371–374.

Winthrop, John. "A Model of Christian Charity." Massachusetts Historical Society. Papers of the Winthrop Family, vol. 2. 1630 Journal (April 12, 1630).

Food and Drink

Carter, Susannah. *The Frugal Housewife, or Complete Woman Cook*. Boston: Edes & Gill, 1772.

Concise Observations on the Nature of Our Common Food, so Far as It Tends to Promote or Injure Health. London: W. Justins, 1787.

Davis, William T. *Plymouth Memories of an Octogenarian*. Plymouth, Mass.: Bittinger Bros., 1906.

Gardiner, Anne Gibbons. *Mrs. Gardiner's Receipts from 1763*. Reprint. Hallowell, Me.: White & Horne, 1938.

Jackson, Sarah. *The Director: or Young Woman's Best Companion*. London: S. Crowder and H. Woodgate, 1754.

Lightbody, James. *Every Man His Own Gauger*. . . . London: private press, 1695.

Smith, Eliza. *The Compleat Housewife; or, Accomplish'd Gentlewoman's Companion*. London: J. Pemberton, 1730.

Contemporary Histories

Bennett, Joseph. "Bennett's History of New England: Boston in 1740." *Proceedings of the Massachusetts Historical Society* 5 (1860–1862): 108–126.

Burke, William, and Edmund Burke. *An Account of the European Settlements in America: In Six Parts*. . . ., vol. 2. London: R. & J. Dodsley, 1757.

Hutchinson, Thomas. *The History of the Province of Massachusetts Bay*, 3 vols. London: John Murray, 1778.

Hutchinson, Thomas. *The Witchcraft Delusion of 1692*. Boston: private press, 1870.

An Impartial History of the War in America, Between Great Britain and Her Colonies.... London: R. Faulder and J. Milliken, 1780.

Oliver, Peter. *Peter Oliver's Origin & Progress of the American Rebellion: A Tory View*. Douglass Adair and John A. Schutz, eds. Stanford, Calif.: Stanford Univ. Press, 1961.

Pemberton, Thomas. "A Topographical and Historical Description of Boston, 1794; by the Author of the Historical Journal of the American War." *Massachusetts Historical Society Collections* 3, 1st series (1794): 241–304.

Shaw, Charles. *A Topographical and Historical Description of Boston*. Boston: Oliver Spear, 1817.

Warren, Mercy Otis. *History of the Rise, Progress and Termination of the American Revolution*, vol. 1. Boston: Manning and Loring, 1805.

Winthrop, John. *Winthrop's Journal, "History of New England," 1630–1649*, vol. 1. James Kendall Hosmer, ed. New York: Charles Scribner's Sons, 1908.

Other Primary Sources

Bickerstaff's Boston Almanack. . . . Boston: Mills and Hicks, 1775.

Billings, William. *New-England Psalm-Singer: Or American Chorister*. Boston: Edes & Gill, 1770.

Boylston, Zabdiel. *An Historical Account of the Small-pox Inoculated in New England, Upon All Sorts of Persons, Whites, Blacks and of All Ages and Constitutions*. Boston: S. Chandler, 1726.

Boylston, Zabdiel. *Some Account of What Is Said of Inoculating or Transplanting the Small Pox. . . .* Boston: S. Gerrish, 1721.

Broadsides, Ballads &c. Printed in Massachusetts, 1639–1800. Worthington Chauncey Ford, ed. Boston: Massachusetts Historical Society, 1922.

Buchan, William. *Domestic Medicine; or the Family Physician*. Edinburgh: Balfour, Auld, and Smellie, 1769.

A Catalogue of Books, Imported and to Be Sold by Henry Knox. Boston: private press, 1773.

Copeland, David A. *Debating Issues in Colonial Newspapers. Primary Documents on Events of the Period*. Westport, Conn.: Greenwood Press, 2000.

The Dying Groans of Levi Ames, Who Was Executed at Boston, the 21st of October, 1773 for Burglary. Boston, 1773 [broadside].

A Pocket Almanack for the Year of Our Lord 1782. Boston: T. & J. Fleet, 1782.

Prynne, William. *Histrio-Mastix, The Players Scourge or, Actors Tragaedie, Divided into Two Parts. . . .* London: Michael Sparke, 1633.

Wheatley, Phillis. *The Poems of Phillis Wheatley*, Julian D. Mason Jr., ed. Chapel Hill, N.C.: Univ. of North Carolina Press, 1989.

Wheatley, Phillis. *Poems on Various Subjects, Religious and Moral*. London: A. Bell, 1773.

Wheatley, Phillis. *The Writings of Phillis Wheatley*, Vincent Carretta, ed. New York: Oxford Univ. Press, 2019.

EARLY HISTORIES

Bacon, Edwin M. *Rambles Around Old Boston*. Boston: Little, Brown, and Co., 1921.

Bowen, Lorenzo H. *Bowen's Picture of Boston . . . to Which Is Prefixed the Annals of Boston*. 2nd ed. Boston: Lilly Wait & Co., 1833.

Cassell's Illustrated History of England, vol. 5. London: Cassell Petter & Galpin, 1865.

Crawford, Mary Caroline. *Social Life in Old New England*. Boston: Little, Brown, and Co., 1914.

Dearborn, Nathaniel. *Dearborn's Reminiscences of Boston, and Guide Through the City and Environs*. Boston: Nathaniel Dearborn, 1851.

Dowst, Henry P. *Random Notes of Boston*. Boston: H. B. Humphrey, 1913.

Drake, Francis S. *The Town of Roxbury: Its Memorable Persons and Places*. Roxbury, Mass.: private press, 1878.

Drake, Samuel G. *The History and Antiquities of Boston . . . From Its Settlement in 1630, to the Year 1770*. Boston: Luther Stevens, 1856.

Drake, Samuel Adams. *Old Landmarks and Historic Personages of Boston*. Boston: Little, Brown, and Co., 1900.

Ellis, George E. *March 17th, 1876. Celebration of the Centennial Anniversary of the Evacuation of Boston by the British Army*. Boston: A. Williams & Co., 1876,

Frothingham, Richard, Jr. *The History of Charlestown, Massachusetts*. Charlestown: Charles P. Emmons, 1845.

Hunnewell, James F. *A Century of Town Life: A History of Charlestown, Massachusetts, 1775–1887*. Boston: Little, Brown, and Co., 1888.

Lodge, Henry Cabot. *Historic Towns: Boston*. New York: Longmans, Green, and Co., 1891.

Porter, Edward G. *Rambles in Old Boston, New England*. Boston: Cupples and Hurd, 1887.

Quincy, Josiah. *A Municipal History of the Town and City of Boston, During Two Centuries from September 17, 1630, to September 17, 1830*. Boston: Charles A. Little and James Brown, 1852.

Sabine, Lorenzo. *Biographical Sketches of Loyalists of the American Revolution*. 2 vols. Boston: Little, Brown, and Co., 1864.

Savage, Edward H. *Boston Events: A Brief Mention and the Date of More Than 5,000 Events That Transpired in Boston from 1630 to 1880*. Boston: Tolman & White, 1884.

Sawyer, Timothy T. *Old Charlestown, Historical, Biographical, Reminiscent.* Boston: James H. West, 1902.

Shurtleff, Nathaniel B. *A Topographical and Historical Description of Boston.* 3rd ed. Boston: Rockwell and Churchill, 1891.

Snow, Caleb. *A History of Boston, the Metropolis of Massachusetts, from Its Origin to the Present Period.* 2nd ed. Boston: Abel Bowen, 1828.

Thomas, Isaiah. *The History of Printing in America, with a Biography of Printers,* vol. 1. New York: Burt Franklin, 1874.

Thwing, Annie Haven. *The Crooked and Narrow Streets of the Town of Boston, 1630–1822.* Boston: Marshall Jones, 1920.

Wheildon, William W. *Curiosities of History: Boston, September Seventeenth, 1630–1880.* Boston: Lee and Shepard, 1880.

Winsor, Justin, ed. *The Memorial History of Boston: The Early and Colonial Periods,* vol. 1. Boston: James R. Osgood and Co., 1881.

Winsor, Justin, ed. *The Memorial History of Boston: The Provincial Period,* vol. 2. Boston: James R. Osgood and Co., 1881.

Winsor, Justin, ed. *The Memorial History of Boston: The Revolutionary Period,* vol. 3. Boston: James R. Osgood and Co., 1882.

SECONDARY SOURCES

General Revolution

Bailyn, Bernard. *The Ideological Origins of the American Revolution.* Cambridge, Mass.: Harvard Univ. Press, 1967.

Breen, T. H. *The Marketplace of Revolution: How Consumer Politics Shaped American Independence.* New York: Oxford University Press, 2004.

Carp, Benjamin L. *Defiance of the Patriots: The Boston Tea Party and the Making of America.* New Haven, Conn.: Yale University Press, 2010.

Deming, Brian. *Boston and the Dawn of American Independence.* Yardley, Pa.: Westholme, 2015.

Deshler, Charles D. “How the Declaration Was Received in the Old Thirteen.” *Harper's New Monthly Magazine* (July 1892): 174–175.

Hoock, Holger. *Scars of Independence: America's Violent Birth.* New York: Crown, 2017.

Maier, Pauline. “John Wilkes and American Disillusionment with Britain.” *The William and Mary Quarterly* 20, no. 3 (July 1963): 373–395.

Maier, Pauline. *From Resistance to Revolution: Colonial Radicals and the Development of American Opposition to Britain, 1765–1776*. New York: W. W. Norton, 1972.

Middlekauff, Robert. *The Glorious Cause: The American Revolution, 1763–1789*. New York: Oxford University Press, 1982.

Morgan, Edmund S., and Helen Morgan. *The Stamp Act Crisis: Prologue to Revolution*. Chapel Hill, N.C.: University of North Carolina Press, 1953.

Nash. Gary B. *The Unknown American Revolution: The Unruly Birth of Democracy and the Struggle to Create America*. New York: Viking, 2005.

Peterson, Mark. *The City-State of Boston: The Rise and Fall of an Atlantic Power, 1630–1865*. Princeton, N.J.: Princeton University Press, 2019.

Raphael, Ray. *A People's History of the American Revolution*. New York: New Press, 2001.

Syrett, David. "Town-Meeting Politics in Massachusetts, 1776–1786." *The William and Mary Quarterly* 21, no. 3 (July 1964): 352–366.

Taylor, Alan. *American Revolutions: A Continental History, 1750–1804*. New York: W. W. Norton, 2016.

Warner, Willam B. "The Invention of a Public Machine for Revolutionary Sentiment: The Boston Committee of Correspondence." *The Eighteenth Century* 50, no. 2/3 (Summer/Fall 2009): 145–164.

Wood, Gordon S. *The Radicalism of the American Revolution*. New York: Knopf, 1991.

Young, Alfred F. "English Plebeian Culture and Eighteenth-Century American Radicalism." In *The Origins of Anglo-American Radicalism*. Margaret Jacob and James Jacob, eds. London: George Allen & Unwin, 1984.

Young, Alfred F. *Liberty Tree: Ordinary People and the American Revolution*. New York: New York University Press, 2006.

Young, Alfred F. "Revolution in Boston? Eight Propositions for Public History on the Freedom Trail." *The Public Historian* 25, no. 2 (Spring 2003): 17–41.

Zabin, Serena. *The Boston Massacre: A Family History*. Boston: Houghton Mifflin Harcourt, 2020.

Public Figures

Anderson, George P. "Ebenezer Mackintosh: Stamp Act Rioter and Patriot." *Colonial Society of Massachusetts*, Transactions 26 (1924): 15–64.

Bailyn, Bernard. *The Ordeal of Thomas Hutchinson*. Cambridge, Mass.: Belknap Press, 1974.

Barbier, Brooke. *King Hancock: The Radical Influence of a Moderate Founding Father*. Cambridge, Mass.: Harvard University Press, 2023.

Baxter, W.T. *The House of Hancock: Business in Boston, 1724–1775*. Cambridge, Mass.: Harvard University Press, 1945.

Boston University Graduate History Club. "Paul Revere: Early Life." Paul Revere Heritage Project (2007). http://www.paul-revere-heritage.com

Cleary, Patricia. *Elizabeth Murray: A Woman's Pursuit of Independence in Eighteenth-Century America.* Amherst, Mass.: University of Massachusetts Press, 2000.

Curran, Emily, and Jill Sanderson. *Phillis Wheatley and the Origins of African American Literature.* Boston: Old South Association, 1999.

Duffy, Shannon E. "An Enlightened American: The Political Ideology of Thomas Hutchinson on the Eve of the Revolutionary Crisis." PhD diss., University of Maryland, 2008

Ellis, Joseph J. *First Family: Abigail and John Adams*. New York: Knopf, 2010.

Erkkila, Betsy. "Phillis Wheatley on the Streets of Revolutionary Boston and in the Atlantic World." *Early American Literature* 56, no. 2 (2021): 351–372.

Ferguson, James R. "Reason in Madness: The Political Thought of James Otis." *The William and Mary Quarterly* 36, no. 2 (1979), 194–214.

Ferling, John. *John Adams: A Life*. New York: Oxford University Press, 2010.

Fischer, David Hackett. *Paul Revere's Ride*. New York: Oxford University Press, 1994.

Forbes, Esther. *Paul Revere and the World He Lived In*. Boston: Houghton Mifflin, 1942.

Forman, Samuel. *Dr. Joseph Warren: The Boston Tea Party, Bunker Hill, and the Birth of American Liberty*. Gretna, La.: Pelican Publishing Co., 2011.

Fowler, William M., Jr. *The Baron of Beacon Hill: A Biography of John Hancock*. Boston: Houghton Mifflin, 1980.

Fowler, William M., Jr. *Samuel Adams: Radical Puritan*. New York: Longman, 1997.

Frothingham, Richard, Jr. *Life and Times of Joseph Warren*. Boston: Little, Brown and Co., 1865.

Gelles, Edith B. *Abigail Adams: A Writing Life*. New York: Routledge, 2002.

Hosmer, James K. *American Statesmen: Samuel Adams*. Boston: Houghton, Mifflin and Co., 1890.

Levernier, James A. "Phillis Wheatley and the New England Clergy." *Early American Literature* 26, no. 1 (1991): 21–38.

Maier, Pauline. "Coming to Terms with Samuel Adams." *The American Historical Review* 81, no. 1 (Feb. 1976): 12–37.

Miller, John C. *Sam Adams: Pioneer in Propaganda*. Stanford, Calif.: Stanford University Press, 1936.

Puls, Mark. *Samuel Adams: Father of the American Revolution*. New York: Palgrave Macmillan, 2006.

Ryerson, Richard Alan. *John Adams's Republic: The One, the Few, and the Many*. Baltimore: Johns Hopkins Univ. Press, 2016.

Sankovitch, Nina. *American Rebels: How the Hancock, Adams, and Quincy Families Fanned the Flames of Revolution*. New York: St. Martin's Press, 2020.

Schiff, Stacy. *The Revolutionary: Samuel Adams*. New York: Little, Brown and Co., 2022.

Smith, John L., Jr. *The Unexpected Abigail Adams: A Woman "Not Apt to Be Intimidated."* Yardley, Pa.: Westholme, 2024.

Smith, Page. *John Adams*. 2 vols. New York: Doubleday, 1962.

Unger, Harlow Giles. *John Hancock: Merchant King and American Patriot*. Hoboken, N.J.: John Wiley & Sons, 2000.

Wells, William V. *The Life and Public Services of Samuel Adams,* 2 vols. Boston: Little, Brown, and Company, 1865.

Wesley, Charles H. *Prince Hall: Life and Legacy*. Washington, D.C.: United Supreme Council, Southern Jurisdiction, Prince Hall Affiliation, 1977.

Zagarri, Rosemarie. *A Woman's Dilemma: Mercy Otis Warren and the American Revolution*. Wheeling, Ill.: Harlan Davidson, 1995.

War and Military Occupation

Alden, John Richard. *General Gage in America, Being Principally a History of His Role in the American Revolution*. New York: Greenwood Press, 1948.

Archer, Richard. *As If an Enemy's Country: The British Occupation of Boston and the Origins of Revolution*. New York: Oxford University Press, 2010.

Atkinson, Rick. *The British Are Coming: The War for America, Lexington to Princeton, 1775–1777*. New York: Henry Holt, 2019.

Brooks, Victor. *The Boston Campaign: April 1775–March 1776*. Conshohocken, Penn.: Combined Publishing, 1999.

Brown, Richard D. "The Confiscation and Disposition of Loyalists' Estates in Suffolk County, Massachusetts." *The William and Mary Quarterly* 21, no. 4 (Oct. 1964): 534–550.

Conway, Stephen. "'The Great Mischief Complain'd of': Reflections on the Misconduct of British Soldiers in the Revolutionary War." *The William and Mary Quarterly* 47, no. 3 (July 1990): 370–390.

Conway, Stephen. "To Subdue America: British Army Officers and the Conduct of the Revolutionary War." *The William and Mary Quarterly* 43, no. 3 (July 1986): 381–407.

Frothingham, Richard, Jr. *The Battle-Field at Bunker Hill: with a Relation of the Action by William Prescott and Illustrative Documents.* Boston: private press, 1876.

Frothingham, Richard, Jr. *The Centennial: Battle of Bunker Hill.* Boston: Little, Brown, and Co., 1875.

Frothingham, Richard, Jr. *History of the Siege of Boston, and of the Battles of Lexington, Concord, and Bunker Hill.* Boston: Charles C. Little and James Brown, 1851.

Galvin, John R. *The Minute Men, The First Fight: Myths & Realities of the American Revolution.* Washington, D.C.: Pergamon-Brassey's, 1989.

Gross, Robert A. *The Minutemen and Their World.* Reprint. New York: Hill and Wang, 2001.

Ketchum, Richard R. *Decisive Day: The Battle for Bunker Hill.* Reprint. New York: Henry Holt, 1999.

Messer, Peter. "A Scene of Villainy Acted by a Dirty Banditti, as Must Astonish the Public." *The New England Quarterly* 90, no. 4 (Dec. 2017): 502–539.

Naval Documents of the American Revolution, vol. 1, William Bell Clark, ed. Washington, D.C.: U.S. Govt. Printing Office, 1964.

Philbrick, Nathaniel. *Bunker Hill: A City, A Siege, A Revolution.* New York: Viking, 2013.

Starkey, Armstrong. "Paoli to Stony Point: Military Ethics and Weaponry During the American Revolution." *The Journal of Military History* 58, no. 1 (Jan. 1994): 7–27.

War & Society in the American Revolution: Mobilization and Home Fronts. John Resch and Walter Sargent, eds. DeKalb, Ill.: Northern Illinois University Press, 2007.

Trade and Commerce

Boston National Historical Park. "Piecing Together the Atlantic Empire of Peter Faneuil." National Park Service. Accessed July 29, 2024. https://www.nps.gov/articles/000/piecing-together-the-atlantic-empire-of-peter-faneuil.htm.

Breen, T.H. "An Empire of Goods: The Anglicization of Colonial America, 1690–1776." *Journal of British Studies* 25, no. 4 (Oct. 1986): 467–499.

Bushman, Richard L. "Shopping and Advertising in Colonial America." In *Of Consuming Interests: The Style of Life in the Eighteenth Century*. Cary Carson, Ronald Hoffman, and Peter J. Albert, eds. Charlottesville, Va.: University Press of Virginia, 1994.

Conway, Stephen. "British Governments, Colonial Consumers, and Continental European Goods in the British Atlantic Empire, 1763–1775." *The Historical Journal* 58, no. 3 (September 2015): 711–732.

Entrepreneurs: The Boston Business Community, 1700–1850. Conrad Edick Wright and Katheryn P. Viens, eds. Boston: Massachusetts Historical Society, 1997.

Harlow, Ralph Volney. "Aspects of Revolutionary Finance, 1775–1783." *The American Historical Review* 35, no. 1 (Oct. 1929): 46–68.

McCusker, John J. "The Rum Trade and the Balance of Payments of the Thirteen Continental Colonies, 1650–1775." *The Journal of Economic History* 30, no. 1 (March 1970): 244–247.

Morison, Samuel Eliot. "The Commerce of Boston on the Eve of Revolution." *American Antiquarian Society* 32 (April 1922): 24–51.

Newell, Margaret E. "A Revolution in Economic Thought: Currency and Development in Eighteenth-Century Massachusetts." In *Entrepreneurs: The Boston Business Community, 1700–1850*. Conrad Edick Wright and Katheryn P. Viens, eds. Boston: Massachusetts Historical Society, 1997.

Shammas, Carol. "Consumer Behavior in Colonial America." *Social Science History* 6, no. 1 (Winter 1982): 67–86.

Smith, Barbara Clark. "The Politics of Price Control in Revolutionary Massachusetts, 1774–1780." PhD diss., Yale University, 1983.

Smith, S.D. "The Market for Manufactures in the Thirteen Continental Colonies, 1698–1776." *The Economic History Review* 51, no. 4 (Nov. 1998): 676–708.

Tyler, John W. "Persistence and Change Within the Boston Business Community, 1775–1790." In *Entrepreneurs: The Boston Business Community, 1700–1850*. Conrad Edick Wright and Katheryn P. Viens, eds. Boston: Massachusetts Historical Society, 1997.

Tyler, John W. *Smugglers and Patriots: Boston Merchants and the Advent of the American Revolution*. Boston: Northeastern University Press, 1986.

Maritime History

Baker, William Avery. "Vessel Types in Colonial Massachusetts." *Colonial Society of Massachusetts* 52 (1980): 3–29.

Balicki, Joseph F. "Wharves, Privies, and the Pewterer: Two Colonial Period Sites on the Shawmut Peninsula." *Historical Archaeology* 32, no. 3 (1998): 99–120.

Brunsman, Denver. "The Knowles Atlantic Impressment Riots of the 1740s." *Early American Studies* 5, no. 2 (Fall 2007): 324–366.

Farr, James. "A Slow Boat to Nowhere: The Multi-Racial Crews of the American Whaling Industry." *The Journal of Negro History* 68, no. 2 (Spring 1983): 159–170.

Frayler, John. "The Great Age of Duck." *Pickled Fish and Salted Provisions: Historical Musings from Salem Maritime NHS* 7, no. 4 (2005): 3–7.

Gilje, Paul A. *Liberty on the Waterfront: American Maritime Culture in the Age of Revolution*. Philadelphia: University of Pennsylvania Press, 2004.

Gilje, Paul A. "Loyalty and Liberty: The Ambiguous Patriotism of Jack Tar in the American Revolution." *Pennsylvania History: A Journal of Mid-Atlantic Studies* 67, no. 2 (Spring 2000): 165–193.

Johnson, Bob. "A Peculiarly Valuable Oil: Energy and the Ecology of Production on an Early American Whale Ship." *The Journal of the Society for Industrial Archeology* 40, no. 1/2 (2014): 33–50.

Lemisch, Jesse. "Jack Tar in the Streets: Merchant Seamen in the Politics of Revolutionary America." *The William and Mary Quarterly* 25, no. 3 (July 1968): 371–407.

Morison, Samuel Eliot. *Maritime History of Massachusetts, 1783–1860*. Boston: Houghton Mifflin, 1921.

Norton, Mary Beth. "The Seventh Tea Ship." *The William and Mary Quarterly* 73, no. 4 (Oct. 2016): 681–710.

Old Shipping Days in Boston. Boston: State Street Trust Co., 1918.

Olmsted Center for Landscape Preservation. *Cultural Landscape Report for the Boston Harbor Islands: Boston Harbor Islands National & State Park. Volume I: Historical Overview*. Boston: National Park Service, U.S. Dept. of the Interior, 2017.

Patton, Robert H. *Patriot Pirates: The Privateer War for Freedom and Fortune in the American Revolution*. New York: Pantheon, 2008

Pitt, Steven J. "Building and Outfitting Ships in Colonial Boston." *Early American Studies* 13, no. 4 (Fall 2015): 881–907.

President and Fellows of Harvard College. "Long Wharf." *Bulletin of the Business Historical Society* 9, no. 2 (March 1935): 17–22.

Stevens, Christopher, et al. *Cultural Landscape Report for Charlestown Navy Yard*. Boston: National Park Service, 2005.

Watson, D. H. "Joseph Harrison and the Liberty Incident." *The William and Mary Quarterly* 20, no. 4 (Oct. 1963): 585–595.

Physical Conditions and Sites

Barber, Samuel. *Boston Common, A Diary of Notable Events, Incidents, and Neighboring Occurrences.* 2nd ed. Boston: Christopher Publishing House, 1916.

Beagle, Jonathan M. "'The Cradle of Liberty': Faneuil Hall and the Political Culture of Eighteenth-Century Boston." PhD diss., Univ. of New Hampshire, 2003.

Boston Landmarks Commission. *City Square Historical & Archaeological Site.* Boston: Landmarks Commission, Environment Department, 1992.

Boston Landmarks Commission. *Report on the Potential Designation of the Old State House as a Landmark. . . .* Boston: Boston Landmarks Commission, 1994.

Boston Parks and Recreation Department. "History of Eliot Burying Ground: A Community Undertaking." *Historic Burying Grounds Initiative Newsletter* 2, no. 2 (2012): 1–11.

Chamberlain, Allen. *Beacon Hill: Its Ancient Pastures and Early Mansions.* Boston: Houghton Mifflin, 1925.

Chartier, Craig S. *An Archaeological Reevaluation of the Great House/Three Cranes Tavern (1629–1775), Charlestown, Massachusetts.* New Bedford, Mass.: Plymouth Archaeological Rediscovery Project, 2016.

Conroy, Thomas E., III. "The Politics of Style: Building, Builders, and the Creation of Federal Boston." PhD diss., University of Massachusetts Amherst, 2005.

Goldfeld, Alex R. *The North End: A Brief History of Boston's Oldest Neighborhood.* Charleston, S.C.: The History Press, 2009.

Hedges, Hillary Rayport, et al. "Historic Paving and Sidewalks in New England." Archipedia New England. Accessed on January 11, 2025. www.archipedianewengland.org/1600-1699/historic-paving-and-sidewalks-in-new-england/.

Historic Boston, Inc. "Commercial Casebook: Upham's Corner, Dorchester." 2015, Accessed on October 8, 2024. https://historicboston.org/wp-content/uploads/Casebook-Uphams-Corner.pdf.

"Hutchinson House." *American Magazine of Useful and Entertaining Knowledge* 2, no. 1 (September 1835): 237.

Kaye, Clifford A. *The Geology and Early History of the Boston Area of Massachusetts, A Bicentennial Approach.* Washington, D.C.: U.S. Govt. Printing Office, 1976.

Klee, Jeffrey. "Civic Order on Beacon Hill." *Buildings & Landscapes: Journal of the Vernacular Architecture Forum* 15 (Fall 2008): 43–57.

Massachusetts Historical Commission. *MHC Reconnaissance Survey Town Report.* Boston: Massachusetts Historical Commission, 1981.

Massachusetts Historical Commission. "Three Cranes Tavern." Archaeological Exhibits Online. Accessed on April 3, 2025. https://www.sec.state.ma.us/divisions/mhc/archaeology/exhibits/three-cranes.htm.

McDonald, E. *Old Copp's Hill and Burial Ground with Historical Sketches.* Boston: W.F. Brown & Co., 1879.

The Old Town-House of Boston. 2nd ed. Boston: Conant & Newhall, 1883.

Robbins, Chandler. *A History of the Second Church, or Old North Church, in Boston.* Boston: John Wilson & Son, 1852.

Seasholes, Nancy S., ed. *The Atlas of Boston History.* Chicago: Univ. of Chicago Press, 2019.

Seasholes, Nancy S. "Filling Boston's Mill Pond." *Historical Archaeology* 32, no. 3 (1998): 121–136.

Seasholes, Nancy S. *Gaining Ground: A History of Landmaking in Boston.* Cambridge, Mass.: MIT Press, 2003.

Shammas, Carole. "The Housing Stock of the Early United States: Refinement Meets Migration." *The William and Mary Quarterly* 64, no. 3 (July 2007): 549–590.

Shammas, Carol. "The Space Problem in Early United States Cities." *The William and Mary Quarterly* 57, no. 3 (July 2000): 505–542.

Shurtleff, Nathaniel B. "Notable Places: The Green Dragon Tavern." *The Historical Magazine* 3rd series, no. 1 (1872): 28–31.

Smith, John L., Jr. "Visiting Boston's Liberty Tree Site." Journal of the American Revolution, April 21, 2015. https://allthingsliberty.com/2015/04/visiting-bostons-liberty-tree-site/.

Sweetser, M.F. *King's Handbook of Boston Harbor*, 3rd ed. Boston: Moses King Corp., 1888.

Wheildon, William W. *Sentry, or Beacon Hill; The Beacon and the Monument of 1635 and 1790.* Boston: Lee and Shepard, 1877.

Whitehill, Walter Muir, and Lawrence W. Kennedy. *Boston: A Topographical History*, 3rd Ed. Cambridge, Mass.: Belknap Press, 2000.

Religion

Akers, Charles W. *Called Unto Liberty: A Life of Jonathan Mayhew.* Cambridge, Mass.: Harvard University Press, 1964.

Akers, Charles W. *The Divine Politician: Samuel Cooper and the American Revolution in Boston*. Boston: Northeastern University Press, 1982.

Akers, Charles W. "Religion and the American Revolution: Samuel Cooper and the Brattle Street Church." *The William and Mary Quarterly* 35, no. 3 (July 1978): 477–498.

Baldwin, Alice M. *The New England Clergy and the American Revolution*. New York: Frederick Ungar, 1958.

Bonomi, Patricia U., and Peter R. Eisenstadt. "Church Adherence in the Eighteenth-Century British American Colonies." *The William and Mary Quarterly* 39, no. 2 (April 1982): 245–286.

Carter, Michael S. "'A Traiterous Religion': Indulgences and the Anti-Catholic Imagination in Eighteenth-Century New England." *The Catholic Historical Review* 99, no. 1 (Jan. 2013): 52–77.

Cogliano, Francis D. *No King, No Popery: Anti-Catholicism in Revolutionary New England*. Westport, Conn.: Greenwood Press, 1996.

Emerson, William. *An Historical Sketch of the First Church in Boston, from Its Formation to the Present Period*. Boston: Munroe & Francis, 1812.

Foote, Henry Wilder. *Annals of King's Chapel, from the Puritan Age of New England to the Present Day*, vol. 2. Boston: Little, Brown, and Co., 1896.

Griffin, Edward M. *Old Brick: Charles Chauncy of Boston, 1705-1787*. Minneapolis: University of Minnesota Press, 1980.

Hill, Hamilton Andrews. *History of the Old South Church (Third Church), Boston 1669–1884*, vol. 2. Boston: Houghton Mifflin and Co., 1890.

Lothrop, Samuel Kirkland. *A History of the Church in Brattle Street, Boston*. Boston: Crosby and Nichols, 1851.

Lubert, Howard. "Jonathan Mayhew: Conservative Revolutionary." *History of Political Thought* 32, no. 4 (2011), 589–616.

Marini, Stephen R. *Radical Sects of Revolutionary New England*. Cambridge, Mass.: Harvard University Press, 1982.

McGunigal, Lisa. "The Criminal Trial of Anne Hutchinson: Ritual, Religion, and Law." *Mosaic: An Interdisciplinary Critical Journal* 49, no. 2 (June 2016): 149–166.

Moerschel, Lesley Ann. "'In Ye Service of the Lord': Boston's Churches, Public Discourse, and the American Revolution." PhD diss., Washington State University, 2012.

Monaghan, E. Jennifer. "Family Literacy in Early 18th-Century Boston: Cotton Mather and His Children." *Reading Research Quarterly* 26, no. 4 (Autumn 1991): 342–370.

Mullins, J. Patrick. *Father of Liberty: Jonathan Mayhew and the Principles of the American Revolution*. Lawrence, Ks.: University Press of Kansas, 2017.

Perry, William Stevens. *Papers Relating to the History of the Church in Massachusetts, A.D. 1676–1785*. Boston: private press, 1873.

Rossiter, Clinton. "The Life and Mind of Jonathan Mayhew." *William and Mary Quarterly* 3rd series, no. 7 (1950): 531–558.

Schneider, Deborah Lucas. "Anne Hutchinson and Covenant Theology." *The Harvard Theological Review* 103, no. 4 (October 2010): 485–500.

Stout, Harry S. *The Divine Dramatist: George Whitefield and the Rise of Modern Evangelicalism*. Grand Rapids, Mich.: Eerdmans Co., 1991.

Thornton, John Wingate. *The Pulpit of the American Revolution*. Boston: D. Lothrop & Co., 1876.

Economic and Social Conditions

Bridenbaugh, Carl. *Cities in the Wilderness: The First Century of Urban Life in America, 1625-1742*. New York: Ronald Press, 1938.

Carr, Jacqueline Barbara. *After the Siege: A Social History of Boston, 1775–1800*. Boston: Northeastern University Press, 2005.

Carr, Jacqueline Barbara. "A Change 'As Remarkable as the Revolution Itself': Boston's Demographics, 1780–1800." *The New England Quarterly* 73, no. 4 (Dec. 2000): 583–602.

Dayton, Cornelia H., and Sharon V. Salinger. *Robert Love's Warnings: Searching for Strangers in Colonial Boston*. Philadelphia: Univ. of Pennsylvania Press, 2014.

Glaeser, Edward L. "Reinventing Boston: 1630–2003." *Journal of Economic Geography* 5, no. 2 (April 2005): 119–153.

Henretta, James A. "Economic Development and Social Structure in Colonial Boston." *The William and Mary Quarterly* 22, no. 1 (Jan. 1965): 75–92.

Huang, Nian-Sheng. "Financing Poor Relief in Colonial Boston." *Massachusetts Historical Review* 8 (2006): 72–103.

Jones, Douglas Lamar. "The Strolling Poor: Transiency in Eighteenth Century Massachusetts." *Journal of Social History* 8 (1975): 28–54.

Kulikoff, Allan. "The Progress of Inequality in Revolutionary Boston." *The William and Mary Quarterly* 28, no. 3 (July 1971): 375–412.

Nash, Gary B. *The Urban Crucible: The Northern Seaports and the Origins of the American Revolution.* Cambridge, Mass.: Harvard University Press, 1986.

Nash, Gary B. "Urban Wealth and Poverty in Pre-Revolutionary America." *The Journal of Interdisciplinary History* 6, no. 4 (Spring 1976): 545–584.

Nellis, Eric G., ed. "The Almshouse and Workhouse." *Colonial Society of Massachusetts* 69 (2007): 57–102.

Nellis, Eric G., ed. "The Historical Setting: the Boston Poor and the Records of the Overseers." *Colonial Society of Massachusetts* 69 (2007): 18–40.

Nellis, Eric G. "Misreading the Signs: Industrial Imitation, Poverty, and the Social Order in Colonial Boston." *The New England Quarterly* 59, no. 4 (Dec. 1986): 486–507.

Towner, Lawrence W. "The Indentures of Boston's Poor Apprentices: 1734–1805." *Colonial Society of Massachusetts, Transactions* 43 (1962): 417–468.

Warden, G. B. "Inequality and Instability in Eighteenth-Century Boston: A Reappraisal." *The Journal of Interdisciplinary History* 6, no. 4 (Spring 1976): 585–620.

Wright, Carroll D. *History of Wages and Prices in Massachusetts: 1752–1883.* Boston: Wright & Potter, 1885.

Young, Alfred F. "George Robert Twelves Hewes (1742-1840): A Boston Shoemaker and the Memory of the American Revolution." *The William and Mary Quarterly* 38, no. 4 (October 1981): 561–623.

Young, Alfred F. *The Shoemaker and the Tea Party: Memory and the American Revolution.* Boston: Beacon Press, 1999.

Women in the Revolution

Carr, Jacqueline Barbara. "Marketing Gentility: Boston's Businesswomen, 1780-1830." *The New England Quarterly* 82, no. 1 (March 2009): 25–55.

Cleary, Patricia. "'She Merchants' of Colonial America: Women and Commerce on the Eve of the Revolution." PhD diss., Northwestern University, 1989.

Cleary, Patricia. "Who Shall Say We Have Not Equal Abilitys with the Men. . . . Women of Commerce in Boston, 1750–1776." In *Entrepreneurs: The Boston Business Community, 1700–1850.* Conrad Edick Wright and Katheryn P. Viens, eds. Boston: Massachusetts Historical Society, 1997.

Crane, Elaine Forman. *Ebb Tide in New England: Women, Seaports, and Social Change, 1630–1800.* Boston: Northeastern University Press, 1998.

Erkkila, Betsy. "Revolutionary Women." *Tulsa Studies in Women's Literature* 6, no. 2 (Autumn 1987):189–223.

Hartigan-O'Connor, Ellen. "'She Said She Did Not Know Money'": Urban Women and Atlantic Markets in the Revolutionary Era." *Early American Studies* 4, no. 2 (Fall 2006): 322–352.

Kerber, Linda K. *The Women of the Republic: Intellect and Ideology in Revolutionary America.* Chapel Hill, N.C.: University of North Carolina Press, 1980.

Keyssar, Alexander. "Widowhood in Eighteenth-Century Massachusetts: A Problem in the History of the Family." *Perspectives in American History* 8 (1974): 83–122.

Main, Gloria L. "Gender, Work, and Wages in Colonial New England." *The William and Mary Quarterly* 51, no. 1 (Jan. 1994): 39–66.

Miller, Marla R. "Gender, Artisanry, and Craft Tradition in Early New England: The View Through the Eye of a Needle." *The William and Mary Quarterly* 60, no. 4 (Oct. 2003): 743–776.

Miller, Marla R. "The Last Mantuamaker: Craft Tradition and Commercial Change in Boston, 1760–1845." *Early American Studies* 4, no. 2 (Fall 2006): 372–424.

Norton, Mary Beth. "Eighteenth-Century American Women in Peace and War: The Case of the Loyalists." *The William and Mary Quarterly* 33, no. 3 (July 1976): 386–409.

Norton, Mary Beth. *Liberty's Daughters: The Revolutionary Experience of American Women, 1750–1800.* Boston: Scott, Foresman and Co., 1980.

Shammas, Carole. "Early American Women and Control over Capital." In *Women in the Age of the American Revolution*, Ronald Hoffman and Peter J. Albert, eds. Charlottesville, Va.: Univ. Press of Virginia, 1989: 134–154.

Smith, Daniel Scott. "Female Householding in Late Eighteenth-Century America and the Problem of Poverty." *Journal of Social History* 28, no. 1 (Autumn 1994): 83–107.

Ulrich, Laura Thatcher. *Good Wives: Image and Reality in the Lives of Women in Northern New England, 1650-1750.* New York: Knopf, 1982.

Ulrich, Laurel Thatcher. "Wheels, Looms, and the Gender Division of Labor in Eighteenth-Century New England." *The William and Mary Quarterly* 55, no. 1 (Jan. 1998): 3–38.

Young, Alfred F. "The Women of Boston: 'Persons of Consequence' in the Making of the American Revolution." In *Women and Politics in the Age of the Democratic Revolution*, Harriet B. Applewhite and Darline G. Levy, eds. Ann Arbor: University of Michigan Press, 1990.

Racial Conditions

Bailey, Ronald. "The Slave(ry) Trade and the Development of Capitalism in the United States: The Textile Industry in New England." *Social Science History* 14, no. 3 (Autumn 1990): 373–414.

Brooks, Joanna. "The Early American Public Sphere and the Emergence of a Black Print Counterpublic." *The William and Mary Quarterly* 62, no. 1 (Jan. 2005), 67–92.

Brooks, Joanna. "Prince Hall, Freemasonry, and Genealogy." *African American Review* 34, no. 2 (Summer 2000): 197–216.

Davis, Harry E. *A History of Freemasonry Among Negroes in America*. Cleveland: United Supreme Council (AASR), 1946.

Davis, Thomas J. "Emancipation Rhetoric, Natural Rights, and Revolutionary New England: A Note on Four Black Petitions in Massachusetts, 1773–1777." *The New England Quarterly* 62, no. 2 (June 1989): 248–263.

Desrochers, Robert E., Jr. "Slave-for-Sale Advertisements and Slavery in Massachusetts, 1704-1781." *The William and Mary Quarterly* 59, no. 3 (July 2002): 623–664.

Donnan, Elizabeth. "The New England Slave Trade After the Revolution." *The New England Quarterly* 3, no. 2 (April 1930): 251–278.

Gilje, Paul A., and Howard B. Rock. "'Sweep O! Sweep O!': African-American Chimney Sweeps and Citizenship in the New Nation." *The William and Mary Quarterly* 51, no. 3 (July 1994): 507–538.

Horton, James Oliver, and Lois E. Horton. *Black Bostonians: Family Life and Community Struggle in the Antebellum North*. New York: Holmes & Meier, 1997.

Landon, David B., and Teresa D. Bulger. "Constructing Community: Experiences of Identity, Economic Opportunity, and Institution Building at Boston's African Meeting House." *International Journal of Historical Archaeology* 17, no. 1 (March 2013): 119–142.

MacEachern, Elaine. "Emancipation of Slavery in in Massachusetts: A Reexamination 1770-1790." *The Journal of Negro History* 55, no. 4 (Oct. 1970): 289–306.

Nash, Gary. "African Americans in the Early Republic." *OAH Magazine of History* 14, no. 2 (Winter 2000): 12–16.

Nell, William C. *The Colored Patriots of the American Revolution, with Sketches of Several Distinguished Colored Persons*. Boston: Robert F. Wallcut, 1855.

Newton, Ross. "'Persons of Worthy Character': Slaves, Servants, and Masters at Boston's Old North Church." *Journal of the North End Historical Society* 1, no. 1 (March 2012): 51–69.

Piersen, William D. *Black Yankees: The Development of an Afro-American Subculture in Eighteenth-Century New England.* Amherst, Mass.: University of Massachusetts Press, 1988.

Quintal, George, Jr. *Patriots of Color: "A Peculiar Beauty and Merit," African Americans and Native Americans at Battle Road & Bunker Hill.* Washington, D.C.: National Park Service, 2004.

Stewart, James Brewer. "Modernizing 'Difference': The Political Meanings of Color in the Free States, 1776-1840." *Journal of the Early Republic* 19, no. 4 (Winter 1999): 691–712.

Wade, Melvin. "'Shining in Borrowed Plumage': Affirmation of Community in the Black Coronation Festivals of New England (c. 1750–c. 1850)." *Western Folklore* 40, no. 3 (July 1981): 211–231.

White, Shane. "'It Was a Proud Day': African Americans, Festivals, and Parades in the North, 1741–1834." *The Journal of American History* 81, no. 1 (June 1994): 13–50.

White, Shane. "Slavery in the North." *OAH Magazine of History* 17, no. 3 (April 2003): 17–21.

Crime and Social Disorder

Bourne, Russell. *Cradle of Violence: How Boston's Waterfront Mobs Ignited the American Revolution.* Hoboken, N.J.: John Wiley & Sons, 2006.

Bridenbaugh, Carl. *Cities in Revolt; Urban Life in America, 1743-1776.* New York: Knopf, 1955.

Brunsman, Denver. "The Knowles Atlantic Impressment Riots of the 1740s." *Early American Studies* 5, no. 2 (Fall 2007): 324–366.

Butler, James Davie. "British Convicts Shipped to American Colonies." *The American Historical Review* 2, no. 1 (Oct. 1896): 12–33.

Cogliano, Francis. "Deliverance from Luxury: Pope's Day, Conflict and Consensus in Colonial Boston, 1745–1765." *Studies in Popular Culture* 15, no. 2 (1993): 15–28.

Ekirch, A. Roger. "Bound for America: A Profile of British Convicts Transported to the Colonies, 1718–1775." *The William and Mary Quarterly* 42, no. 2 (April 1985): 184–200.

Flaherty, David H. "Crime and Social Control in Provincial Massachusetts." *The Historical Journal* 24, no. 2 (June 1981): 339–360.

Gottlieb, Gabriele. "Theater of Death: Capital Punishment in Early America, 1750–1800." PhD diss., University of Pittsburgh, 2005.

Greenberg, Douglas. "Crime, Law Enforcement, and Social Control in Colonial America." *The American Journal of Legal History* 26, no. 4 (Oct. 1982): 293–325.

Hersey, Frank W. C. "The Misfortunes of Dorcas Griffiths." *Colonial Society of Massachusetts, Transactions* 34 (1937): 13–25.

Irvin, Benjamin H. "Tar, Feathers, and the Enemies of American Liberties, 1768-1776." *The New England Quarterly* 76, no. 2 (June 2003): 197–238.

Kealey, Linda. "Patterns of Punishment: Massachusetts in the Eighteenth Century." *The American Journal of Legal History* 30, no. 2 (April 1986): 163–186.

Lloyd, Joanne. "Beneath the 'City on the Hill': The Lower Orders, Boston 1700–1850." PhD diss., Boston College, 2007

Maier, Pauline. "Popular Uprisings and Civil Authority in Eighteenth-Century America." *The William and Mary Quarterly* 27, no. 1 (Jan. 1970): 3–35.

Preyer, Kathryn. "Penal Measures in the American Colonies: An Overview." *The American Journal of Legal History* 26, no. 4 (Oct. 1982): 326–353.

Schlesinger, Arthur Meier. "Political Mobs and the American Revolution, 1765-1776." *Proceedings of the American Philosophical Society* 99, no. 4 (Aug. 30, 1955): 244–250.

"The Second Stamp Act Riots, 26 August 1765." Tyler, John W., and Elizabeth Dubrulle, eds. *Colonial Society of Massachusetts* 84 (2014): 285–316.

Smith, Barbara Clark. "Food Rioters and the American Revolution." *The William and Mary Quarterly* 51, no. 1 (January 1994): 3–38.

Tager, Jack. *Boston Riots: Three Centuries of Social Violence*. Boston: Northeastern Univ. Press, 2001.

Tyler, John W. "'Such Ruins Were Never Seen in America': The Looting of Thomas Hutchinson's House at the Time of the Stamp Act Riots." *Colonial Society of Massachusetts* 88 (2016): 150–151.

Wood, Gordon S. "A Note on Mobs in the American Revolution." *The William and Mary Quarterly* 23, no. 4 (October 1966): 635–642.

Young, Alfred F. "Pope's Day: Tar and Feathers, and Cornet Joyce, Jun.: From Ritual to Rebellion in Boston, 1745–1775." *Bulletin of the Society for the Study of Labour History* 27 (1973): 27–59.

Medicine and Disease

Becker, Ann M. "Smallpox in Washington's Army: Strategic Implications of the Disease During the American Revolutionary War." *Journal of Military History* 68, no. 2 (2004): 381–430.

Blake, John B. *Public Health in the Town of Boston: 1630–1822*. Cambridge, Mass.: Harvard University Press, 1959.

Blake, John B. "Smallpox Inoculation in Colonial Boston." *Journal of the History of Medicine and Allied Sciences* 8, no. 3 (July 1953): 284–300.

Cash, Philip. *Medicine in Colonial Massachusetts, 1620–1820*. Boston: Colonial Society of Massachusetts, 1980.

Fenn, Elizabeth A. "Biological Warfare in Eighteenth-Century North America: Beyond Jeffery Amherst." *The Journal of American History* 86, no. 4 (March 2000): 1552–1580.

Fenn, Elizabeth A. *Pox Americana: The Great Smallpox Epidemic of 1775–82*. New York: Hill and Wang, 2001.

Griffenhagen, George P., and James Harvey Young. *Old English Patent Medicines in America*. U.S. National Museum Bulletin 218. Washington, D.C.: Smithsonian Institution, 1959.

Kass, Amalie M. "Boston's Historic Smallpox Epidemic." *Massachusetts Historical Review* 14 (2012): 1–51.

Mager, Gerald Marvin. "Zabdiel Boylston: Medical Pioneer of Colonial Boston." PhD diss., University of Illinois, Urbana-Champaign, 1975.

Schuetze, Sarah. "Carrying Home the Enemy: Smallpox and Revolution in American Love and Letters, 1775–76." *Early American Literature* 53, no. 1 (2018): 97–125.

Shryock, Richard Harrison. *Medicine and Society in America: 1660–1860*. New York: New York University Press, 1960.

Silva, Cristobal. *Miraculous Plagues: An Epidemiology of Early New England Narrative*. New York: Oxford University Press, 2011.

Winslow, Ola Elizabeth. *The Destroying Angel: The Conquest of Smallpox in Colonial Boston*. Boston: Houghton Mifflin, 1974.

Food and Tavern Culture

Balfour, David F. "The Taverns of Boston in Ye Olden Time." *The Bay State Monthly* 2, no. 2 (1884): 164–207.

Booth, Sally Smith. *Hung, Strung & Potted: A History of Eating in Colonial America*. New York: Clarkson N. Potter, 1971.

Bowen, Joanne. "To Market, to Market: Animal Husbandry in New England." *Historical Archaeology* 32, no. 3 (1998): 137–152.

Brown, John Hull. *Early American Beverages*. Rutland, Vt.: Charles E. Tuttle, 1966.

Cheek, Charles D. "Massachusetts Bay Foodways: Regional and Class Influences." *Historical Archaeology* 32, no. 3 (1998): 153–172.

Conroy, David W. *In Public Houses: Drink and the Revolution of Authority in Colonial Massachusetts*. Chapel Hill, N.C.: University of North Carolina Press, 1995.

Drake, Samuel Adams. *Old Boston Taverns and Tavern Clubs*. Boston: W.A. Butterfield, 1917.

Earle, Alice Morse. *Stage-Coach and Tavern Days*. New York: Macmillan Co., 1900.

Friedmann, Karen J. "Victualling Colonial Boston." *Agricultural History* 47, no. 3 (July 1973): 189–205.

Gifford, George E., Jr. "Botanic Recipes in Colonial Massachusetts, 1620–1820." *Colonial Society of Massachusetts* 57 (1980): 263–288.

Hancock, David. "Markets, Merchants, and the Wider World of Boston Wine, 1700–1775." In *Entrepreneurs: The Boston Business Community, 1700–1850*. Conrad Edick Wright and Katheryn P. Viens, eds. Boston: Massachusetts Historical Society, 1997.

Hooker, Richard J. "The American Revolution Seen Through a Wine Glass." *The William and Mary Quarterly* 11, no. 1 (Jan. 1954): 52–77.

Landon, David B. "Feeding Colonial Boston: A Zooarchaeological Study." *Historical Archaeology* 30, no. 1 (1996): 1-153.

Salinger, Sharon V. *Taverns and Drinking in Early America*. Baltimore: Johns Hopkins Univ. Press, 2002.

Watkins, Walter K. *Ye Crown Coffee House, A Story of Old Boston*. Boston: Henderson & Ross, 1916.

Other Secondary Sources

Alexander, Kimberley S. *Fashioning the New England Family*. Boston: Massachusetts Historical Society, 2021.

Bullock, Steven C. "The Revolutionary Transformation of American Freemasonry, 1752-1792." *The William and Mary Quarterly* 47, no. 3 (July 1990): 347–369.

Bullock, Steven C., and Sheila McIntyre. "The Handsome Tokens of a Funeral: Glove-Giving and the Large Funeral in Eighteenth-Century New England." *The William and Mary Quarterly* 69, no. 2 (April 2012): 305–346.

Carp, Benjamin L. "Fire of Liberty: Firefighters, Urban Voluntary Culture, and the Revolutionary Movement." *The William and Mary Quarterly* 58, no. 4 (Oct. 2001): 781–818.

Crist, Elizabeth B. "'Ye Sons of Harmony': Politics, Masculinity, and the Music of William Billings in Revolutionary Boston." *The William and Mary Quarterly* 60, no. 2 (April 2003): 333–354.

Forbes, Harriette Merrifield. *Gravestones of Early New England and the Men Who Made Them, 1653–1800*. Boston: Houghton Mifflin, 1927.

Foster, Thomas. *Sex and the Eighteenth-Century Man: Massachusetts and the History of Sexuality in America*. Boston: Beacon Press, 2006.

Hayward, Arthur H. *Colonial and Early American Lighting*, 3rd ed. New York: Dover, 1962.

Lewis, Ann-Eliza H. *Highway to the Past: The Archaeology of Boston's Big Dig*. Boston: Massachusetts Historical Commission, 2001.

Ludwig, Allan I. *Graven Images: New England Stonecarving and Its Symbols, 1650–1815*. Middletown, Conn.: Wesleyan University Press, 1966.

McKay, David. "Opera in Colonial Boston." *American Music* 3, no. 2 (Summer 1985): 133–142.

Morgan, Edmund S. "Puritan Hostility to the Theatre." *Proceedings of the American Philosophical Society* 110, no. 5 (Oct. 27, 1966): 340–347.

Newman, Simon P. *Parades and the Politics of the Street: Festive Culture in the Early American Republic*. Philadelphia: University of Pennsylvania Press, 1997.

Schorow, Stephanie. *Boston on Fire: A History of Fires and Firefighting in Boston*. Beverly, Mass.: Commonwealth Editions, 2003.

Seybolt, Robert Francis. *The Public Schools of Colonial Boston, 1635–1775*. Cambridge, Mass.: Harvard University Press, 1935.

Warwick, Edward, and Henry C. Pitz. *Early American Costume*. New York: Century Corp., 1929.

Widmer, Ted. "Forefathers' Day, the Forgotten Pilgrim Holiday." *Boston Globe*, Nov. 23, 2014.

York, Neil Longley. *Mechanical Metamorphosis: Technological Change in Revolutionary America*. Westport, Conn.: Greenwood Press, 1985.

SELECTED NOTES

The notes that follow are grouped by chapter. Each note is anchored to a distinctive phrase from the main text, allowing the reader to locate the corresponding passage with precision.

INTRODUCTION

"numbers are gone already": *Report of the Record Commissioners, 1742–1757*, 240. **"The Inhabitants of the Colonies were a Race of Smugglers"**: Oliver, *Origin & Progress*, 60. **"are of one Mind about the Governor"**: Adams, J., *Diary and Autobiography*, vol. 1, 329. **"the first Leader of Dirty Matters"**: Maier, *From Resistance to Revolution*, 129. **"it is certain that our safety & quiet"**: Hulton, *Letters*, 17. **"drunkenness, debaucheries, and other extravagances"**: Conroy, *In Public Houses*, 251. **"to state the rights of the colonists"**: Adams, S., "Rights of the Colonists," In *The Writings of Samuel Adams*, vol. 2, 350. **"the foulest, subtlest and most venomous serpent"**: Warner, "Invention of a Public Machine," 153. **"There must be an Abridgment"**: Hutchinson, Letter to Thomas Whately, January 20, 1769. In "Correspondence," vol. 2. **"the ill effects of tea on the constitution"**: Upton, "Proceedings of Ye Body," 298. **"Poor Unhappy Boston"**: Rowe, *Letters and Diary*, 273. **"The Town of Boston, for ought I can see"**: Adams, J., *My Dearest Friend*, 29. **"now a very gloomy place, the Streets almost empty"**: Hulton, *Letters*, 73. **"With all the support furnished by a royal governor"**: Winsor, *Memorial History*, 57. **"the most vile, profane, blackguard language"**: Andrews, "Letters," 400. **"nothing but the Bayonet & Torch"**: Conway, "To Subdue America," 392. "arrest the principal actors and abettors": Alden, *General Gage*, 241. "The country militia, in great numbers": Thacher, *Military Journal*, 20. **"an open and avowed Rebellion"**: George III, Proclamation. **"Pork and beans one day"**: Andrews, "Letters," 408. **"diarrhea, dysentery, food poisoning, malnutrition"**: Carr, *After the Siege*, 27. **"I can do little for God & his people"**: Moerschel, "In Ye Service of the Lord," 199. **"The ministerial butchers have robbed the warehouses"**: Taylor, "Evacuation of Boston," 231. **"There never was such Destruction & Outrage"**: Rowe, *Letters and Diary*, 302. **"They look like a forest"**: Winsor, *Memorial History*,

180. **"While [we were] marching through the streets"**: Thacher, *Military Journal*, 43–44. **"detachment of artillery in King Street"**: Thacher, *Military Journal*, 48.

CHAPTER 1: THE HARBOR AND HARBORSIDE

"in 20 minutes the whole was in flames": Kemble, "Journals," 74. **"We never thought ourselves more safe from the Sons of Violence"**: Hulton, *Letters*, 28. **"a City upon a Hill [where] the eyes of all people are upon us"**: Winthrop, "Model of Christian Charity." **"the longest wharf on the continent"**: Bacon, *Rambles Around Old Boston*, 163. **"with insolent Parade, Drums beating, Fifes playing"**: President and Fellows, "Long Wharf," 18. **"the enemy with a malicious assiduity"**: Washington, *Papers*, 458. **"impotent, lame or otherwise infirme"**: Dayton and Salinger, *Robert Love's Warnings*, 11. **"I warn you to depart"**: Dayton and Salinger, *Robert Love's Warnings*, 15. **"vicious" or having "criminal tendencies"**: Flaherty, "Crime and Social Control," 347. **"Dirt Dung Carrion or any Rubbish into the Streets"**: *Report of the Record Commissioners*, 1764–1768, 130. **"the loathsome vice of Drunkennesse and other disorders"**: Winthrop, "For Preventing Drunkenness," 371. **"divine affliction, and a warning of eternal damnation"**: Salinger, *Taverns and Drinking*, 137; quoting Mather, "Sober Considerations," 1–2, 5. **"idleness, drunkenness, profane cursing and swearing"**: *Report of the Record Commissioners*, 1758–1769, 274. **"This small building was tumbled into the water"**: Snow, *History of Boston*, 109, 259. **"a wheelbarrow-way of full five feet"**: Thwing, *Crooked and Narrow Streets*, 130. **"cassowaries, learned pigs, learned horses"**: Earle, *Stage-Coach and Tavern Days*, 198. **"a very stinking puddle"**: Seasholes, *Gaining Ground*, 38. **"a receptacle for every species of filth, and a public nuisance"**: Quincy, *Municipal History*, 75. **"crowded late medieval tradition of the City of London"**: Whitehill and Kennedy, *Topographical History*, 17. **"house of bad repute"**: Drake, *Old Boston Taverns*, 67. **"notorious resort of doubtful repute"**: Drake, *Old Landmarks*, 131. **"And on the broken pavement here and there"**: Drake, *Old Landmarks*, 153. **"several Houses of This town, where there are young Women"**: Mather, *Diary*, 229. One of them was Mather's own son 'Cresy': Mather, *Diary*, 484. **"quarrling fighting tipling & drinking to Excess"**: Dayton and Salinger, *Robert Love's Warnings*, 111. **"indecent exhibitions at their windows"**: Bridenbaugh, *Cities in Revolt*, 317. **"there is more Wickedness in many taverns"**: Lloyd, "Beneath the 'City on the Hill,'" 145. **"Wherever the haunts of sailors"**: Gilje, *Liberty on the Waterfront*, 71.

CHAPTER 2: THE NORTH END

"Jack Tars," or even "Jolly Tars": Gilje, "Loyalty and Liberty," 170–171. **"the most spectacular series of impressment riots"**: Brunsman, "Knowles Atlantic

Impressment Riots," 324. **"putting a shingle on her front door"**: Lloyd, "Beneath the 'City on the Hill,'" 120. **"ample allotments of grog"**: Patton, *Patriot Pirates*, 114. **"legalized piracy" of privateering:** Gilje, *Liberty on the Waterfront*, 90. **"a rage for privateering"**: Adams, A., Letter to John Adams, Sept. 29, 1776. In *Adams Family Correspondence*, vol. 2. **"I run the Gauntlet near 200 Yards"**: Watson, "Joseph Harrison," 590. **"unparalleled barbarity" in which "our brethren were murdered"**: Lathrop, *A Sermon Occasioned*, 5–6, 9. **"a nest of traitors"**: Moerschel, "In Ye Service of the Lord," 1. **"a number of evil-minded men"**: Robbins, *History of the Second Church*, 129. **"can have them replaced with Artificial Ones"**: Crawford, *Social Life*, 133. **"undaunted by the insolent Menaces"**: Revere, Sons of Liberty Bowl Inscription. **"the whole exhibition was so well executed"**: Snow, *History of Boston*, 285. **"the Hutchinson family was very ancient"**: Hutchinson, *American Magazine*, 237. **"an apologist for most of their oppressive measures"**: Hutchinson, *American Magazine*, 237. **"The hellish crew fell upon my house"**: Hutchinson, Letter to Richard Jackson, August 30, 1765. In "Correspondence," vol. 1. **"a War of Plunder, general levelling"**: Nash, "Urban Wealth and Poverty," 581. **"patriarch of pedagogues"**: Porter, *Rambles in Old Boston*, 139. **"the father of good writing in Boston"**: Porter, *Rambles in Old Boston*, 140. **"daughters who every day experience the want of it"**: Adams, A., Letter to John Adams, August 14, 1776. In *Adams Family Correspondence*, vol. 2. **"poor Boston May God sanctify our distresses"**: Eliot, Letter to His Son, April 23, 1775. **"Consignees of Tea took up the Brethren's time"**: Shurtleff, "Notable Places," 30. **"they tinge the Minds of the People"**: Adams, J., August 14, 1769, *Diary and Autobiography*, vol. 1, 329.

CHAPTER 3: OFFICIAL BOSTON

"the middle Market-House in this Town": Tager, *Boston Riots*, 34. **"The audience at this was thrown into dire confusion"**: Winsor, *Memorial History*, vol. 3, 161–162. **"He has licenced the Instruments of his hostile Oppressions"**: *Report of the Record Commissioners*, 1770–1777, 237. **"Extortions of every kind"**: Carr, *After the Siege*, 120. **"Here we follow the fashions in England"**: Hulton, *Letters*, 45. **"a droll figure of a young lady [in] a tasty head Dress"**: Winslow, *Diary*, 63. **"our Dress would not be So elegant"**: Adams, J., Letter to James Warren, Oct. 20, 1775. In *Papers of John Adams*, vol. 3. **"becomes monstrous, and ridiculous"**: Foster, *Sex and the Eighteenth-Century Man*, 112–114. **"they should not walk in great boots"**: Winsor, *Memorial History*, vol. 1, 483. **"the industry and frugality of American ladies"**: Norton, *Liberty's Daughters*, 166 **"I choose to wear as much of our own manufactory"**: Winslow, *Diary*, 32. **"Ladies of the highest rank and Influence"**: Crawford, *Social Life*, 253. **"It is desired that the Sons and Daughters of LIBERTY"**: Erkkila, "Revolutionary Women," 211. **"A New Touch on the Times"**: Gutridge, *A New Touch on the Times.* **"the chosen resort of the patriot**

leaders": Bacon, *Rambles Around Old Boston*, 164. **"Every one with this writ may be a tyrant"**: Adams, J., "Abstract of the Argument," c. April 1761. In *Legal Papers of John Adams*, vol. 2, 134–144. **"Then and there the Child Independence was born"**: Adams, J., Letter to William Tudor, March 29, 1817. In *Works of John Adams*, vol. 10. **condemning the state of the "American peazant"**: Tyler, *Smugglers and Patriots*, 92. **Otis called the commissioners "superlative blockheads"**: Archer, *As If an Enemy's Country*, 156. **"a number of sticks at once were over Mr. Otis's head"**: Adams, S., *Boston Gazette*, September 25, 1769; quoted in *Writings of Samuel Adams*, 381. **he even "got into a mad Freak"**: Rowe, *Letters and Diary*, 199. **"a living Monument of the Justice of Heaven"**: Oliver, *Origin & Progress*, 36. **"all New England is deploring the irreparable loss"**: Thacher, *Military Journal*, 15. **"Bloody Massacre Perpetrated on King Street"**: Revere, "The Bloody Massacre." **"attacked the people with their bayonets"**: Bowdoin, et al., *Short Narrative*, 30. **"a very gross abuse of language"**: *Fair Account*, 21. **"there are witnesses who swear"**: Bowdoin, et al., *Short Narrative*, 7–8. **"scarcely ever with dry eyes"**: Adams, J., Letter to Jedidiah Morse, January 5, 1816. In *Works of John Adams*, vol. 10 **"not only as the stench occasioned by the troops"**: Drake, *Old Landmarks*, 89–90. **"shouting and huzzaing, and threatening life"**: Adams, J., quoted in *Trial of William Wemms*, 174–176. **"Facts are stubborn things"**: Adams, J., quoted in *Trial of William Wemms*, 177. **"one of the most gallant, generous, manly, disinterested Actions"**: Adams, J., *Diary and Autobiography*, vol. 2, 79. **"We hold these truths to be self-evident"**: Declaration of Independence, July 4, 1776. **"God save our American States!"**: Adams, A., Letter to John Adams, July 21, 1776. In *Adams Family Correspondence*, vol. 2. **"a great Confusion"**: Rowe, *Letters and Diary*, 313. **"May the foundation of our new Constitution"**: Adams, A., Letter to John Adams, July 21, 1776. In *Adams Family Correspondence*, vol. 2. **"You will think me transported with Enthusiasm"**: Adams, J., Letter to Abigail Adams, July 3, 1776. In *Adams Family Correspondence*, vol. 2.

CHAPTER 4: THE TOWN CENTER

"For God's sake take care of your Men": Knox quoted in Adams, J., "Rex v. Preston," in *Legal Papers of John Adams*, vol. 3, 55. **"I find Common Sense is working a powerful change"**: Young, *Liberty Tree*, 270–271. **"a French bastard landing with an armed banditti"**: Paine, *Common Sense*, 26. **"The more simple a thing is, the less liable it is to be disordered"**: Paine, *Common Sense*, 11. **"so democratical, without any restraint"**: Adams, J., *Diary and Autobiography*, vol. 3, 332–333. **Some call his brand of religion "polemical divinity"**: Pemberton, "Topographical and Historical Description," 301. **"Surely he would not suffer the town"**: Hutchinson, *History of the Province*, 329n–330. **"Force may for a while keep the people under restraint"**: Chauncy, *Letter to a Friend*. **"scarcely a patriot club**

was without a divine": Miller, *Pioneer in Propaganda*, 37. **"Gutters of Sedition" and preach "*it was no Sin to kill the Tories*"**: Oliver, *Origin & Progress*, 104–106. **"That fine preacher, called a teacher"**: Griffin, *Old Brick*, 141. **something called "the holy Kiss"**: Dayton and Salinger, *Robert Love's Warnings*, 132. **the authorities called "ravings and blasphemies"**: Winsor, *Memorial History*, vol. 1, 180. **"a covetous and deceitful rotten heart"**: Norton, *New-England's Ensigne*. **"a Woman that Preaches better Gospel"**: McGunigal, "Criminal Trial," 150. **"a woman of ready wit and bold spirit"**: *Winthrop's Journal*, 195. **Winthrop and his allies labeled her an "opinionist"**: Schneider, "Anne Hutchinson," 487. **radical patriots occasionally invoke him as a "glorious fellow"**: Young, *Liberty Tree*, 162–164. **"the spiritual siege of our churches"**: Mayhew, *Observations*, 48–49. **"much more to be dreaded from the growth of POPERY"**: Moerschel, "In Ye Service of the Lord," 140. **"the good people of [New England] are threaten'd"**: Winslow, *Diary*, 14. **"we have the prospect of a fiery trial"**: Moerschel, "In Ye Service of the Lord," 188. **"The Sons of Liberty have almost killed one of my Church"**: Samuel Peters, *Boston Evening Post*, Oct. 24, 1774; quoted in Foote, *Annals*, 304. **"an entire disconnection with Great Britain"**: Foote, *Annals*, 320. **"Here women were taken from a huge cage"**: Breck, *Recollections*, 36–37. **"in this country you need not be told"**: Adams, A., Letter to John Adams, June 30, 1778. In *Adams Family Correspondence*, vol. 3. **"Frugality, Industry and Economy are the Lessons of the day"**: Adams, A., Letter to Mercy Warren, April 13, 1776. In *Adams Family Correspondence*, vol. 1. **"A melancholy sight . . . which evinces the barbarity of the foe"**: Adams, A., Letter to Mercy Warren, April 17, 1776. In *Adams Family Correspondence*, vol. 1. **"We are no ways dispirited here"**: Adams, A., Letter to John Adams, September 20, 1776. In *Adams Family Correspondence*, vol. 2. **"I wish most sincerely there was not a Slave in the province"**: Adams, A., Letter to John Adams, September 22, 1774. In *Adams Family Correspondence*, vol. 1. "I desire you would Remember the Ladies": Adams, A., Letter to John Adams, March 31, 1776. In *Adams Family Correspondence*, vol. 1. **"He is very saucy to me in return"**: Adams, A., Letter to Mercy Warren, April 27, 1776. In *Adams Family Correspondence*, vol. 1. **the greatest aspiration of some is to become a "she-merchant"**: Carr, "Marketing Gentility," 29. **public denunciation as "Enemies to their country"**: Young, *Liberty Tree*, 115. **"will bring disgrace upon themselves"**: "Sons and Daughters of Liberty Unite." **"filthy and defaced condition"**: Lothrop, *History of the Church*, 108. **"a voice melodious in the tones of a delicate flute"**: Akers, "Religion and the American Revolution," 481. "I rejoice in a preacher who has some warmth": Adams, A., Letter to John Adams, August 5, 1776. In *Adams Family Correspondence*, vol. 2. **"Dr. Cooper and others were excellent hands"**: Adams, J., Letter to William Tudor, January 24, 1817. In *Works of John Adams*, vol. 10. **"Let tyrants shake their iron Rod"**: Billings, *New-England Psalm-Singer*, 132. **"the wanton gestures; the amorous kisses"**: Prynne, *Histrio-Mastix*, 374. **"tend[s] generally to increase immorality"**: Felt, *Annals*, 42.

"every species of extravagance and dissipation": "Articles of Association," 78. **"One of our most bawling demagogues and voluminous writers"**: Bourne, *Cradle of Violence,* 205. **"The hearts of Britons and Americans"**: Warren, J., "Oration," March 6, 1775, 20. **"Our streets are again filled with armed men"**: Warren, J., "Oration," March 6, 1775, 21. **"the soldiers began to yell, "O fie! O fie!"**: Hill, *History of the Old South Church,* 172. **"his memory will be revered by every lover of his country"**: Warren, *History of the Rise*, 223.

CHAPTER 5: WEST BOSTON AND BEACON HILL

he "read it, till the Substance of it was incorporated into my Nature": Adams, J., Letter to Thomas Jefferson, July 18, 1818. In *Papers of Thomas Jefferson*, vol. 13. **"more readily embraced by a man after his brains are knocked out"**: Mayhew, *Seven Sermons*, 63. **"natural religion" that valued "beauty, order, harmony and design"**: Mayhew, *Seven Sermons*, 24, 150–152. **"One of the most Seditious Sermons ever delivered"**: Moerschel, "In Ye Service of the Lord," 80. **"from the bottom of my heart I detest these proceedings"**: Mayhew, J., Letter to Thomas Hutchinson, August 27, 1765. In Tyler and Dubrulle, "Second Stamp Act Riots." **"our soul is escaped as a bird from the snare of the fowlers"**: Mayhew, *The Snare Broken*, 8. **"maddening the corrupt, frightening the timid"**: Thornton, *Pulpit of the American Revolution*, 43. **designates anyone born to such a union a "molatto bastard child"**: Lloyd, "Beneath the 'City on the Hill,'" 49. **"Negro Boys & Girls, duly Imported"**: Desrochers, "Slave-for-Sale Advertisements," 625. **"It is most certain that all Men, as they are the Sons of Adam"**: Sewell, *Selling of Joseph*, 1. **earning him only "frowns and hard words"**: Desrochers, "Slave-for-Sale Advertisements," 641. **comparing him to an "Oriental prince"**: Winsor, *Memorial History*, vol. 3, 171. **"Ye dark designing knaves, ye murderers, parricides!"**: Hancock, "Oration," March 5, 1774, 15. **calling them the "strolling poor"**: Jones, "Strolling Poor," 45–46. **"venereal disease ('the French pox')"**: Nellis, "Almshouse and Workhouse," 66. **"[I]t is rather a dungeon than a hospital"**: Pemberton, "Topographical and Historical Description." 251. **with a watchman to provide the "discipline of the whip"**: Pemberton, "Topographical and Historical Description." 252. **Unlike the "deserving poor" in the Almshouse, the "immoral poor"**: Nellis, "Almshouse and Workhouse," 68–72.

CHAPTER 6: THE COMMON AND THE LIBERTY TREE

"the ground was covered with beehives and serpents": Drake, *History and Antiquities*, 723. **"The rum is so cheap that it debauches both navy and army"**: Pitcairn, John, Letter to Lord Sandwich, March 4, 1775. In *Naval Documents*, vol. 1, 124–125. **"their ribs are laid quite bare"**: Andrews, "Letters," 397. **"Punch, Wine,**

Pipes and Tobacco, Biscuit and Cheese": Adams, J., *Diary and Autobiography*, vol. 1, 294. **crying out "South End forever!":** Thomas, *History of Printing*, xxx [intro p. 30]. **shouting "with the utmost Rage and fury":** Tager, *Boston Riots*, 48. **"Don't you hear my little bell / Go chink, chink, chink?":** Drake, *History and Antiquities*, 662n. **"Captain General of the Liberty Tree":** Anderson, "Ebenezer Mackintosh," 29. **a different label: "the consummate rioter":** Bourne, *Cradle of Violence*, 74. **"Liberty, Property and No Stamps!":** Anderson, "Ebenezer Mackintosh," 32. **feted the gang leaders in a "Union Feast":** Cogliano, *No King, No Popery*, 33. **"Love and Unity—The American Whig":** Tager, *Boston Riots*, 50. **broadsides threatened "parricides" with damnation:** Fowler, *Samuel Adams*, 82. "[H]e was stripped Stark naked": Hulton, *Letters*, 70–71. **"This was looked upon by me & every Sober man":** Rowe, *Letters and Diary*, 261. **he said was accomplished by his "chickens":** Young, *Shoemaker and the Tea Party*, 100. **their loyalist allies faced a "tree ordeal":** Oliver, *Origin & Progress*, 54. **the tree was "consecrated as an Idol for the Mob to worship":** Oliver, *Origin & Progress*, 54. **"Armed with axes, they made a furious attack upon it":** *Essex Gazette*, Aug. 31, 1775, quoted in Drake, *Old Landmarks*, 397.

CHAPTER 7: THE SOUTH END

"they are more famous for the quantity and cheapness": Burke, *An Account*, 168. **"If Taxes are laid upon us in any shape":** Adams, S., Instruction to Representatives. **"it is destructive to the morals":** *Report of the Record Commissioners*, 1758–1769, 228. **it causes "idleness, poverty, and disgrace":** Pemberton, "Topographical and Historical Description," 277–278. **"persons of the best character and best Estate":** Hutchinson, Letter to Lord Hillsborough, April 19, 1771. In "Correspondence of Thomas Hutchinson," vol. 4. **"There must be an Abridgment":** Hutchinson, Letter to Thomas Whately, January 20, 1769. In "Correspondence," vol. 2. **"the Destruction of the Charter and Constitution":** Massachusetts House of Representatives, "Resolves Respecting Certain Letters," 516–517. **"entire satisfaction we feel":** Address of the Merchants and Others of Boston, to Gov. Hutchinson, May 30, 1774. In Curwen, *Journals and Letters*, 423–424. **they were "worthless wretches" no better than prostitutes:** Boston Committee of Correspondence, Letter to New York Committee, quoted in Tyler, *Smugglers and Patriots*, 218. **"Such is the detestation in which that tool of tyrants":** Andrews, "Letters," 328. **"dark, intriguing, insinuating, haughty and ambitious":** Warren, *History of the Rise*, 79. **These massive assemblies of "the Body of the People":** Adams, S., *Writings*, vol. 4, 93. **"consist[ing] principally of the lower ranks of people":** Hutchinson, "Correspondence," vol. 5, 359. **"we are called on to defend our liberty and privileges":** Hill, *History of the Old South Church*, 93. **"Shadow of a Man, scarce able to support his withered Carcass":** Upton, "Proceedings of Ye Body," 293. **"Whether a little Salt Water would not do it good":** Upton, "Proceedings of Ye

Body," 294. **"My Fellow Countrymen, we have now put our Hands"**: Upton, "Proceedings of Ye Body," 296. **"then we shall have Tea enough"**: Carp, *Defiance*, 120. **"This meeting can do nothing more to save the country"**: Hill, *History of the Old South Church*, 153. **"Tis thus with thee O Britain keeping down"**: Wheatley, "America," in *Writings*, 22. **"In heavens eternal court it was decreed"**: Wheatley, "On the Death of Mr. Snider Murder'd by Richardson," in *Poems of Wheatley*, 131. **"I, young in life, by seeming cruel fate"**: Wheatley, "To the Right Honourable William, Earl of Dartmouth," in *Poems on Various Subjects*, 74. **"I am now upon my own footing"**: Wheatley, Letter to David Wooster, Oct. 18, 1773. **"style and manner exhibit a striking proof"**: Washington, Letter to Phillis Wheatley, February 28, 1776. In *Papers of Washington*, vol. 3. **"I went to see the black Poetess"**: Franklin, B., Letter to Jonathan Williams, Sr., July 7, 1773. In *Papers of Franklin*, vol. 3. **"bought office with money, and was as rapacious"**: Sabine, *Biographical Sketches*, 154. **"Governor, Lieutenant-Governor, Secretary, and Chief Justice"**: Adams, J., Letter to William Tudor, March 11, 1818. In *Works of John Adams*, vol. 10. **"threaten[ing] vengeance on the defenceless workmen"**: Bowdoin, et al., *Short Narrative*, 6. **"Well then, go clean my shit house!"**: Bourne, *Cradle of Violence*, 155. **"began taking down houses at the South End"**: Newell, "Journal," 268. **"seen drunk in the Streets & about the different Wharfs"**: Howe, *Orderly Book*, 231. **"Houses have been forced open and Robbed"**: Howe, *Orderly Book*, 237. **"Any Person detected setting Fire to the Town"**: Howe, *Orderly Book*, 230. **"tends to destroy discipline among the Troops"**: Kemble, "Journals," 382. **"in a decayed situation and constantly washing away"**: Pemberton, "Topographical and Historical Description," 249. **"A tea-pot tonight!" and "Hurrah for Griffin's Wharf!"**: Bourne, *Cradle of Violence*, 191. **"hideous Yelling in the Street"**: Upton, "Proceedings of Ye Body," 298. **"cloth'd in Blankets with the heads muffled"**: Andrews, "Letters," 326. **"Some were in the hold immediately"**: Edes, *Pioneer Printer*, 61–62. **"If we have not passed the Rubicon this winter"**: Hutchinson, *Diary and Letters*, 139. **"This is the most magnificent . . ."**: Adams, J., *Diary and Autobiography*, vol. 2, 85–87. **"Is it lawful to resist the Supreme Magistrate?"**: Fowler, *Samuel Adams*, 25. **"keep the attention of his fellow citizens"**: Maier, "Coming to Terms," 24. **"whether there is a greater incendiary"**: Hutchinson, Letter to John Pownall, August 1771. In "Correspondence," vol. 4, 228. **wield the "iron Hand of Tyranny"**: Adams, Samuel. Letter to *Boston Gazette*, October 5, 1772. Quoted in *Writings*, vol. 2, 336. **"understood human Nature, in low life, so well"**: Oliver, *Origin & Progress*, 39. "to draw a Picture of the Devil": Oliver, *Origin & Progress*, 39. **"The ultimate wish and desire of the High Government party"**: Andrews, "Letters," 340. **They valued him "for his good sense"**: Andrews, "Letters," 340. **"truly the *Man of the Revolution*"**: Hosmer, *American Statesmen*, 365. **"We may look up to Armies for our Defence"**: Adams, *Writings*, vol. 3, 235. **"whose offenses are of too flagitious a nature"**: Gage,

Proclamation of Amnesty. "[They] **wantonly mutilated the interior**": Wells, *Life and Public Services*, vol. 2, 380.

CHAPTER 8: THE CHARLESTOWN PENINSULA

"The Regulars are coming out!": Fischer, *Paul Revere's Ride*, 109. **Congress directed that Bunker Hill "be securely kept and defended"**: White, Benjamin. Committee of Safety, Massachusetts. Order to Artemus Ward, June 15, 1775. In *Journals of the Provincial Congress*. **"Prescott will fight you to the gates of hell"**: Graydon, *Memoirs*, 424. **"I will never be taken alive"**: Frothingham, *History of the Siege*, 123n. **"carcass balls"—a combustible mix of gunpowder:** Brooks, *Boston Campaign*, 158. **General Burgoyne saw "great pyramids of fire"**: Burgoyne, John. Dispatch to Lord Stanley. June 25, 1775. In *Cassell's Illustrated History*, 125. **"Fire was communicated to a number of houses"**: Thacher, *Military Journal*, 28–29. **"a horrid breastwork to fire from"**: Philbrick, *Bunker Hill*, 223. buckshot known as "Yankee peas": Atkinson, *British Are Coming*, 103. **Yelling "Fight, conquer or die!"**: Frothingham, *Battle-Field*, 32. **"the most melancholy scene ever beheld"**: Frothingham, *History of the Siege*, 194. **"The die is now cast"**: Bourne, *Cradle of Violence*, 227. **"The loss we have sustained here"**: Gage, Thomas. Letter to Lord Barrington, June 26, 1775. In *Spirit of 'Seventy-Six*, 134.

CHAPTER 9: THE NECK, ROXBURY, AND DORCHESTER

"the streets and Neck lined with wagons": Andrews, "Letters," 402. **"the terrors of a frowning God"**: *Dying Groans of Levi Ames.* **her supposed "turbulent and quarrelsome" nature:** Winsor, *Memorial History*, vol. 2, 139. **"The jury brought her in guilty"**: Winsor, *Memorial History*, vol. 2, 139. the authorities had "warned out" of town: Dayton and Salinger, *Robert Love's Warnings*, 109. **"desolate and forbidding in the extreme"**: Drake, *Old Landmarks*, 420. **"I never drank wine in my life"**: Winsor, *Memorial History*, vol. 1, 402. **"Roxbury looks more injured than Boston"**: Adams, A., Letter to John Adams, May 27, 1776. In *Adams Family Correspondence*, vol. 1. **"Nothing struck me with more horror"**: Drake, *Town of Roxbury*, 80. **"State pirates, thieves, robbers and traitors"**: Drake, *History and Antiquities*, 768. **"strong halters, firm blocks, and sharp axes"**: Wells, *Life and Public Services*, vol. 1, 270. **"This is cultivating the Sensations of Freedom"**: Adams, J., Monday, August 14, *Diary and Autobiography*, vol. 1. **"I hope to give you joy of Boston"**: Adams, A., Letter to John Adams, March 2, 1776. In *Adams Family Correspondence*, vol. 1. **"as if heaven and earth were engaged"**: Newell, "Journal," 272. **1,200 men brought up a series of "chandeliers"**: Atkinson, *British Are Coming*, 258–260. **"to break the ranks and legs of the assailants"**: Thacher, *Military Journal*, 41. **"avenge the death of your brethren"**: Nell, *Colored Patriots*, 17. "The rebels have done more in one night": Sweetser, *King's Handbook*, 119. **"he has no intention of destroying the Town"**: Newell, "Journal," 273.

PRACTICAL MATTERS

"lewd and idle and dissolute persons": Lloyd, "Beneath the 'City on the Hill,'" 131. **selling "small meat" like chickens and pigeons:** Friedmann, "Victualling Colonial Boston," 197. *Beef Ragout* recipe: Carter, *Frugal Housewife*, 105. *Oyster Pie* recipe: Carter, *Frugal Housewife*, 117. *A Poor Man's Pudding* recipe: Carter, *Frugal Housewife*, 139–140. *A Whipt Syllabub* recipe: Carter, *Frugal Housewife*, 143. "*To Make Elder-Ale*": Smith, *Compleat Housewife*, 223. **"made 90 Barrels of Cider in one Year"**: Hulton, *Letters*, 42. **"If the Ancients drank Wine as our People drink rum"**: Adams, J., *Diary and Autobiography*, vol. 3, 229–231. **"our treat was nuts, raisins, Cakes, Wine, punch"**: Winslow, *Diary*, 17. **"*To Make Birch Wine*"**: Smith, *Compleat Housewife*, 209. **"*To Make Cherry Brandy*"**: Smith, *Compleat Housewife*, 206. **tea has been called "the Ladies favorite Liquor"**: Carp, *Defiance of the Patriots*, 64. **"*An Opening Drink*"**: Smith, *Compleat Housewife*, 242. **"I am fearful of the small pox"**: Adams, A., Letter to John Adams, March 31, 1776. In Adams, C.F., *Familiar Letters*. **"the Offal near many of the Commissaries Stalls"**: Blake, *Public Health*, 145. **"Dirt Dung Garbage Carcass Carrion Shavings"**: *Report of the Record Commissioners*, 1742–1757, 323. **"malignant Vapours proceeding from dead Bodies"**: Blake, *Public Health*, 100. **patent medicine such as "Pectoral Balsam of Honey"**: Blake, *Public Health*, 121. **"levying war against the King"**: Maier, "Popular Uprisings," 21. **"Rum, Sugar, Molasses, Cotton-Wool, coffee, Cocoa"**: *Report of the Record Commissioners*, 1770–1777, 262. **"There has been much rout and Noise in the Town"**: Adams, A., Letter to John Adams, July 30, 1777. In *Adams Family Correspondence*, vol. 2. **"In the evening, a large Mob Assembled"**: Rowe, *Letters and Diary*, 194. **"large baked Indian whortleberry pudding"**: Widmer, "Forefathers' Day." **"completely tarred and feathered, representing a he Devil"**: Andrews, "Letters," 393. **"Men dishonor Christ more in the twelve days of Christmas"**: Latimer, quoted in Mather, *Grace Defended*, 20. **a five-shilling fine as the "Penalty for Keeping Christmas"**: *Records of the Governor*, vol. 4, 366. litany of holidays and "remarkable days": *Pocket Almanack*, 9.

ABOUT THE AUTHOR

J. D. DICKEY is an author of narrative nonfiction about American history, society, and culture. His book *Empire of Mud*, covering the troubled landscape of nineteenth-century Washington, DC, was a *New York Times* bestseller, and his Civil War book, *Rising in Flames*, was praised by *The Wall Street Journal* as "absolutely spellbinding." Dickey has written articles on a broad range of historical, political, and travel-related topics for *TIME*, *The Wall Street Journal*, LitHub, and more, and he has appeared in media from C-SPAN's *Book TV* to *PBS NewsHour* to Public Radio International's *The Takeaway*. He has lectured for the New-York Historical Society, the Pritzker Military Museum & Library, the Atlanta History Center, and the US Army War College.